American Literature and Language

AMERICAN STUDIES INFORMATION GUIDE SERIES

Series Editor: Donald Koster, Professor of English Emeritus, Adelphi University, Garden City, New York

Also in this series:

AFRO-AMERICAN LITERATURE AND CULTURE SINCE WORLD WAR II—*Edited by Charles D. Peavy*

AMERICAN ARCHITECTURE AND ART—*Edited by David M. Sokol*

AMERICAN POPULAR CULTURE—*Edited by Larry Landrum**

THE AMERICAN PRESIDENCY—*Edited by Kenneth E. Davison**

AMERICAN RELIGION AND PHILOSOPHY—*Edited by Ernest R. Sandeen and Frederick Hale*

AMERICAN STUDIES—*Edited by David W. Marcell*

HISTORY OF THE UNITED STATES OF AMERICA—*Edited by Ernest Cassara*

JEWISH WRITERS OF NORTH AMERICA—*Edited by Ira Bruce Nadel*

THE RELATIONSHIP OF PAINTING AND LITERATURE—*Edited by Eugene L. Huddleston and Douglas A. Noverr*

SOCIOLOGY OF AMERICA—*Edited by Charles Mark*

TECHNOLOGY AND VALUES IN AMERICAN CIVILIZATION—*Edited by Stephen H. Cutcliffe, Judith A Mistichelli, and Christine M. Roysdon*

WOMAN IN AMERICA—*Edited by Virginia R. Terris*

*in preparation

The above series is part of the

GALE INFORMATION GUIDE LIBRARY

The Library consists of a number of separate series of guides covering major areas in the social sciences, humanities, and current affairs.

General Editor: Paul Wasserman, Professor and former Dean, School of Library and Information Services, University of Maryland

Managing Editor: Denise Allard Adzigian, Gale Research Company

American Literature and Language

A GUIDE TO INFORMATION SOURCES

Volume 13 in the American Studies Information Guide Series

Donald N. Koster

Emeritus Professor of English
Adelphi University
Garden City, New York

Gale Research Company
Book Tower, Detroit, Michigan 48226

Library of Congress Cataloging in Publication Data

Koster, Donald Nelson, 1910-
American literature and language.

(American studies information guide series ; v. 13)
(Gale information guide library)
Includes indexes.
1. American literature—Bibliography. 2. Reference books—American literature—Bibliography. 3. English language—Bibliography. 4. Reference books—English language—Bibliography. I. Title.
Z1225.K68 [PS88] 016. 81 82-2917
ISBN 0-8103-1258-1 AACR2

TO ROSEMARY

VITA

Donald Nelson Koster is emeritus professor of English at Adelphi University, Garden City, New York, where he taught American literature and directed the interdepartmental program in American Studies. He earned his A.B., M.S., and Ph.D. degrees at the University of Pennsylvania, where he taught before going to Adelphi University. He was for many years bibliographer of the American Studies Association, for which he organized and directed a number of bibliographical projects, the results of which appeared in AMERICAN QUARTERLY.

Koster is the author of TRANSCENDENTALISM IN AMERICA (Twayne, 1975) and DIVORCE IN THE AMERICAN DRAMA (University of Pennsylvania, 1942), as well as of many articles appearing in such publications as AMERICAN QUARTERLY, AMERICAN STUDIES, AMERICAN STUDIES: AN INTERNATIONAL NEWSLETTER, AMERICAN TRANSCENDENTAL QUARTERLY, PENNSYLVANIA GAZETTE, and ADELPHI QUARTERLY. He is currently series editor of Gale Research Company's American Studies Information Guide Series in which this volume appears.

CONTENTS

ACKNOWLEDGMENTS

It is a pleasant obligation to acknowledge the resources of the Van Pelt Library at the University of Pennsylvania, where most of the research for this book was done, as well as the willing assistance of its capable staff when help was needed. I am also grateful to the editor of the Gale Information Guide Library, Denise Allard Adzigian, for her patience in bearing with me and in responding promptly to my queries. Above all, I am appreciative of the encouragement and forebearance of my wife, Rosemary, and of my family, who never complained of my spending, over the past many months, far more time with this bibliography than with them.

INTRODUCTION

It is, of course, a truism to say that the language and literature of a civilization are its most essential building blocks. Without them, no culture would be possible, for the communication of ideas would be all but eliminated. It follows, therefore, that systematic examination of these building blocks is desirable and that tools for such examination may be quite necessary.

This guide to information about American literature and the language which is its medium of expression is offered, then, as an aid to the serious study of these vital aspects of the civilization that has come to be called American. True, many such aids already exist, but each is different from the others, and each has its points of strength and weakness. The necessity for new ones to appear with some frequency should be apparent in that literature and language grow and change rapidly, as does the scholarship related to them.

A few words should be said about the nature of this guide--its objectives and its limitations. To begin with, it is not intended to be complete, a state that would be unachievable were all the bibliographers in the United States to work on it every minute of every day for the next century. Indeed, it is highly selective, the inclusion of items being dependent on my judgment of their value to a guide of this sort. For example, the list of individual authors included in the literature section is infinitesimal when compared with the number of writers whose work has been published in the course of America's history. Nevertheless, it is an impressive list, drawn up according to certain criteria: (1) the existence of a sizeable body of biographical and critical books about the authors and their works; (2) the importance attributed to the authors in their time; (3) their intrinsic merit as literary artists according to critical judgments, my own included; (4) the extent to which study of their works is continuing.

The omission of certain names considered by others to be important enough for inclusion may be attributed not only to my own predilections but more importantly to the fact that most, if not all, of the biographical or critical attention paid to them has been published in periodicals or exists in unpublished doctoral dissertations, neither of which I have chosen to include.

Introduction

For both the literature and language sections, the items chosen for inclusion are either published books or pamphlets written in English or translated into English. Articles and essays published in periodicals have not been used unless they are part of a collection published in book form. To include periodical pieces would be to exceed by many hundreds of pages the space available to me. Furthermore, by the very manner of their publication, they tend to be more ephemeral than do books. Even so, the inclusion of items has been subjected to a rigorous control, in that for certain writers--Emerson, Whitman, Henry James, Melville, and Hawthorne, for example--the listing of all secondary book sources would necessitate the publication of this volume in several volumes.

My plan is fairly straightforward. The section on literature opens with a subsection on bibliographies likely to be useful to the student at every level. A subsection of more or less general cultural background books follows, and, in turn, subsections on literary biography, literary history, and literary criticism. Then comes by far the largest subsection: the studies, biographical and critical, of individual authors. In the interest of conserving space, no attempt has been made to list each author's own works, for such listings are readily available elsewhere. Thus, only secondary sources are mentioned.

The section on language, being relatively brief, has not been divided into subsections. Once again, the field of possibilities for inclusion was large. Therefore, my decision was to list only representative books that seemed to me to be of high quality and genuine value to the potential user. The aim was judicious selectivity.

I have tried to make reasonably descriptive and, frequently, evaluative annotations to accompany the items listed throughout. The temptation to write lengthy accounts was present more often than not, but the restraint imposed by the limits of the series format triumphed over the verbosity which might have resulted in the absence of such limits. In those instances in which direct quotation has been used, it should be understood that the words within the quotation marks are those of the book's author unless otherwise indicated.

Although works are included herein which were originally published a century or more ago, the attempt has been made to emphasize the inclusion of scholarship of much more recent vintage. In particular, books published after 1950 tend to predominate; in fact, a large number of the volumes cited have appeared within the last decade. This emphasis on recent scholarship helps, of course, to make this guide much more than an echo of bibliographies past. Nevertheless, there were many books from the distant past that demanded inclusion because of their importance, their acquired stature, or because nothing else has come along to replace them. Such books, many of which have received the tribute of being reprinted, have, within reason, been included.

ACRONYMS

TUSAS	Twayne's United States Authors Series
UMPAW	University of Minnesota Pamphlets on American Writers

Part 1

LITERATURE

A. GENERAL AIDS

1. BIBLIOGRAPHIES, CHECKLISTS, INDEXES, AND REFERENCE GUIDES

1 BIBLIOGRAPHIC INDEX; A CUMULATIVE INDEX TO BIBLIOGRAPHIES, 1937-- . New York: H.W. Wilson, 1938-- . Annual.

Invaluable and indispensable tool.

2 Blanck, Jacob, comp. BIBLIOGRAPHY OF AMERICAN LITERATURE. New Haven, Conn.: Yale University Press, 1955-- .

A monumental descriptive author bibliography, compiled for the Bibliographical Society of America. To date six volumes published, with the alphabetical treatment through the work of Thomas William Parsons.

3 Brenni, Vito Joseph. THE BIBLIOGRAPHIC CONTROL OF AMERICAN LITERATURE 1920-1975. Metuchen, N.J., and London: Scarecrow Press, 1979. vii, 210 p.

An invaluable book for information about bibliographies of American literature, both general and specialized, published between 1920 and 1975.

4 Bristol, Roger P., ed. SUPPLEMENT TO CHARLES EVANS' AMERICAN BIBLIOGRAPHY. Charlottesville: University Press of Virginia, 1970. xix, 636 p. Index published separately in 1971.

Adds hundreds of items overlooked by Evans (see no. 9).

5 Burke, W.J., and Howe, Will D., eds. AMERICAN AUTHORS AND BOOKS, 1640 TO THE PRESENT DAY. 3d ed. rev. by Irving Weiss and Anne Weiss. New York: Crown, 1972. 719 p.

Gives alphabetical listing of American authors and their works in chronological order.

6 Cassara, Ernest, ed. HISTORY OF THE UNITED STATES OF AMERICA: A GUIDE TO INFORMATION SOURCES. American Studies Information Guide Series, vol. 3. Detroit: Gale Research Co., 1977. xxi, 459 p.

An amply annotated bibliography of approximately two thousand items.

7 COMPREHENSIVE DISSERTATION INDEX, 1861-1972. 37 vols. Ann Arbor, Mich.: Xerox University Microfilms, 1973.

University Microfilms International has provided annual supplements since 1973.

8 Davis, Lloyd, and Irwin, Robert, eds. CONTEMPORARY AMERICAN POETRY: A CHECKLIST. Metuchen, N.J.: Scarecrow Press, 1975. iv, 179 p.

A guide to American poetry of the 1950s and 1960s, the "postmodern" as opposed to the "modern" period of 1890-1945.

9 Evans, Charles, ed. AMERICAN BIBLIOGRAPHY: A CHRONOLOGICAL DICTIONARY OF ALL BOOKS, PAMPHLETS AND PERIODICAL PUBLICATIONS PRINTED IN THE UNITED STATES OF AMERICA FROM THE GENESIS OF PRINTING IN 1639 DOWN TO AND INCLUDING THE YEAR 1820. Chicago: For the author by Blakely Press, 1902.

Invaluable tool. Contains bibliographical and biographical notes. Evans died before getting beyond 1800.

10 French, William P.; Fabre, Michel J.; and Singh, Amritjit, eds. AFRO-AMERICAN POETRY AND DRAMA 1760-1975: A GUIDE TO INFORMATION SOURCES; Fabre, Geneviève E., ed. AFRO-AMERICAN DRAMA, 1850-1975. American Literature, English Literature, and World Literatures in English Information Guide Series, vol. 17. Detroit: Gale Research Co., 1979. ix, 493 p.

The poetry section is virtually unannotated; the drama section contains many brief annotations as well as many unannotated entries. Lists books and periodical articles.

11 Friedel, Frank Burt, ed., with assistance of Richard K. Showman. HARVARD GUIDE TO AMERICAN HISTORY. 2 vols. Rev. ed. Cambridge, Mass.: Belknap Press of Harvard University Press, 1974. Bibliog. Earlier editions edited by Oscar Handlin et al.

Divided into six parts: (1) "Status, Methods, and Presentation"; (2) "Materials and Tools"; (3) "Colonial History and the Revolution, 1492-1788"; (4) "National Growth, 1789-1865"; (5) "The Rise of Modern America, 1865-1900"; (6) "America in the Twentieth Century." Unannotated.

12 Gohdes, Clarence, ed. BIBLIOGRAPHICAL GUIDE TO THE STUDY OF THE LITERATURE OF THE U.S.A. 4th ed. rev. and enl. Durham, N.C.: Duke University Press, 1976. xii, 173 p.

Provides lists of books useful to "the professional student of the literature of the United States in the acquiring of information and in the techniques of research." Intended to help college teachers of American literature, reference librarians, and graduate students writing master's or doctor's theses.

13 Hart, James D., ed. THE OXFORD COMPANION TO AMERICAN LITERATURE. 4th ed. New York: Oxford University Press, 1965. ix, 991 p.

In alphabetic arrangement, the work includes short biographies and bibliographies of American authors, about nine hundred summaries of important American novels, stories, essays, poems, and plays; definitions and outlines of literary schools and movements; information on literary societies, and on other matters related to writing in America. A useful reference work.

14 Hatch, James V., and Abdullah, Omanii, comps. and eds. BLACK PLAYWRIGHTS, 1823-1977: AN ANNOTATED BIBLIOGRAPHY OF PLAYS. New York and London: R.R. Bowker, 1977. xxi, 319 p.

Lists over twenty-seven hundred plays by about nine hundred black American playwrights. The annotations are very brief and descriptive, not evaluative. Besides being a tool for scholars, the bibliography is designed to assist directors and producers searching for plays to meet their production requirements.

15 Havlice, Patricia Pate, ed. INDEX TO AMERICAN AUTHOR BIBLIOGRAPHIES. Metuchen, N.J.: Scarecrow Press, 1971. vii, 204 p.

Gathers together as many American author bibliographies as possible that have been published in periodicals.

16 Kirby, David K., ed. AMERICAN FICTION TO 1900: A GUIDE TO INFORMATION SOURCES. American Literature, English Literature, and World Literatures in English Information Guide Series, vol. 4. Detroit: Gale Research Co., 1975. xvii, 296 p.

Briefly annotated bibliographies on forty-one authors, including both book-length and periodical sources.

17 Kolb, Harold H., Jr. A FIELD GUIDE TO THE STUDY OF AMERICAN LITERATURE. Charlottesville: University Press of Virginia, 1976. xii, 136 p.

A very useful guide for students at all levels from undergraduate through graduate and beyond. Divided into six sections: (1) "Bibliographies," (2) "Literary History and Criticism," (3) "Reference Works," (4) "Editions and Series," (5) "Anthologies," (6) "Journals." There is an author, subject, and genre index.

18 Leary, Lewis, ed. ARTICLES ON AMERICAN LITERATURE, 1900-1950. Durham, N.C.: Duke University Press, 1954. xv, 437 p.

A listing of articles written in English and appearing in pertinent periodicals through the period indicated. Unannotated.

19 Library of Congress. General Reference and Bibliography Division. A GUIDE TO THE STUDY OF THE UNITED STATES OF AMERICA. Washington, D.C.: Library of Congress, 1960. xv, 1,193 p. SUPPLEMENT 1956-1965, 1976. x, 526 p.

Roy P. Basler and his staff have made in these volumes an invaluable tool for the study of American civilization in its manifold activities from literature to sports and recreation. Annotated, sometimes very fully.

20 LITERARY WRITINGS IN AMERICA: A BIBLIOGRAPHY. 8 vols. Millwood, N.Y.: KTO Press, 1977.

The long-delayed publication of the research project begun at the University of Pennsylvania in 1938 under the supervision of Edward H. O'Neill for the Historical Records Survey of the Federal Works Progress Administration (later called Works Projects Administration or WPA). The bibliography attempts a complete listing of creative American literature written between 1850 and 1940. These volumes are the result of photo-offsetting the entire card catalog of over 250,000 cards garnered from the searching of over two thousand volumes of magazines, over five hundred volumes of literary history and criticism, and more than one hundred bibliographies. Each entry, when possible, is categorized as to its nature (verse, novel, etc.).

21 Mainiero, Lina, ed. AMERICAN WOMEN WRITERS: A CRITICAL REFERENCE GUIDE FROM COLONIAL TIMES TO THE PRESENT. 4 vols. to date. New York: Frederick Ungar, 1979, 1980-- .

Provides biographical sketches for almost fifteen hundred American women writers, including writers of reputation; popular writers; nontraditional writers--of diaries, letters, autobiographies; children's writers; and writers known for extraliterary achievements who have had a wide general readership. For each, critical consideration of the works, biographical data, complete primary bibliography and selected secondary bibliography are included.

22 Margolies, Edward, and Bakish, David, eds. AFRO-AMERICAN FICTION, 1853-1976: A GUIDE TO INFORMATION SOURCES. American Literature, English Literature, and World Literatures in English Information Guide Series, vol. 25. Detroit: Gale Research Co., 1979. xviii, 161 p.

In four chapters: (1) "Checklist of Novels," (2) "Short Story Collections," (3) "Major Authors--Secondary Sources," and (4) "Bibliographies and General Studies." An appendix provides a chronological bibliography. Annotations are very brief or nonexistent.

23 Marshall, Thomas F., ed. AN ANALYTICAL INDEX TO AMERICAN LITERATURE VOLUMES I-XXX, MARCH 1929-JANUARY 1959. Durham, N.C.: Duke University Press, 1963. vii, 253 p.

Indexes the leading scholarly journal devoted exclusively to articles in American literature. In two parts: (1) "Author-Subject Index"; (2) "Book Review Index."

24 Meserve, Walter J., ed. AMERICAN DRAMA TO 1900: A GUIDE TO INFORMATION SOURCES. American Literature, English Literature, and World Literatures in English Information Guide Series, vol. 28. Detroit: Gale Research Co., 1980. xviii, 254 p.

In two parts: (1) "Critical, Historical and Reference Resources"; (2) "Individual Dramatists," thirty-four of whom are included. Annotations are either lacking or very brief.

25 Nadel, Ira Bruce, ed. JEWISH WRITERS OF NORTH AMERICA: A GUIDE TO INFORMATION SOURCES. American Studies Information Guide Series, vol. 8. Detroit: Gale Research Co., 1981. xix, 493 p.

In four parts: (1) "General Reference Guides," (2) "Poets," (3) "Novelists and Short-Story Writers," (4) Dramatists." Includes Canadian as well as U.S. writers. Lists primary materials and provides extensive, annotated secondary source materials for each writer. Two appendixes: "Yiddish Literature" and "Checklists of Additional American- and Canadian-Jewish Writers."

26 Nilon, Charles H., ed. BIBLIOGRAPHY OF BIBLIOGRAPHIES IN AMERICAN LITERATURE. New York and London: R.R. Bowker, 1970. xi, 483 p.

In addition to listing materials dealing with American literature, it lists some tools for the study of American history, the history of publishing and printing in America, biography, newspapers, and other subjects. These entries are useful to students in American studies.

27 Peavy, Charles D., ed. AFRO-AMERICAN LITERATURE AND CULTURE SINCE WORLD WAR II: A GUIDE TO INFORMATION SOURCES. American Studies Information Guide Series, vol. 6. Detroit: Gale Research Co., 1979. xiv, 302 p.

In two parts: (1) subjects; (2) individual authors, of whom there are fifty-six. Well annotated.

28 Reardon, Joan, and Thorsen, Kristine A., eds. POETRY BY AMERICAN WOMEN, 1900-1975: A BIBLIOGRAPHY. Metuchen, N.J., and London: Scarecrow Press, 1979. vii, 674 p.

Some fifty-five hundred American women who have published at least one volume of poetry are listed alphabetically. Unannotated.

29 Robbins, J. Albert, and Woodress, James, eds. AMERICAN LITERARY SCHOLARSHIP, AN ANNUAL. Durham, N.C.: Duke University Press, 1963-- .

Edited in alternate years by Robbins and Woodress, this valuable work contains bibliographical essays by specialists on scholarly publication during the title year under the following headings. Part 1. Emerson, Thoreau, and transcendentalism; Hawthorne; Poe; Melville; Whitman and Dickinson; Mark Twain; Henry James; Pound and Eliot; Faulkner; Fitzgerald and Hemingway. Part 2. Literature to 1800; nineteenth-century literature; fiction: 1900 to the 1930s; fiction: the 1930s to the 1950s; fiction: the 1950s to the present; poetry: 1900 to the 1930s; poetry: the 1930s to the present; drama; black literature; themes, topics, and criticism; foreign scholarship.

30 Sandeen, Ernest R., and Hale, Frederick, eds. AMERICAN RELIGION AND PHILOSOPHY: A GUIDE TO INFORMATION SOURCES. American Studies Information Guide Series, vol. 5. Detroit: Gale Research Co., 1978. xvi, 377 p.

Provides a well annotated listing of recent secondary literature and key primary documents, with special attention to the relationship of religion and philosophy with the rest of American culture.

31 Shaw, Ralph R., and Shoemaker, Richard H., eds. AMERICAN BIBLIOGRAPHY, A PRELIMINARY CHECKLIST FOR 1801-1819. 22 vols. New York: Scarecrow Press, 1958-66.

Continues Evans's work (see no. 9).

32 Shoemaker, Richard H., ed. A CHECKLIST OF AMERICAN IMPRINTS FOR 1820-1829. 10 vols. New York: Scarecrow Press, 1964-71.

Pushes beyond Evans's original goal of 1820. A title index was compiled by M. Frances Cooper and published by Scarecrow in 1972, and an author index in 1973.

33 Terris, Virginia R., ed. WOMAN IN AMERICA: A GUIDE TO INFORMATION SOURCES. American Studies Information Guide Series, vol. 7. Detroit: Gale Research Co., 1980. xviii, 520 p.

Contains an excellent section on women in American literature.

34 Woodress, James, ed. AMERICAN FICTION, 1900-1950: A GUIDE TO INFORMATION SOURCES. American Literature, English Literature, and World Literatures in English, vol. 1. Detroit: Gale Research Co., 1974. xxii, 260 p.

Contains a general bibliography section and forty-four individual bibliographical essays. The essays give much helpful information, but the essay method makes for some difficulty in finding it quickly.

35 _____. DISSERTATIONS IN AMERICAN LITERATURE, 1891-1955. Durham, N.C.: Duke University Press, 1957. x, 100 p.

A useful listing arranged according to subject fields. About half the number is on individual authors.

36 Wright, Lyle H., ed. AMERICAN FICTION, 1774-1850. 2d ed., rev. San Marino, Calif.: Huntington Library, 1969. xviii, 411 p.

Alphabetical listing by author.

37 _____. AMERICAN FICTION, 1851-1875. San Marino, Calif.: Huntington Library, 1965. xviii, 438 p.

38 _____. AMERICAN FICTION, 1876-1900. San Marino, Calif.: Huntington Library, 1966. xix, 683 p.

39 Yannella, Donald, and Roch, John H., eds. AMERICAN PROSE TO 1820: A GUIDE TO INFORMATION SOURCES. American Literature, English Literature, and World Literatures in English Information Guide Series, vol. 26. Detroit: Gale Research Co., 1979. xxii, 653 p.

An excellent compilation with helpful annotations, containing 2,957 items. Included are 139 authors, many of them all but forgotten names. The long section on general and specific references is unusually thorough.

2. BIOGRAPHICAL REFERENCE AIDS

40 Helterman, Jeffrey, and Layman, Richard, eds. AMERICAN NOVELISTS SINCE WORLD WAR II. Dictionary of Literary Biography, vol. 2. Detroit: Gale Research Co., 1978. xi, 557 p. Illus.

Contains biographical sketches of eighty writers from James Agee through Richard Yates who either began writing novels after 1945 or have done their most important work since that year. Full bibliographies of each author's books are provided, as are selected bibliographies of critical work about him.

41 Myerson, Joel, ed. THE AMERICAN RENAISSANCE IN NEW ENGLAND. Dictionary of Literary Biography, vol. 1. Detroit: Gale Research Co., 1978. 224 p. Illus.

Biographical sketches of ninety-eight authors who participated in the American Renaissance in the years 1830 to 1860. Bibliographies of primary and secondary sources for each.

42 _____. ANTEBELLUM WRITERS IN NEW YORK AND THE SOUTH. Dictionary of Literary Biography, vol. 3. Detroit: Gale Research Co., 1979. x, 383 p. Illus.

Biographical sketches of sixty-seven authors "who wrote or began writing their major works during the period 1820 to 1860." Writers considered to be major are Bryant, Calhoun, Cooke, Cooper, E.A. Duyckinck, Greeley, Harris, Herbert, Irving, Kennedy, Longstreet, Melville, Poe, Simms, and Whitman. Bibliographies of significant works by and about each author.

43 Rood, Karen Lane, ed. AMERICAN WRITERS IN PARIS, 1920-1939. Dictionary of Literary Biography, vol. 4. Detroit: Gale Research Co., 1980. xv, 426 p. Illus.

Biographical sketches of ninety-nine American writers, journalists, editors, and publishers who went to France between the two World Wars. Concentration is on the years they spent in France. Brief bibliographies of secondary sources are appended.

3. GENERAL HISTORIES

44 Ahlstrom, Sydney E. A RELIGIOUS HISTORY OF THE AMERICAN PEOPLE. New Haven, Conn., and London: Yale University Press, 1972. xvi, 1,158 p. Illus., Bibliog.

Provides a superb social as well as religious background for the study and better understanding of American literature.

45 Allen, Frederick Lewis. ONLY YESTERDAY: AN INFORMAL HISTORY OF THE NINETEEN-TWENTIES. New York: Harper, 1931. Perennial Library ed., 1964. viii, 312 p.

A widely read social history of the eleven years between the end of World War I and the crash of the New York stock market on 13 November 1929.

46 Beard, Charles A.; Beard, Mary R.; and Beard, William. THE BEARDS' NEW BASIC HISTORY OF THE UNITED STATES. Garden City, N.Y.: Doubleday, 1960. 547 p. Illus.

A clearly written and concise history of the nation up to 1960. Useful to college undergraduates.

47 Beer, Thomas. THE MAUVE DECADE: AMERICAN LIFE AT THE END OF THE NINETEENTH CENTURY. New York: Knopf, 1926. 268 p. Reprint. New York: Vintage Books, 1960. xxii, 193 p., vi.

Breezy social history that, although not totally reliable, became a minor classic.

48 Boorstin, Daniel J. THE AMERICANS: THE COLONIAL EXPERIENCE. New York: Random House, 1958. 434 p. Bibliog.

From the beginnings to the Revolution.

49 _____. THE AMERICANS: THE NATIONAL EXPERIENCE. New York: Random House, 1965. 517 p. Bibliog. notes.

Devoted largely to the nineteenth century, which saw the forging of a nation. Cultural history of the first order.

50 _____. THE AMERICANS: THE DEMOCRATIC EXPERIENCE. New York: Random House, 1973. xiv, 717 p. Bibliog. notes.

The final volume of the trilogy, it runs from the Reconstruction era down to 1972.

51 Carter, Paul A. ANOTHER PART OF THE TWENTIES. New York: Columbia University Press, 1977. xiii, 229 p.

An interesting attempt to describe the America of the 1920s that is not reflected in the books about the jazz age or the roaring twenties.

52 Commager, Henry Steele. THE AMERICAN MIND: AN INTERPRETATION OF AMERICAN THOUGHT AND CHARACTER SINCE THE 1880'S. New Haven, Conn., and London: Yale University Press, 1950. ix, 476 p. Bibliog.

An individualistic but well supported analysis of a way of thinking and acting that Commager sees as unique.

53 Curti, Merle. THE GROWTH OF AMERICAN THOUGHT. New York and London: Harper, 1943. xx, 848 p. Bibliog. note.

The classic intellectual history of the American people.

54 Jones, Howard Mumford. O STRANGE NEW WORLD; AMERICAN CULTURE: THE FORMATIVE YEARS. New York: Viking, 1964. xiv, 464 p. Illus.

An imaginative look at the development of a distinctive culture during the colonial period and into the early years of the Republic.

55 Lerner, Max. AMERICA AS A CIVILIZATION; LIFE AND THOUGHT IN THE UNITED STATES TODAY. New York: Simon and Schuster, 1957. xiii, 1,036 p. Bibliog.

Lerner says that the purpose of this very big book is to grasp "the pattern and inner meaning of contemporary American civilization and its relation to the world of today." The chapter headings indicate the scope of the work: "Heritage," "The Idea of American Civilization," "People and Place," "The Culture of Science and the Machine," "Capitalist Economy and Business Civilization," "The Political System," "Class and Status in America," "Life Cycle of the American," "Character and Society," "Belief and Opinion," "The Arts and Popular Culture," "America as a World Power."

56 Morris, Richard B., ed. ENCYCLOPEDIA OF AMERICAN HISTORY. Enl. and updated. New York: Harper and Row, 1970. xiv, 850 p. Illus., maps.

The aim of this helpful tool is to provide in a single volume of standard size the essential facts about American life and institutions. Organization is both chronological and topical. There are three main sections: "Basic Chronology," "Topical Chronology," "Biographies of 300 Notable Americans."

57 Perkins, Dexter, and Van Deusen, Glyndon G. THE UNITED STATES OF AMERICA: A HISTORY. 1962. 2 vols. 2d ed. Vol. 1: TO 1876. xiii, 818 p. Bibliog. Intro. Vol. 2: SINCE 1865. xiii, 893 p. Bibliog. Intro. New York: Macmillan, 1968.

An excellent basic history.

4. LITERARY HISTORIES

58 Aaron, Daniel. THE UNWRITTEN WAR: AMERICAN WRITERS AND THE CIVIL WAR. New York: Knopf, 1973. xix, 385 p., xiv.

Argues that, with a few notable exceptions, American writers have said nothing revealing "about the meaning, if not the causes, of the War." However, Aaron shows that the War "touched and engaged a number of writers." Among those discussed are Simms, Dr. Holmes, James Russell Lowell, Emerson, Hawthorne, Whitman, Melville, Henry Adams, Henry James, Howells, Mark Twain, DeForest, Bierce, Tourgee, Stephen Crane, Frederic, Lanier, Cable, Tate, Warren, and Faulkner.

59 Austen, Roger. PLAYING THE GAME: THE HOMOSEXUAL NOVEL IN AMERICA. Indianapolis and New York: Bobbs-Merrill, 1977. xv, 240 p. Bibliog.

Attempts to select "the relevant male fiction--veiled or unveiled--that has appeared in this country over the past hundred years and place it in simple chronological order, adding bits of background on the author and gay life as it seems to have been lived at the time."

60 Barnett, Louise K. THE IGNOBLE SAVAGE: AMERICAN LITERARY RACISM, 1790-1890. Contributions in American Studies, no. 18. Westport, Conn.: Greenwood Press, 1975. xii, 220 p. Bibliog.

Traces the development in our literature of the stereotype of the bad Indian, particularly in the popular romances of the nineteenth century. A very few writers, like Hawthorne and Melville, ironically penetrate the stereotyped views found in the frontier romance by revealing them to be white rationalizations that smooth over dark truths, the basic one being that "the white men's destruction of primitive peoples is the true barbarism which the aggressors avoid recognizing by labeling their victims savages."

61 Bogard, Travis; Moody, Richard; and Meserve, Walter J. AMERICAN DRAMA. The Revels History of Drama in English, vol. 8. New York: Methuen, 1977. 373 p. Bibliog.

An encyclopedic history with an extensive bibliography and a useful chronological table listing important events, first performances of American plays, and birth and death dates of playwrights.

62 Bone, Robert. THE NEGRO NOVEL IN AMERICA. New Haven, Conn., and London: Yale University Press, 1958. Rev. ed. 1965. x, 289 p. Bibliog.

Ranges from 1853, when William Brown's CLOTEL was published, to 1962, which marked the publication of Baldwin's ANOTHER COUNTRY. Not only is this an excellent sociohistorical study, but also it contains incisive criticism of the novels of the later years.

63 Brodbeck, May; Gray, James; and Metzger, Walter. AMERICAN NON-FICTION, 1900-1950. Twentieth Century Literature in America Series. Chicago: Henry Regnery, 1952. vii, 198 p. Bibliog.

Brodbeck reviews philosophy; Gray, the journalist as literary man; and Metzger, American social thought.

64 Brooks, Van Wyck. MAKERS AND FINDERS: A HISTORY OF THE WRITER IN AMERICA. 5 vols. Vol. 1: THE WORLD OF WASHINGTON IRVING, 1944, 495 p.; vol. 2: THE FLOWERING OF NEW ENGLAND, 1815-1865, 1936. Rev. 1940. 550 p.; vol. 3: THE TIMES OF MELVILLE AND WHITMAN, 1947. 489 p.; vol. 4: NEW ENGLAND: INDIAN SUMMER, 1865-1915, 1940. 557 p.; vol. 5: THE CONFIDENT YEARS: 1885-1915, 1952. 627 p. New York: Dutton.

The five volumes cover: from about 1800 through Poe and the early 1840s; the Boston of Gilbert Stuart through Lowell's essays and the Saturday Club; Irving's New York through Mark Twain in the East; Dr. Holmes's Boston through the pre-World War I years; and New York in the 1880s through the "younger generation" of 1915 in New York, and O'Neill and others.

Written in a flowing style without the impediments of scholarly apparatus, with dextrous use of quotations from many of the authors treated, this is social and cultural, as well as literary, history.

65 Brooks, Van Wyck, and Bettmann, Otto L. OUR LITERARY HERITAGE: A PICTORIAL HISTORY OF THE WRITER IN AMERICA. New York: Dutton, 1956. ix, 241 p.

Based on the five volumes of Brooks's MAKERS AND FINDERS, the book is a happy blending of Brooks's text and Bettmann's remarkable collection of photographs and pictures.

66 Brunvand, Jan Harold. THE STUDY OF AMERICAN FOLKLORE: AN INTRODUCTION. New York: Norton, 1968. xii, 383 p.

Presents in a systematic way the types of folklore found in the United States, and suggests some of the links between American folklore and its parent traditions. Limited to folklore transmitted in English, this is an excellent introduction to the field.

67 Cady, Edwin H. THE LIGHT OF COMMON DAY: REALISM IN AMERICAN FICTION. Bloomington and London: Indiana University Press, 1971. 224 p.

Attempts to define realism and to contrast it to romance and naturalism, and to study its practice in certain works and writers.

68 Cargill, Oscar. INTELLECTUAL AMERICA: IDEAS ON THE MARCH. New York: Macmillan, 1941. xxi, 777 p.

An examination of American ideologies from 1890 to 1940. In six parts: (1) The Invading Forces, French Naturalism and Decadence, German Absolutism, English Liberalism, and Their Purveyors; (2) The Naturalists; (3) The Decadents; (4) The Primitivists; (5) The Intelligentsia; (6) The Freudians.

69 Cowie, Alexander. THE RISE OF THE AMERICAN NOVEL. New York: American Book Co., 1948. xii, 877 p. Bibliog.

Although ending with 1940, this is a reliable standard history from the beginnings to that date.

70 Cunliffe, Marcus. THE LITERATURE OF THE UNITED STATES. 3d ed. rev. Harmondsworth, Engl.: Penguin, 1968. 409 p.

Although by a British scholar, this is the best short history of the full range of American literature from colonial times to the near present.

71 Dorson, Richard M. AMERICAN FOLKLORE AND THE HISTORIAN. Chicago and London: University of Chicago Press, 1971. xii, 239 p.

A collection of the author's essays written over twenty-five years, in which he attempts to convey his sense of the values of folklore for American cultural and literary history. The essays entitled "The Identification of Folklore in American Literature" and "Folklore in American Literature: A Postscript" are particularly pertinent.

72 ______. AMERICAN FOLKLORE: WITH REVISED BIBLIOGRAPHICAL NOTES. Chicago History of American Civilization, no. 4. Chicago: University of Chicago Press, 1977. xi, 338 p. Bibliog.

An excellent historical survey of the development of the major folk traditions.

73 Edmiston, Susan, and Cirino, Linda D. LITERARY NEW YORK: A HISTORY AND GUIDE. Boston: Houghton Mifflin, 1976. xix, 409 p. Illus.

A fascinating book, organized around a series of neighborhood tours with street maps that take the reader or visitor to every section in the city which writers lived in, worked in, or wrote about. The illustrations (photographs) are numerous and excellent. Areas covered are Lower Manhattan, Greenwich Village, Lower East Side, Gramercy Park, Chelsea, Midtown, East Side, West Side, Harlem, Bronx, Queens, Staten Island, Brooklyn, and Brooklyn Heights.

74 Gregory, Horace, and Zaturenska, Marya. A HISTORY OF AMERICAN POETRY 1900-1940. New York: Harcourt, Brace, 1946. xi, 524 p. Bibliog.

The best critical history of a vital era in American poetry. Divided into four parts and an epilogue: (1) the "Twilight Interval" from William Vaughan Moody to E.A. Robinson; (2) the "Poetic Renaissance," from Harriet Monroe and Frost to Masters, Lindsay, and Sandburg; (3) the 1920s, from Millay to Eliot; (4) the 1930s from the Benets to Hart Crane; and the epilogue, on "Recent American Poetry," with some discussion of Jarrell, Prokosch, Eberhart, Robert Fitzgerald, Brinnin, Rexroth, and others.

75 Hart, James. THE POPULAR BOOK; A HISTORY OF AMERICA'S LITERARY TASTE. New York: Oxford University Press, 1950. ix, 351 p. Illus. Bibliog. checklist.

A highly readable and often fascinating history of the books America was reading from the colonial beginnings down through 1949.

76 Hoffman, Frederick J. THE MODERN NOVEL IN AMERICA, 1900-1950. Chicago: Regnery, 1951. viii, 216 p. Bibliog.

Examines the twentieth-century American novel in terms of what is seen as the two primary issues involved in its progress: James's preoccupation with technique and method, and the naturalists' concern for social relevance. Chapters on James, Howells and the art of fiction, prewar naturalism, Cather and Glasgow, Stein, the novel between wars, violence and rhetoric in the 1930s, and the 1940s.

77 Horton, Rod W., and Edwards, Herbert W. BACKGROUNDS OF AMERICAN LITERARY THOUGHT. 3d ed. Englewood Cliffs, N.J.: Prentice-Hall, 1974. x, 630 p. Bibliog.

A very useful book for the undergraduate student in particular. It provides in compact and relatively simple form historical and intellectual materials necessary to a genuine understanding of major American writers. The intellectual, social, political, and economic currents underlying American literature are examined, and an attempt is made to define such concepts and movements as the Enlightenment, Transcendentalism, Pragmatism, Marxism, Naturalism, and Existentialism.

78 Howard, Helen Addison. AMERICAN INDIAN POETRY. Boston: Twayne, 1979. 191 p. Bibliog.

A survey of the poetry of North American Indians which is "intended as an introduction to both the earlier works and to the nineteenth-century preserved metrical compositions of Indian bards from representative tribes in all cultural areas throughout the United States."

79 Howard, Leon. LITERATURE AND THE AMERICAN TRADITION. Garden City, N.Y.: Doubleday, 1960. 354 p.

Attempts to answer the question: "Does the literary history of America reveal the existence of an attitude of mind consistent and durable enough to be called an aspect of the national character?" Examining the literature from the beginnings to the present, Howard concludes that it does, and that the attitude is "a belief in the creative power of the human spirit to endure and prevail and to exist in the meanest and queerest of individuals." This is the tradition.

80 Hubbell, Jay B. THE SOUTH IN AMERICAN LITERATURE, 1607-1900. Durham, N.C.: Duke University Press, 1954. xix, 987 p. Bibliog.

The standard history of American southern writing, it is divided thus: (1) "The Colonial Period, 1607-1765"; (2) "The American Revolution, 1765-1789"; (3) "The Era of Good Feeling, 1789-1830"; (4) "The Road to Disunion, 1830-1865"; (5) "The New South, 1865-1900"; (6) "Epilogue: The Twentieth Century (up to 1953)."

81 Kazin, Alfred. ON NATIVE GROUNDS, AN INTERPRETATION OF MODERN AMERICAN PROSE LITERATURE. New York: Harcourt, Brace, 1942. xiii, 541 p. Abridged with a new postscript. Garden City, N.Y.: Doubleday, 1956. xiv, 425 p.

In three parts: (1) "The Search for Reality (1890-1917)," (2) "The Great Liberation (1918-1929)," (3) "The Literature of Crisis (1930-1940)."

82 Keiser, Albert. THE INDIAN IN AMERICAN LITERATURE. New York: Oxford University Press, 1933. Reprint. New York: Octagon Books, 1975. vi, 312 p. Bibliog.

Follows the treatment of the Indian from the Pocahontas legend to Edna Ferber's CIMARRON.

83 Koster, Donald N. TRANSCENDENTALISM IN AMERICA. World Leaders Series. Boston: Twayne, 1975. 126 p. Bibliog.

The only book that tells the story of Transcendentalism in the United States from its beginnings up to the present time. The ten chapters are: "Definitions"; "Major Influences"; "The Transcendental Club, Brook Farm and Fruitlands, the Movement in the West"; "Transcendental Journals and the Transcendentalist Aesthetic"; "Emerson"; "Thoreau"; "Whitman"; "Other Important Transcendentalists"; "Critics of Transcendentalism"; "Influences of Transcendentalism on American Life and Literature."

84 Leisy, Ernest E. THE AMERICAN HISTORICAL NOVEL. Norman: University of Oklahoma Press, 1950. x, 280 p.

This outline of the development of the historical novel is arranged according to historical backgrounds: (1) "Colonial America," (2) "The American Revolution and Its Aftermath," (3) "The Westward Movement," (4) The Civil War and Reconstruction," (5) "National Expansion."

85 Martin, Jay. HARVESTS OF CHANGE: AMERICAN LITERATURE 1865-1914. Englewood Cliffs, N.J.: Prentice-Hall, 1967. xv, 382 p.

Tries to show how and why the period was particularly rich with "relatedness . . . among people, ideas, convictions, and the institutions of society." The effects of this relatedness on our literature is the theme of this study.

86 Marx, Leo. THE MACHINE IN THE GARDEN; TECHNOLOGY AND THE PASTORAL IDEAL IN AMERICA. New York: Oxford University Press, 1964. 392 p. Illus.

Shows the effects of machine technology upon consciousness by exploring American literary response to the general culture. The acceptance by Emerson and Whitman of the machine's invasion of the Edenic garden that had been pastoral America becomes unreconciled tension in Hawthorne, Melville, and Mark Twain, and finally terror for Scott Fitzgerald. An important study.

87 Miller, Perry. THE RAVEN AND THE WHALE: THE WAR OF WORDS AND WITS IN THE ERA OF POE AND MELVILLE. New York: Harcourt, Brace and World, 1956. viii, 370 p.

The fascinating account of the influence of Evert Augustus Duyckinck and Lewis Gaylord Clark on the careers and reputations of Melville and Poe.

88 Miller, Wayne Charles. AN ARMED AMERICA; ITS FACE IN FICTION: A HISTORY OF THE AMERICAN MILITARY NOVEL. New York: New York University Press, 1970. xvi, 294 p. Bibliog.

From Cooper's THE SPY through DR. STRANGELOVE. Unfortunately, the study is marred by poor proofreading, for example, "Senator Eugent J. McCarthy" or "material" for "materiel."

89 Millgate, Michael. AMERICAN SOCIAL FICTION, JAMES TO COZZENS. Edinburgh and London: Oliver and Boyd, 1964. x, 217 p.

A British critic discusses American novels between 1877, the publication date of James's THE AMERICAN, and 1957, the date of Cozzens's BY LOVE POSSESSED, which deliberately create an image of the society in which their characters move. James, Howells, Norris, Wharton, Dreiser, Anderson, Lewis, Fitzgerald, Dos Passos, and Cozzens are the principal writers discussed.

90 Mott, Frank Luther. AMERICAN JOURNALISM; A HISTORY, 1690-1960. 3d ed. New York: Macmillan, 1962. 901 p. Illus.

The standard history.

91 _____. GOLDEN MULTITUDES; THE STORY OF BEST SELLERS IN THE UNITED STATES. New York: Macmillan, 1947. Reissue. New York: R.R. Bowker, 1960. xii, 357 p. Bibliog.

A lively account of America's reading tastes.

92 _____. A HISTORY OF AMERICAN MAGAZINES. 5 vols. Cambridge, Mass.: Harvard University Press, 1966. Illus.

Runs from 1741 through 1930.

93 Murdock, Kenneth B. LITERATURE AND THEOLOGY IN COLONIAL NEW ENGLAND. Cambridge, Mass.: Harvard University Press, 1949. xi, 235 p.

Easily the best study of early New England literature and the influence on it of theology.

94 Parrington, Vernon Louis. MAIN CURRENTS IN AMERICAN THOUGHT: AN INTERPRETATION OF AMERICAN LITERATURE FROM THE BEGINNINGS TO 1920. 3 vols. Vol. 1: THE COLONIAL MIND, 1620-1800, 1927. xvii, 413 p. bibliog.; vol. 2: THE ROMANTIC REVOLUTION IN AMERICA, 1800-1860, 1927. xxii, 493 p. bibliog.; vol. 3: THE BEGINNINGS OF CRITICAL REALISM IN AMERICA, 1860-1920 COMPLETED TO 1900 ONLY. New York: Harcourt, Brace, 1930. xxxix, 429 p. Bibliog.

American literature assessed from the point of view of agrarian liberalism. Parrington's evaluation of American writers has been strongly challenged by many critics; for example, he dismisses Poe in two pages saying that he "lies quite outside the main current of American thought." Despite Parrington's biases, his work has the advantage of a firmly held critical point of view.

95 Pattee, Fred Lewis. THE DEVELOPMENT OF THE AMERICAN SHORT STORY: AN HISTORICAL SURVEY. New York: Harper, 1923. Reprint. New York: Biblo and Tannen, 1975. v, 388 p.

A classic survey that is still useful. Begins with Irving and ends with O. Henry and his influence.

96 Pizer, Donald. REALISM AND NATURALISM IN NINETEENTH-CENTURY AMERICAN LITERATURE. Cross-Currents/Modern Critiques. Carbondale and Edwardsville: Southern Illinois University Press, 1966. xv, 176 p. Bibliog.

Attempts to answer two major questions: "how can one best describe realism and naturalism in nineteenth-century American fiction, and what is the relationship between the literary criticism of the age and the emergence and nature of realism and naturalism?"

97 Quinn, Arthur Hobson, ed. AMERICAN FICTION: AN HISTORICAL AND CRITICAL SURVEY. New York and London: Appleton-Century, 1936. xxiii, 805 p. Bibliog.

Treats both the novel and the short story. Ranges from the work of Franklin, Hopkinson, and Brackenridge to that of Mary Austin, Dorothy Canfield, and Susan Glaspell.

98 ______. A HISTORY OF THE AMERICAN DRAMA FROM THE BEGINNING TO THE CIVIL WAR. New York and London: Harper, 1923. xv, 486 p. Bibliog.

The first volume of Quinn's monumental history, which remains the standard in its field. Contains a valuable list of American plays from 1665 to 1860.

99 ______. A HISTORY OF THE AMERICAN DRAMA FROM THE CIVIL WAR TO THE PRESENT DAY. 2 vols. in 1. Rev. ed. New York: F.S. Crofts, 1936. xxv, 728 p. illus. Bibliog. Playlist.

The revised edition of the original 1927 edition, this was published as a single volume and contains an additional chapter covering the period 1927-36. Begins with the work of Augustin Daly, and ends with the early work of such playwrights as Rose Franken, Lillian Hellman, and S.N. Behrman.

100 ______. THE LITERATURE OF THE AMERICAN PEOPLE: AN HISTORICAL AND CRITICAL SURVEY. New York: Appleton-Century-Crofts, 1951. xix, 1,172 p. Bibliogs.

In this wide-ranging, four-part survey part 1, "The Colonial and Revolutionary Period," is the work of Kenneth B. Murdock; part 2, "The Establishment of National Literature," that of Professor Quinn; part 3, "The Later Nineteenth Century," that of Clarence Gohdes; and part 4, "The Twentieth Century," that of George F. Whicher. The bibliographies are excellent.

101 Rourke, Constance. AMERICAN HUMOR: A STUDY OF THE NATIONAL CHARACTER. New York: Harcourt, Brace, 1931. 253 p. Bibliog. note.

The classic account of the development of American humor in literature, and of its importance as an index to the character of Americans.

102 Smith, Henry Nash. VIRGIN LAND: THE AMERICAN WEST AS SYMBOL AND MYTH. Cambridge, Mass.: Harvard University Press, 1950. Reprint. New York: Vintage Books, 1957. viii, 305 p., vi.

A major study that traces the impact of the West "on the consciousness of Americans and follows the principal consequences of this impact in literature and social thought down to Turner's formulation of it." In three books: "Passage to India," "The Sons of Leatherstocking," "The Garden of the World."

103 Smith, Herbert F. THE POPULAR AMERICAN NOVEL, 1865-1920. TUSAS, no. 372. Boston: Twayne, 1980. 192 p. Bibliog.

An interesting history of the American novel of the period, which emphasizes the minor writers. The main criterion for inclusion is social and cultural significance, not literary artistry. The reader will find himself in touch with many novelists included in no standard history of American letters.

104 Sonnichsen, C.L. FROM HOPALONG TO HUD: THOUGHTS ON WESTERN FICTION. College Station and London: Texas A & M University Press, 1978. 201 p. Bibliog.

Suggests that the continued vitality of the myth of the West as seen in fiction arises from "a natural and normal hunger for a heroic past."

105 Spiller, Robert E. THE CYCLE OF AMERICAN LITERATURE: AN ESSAY IN HISTORICAL CRITICISM. New York: Macmillan, 1955. xv, 318 p.

Reviews the history of American literature and finds that it moves in cycles. Romanticism led the way to the first great literary renaissance in America and it was "the literary expression of the Atlantic seaboard Republic." It died out and was replaced by a second renaissance, led by "the rise of realism and the ultimate dominance of the West after 1870."

106 Spiller, Robert E., et al. LITERARY HISTORY OF THE UNITED STATES. 4th ed. rev. 2 vols. New York: Macmillan, 1974. Originally published in 1946.

The best full-scale history of American literature available. Many distinguished scholars have contributed to its writing. The second volume is entirely devoted to an extensive and valuable bibliography, organized in sections: "Guide to Resources," "Bibliographies of Literature and Culture," "Bibliographies of Movements and Influences," "Bibliographies of Individual Authors."

107 Stauffer, Donald Barlow. A SHORT HISTORY OF AMERICAN POETRY. New York: Dutton, 1974. xvii, 459 p. Bibliog.

A useful brief history that ranges from early colonial to contemporary poetry, such as that of Allen Ginsberg, Gary Snyder, Denise Levertov, and Imamu Amiri Baraka.

108 Stout, Janis P. SODOMS IN EDEN: THE CITY IN AMERICAN FICTION BEFORE 1860. Contributions in American Studies, no. 19. Westport, Conn., and London: Greenwood Press, 1976. x, 161 p. Bibliog.

Discusses early urban stereotypes in popular fiction, and then devotes a chapter to the "urban Gothicists," Brockden Brown, Lippard, and Poe; another to Cooper and others; a third to Hawthorne; and a final one to Melville.

109 Taylor, Walter Fuller. THE ECONOMIC NOVEL IN AMERICA. Chapel Hill: University of North Carolina Press, 1942. Reprint. New York: Octagon Books, 1964, 1969, 1973. xi, 378 p. Bibliog.

Examines the development from about 1865 to 1900 of a body of fiction that presented a "coherent and incisive critique of capitalistic industrialism." Major writers treated are Mark Twain, Hamlin Garland, Edward Bellamy, Howells, and Norris.

110 Trent, William P.; Erskine, John; Sherman, Stuart P.; and Carl Van Doren, eds. THE CAMBRIDGE HISTORY OF AMERICAN LITERATURE. 4 vols. New York: Putnam, 1917-21. 2,114 p. Bibliogs.

Although superseded in many respects by later works, some of the essays remain important, and the bibliographies are quite comprehensive for their time.

111 Tyler, Moses Coit. A HISTORY OF AMERICAN LITERATURE, 1607-1765. New York: Putnam, 1878. Reissue. Ithaca, N.Y.: Cornell University Press, 1949. xxxiii, 551 p.

The classic history of the pre-revolutionary period.

112 Voss, Arthur. THE AMERICAN SHORT STORY: A CRITICAL SURVEY. Norman: University of Oklahoma Press, 1973. xi, 399 p. Bibliog.

Like Fred Pattee's (no. 95), this survey begins with Irving, but ends with a chapter on the short story since 1940, in which the works of Welty, Mary McCarthy, Stafford, Powers, Salinger, Malamud, and O'Connor are considered.

113 Wagenknecht, Edward. CAVALCADE OF THE AMERICAN NOVEL. New York: Holt, Rinehart and Winston, 1952. xv, 575 p. Bibliog.

Ranges "from the birth of the nation to the middle of the twentieth century," beginning with Brockden Brown and Brackenridge and ending with Steinbeck and Marquand.

114 Waggoner, Hyatt H. AMERICAN POETS FROM THE PURITANS TO THE PRESENT. Boston: Houghton Mifflin, 1968. xxi, 740 p. Bibliog.

Begins with the New England Puritan poets and concludes with the work of Roethke, Dickey, Robert Kelly, Robert Duncan, and Denise Levertov. Treats fewer poets than does Stauffer (see no. 107), but with somewhat greater depth. The book is organized around the idea that Emerson is the central figure in American poetry, "essential both as spokesman and as catalyst" and "essential for our understanding of those poets not numbered among his poetic sons."

115 Weales, Gerald. AMERICAN DRAMA SINCE WORLD WAR II. New York: Harcourt, Brace and World, 1962. ix, 246 p.

A critical description of American plays produced between 1945 and 1961. Criteria for inclusion were one of the following: intrinsic merit, being written by an established playwright, and length of run on or off Broadway.

116 _____. THE JUMPING-OFF PLACE: AMERICAN DRAMA IN THE 1960'S. New York: Macmillan, 1969. xii, 306 p.

Continues Weales's (no. 115) critical description of American plays. Notes that the distinction between on and off Broadway was all but eliminated in the 1960s. The title suggests that there is an implicit difference between the drama of the 60s and that of the 40s and 50s: "a sense of newness, of departure, of possibility."

117 Westbrook, Wayne W. WALL STREET IN THE AMERICAN NOVEL. New York and London: New York University Press, 1980. vii, 213 p.

Studies the treatment of finance in the work of many American writers, among them Hawthorne, Melville, James, Howells, Wharton, Norris, Dreiser, Auchincloss.

5. GENERAL CRITICAL STUDIES

118 Aldridge, John W. AFTER THE LOST GENERATION: A CRITICAL STUDY OF THE WRITERS OF TWO WARS. New York: McGraw-Hill, 1951. xiii, 263 p.

A book that created a stir upon its publication and which remains instructive, it studies the American writers of the two world wars and contrasts them. Hemingway, Fitzgerald, and Dos Passos are in the older group; Mailer, Lowry, Bourjaily, Merle Miller, Capote, Vidal, Buechner, Bowles, Irwin Shaw, Burns, and Hayes in the younger. Aldridge sees an emptiness in the fiction of the latter group, who are viewed as victims of a failure of values and the absence of a community of art in the contemporary world, "a symptom of the general debility of the times as a whole."

119 ______. IN SEARCH OF HERESY: AMERICAN LITERATURE IN AN AGE OF CONFORMITY. New York: McGraw-Hill, 1956. Reprint. Westport, Conn.: Greenwood Press, 1974. ix, 208 p.

A series of provocative essays that revolve around the theme that a new intellectual conformism has enveloped our writers, who have increasingly been adopting the values of institutional orthodoxy.

120 Blake, Nelson Manfred. NOVELISTS' AMERICA: FICTION AS HISTORY, 1910-1940. Syracuse, N.Y.: Syracuse University Press, 1969. xiii, 279 p. Illus. Bibliog.

Probes the use of fiction as a source in the search for historical truth. Examines aspects of American life as viewed from the perspective of eight important novelists: Lewis, Fitzgerald, Faulkner, Wolfe, Steinbeck, Dos Passos, Farrell, and Wright.

121 Bluefarb, Sam. THE ESCAPE MOTIF IN THE AMERICAN NOVEL: MARK TWAIN TO RICHARD WRIGHT. Columbus: Ohio State University Press, 1972. xii, 173 p.

A discussion of eight novels that employ the frequently used motif of flight, or escape. They are HUCKLEBERRY FINN; THE DAMNATION OF THERON WARE; WINESBURG, OHIO (which the author regards as a novel because of the linkage of the stories); THREE SOLDIERS; A FAREWELL TO ARMS; THE GRAPES OF WRATH; THE HEART IS A LONELY HUNTER; and NATIVE SON.

122 Canby, Henry Seidel. CLASSIC AMERICANS: A STUDY OF EMINENT AMERICAN WRITERS FROM IRVING TO WHITMAN, WITH AN INTRODUCTORY SURVEY OF THE COLONIAL BACKGROUND OF OUR NATIONAL LITERATURE. New York: Harcourt, Brace, 1931. Reprint. New York: Russell and Russell, 1959. xvii, 371 p. Bibliog.

A long opening chapter on "The Colonial Background" is followed by a chapter each on Irving, Cooper, Emerson, Thoreau, Hawthorne and Melville, Poe, and Whitman. Canby's opinions are often stated as fact.

123 Cooperman, Stanley. WORLD WAR I AND THE AMERICAN NOVEL. Baltimore: Johns Hopkins Press, 1967. xii, 271 p. Bibliog.

The war fiction of Willa Cather, Theodore Fredenburgh, Dos Passos, James Stevens, Elliot Paul, Faulkner, Thomas Boyd, Cummings, and Hemingway is studied as an "echo of meaning" for "those who are interested in understanding why Americans do tend to embark on so many crusades, and why they so often trip over their own ideals in the process."

124 Cowley, Malcolm. EXILE'S RETURN: A LITERARY ODYSSEY OF THE 1920'S. Rev. ed. New York: Viking, 1951. 322 p.

The story to 1930 "of what used to be called the lost generation of American writers." This is the revised version of the book published originally in 1934.

125 _____. A MANY-WINDOWED HOUSE: COLLECTED ESSAYS ON AMERICAN WRITERS AND AMERICAN WRITING. Edited with introduction by Henry Dan Piper. Carbondale and Edwardsville: Southern Illinois University Press, 1970. xviii, 261 p.

Fourteen of Cowley's most important essays are here gathered for the first time. Among writers treated are Hawthorne, Whitman, Horatio Alger, Henry James, Lafcadio Hearn, Dreiser, Sherwood Anderson, Ezra Pound, O'Neill, Frost, and Van Wyck Brooks. There are also essays on "American Naturalism," "Criticism," and "Myth in American Writing."

126 Curley, Dorothy Nyren; Kramer, Maurice; and Kramer, Elaine Fialka, eds. MODERN AMERICAN LITERATURE: A LIBRARY OF LITERARY CRITICISM. 4th ed. enl. 3 vols. New York: Frederick Ungar, 1969.

Contains condensed critiques of over 250 modern American authors, as well as a bibliography for each author.

127 Downer, Alan S., ed. THE AMERICAN THEATER TODAY. New York and London: Basic Books, 1967. ix, 212 p.

A book of essays in four parts: (1) an account of theater before World War I by John Hewitt, John Gassner, and Malcolm Goldstein; (2) focus on Broadway by Elliot Norton, Eric Bentley, Goldstein, Esther Jackson, and Gerald Weales; (3) a producer, two playwrights, a lyricist, and a composer of musical comedy discuss their work--Richard Barr, Edward Albee, Murray Schisgal, Sheldon Hernick, and Jerry Bock; and (4) off-Broadway, educational theater, and the relationship between professional theater and the universities, by Bernard Dukore, Edwin Pettet, and Arthur Lithgow. There is an epilogue entitled "The Future of the American Theater" by Downer.

128 Eisinger, Chester E. FICTION OF THE FORTIES. Chicago and London: University of Chicago Press, 1963. 392 p.

A wide-ranging historical-critical account of what the author calls the "age of prose fiction." Chapters on the war novel, on naturalism, on fiction and the liberal reassessment, on the conservative imagination, on the "new" fiction, and on the existential crisis.

129 Fiedler, Leslie A. LOVE AND DEATH IN THE AMERICAN NOVEL. New York: Criterion Books, 1960. xxxiv, 603 p.

In a controversial study, Fiedler asserts that "American literature is distinguished by the number of dangerous and disturbing books in its canon--and American scholarship by its ability to conceal this fact." He concentrates on the themes of love and death as treated by our major writers, and on the duplicity with which those themes are handled. The lengthy analyses of THE SCARLET LETTER, MOBY DICK, and HUCKLEBERRY FINN are especially interesting.

130 Folsom, James K., ed. THE WESTERN: A COLLECTION OF CRITICAL ESSAYS. Englewood Cliffs, N.J.: Prentice-Hall, 1979. viii, 177 p. Bibliog.

David B. Davis on "Ten-Gallon Hero"; W.H. Hutchinson on "Virgins, Villains, and Varmints"; J. Frank Dobie on "Andy Adams, Cowboy Chronicler"; David Mogen on "Owen Wister's Cowboy Heroes"; Max Westbrook on "The Archetypal Ethic of THE OX-BOW INCIDENT"; Vardis Fisher on "The Novelist and His Background"; Fisher and Opal Laurel Holmes on "The Blend of History and Legend"; S. Griswold

Morley on "Cowboy and Gaucho Fiction"; editor Folsom on "English Westerns"; and Richard W. Etulain on "The American Literary West and Its Interpreters: The Rise of a New Historiography."

131 Frohock, W.M. THE NOVEL OF VIOLENCE IN AMERICA. Rev. and enl. ed. Dallas: Southern Methodist University Press, 1957. xi, 238 p.

Studies of Dos Passos, Wolfe, Farrell, Warren, Caldwell, Steinbeck, Faulkner, Hemingway, and Agee.

132 Fussell, Edwin. FRONTIER: AMERICAN LITERATURE AND THE AMERICAN WEST. Princeton, N.J.: Princeton University Press, 1965. xv, 450 p.

Explores the idea of the West in the writing of Cooper, Hawthorne, Poe, Thoreau, Melville, and Whitman.

133 Geismar, Maxwell. THE LAST OF THE PROVINCIALS: THE AMERICAN NOVEL, 1915-1925. Boston: Houghton Mifflin, 1947. xii, 404 p. Bibliog.

Critical studies of H.L. Mencken, Lewis, Cather, Anderson, and Fitzgerald, who are seen as presenting in their work "the final conquest of the American town, and the values of an older rural life, by the New Economic Order of the industrialized cities."

134 Gross, Seymour L., and Hardy, John Edward, eds. IMAGES OF THE NEGRO IN AMERICAN LITERATURE. Patterns of Literary Criticism. Chicago and London: University of Chicago Press, 1966. x, 321 p.

Fifteen essays by well-known writers, critics, and literary scholars, including Tremaine McDowell, Leslie Fiedler, Ralph Ellison, Sidney Kaplan, James M. Cox, Irving Howe, James Baldwin, Robert A. Bone, and the two editors.

135 Hoffman, Daniel G. FORM AND FABLE IN AMERICAN FICTION. New York: Oxford University Press, 1961. xvi, 368 p.

An interesting attempt to discover themes that "profoundly influenced the early masters of American fiction--Irving, Hawthorne, Melville, and Mark Twain."

136 _____, ed. HARVARD GUIDE TO CONTEMPORARY AMERICAN WRITING. Cambridge, Mass., and London: Belknap Press of Harvard University Press, 1979. ix, 618 p.

A critical survey of "the most significant writing in the United States between the end of World War II and the end of the 1970's." Alan Trachtenberg writes on intellectual background; A. Walton Litz on literary criticism;

Leo Braudy on realists, naturalists, and novelists of manners; Lewis P. Simpson on southern fiction; Mark Shechner on Jewish writers; Josephine Hendin on experimental fiction; Nathan A. Scott, Jr., on black literature; Elizabeth Janeway on women's literature; Gerald Weales on drama; and Hoffman on poetry in three chapters--"After Modernism," "Schools of Dissidents," and "Dissidents from Schools."

137 Hoffman, Frederick J. THE ART OF SOUTHERN FICTION: A STUDY OF SOME MODERN NOVELISTS. Crosscurrents/Modern Critiques. Carbondale and Edwardsville: Southern Illinois University Press, 1967. x, 198 p.

Discusses the importance of place in the work of Eudora Welty and Carson McCullers; explores religious consciousness in the fiction of James Agee and Flannery O'Connor; sees the work of Truman Capote, William Goyen, Walker Percy, and Reynolds Price in terms of the "Gothic" and grotesque; and devotes a chapter to an exploration of William Styron's novels.

138 Holman, C. Hugh. WINDOWS ON THE WORLD: ESSAYS ON AMERICAN SOCIAL FICTION. Knoxville: University of Tennessee Press, 1979. xiv, 205 p.

Lively discussions of literary realism, the Southern Provincial in Metropolis, John P. Marquand, Ellen Glasgow, Faulkner, Wolfe, and others.

139 Howard, Richard. ALONE WITH AMERICA: ESSAYS ON THE ART OF POETRY IN THE UNITED STATES SINCE 1950. New York: Atheneum, 1969. xiii, 594 p.

Discusses forty-one poets, each in an essay. Among the best known are John Ashbery, Robert Bly, Gregory Corso, James Dickey, Allen Ginsberg, Daniel Hoffman, John Hollander, Galway Kinnell, Kenneth Koch, Denise Levertov, James Merrill, Frank O'Hara, Sylvia Plath, Adrienne Rich, Anne Sexton, Louis Simpson, W.D. Snodgrass, Gary Snyder, May Swenson, David Wagoner, and James Wright.

140 Levin, Harry. THE POWER OF BLACKNESS: HAWTHORNE, POE, MELVILLE. New York: Knopf, 1958. Reprint. New York: Vintage Books, 1960. xii, 263 p., ix. Bibliog.

A rewarding examination of the works of three great American writers whose work was permeated by visions and symbols of the darker side of life.

141 Lewis, R.W.B. THE AMERICAN ADAM: INNOCENCE, TRAGEDY, AND TRADITION IN THE NINETEENTH CENTURY. Chicago and London: University of Chicago Press, 1955. v, 201 p.

An influential historical-critical study that covers the period 1820-60, primarily in coastal New England, where "the image contrived to embody the most fruitful contemporary ideas was that of the authentic American as a figure of heroic innocence and vast potentialities, poised at the start of a new history." Gradually the image is changed and darkened as innocence encounters tragedy until in the contemporary world "the American as Adam has been replaced by the American as Laocoön," as "a figure struggling to stand upright amid the most violent cross-currents."

142 Matthiessen, F.O. AMERICAN RENAISSANCE; ART AND EXPRESSION IN THE AGE OF EMERSON AND WHITMAN. London and New York: Oxford University Press, 1941. xxiv, 678 p. Illus.

The book has become a classic historical-critical study. Its main subject is "the conceptions held by five of our major writers concerning the function and nature of literature, and the degree to which their practice bore out their theories." The writers are Emerson, Thoreau, Hawthorne, Melville, and Whitman, and it is Matthiessen's contention that their common denominator was their devotion to the possibilities of democracy. The time period covered intensively is the half decade of 1850-55, which is seen as the time of a rebirth or flowering of literary imaginative vitality.

143 Mazzaro, Jerome. POSTMODERN AMERICAN POETRY. Urbana, Chicago, and London: University of Illinois Press, 1980. xi, 203 p.

Essays on seven poets: W.H. Auden, Randall Jarrell, Theodore Roethke, David Ignatow, John Berryman, Sylvia Plath, and Elizabeth Bishop.

144 Milton, John R. THE NOVEL OF THE AMERICAN WEST. Lincoln and London: University of Nebraska Press, 1980. xvi, 341 p.

Not intended to be a definitive history of the western American novel, this nonetheless does trace much of that history although the major emphasis is on the major writers and their right to a place in American letters. Vardis Fisher, A.B. Guthrie, Jr., Frederick Manfred, Walter Van Tilburg Clark, Harvey Fergusson, and Frank Waters are explored in depth.

145 Pilkington, William T., ed. CRITICAL ESSAYS ON THE WESTERN AMERICAN NOVEL. Critical Essays on American Literature. Boston: Twayne, 1980. 296 p. Bibliog.

Twenty-four essays that discuss such writers as Owen Wister, A.B. Guthrie, Jr., Louis L'Amour, and Walter Van Tilburg Clark.

146 Pritchard, John Paul. CRITICISM IN AMERICA: AN ACCOUNT OF THE DEVELOPMENT OF CRITICAL TECHNIQUES FROM THE EARLY PERIOD OF THE REPUBLIC TO THE MIDDLE YEARS OF THE TWENTIETH CENTURY. Norman: University of Oklahoma Press, 1956. x, 325 p. Bibliog. notes.

A survey of American literary criticism from 1800. Treated are Emerson and his circle, Poe, minor critics of 1837-55, Whitman, the Brahmins, the Realists, the Impressionists, Regionalists and Nationalists; the New Humanists and their opponents; the New Criticism, and recent practising critics such as T.K. Whipple, Edmund Wilson, the later Van Wyck Brooks, and the Chicago Critics.

147 Pritchard, William H. LIVES OF THE MODERN POETS. New York: Oxford University Press, 1980. xii, 316 p.

Attempts to provide introductions to, and revaluations of, "the nine most interesting and important poets writing in English in the first part of this century." Two are British--Hardy and Yeats--the remainder are American: Robinson, Frost, Pound, Eliot, Stevens, Hart Crane, and William Carlos Williams.

148 Tanner, Tony. THE REIGN OF WONDER: NAIVETY AND REALITY IN AMERICAN LITERATURE. Cambridge, Engl.: Cambridge University Press, 1965. New York: Perennial Library, Harper and Row, 1967. Paper. viii, 388 p.

A stimulating attempt by a British scholar to show that many American writers worked to develop a new angle of vision through a recurring use of wonder and naivety of response that concentrates on the present to the virtual exclusion of the past. The book is in four parts: (1) "The Transcendentalists"; (2) "Mark Twain"; (3) "The Twentieth Century," with chapters on Stein, Sherwood Anderson, and Hemingway; (4) "Henry James."

149 Wilson, Edmund. PATRIOTIC GORE: STUDIES IN THE LITERATURE OF THE AMERICAN CIVIL WAR. New York: Oxford University Press, 1962. xxxii, 816 p.

A masterful examination of the writings of Americans, North and South, literary and nonliterary, centering on the Civil War.

B. INDIVIDUAL AUTHOR BIBLIOGRAPHIES

HENRY BROOKS ADAMS (1838-1918)

150 Adams, James Truslow. HENRY ADAMS. New York: Albert and Charles Boni, 1933. 246 p. Bibliog.

The first biography of Adams, originally intended for a collected edition of Henry Adams's WORKS. Still of value, but superseded by the work of Samuels (see nos. 166-168).

151 Auchincloss, Louis. HENRY ADAMS. UMPAW, no. 93. Minneapolis: University of Minnesota Press, 1971. 48 p. Bibliog.

Suggests that "Prayer to the Virgin of Chartres" synthesizes Adams's philosophy.

152 Baym, Max I. THE FRENCH EDUCATION OF HENRY ADAMS. New York: Columbia University Press, 1951. Reprint. New York: Kraus Reprint Co., 1969. xii, 358 p.

Studies the indebtedness of Adams to French thought through a close examination of Adams's own books with his scorings and marginalia.

153 Bishop, Ferman. HENRY ADAMS. TUSAS, no. 293. Boston: Twayne, 1979. 157 p. Bibliog.

An introduction to Adams through close examination of some of the minor essays and all of the major works. Adams's use of satire is stressed. Very helpful for the reader who is relatively unacquainted with the subject.

154 Blackmur, R.P. HENRY ADAMS. Edited by Veronica A. Makowsky. New York and London: Harcourt Brace Jovanovich, 1980. xxvii, 354 p.

When Blackmur died in 1965 he left about seven hundred pages of manuscript and several boxes of notes on Adams.

He had planned a book that would be a full portrait of the man and his work. Working from the typescripts, the editor has given us the book Blackmur might have done.

155 Conder, John J. A FORMULA OF HIS OWN: HENRY ADAMS'S LITERARY EXPERIMENT. Chicago and London: University of Chicago Press, 1970. xiv, 202 p. Bibliog.

Sees CHARTRES and EDUCATION as a single unit of art.

156 Dusinberre, William. HENRY ADAMS: THE MYTH OF FAILURE. Charlottesville: University Press of Virginia, 1980. 250 p.

Views THE EDUCATION as a "purposeful travesty of the meaning of Adams's life." Attempts to recreate that life as part of a revaluation of Adams's literary career.

157 Harbert, Earl N. THE FORCE SO MUCH CLOSER HOME: HENRY ADAMS AND THE ADAMS FAMILY. New York: New York University Press, 1977. xi, 224 p.

The book attempts to demonstrate the overwhelming importance of the family heritage in forming Adams's thought and writing.

158 _____, ed. CRITICAL ESSAYS ON HENRY ADAMS. Boston: Twayne, 1981. 300 p. Bibliog.

The first collection of Adams criticism to be published, it contains essays by leading Adams scholars such as Ernest Samuels, Millicent Bell, J.C. Levenson, R.P. Blackmur, and Henry Steele Commager.

159 _____. HENRY ADAMS: A REFERENCE GUIDE. Boston: G.K. Hall, 1978. xii, 96 p.

The most complete annotated list of published writings about Henry Adams from 1879 to 1975, with emphasis on more recent years. Invaluable.

160 Hume, Robert. RUNAWAY STAR: AN APPRECIATION OF HENRY ADAMS. Ithaca, N.Y.: Cornell University Press, 1951. x, 270 p. Bibliog.

Surveys all of Adams's works.

161 Jordy, William H. HENRY ADAMS: SCIENTIFIC HISTORIAN. New Haven, Conn.: Yale University Press, 1952. xv, 327 p. Bibliog.

Treats with authority the scientific side of Adams's historical work.

162 Levenson, J.C. THE MIND AND ART OF HENRY ADAMS. Boston: Houghton Mifflin, 1957. x, 430 p.

A scholarly and well written analysis of Adams's intellectual and creative achievement against the background of his life and times. The most influential general interpretation of Adams's work.

163 Lyon, Melvin. SYMBOL AND IDEA IN HENRY ADAMS. Lincoln: University of Nebraska Press, 1970. 326 p. Bibliog.

Explicates six works in detail and examines Adams's literary techniques.

164 Mane, Robert. HENRY ADAMS ON THE ROAD TO CHARTRES. Cambridge, Mass.: Harvard University Press, 1971. viii, 288 p. Bibliog.

Sees CHARTRES as Adams's greatest work, and examines Adams's intellectual and artistic development before its composition.

165 Murray, James G. HENRY ADAMS. New York: Twayne, 1974. 171 p. Bibliog.

Sees Adams as "truly the exemplar" of Emerson's "man thinking."

166 Samuels, Ernest. HENRY ADAMS: THE MAJOR PHASE. Cambridge, Mass.: Belknap Press of Harvard University Press, 1964. xv, 687 p.

Spans the last twenty-eight years of Adams's life, the period Adams liked to call his "posthumous existence."

167 _____. HENRY ADAMS: THE MIDDLE YEARS. Cambridge, Mass.: Belknap Press of Harvard University Press, 1958. xiv, 514 p.

Biographical and critical study of the main part of Adams's life. Covers the period 1877-90.

168 _____. THE YOUNG HENRY ADAMS. Cambridge, Mass.: Harvard University Press, 1948. xiv, 378 p.

Tells the story of the earlier Henry Adams as reconstructed from contemporary materials, especially those related to his intellectual and literary growth. Covers the period from 1854-77.

169 Stevenson, Elizabeth. HENRY ADAMS, A BIOGRAPHY. New York: Macmillan, 1955. xiv, 425 p. Bibliog.

Sees Adams as a man whose goal was the control of power and whose gift and flaw was pride.

170 Wagner, Vern. THE SUSPENSION OF HENRY ADAMS: A STUDY OF MANNER AND MATTER. Detroit: Wayne State University Press, 1969. 268 p. Bibliog.

Uses the "major formal works"--HISTORY, CHARTRES, EDUCATION--to portray Adams as a great stylist.

CONRAD AIKEN (1889-1973)

171 Denney, Reuel. CONRAD AIKEN. UMPAW, no. 38. Minneapolis: University of Minnesota Press, 1964. 48 p. Bibliog.

Brief but cogent analysis of Aiken's prose and poetry. Sees Aiken as speaking in terms of a creed liberalism.

172 Hoffman, Frederick J. CONRAD AIKEN. TUSAS, no. 17. New York: Twayne, 1962. 172 p. Bibliog.

A reliable introduction to the life and work.

173 Martin, Jay. CONRAD AIKEN: A LIFE OF HIS ART. Princeton, N.J.: Princeton University Press, 1962. ix, 280 p.

Close analysis of the poetry, fiction, and critical writing. Attempts to trace the continuing development of Aiken as an artist.

174 Peterson, Houston. THE MELODY OF CHAOS. New York and Toronto: Longmans, Green, 1931. vii, 280 p.

A study in "complexity and chaos," with the poetry of Aiken as principal theme.

EDWARD ALBEE (1928--)

175 Amacher, Richard E. EDWARD ALBEE. TUSAS, no. 141. New York: Twayne, 1969. 190 p. Bibliog.

Extensive analyses, plot summaries, and explication of each of Albee's ten plays through A DELICATE BALANCE. There is also a biographical sketch.

176 Amacher, Richard E., and Rule, Margaret, comps. EDWARD ALBEE AT HOME AND ABROAD: A BIBLIOGRAPHY. New York: AMS Press, 1973. 95 p.

Provides lists of primary sources (plays, articles, and other works by Albee) and secondary sources (books, dissertations, theses, articles, and reviews) in three groupings: (1) America and England; (2) Germany, Austria, and Switzerland; (3) other countries. Most entries are not annotated; those that are are briefly so.

177 Bigsby, C.W.E. ALBEE. Writers and Critics Series. Edinburgh: Oliver and Boyd, 1969. 120 p. Bibliog.

A British introduction to Albee that presents the conventional biographical sketch and proceeds to examine the early plays, WHO'S AFRAID OF VIRGINIA WOOLF, TINY ALICE, the two adaptations, BALLAD OF THE SAD CAFE and MALCOLM, and finally, A DELICATE BALANCE. Albee's value to the American theater is seen as lying in "his determination to transcend the exhausted naturalism of the Broadway theatre, while establishing an existential drama committed to examining the metaphysical rather than the social or psychological problems of man."

178 Debusscher, Gilbert. EDWARD ALBEE: TRADITION AND RENEWAL. Translated from French by Anne D. Williams. Brussels: Center for American Studies, 1967. viii, 94 p. Bibliog.

Reviews Albee's dramatic career and concludes that he was "the first to integrate the discoveries of the French avant-garde theater." His plays are seen as the first synthesis of the new theater and of the American tradition derived from Ibsen and Strindberg. "He has achieved a theatrical style which belongs only to him, with his disconcerting mixture of minute observation, precise details, and wild invention; with his fusion of reality and daydream."

179 Green, Charles Lee, ed. EDWARD ALBEE: AN ANNOTATED BIBLIOGRAPHY 1968-1977. AMS Studies in Modern Literature, no. 6. New York: AMS Press, 1980. xv, 150 p.

Supplements and complements the English-language section of Amacher and Rule's bibliography (see no. 176). Lists both primary and secondary sources.

180 Paolucci, Anne. FROM TENSION TO TONIC: THE PLAYS OF EDWARD ALBEE. Crosscurrents/Modern Critiques Series. Carbondale and Edwardsville: Southern Illinois University Press, 1972. xiv, 143 p. Bibliog.

A learned analysis of the Albee plays (exclusive of his dramatic adaptations of novels and other plays) in which Albee is seen as "the only playwright, after O'Neill, who shows real growth," the only one to break away from the "message" plays that Paolucci believes "have plagued our theater since O'Neill." He is perceived as the only current playwright committed to serious articulation of the existential questions of our time.

181 Rutenberg, Michael E. EDWARD ALBEE: PLAYWRIGHT IN PROTEST. New York: DBS Publications, 1969. 280 p. Bibliog.

Reviews the plays chronologically from THE ZOO STORY through BOX and QUOTATIONS FROM CHAIRMAN MAO-TSE-TUNG, and establishes the thesis that Albee's early plays are all protests in defense of outcasts of society victimized by the stupid and biased successful elite. In WHO'S AFRAID OF VIRGINIA WOOLF he is seen to change his sociological approach by launching an attack on the hypocrisy and corruption in some circles of our society's intelligentsia, while in the later plays he goes further "into an exploration of modern man's . . . sense of isolation and estrangement from society and his God."

182 Stenz, Anita Maria. EDWARD ALBEE: THE POET OF LOSS. Studies in American Literature, vol. 32. The Hague, Paris, and New York: Mouton, 1978. ix, 146 p. Bibliog.

This recent study of Albee's plays proceeds chronologically from THE ZOO STORY through SEASCAPE, with a chapter devoted to careful analysis of each play as it was first presented in New York. Attempts to clarify the meaning of each. Albee is viewed as focusing on "the twisted human relationships which can evolve within the establishment, on the results of materialism and parasitism, and on the deceptive nature of ambition."

A. BRONSON ALCOTT (1799-1888)

183 Christy, Arthur. THE ORIENT IN AMERICAN TRANSCENDENTALISM: A STUDY OF EMERSON, THOREAU, AND ALCOTT. Columbia University Studies in English and Comparative Literature, no. 68. New York: Columbia University Press, 1932. Reprint. New York: Octagon Books, 1963. xix, 382 p.

The chapter on Alcott, entitled "Alcott the Propagandist," is relatively brief. Christy sees Alcott as making his principal contribution as teacher.

184 Sanborn, F.B., and Harris, William T. A. BRONSON ALCOTT, HIS LIFE AND PHILOSOPHY. 2 vols. Boston: Roberts Brothers, 1893. v, 679 p.

A straightforward memoir composed from biographical material left by Alcott and from materials of such friends as Emerson and Thoreau. The authors write with a profound sympathy toward their subject.

185 Stoehr, Taylor. NAY-SAYING IN CONCORD: EMERSON, ALCOTT, AND THOREAU. Hamden, Conn.: Archon Books, 1979. 179 p.

Alcott is seen, with the two others, as a major transcendentalist.

LOUISA MAY ALCOTT (1832-1888)

186 Anthony, Katharine. LOUISA MAY ALCOTT. New York and London: Knopf, 1938. xiii, 304 p., xi. Bibliog.

Concentrates on the life with little discussion of the work. The approach is Freudian psychoanalytic.

187 Payne, Alma J., ed. LOUISA MAY ALCOTT: A REFERENCE GUIDE. Boston: G.K. Hall, 1980. xix, 87 p.

An annotated and exhaustive bibliography with a valuable introduction.

188 Saxton, Martha. LOUISA MAY; A MODERN BIOGRAPHY OF LOUISA MAY ALCOTT. Boston: Houghton Mifflin, 1977. viii, 428 p. Illus. Bibliog.

A thoroughly researched biography in which Saxton sees Louisa May as a victim of repression who "emptied herself into her books." LITTLE WOMEN is viewed not as her masterpiece, but as "the story of the childhood she would have had if her parents had described it."

189 Stern, Madeline B. LOUISA MAY ALCOTT. Norman: University of Oklahoma Press, 1950. xiii, 424 p. Illus. Bibliog.

A carefully researched and ably written biography with considerable discussion of the literary output.

190 _____. LOUISA'S WONDER BOOK. Juvenile Series, no. 1. Mt. Pleasant: Central Michigan University, 1975. Bibliog.

Contains a major updating of the excellent bibliography included in no. 189.

191 Worthington, Marjorie. MISS ALCOTT OF CONCORD: A BIOGRAPHY. Garden City, N.Y.: Doubleday, 1958. 330 p. Bibliog.

Based primarily on Louisa May's journal and letters, this is a highly readable if occasionally sentimental volume, with distracting introduction of Worthington's own experiences.

JAMES LANE ALLEN (1849-1925)

192 Bottorff, William K. JAMES LANE ALLEN. TUSAS, no. 56. New York: Twayne, 1964. 176 p. Bibliog.

A critical analysis that presents a balanced view of Allen and his work.

193 Knight, Grant C. JAMES LANE ALLEN AND THE GENTEEL TRADITION. Chapel Hill: University of North Carolina Press, 1935. xiii, 313 p. Bibliog.

A biographical treatment that attempts to place Allen within an important frame of reference.

194 Townsend, John Wilson. JAMES LANE ALLEN. Louisville, Ky.: Courier-Journal Job Printing Co., 1927. 124 p.

Contains a biographical sketch and an encomium of Allen and his work.

MAXWELL ANDERSON (1888-1959)

195 Bailey, Mabel Driscoll. MAXWELL ANDERSON: THE PLAYWRIGHT AS PROPHET. London and New York: Abelard-Schuman, 1957. 200 p.

Not a biography, but rather a volume of analytical criticism in which the validity of Anderson's creative principles is tested by examination of his plays.

196 Clark, Barrett H. MAXWELL ANDERSON, THE MAN AND HIS PLAYS. New York: Samuel French, 1933. 32 p.

Pamphlet dealing with Anderson's early years as reporter, poet, and playwright. The plays from WHITE DESERT to BOTH YOUR HOUSES are briefly discussed.

197 Klink, William, ed. MAXWELL ANDERSON AND S.N. BEHRMAN: A REFERENCE GUIDE. Boston: G.K. Hall, 1977. xii, 103 p.

The most complete bibliography on Anderson. Annotated.

198 Shivers, Alfred S. MAXWELL ANDERSON. Boston: Twayne, 1976. 176 p. Bibliog.

Although there are some biographical details, the emphasis is on Anderson's achievement in returning dramatic poetry to the theater.

SHERWOOD ANDERSON (1876-1941)

199 Appel, Paul P., ed. HOMAGE TO SHERWOOD ANDERSON, 1876-1941. Mamaroneck, N.Y.: Paul P. Appel, 1970. 212 p.

A republication in book form of STORY magazine's commemorative issue of March, 1941, in which many of America's leading authors paid tribute to Anderson following his death.

200 Burbank, Rex J. SHERWOOD ANDERSON. TUSAS, no. 65. New York: Twayne, 1964. 159 p. Bibliog.

A useful introduction to the man and his work.

201 Fagin, N. Bryllion. THE PHENOMENON OF SHERWOOD ANDERSON. Baltimore: Rossi-Bryn, 1927. Reprint. New York: Russell and Russell, 1973. xi, 156 p. Bibliog.

An early appreciation of Anderson as an innovator.

202 Howe, Irving. SHERWOOD ANDERSON. American Men of Letters Series. New York: William Sloane Associates, 1951. xiii, 271 p.

A balanced judgment of Anderson as artist, together with a reasonably full biographical account.

203 Rideout, Walter B., ed. SHERWOOD ANDERSON: A COLLECTION OF CRITICAL ESSAYS. Englewood Cliffs, N.J.: Prentice-Hall, 1974. x, 177 p.

A good representative collection.

204 Rogers, Douglas G., ed. SHERWOOD ANDERSON: A SELECTIVE, ANNOTATED BIBLIOGRAPHY. Author Bibliographies Series, no. 26. Metuchen, N.J.: Scarecrow Press, 1976. vi, 157 p.

205 Schevill, James. SHERWOOD ANDERSON: HIS LIFE AND WORK. Denver: Denver University Press, 1951. xvi, 360 p. Bibliog.

A thorough if uncritical survey of Anderson's life and works.

206 Sutton, William A. EXIT TO ELSINORE. Ball State Monograph, no. 7. Muncie, Ind.: Ball State University, 1967. 45 p.

Deals with the period of 1907-13, during Anderson's residence in Elyria, Ohio, a time of crisis and decision culminating in his determination to become a writer.

207 ______. THE ROAD TO WINESBURG: A MOSAIC OF THE IMAGINATIVE LIFE OF SHERWOOD ANDERSON. Metuchen, N.J.: Scarecrow Press, 1972. xiii, 645 p. Bibliog.

Attempts to show the close relationship of Anderson's life to his work. Includes the author's 1967 monograph, EXIT TO ELSINORE.

208 Weber, Brom. SHERWOOD ANDERSON. UMPAW, no. 43. Minneapolis: University of Minnesota Press, 1964. 48 p. Bibliog.

Sees the major theme of Anderson's writing as the tragedy of death in life.

209 White, Ray Lewis, ed. THE ACHIEVEMENT OF SHERWOOD ANDERSON. Chapel Hill: University of North Carolina Press, 1966. 270 p. Bibliog.

An excellent collection of essays on Anderson and his work.

S.N. BEHRMAN (1893-1973)

210 Reed, Kenneth T. S.N. BEHRMAN. Boston: Twayne, 1975. 151 p. Bibliog.

After a biographical chapter, Reed discusses Behrman's plays and then his essays, which he finds superior to the plays. (See also no. 197).

EDWARD BELLAMY (1850-1898)

211 Bowman, Sylvia E. THE YEAR 2000: A CRITICAL BIOGRAPHY OF EDWARD BELLAMY. New York: Bookman Associates, 1958. 404 p. Bibliog.

Approaches LOOKING BACKWARD and EQUALITY from a psychological and sociological viewpoint; thus traces Bellamy's experiences and ideas as well as his reaction to social problems of his time that culminated in his Utopian novels.

212 Bowman, Sylvia E., et al. EDWARD BELLAMY ABROAD; AN AMERICAN PROPHET'S INFLUENCE. New York: Twayne, 1962. xxv, 543 p. Bibliog.

In a series of essays by foreign scholars, Bellamy's influence around the world is assessed. An important bibliography is appended.

213 Morgan, Arthur E. EDWARD BELLAMY. New York: Columbia University Press, 1944. xvii, 468 p. Bibliog.

Views Bellamy as possessed of "one of the most ranging and penetrating minds America has produced." The work as well as the life is thoroughly explored.

SAUL BELLOW (1915--)

214 Clayton, John Jacob. SAUL BELLOW, IN DEFENSE OF MAN. 2d ed. enl. Bloomington and London: Indiana University Press, 1979. xi, 332 p. Bibliog.

An enlargement of the first edition, published by Indiana University Press in 1968. Studies of MR. SAMMLER'S PLANET, TO JERUSALEM AND BACK, and HUMBOLDT'S GIFT are added, and the final section on the unity and development of Bellow's fiction is updated. This most detailed study of Bellow's work is divided into four parts: (1) Introduction, (2) "The Psychic Pattern of Bellow's Fiction," (3) "Studies of Individual Works," (4) "Saul Bellow as a Novelist." Rates Bellow as America's most important living novelist.

215 Cohen, Sarah Blacher. SAUL BELLOW'S ENIGMATIC LAUGHTER. Urbana, Chicago, and London: University of Illinois Press, 1974. 242 p.

The thesis here is that, although Bellow's novels are filled with the details of a degenerating civilization, there is never a total capitulation to despair. "Bellow retaliates with comedy." He employs it, Cohen maintains, "to interrupt, resist, reinterpret, and transcend adversity."

216 Dutton, Robert R. SAUL BELLOW. TUSAS, no. 181. New York: Twayne, 1971. 177 p. Bibliog.

A chapter is devoted to each of the novels through HERZOG, with a final chapter of overview and assessment, and a short supplementary chapter on MR. SAMMLER'S PLANET. The study revolves around the thesis of man as subangelic being.

217 Harris, Mark. SAUL BELLOW, DRUMLIN WOODCHUCK. Athens: University of Georgia Press, 1980. 184 p.

A breezily written account of the author's unsuccessful attempts to become the authorized biographer of Saul Bellow. The portrait of Bellow that emerges is vivid and should be interesting to every reader of his novels.

218 Kulshrestha, Chirantan. SAUL BELLOW: THE PROBLEM OF AFFIRMATION. New Delhi: Arnold-Heinemann, 1978. 174 p. Bibliog.

This Hindu scholar, drawn to Bellow by his books, travels to Chicago to meet and speak at length with Bellow and peruses his manuscripts preliminary to doing this book, which is a valuable study of Bellow's fictional method and a close analysis of DANGLING MAN, SEIZE THE DAY, THE ADVENTURES OF AUGIE MARCH, HERZOG, and MR. SAMMLER'S PLANET.

219 Noreen, Robert G., ed. SAUL BELLOW: A REFERENCE GUIDE. Boston: G.K. Hall, 1978. xiii, 169 p.

Indispensable for scholars. Lists writings about Bellow by year from 1944 through 1976. All items are annotated.

220 Porter, M. Gilbert. WHENCE THE POWER? THE ARTISTRY AND HUMANITY OF SAUL BELLOW. Columbia: University of Missouri Press, 1974. 209 p. Bibliog.

Devotes a chapter to each of the novels, with a final chapter on Bellow's creative vision, which is seen as belonging to the "neotranscendentalist" literary tradition.

221 Rovit, Earl, ed. SAUL BELLOW: A COLLECTION OF CRITICAL ESSAYS. Englewood Cliffs, N.J.: Prentice-Hall, 1975. 176 p. Bibliog.

Essays by Irving Malin, Richard Pearce, M. Gilbert Porter, Ben Siegel, Victoria Sullivan, and Rovit appear here for the first time. Other essays are reprints. A varied collection.

222 Tanner, Tony. SAUL BELLOW. Edinburgh and London: Oliver and Boyd, 1965. 120 p. Bibliog.

A cogent discussion of Bellow's work through HERZOG by an astute British scholar with a special interest in American literature.

223 Trachtenberg, Stanley, ed. CRITICAL ESSAYS ON SAUL BELLOW. Boston: Twayne, 1979. 200 p. Bibliog.

A useful collection that includes an analysis by Daniel Fuchs based on previously unknown Bellow manuscripts.

STEPHEN VINCENT BENET (1898-1943)

224 Fenton, Charles. STEPHEN VINCENT BENET: THE LIFE AND TIMES OF AN AMERICAN MAN OF LETTERS 1898-1943. New Haven, Conn.: Yale University Press, 1958. xv, 436 p. Illus.

A somewhat drawn out biography, although the most reliable source of information on Benet.

225 Stroud, Parry. STEPHEN VINCENT BENET. TUSAS, no. 27. New York: Twayne, 1963. 173 p. Bibliog.

A generally reliable introduction to the life and works.

JOHN BERRYMAN (1914-1972)

226 Arpin, Gary Q. THE POETRY OF JOHN BERRYMAN. Port Washington, N.Y., and London: Kennikat Press, 1978. 111 p. Bibliog.

Imaginative interpretations of the poetry. Berryman's subject is perceived as being the same as his description of Pound's subject matter, "the life of the modern poet." And Arpin feels that "virtually everything he wrote revolved around that theme." His image of the poet is, however, seen as changing through the years.

227 ______, ed. JOHN BERRYMAN: A REFERENCE GUIDE. Boston: G.K. Hall, 1976. xii, 158 p.

This bibliography of writings about Berryman contains descriptive annotations, frequently quite brief. The items are arranged chronologically by year, from 1935 through 1975.

228 Conarroe, Joel. JOHN BERRYMAN: AN INTRODUCTION TO THE POETRY. New York: Columbia University Press, 1977. xxii, 215 p. Bibliog.

Contains a biographical sketch that is obviously indebted to Linebarger's (see no. 230), although adding a few details. There are numerous perceptive analyses of the poetry.

229 Haffenden, John. JOHN BERRYMAN, A CRITICAL COMMENTARY. New York and London: New York University Press, 1980. vii, 216 p. Bibliog.

Berryman's authorized biographer (the biography has not been published as of this writing) here concentrates attention on the long poems, HOMAGE TO MISTRESS BRADSTREET, THE DREAM SONGS, and LOVE AND FAME. Two chapters are devoted to Berryman's notes on THE DREAM SONGS and DELUSIONS, ETC., with commentary by Haffenden.

230 Linebarger, J.M. JOHN BERRYMAN. TUSAS, no. 244. New York: Twayne, 1974. 176 p. Bibliog.

The first full-length study of Berryman's work to be published, it offers, for the Twayne Series, a fairly extended biographical sketch, and a chronological review of the writings. THE DREAM SONGS are seen as bringing together the best of the elements he had experimented with in the earlier verse.

231 Martz, William J. JOHN BERRYMAN. UMPAW, no. 85. Minneapolis: University of Minnesota Press, 1969. 47 p. Bibliog.

The first published monograph on Berryman, it sketches his career and then briefly examines his biography of Stephen Crane, which is viewed as diffuse and uncritical, and analyzes the poetry, which is divided into the early and the later. The difference between the early and later poetry is seen as primarily a striking contrast in style.

232 Stefanik, Ernest C., Jr., ed. JOHN BERRYMAN: A DESCRIPTIVE BIBLIOGRAPHY. Pittsburgh Series in Bibliography. Pittsburgh: University of Pittsburgh Press, 1974. xxix, 285 p.

This indispensable bibliography of Berryman's work is divided into eight sections: (1) "Separate Publications," (2) "First-Appearance Contributions to Books," (3) "Contributions to Periodicals," (4) "Collected Materials Reprinted in Anthologies," (5) "Interviews," (6) "Phono-Recordings," (7) "Dust-Jacket Blurbs," (8) "Poetry Selections." There are two appendixes: (1) chronology of Berryman's publications and (2) periodicals in which Berryman first appeared.

AMBROSE BIERCE (1842-1914?)

233 De Castro, Adolphe Danziger. PORTRAIT OF AMBROSE BIERCE. New York: Century Co., 1929. Reprint. New York: Beekman Publishers, 1974. xiii, 351 p.

An unreliable portrait by one of Bierce's small circle of idolaters.

234 Fatout, Paul. AMBROSE BIERCE, THE DEVIL'S LEXICOGRAPHER. Norman: University of Oklahoma Press, 1951. xv, 349 p. Bibliog.

Useful factual information.

235 ______. AMBROSE BIERCE AND THE BLACK HILLS. Norman: University of Oklahoma Press, 1956. xi, 180 p. Bibliog.

Revises some of the judgments made in his earlier book after a penetrating look, based on primary sources, at a critical period in Bierce's life that had not before been investigated.

236 Grenander, M.E. AMBROSE BIERCE. TUSAS, no. 180. New York: Twayne, 1971. 193 p. Bibliog.

A good, concise biography together with an intensive evaluation of Bierce's more important works.

237 Josephson, Matthew. PORTRAIT OF THE ARTIST AS AMERICAN. New York: Harcourt, Brace, 1930. Reprint. New York: Octagon Books, 1964. xxiii, 308 p.

An early study that took a sympathetic view of Bierce.

238 McWilliams, Carey. AMBROSE BIERCE, A BIOGRAPHY. New York: Albert and Charles Boni, 1929. Reprint. Hamden, Conn.: Archon Books, 1967. xxxi, 358 p. Bibliog. Important new intro.

An early full-length study that retains its value.

239 Neale, Walter. LIFE OF AMBROSE BIERCE. New York: Walter Neale, 1929. Reprint. New York: AMS Press, 1969. 489 p.

An adulatory biography by a friend who regarded Bierce as "the foremost prose writer that this continent so far has produced."

240 O'Connor, Richard. AMBROSE BIERCE, A BIOGRAPHY. Boston: Little, Brown, 1967. 333 p. Bibliog.

In a well written biography the author sees Bierce as "the first notable exponent of black humor in America." Adds little new information.

GEORGE HENRY BOKER (1823-1890)

241 Bradley, Edward Sculley. GEORGE HENRY BOKER, POET AND PATRIOT. Philadelphia: University of Pennsylvania Press; London: H. Milford, Oxford University Press, 1927. Reprint. New York: AMS Press, 1969. xi, 362 p. Bibliog.

This remains the only full-length study of the life and work of a neglected nineteenth-century poet and playwright whose play FRANCESCA DA RIMINI was one of the great stage successes in the history of American drama. Boker was also a founder of the Union League during the Civil War and an American ambassador to Turkey.

HUGH HENRY BRACKENRIDGE (1748-1816)

242 Marder, Daniel. HUGH HENRY BRACKENRIDGE. TUSAS, no. 114. New York: Twayne, 1967. 159 p. Bibliog.

The emphasis is on analysis of Brackenridge's works.

243 Newlin, Claude M. THE LIFE AND WRITINGS OF HUGH HENRY BRACKENRIDGE. Princeton, N.J.: Princeton University Press, 1932. vi, 328 p. Bibliog.

The only full-scale biography of Brackenridge. It does not, however, evaluate his work to any extent.

ANNE BRADSTREET (1612?-1672)

244 Piercy, Josephine K. ANNE BRADSTREET. TUSAS, no. 72. New York: Twayne, 1965. 144 p. Bibliog.

Analyzes Bradstreet's poetry and prose for their revelation of the author's spiritual growth, and studies Bradstreet's development as a writer.

VAN WYCK BROOKS (1886-1963)

245 Hoopes, James. VAN WYCK BROOKS: IN SEARCH OF AMERICAN CULTURE. Amherst: University of Massachusetts Press, 1977. xviii, 346 p.

A full-scale, scholarly, and balanced account of Brooks's life and work, based on extensive research.

245A Nelson, Raymond. VAN WYCK BROOKS: A WRITER'S LIFE. New York: Dutton, 1981. 332 p. Illus.

This new, authorized biography is an excellent complement to Hoopes's book (see no. 245). Taken together, they represent the best work done on Brooks to date.

246 Vitelli, James R. VAN WYCK BROOKS. TUSAS, no. 134. New York: Twayne, 1969. 191 p. Bibliog.

A biographical-critical study in which Vitelli disagrees with the Wasserstrom thesis (see nos. 248-49) that MAKERS AND FINDERS was the major achievement of Brooks's career.

247 ______, ed. VAN WYCK BROOKS: A REFERENCE GUIDE. Boston: G.K. Hall, 1977. xiii, 108 p.

A list of annotated writings about Brooks from 1908 through 1974. Very helpful.

248 Wasserstrom, William. THE LEGACY OF VAN WYCK BROOKS: A STUDY OF MALADIES AND MOTIVES. Carbondale: Southern Illinois University Press, 1971. xviii, 156 p. Bibliog.

Attempts an appraisal of the reasons Brooks's followers abandoned him, and of the reasons for indifference to him among younger critics. Wasserstrom also attempts a vindication of the man. Includes some sixty pages of Brooks's later writings which had not been collected.

249 _____. VAN WYCK BROOKS. UMPAW, no. 71. Minneapolis: University of Minnesota Press, 1968. 48 p. Bibliog.

An imaginative critical essay on the subject and his works.

CHARLES BROCKDEN BROWN (1771-1810)

250 Clark, David Lee. BROCKDEN BROWN AND THE RIGHTS OF WOMEN. Comparative Literature Series, no. 2. Austin: University of Texas, 1922. 48 p.

Traces Brown's interest in the subject, and examines his ALCUIN closely.

251 _____. CHARLES BROCKDEN BROWN, PIONEER VOICE OF AMERICA. Durham, N.C.: Duke University Press, 1952. Reprint. New York: AMS Press, 1966. xi, 363 p. Bibliog.

This is the fullest biography of Brown. Although primary attention focuses on the life, there are chapters on Brown as novelist, as literary critic, as historian, and as journalist.

252 Ringe, Donald A. CHARLES BROCKDEN BROWN. TUSAS, no. 98. New York: Twayne, 1966. 158 p. Bibliog.

Primarily a detailed analysis and critical evaluation of Brown's novels.

253 Rosenthal, Bernard, ed. CRITICAL ESSAYS ON CHARLES BROCKDEN BROWN. Boston: Twayne, 1981. 320 p. Bibliog.

Probably the most substantial collection of critical opinion on Brown yet published. Not only are critiques of him by contemporaries such as Hazlitt and Margaret Fuller included, but also analyses written for this volume by modern Brown specialists such as Nina Baym, Emory Elliot, and Sydney J. Krause. The bibliography is the most extensive one on Brown to date.

254 Vilas, Martin S. CHARLES BROCKDEN BROWN. Burlington, Vt.: Free Press Association, 1904. 66 p.

An early study of Brown's novels marred by infelicities of language and by critical naivete.

255 Warfel, Harry R. CHARLES BROCKDEN BROWN, AMERICAN GOTHIC NOVELIST. Gainesville: University of Florida Press, 1949. xi, 255 p. Bibliog.

The most readable biography of Brown. It is also generally reliable. The plots of the novels are ably recounted, but critical analysis is somewhat sparse.

ORESTES BROWNSON (1803-1876)

256 Gilhooley, Leonard. CONTRADICTION AND DILEMMA: ORESTES BROWNSON AND THE AMERICAN IDEA. New York: Fordham University Press, 1972. xv, 231 p. Bibliog.

The primary focus is an examination of what Brownson had to say about the American idea in his REVIEWS from 1838 to 1860.

257 Lapati, Americo D. ORESTES A. BROWNSON. TUSAS, no. 88. New York: Twayne, 1965. 159 p. Bibliog.

An introduction to the life and thought which serves as an integrated resume of Brownson's contribution to nineteenth-century thought.

258 Maynard, Theodore. ORESTES BROWNSON: YANKEE, RADICAL, CATHOLIC. New York: Macmillan, 1943. xvi, 456 p. Illus., bibliog.

The fullest biography of Brownson. Gives a valuable account of his years as a Roman Catholic.

259 Roemer, Lawrence. BROWNSON ON DEMOCRACY AND THE TREND TOWARD SOCIALISM. New York: Philosophical Library, 1953. xvi, 173 p.

Examines Brownson's political and social principles; reveals his notice of developing trends toward socialism and communism in the nineteenth century.

260 Schlesinger, Arthur M., Jr. ORESTES BROWNSON: A PILGRIM'S PROGRESS. Boston: Little, Brown, 1939. 320 p. Bibliog.

The best study of Brownson's socioeconomic views and of the years prior to the conversion to Catholicism.

261 Sveino, Per. ORESTES A. BROWNSON'S ROAD TO CATHOLICISM. Oslo: Universitetsforlaget and New York: Humanities Press, 1970. 339 p. Bibliog.

Sees Brownson's importance in American intellectual history as lying in his responsiveness to new ideas, an ability to expose the diverse ideologies of his time, and great emotional and intellectual force in presenting his views.

WILLIAM CULLEN BRYANT (1794-1878)

262 Bigelow, John. WILLIAM CULLEN BRYANT. American Men of Letters. Boston: Houghton Mifflin, 1890. Reprint. Detroit: Gale Research Co., 1970. 355 p.

Bryant's long-time friend and associate provides a generous, if uncritical, view of the poet, with many personal reminiscences.

263 Bradley, William Aspenwall. WILLIAM CULLEN BRYANT. English Men of Letters Series. New York and London: Macmillan, 1905. Reprint. Folcroft, Pa.: Folcroft Library Editions, 1973; and Norwood, Pa.: Norwood Editions, 1976. vi, 229 p.

No new biographical material, but considerable criticism of Bryant's poetry, with Bryant seen as second only to Poe as an imaginative American poet.

264 Brown, Charles H. WILLIAM CULLEN BRYANT. New York: Scribner, 1971. 576 p. Illus.

The definitive biography of Bryant to date. Excellent in the account of Bryant as public and political figure. A bit short on analysis of Bryant the poet.

265 Godwin, Parke. A BIOGRAPHY OF WILLIAM CULLEN BRYANT. 2 vols. New York: Appleton, 1883. Vol. 1, 423 p.; vol. 2, 419 p.

Bryant's son-in-law's uncritical but still valuable account of the poet's life.

266 McLean, Albert F., Jr. WILLIAM CULLEN BRYANT. TUSAS, no. 59. New York: Twayne, 1964. 159 p. Bibliog.

An opening chapter of biography is followed by close analysis of the major poems, with a concluding chapter placing Bryant within the total American literary tradition.

267 Nevins, Allan. THE EVENING POST, A CENTURY OF JOURNALISM. New York: Boni and Liveright, 1922. ix, 590 p.

Most of the book is devoted to a valuable account of Bryant's career as editor of the influential newspaper, with Bryant viewed as a political liberal.

268 Peckham, Harry Houston. GOTHAM YANKEE: A BIOGRAPHY OF WILLIAM CULLEN BRYANT. New York: Vantage Press, 1950. Reprint. New York: Russell and Russell, 1971. 228 p. Bibliog.

A popularized treatment of Bryant that is cliche ridden. Offers little that is new.

269 Phair, Judith Turner, ed. A BIBLIOGRAPHY OF WILLIAM CULLEN BRYANT AND HIS CRITICS, 1808-1972. Troy, N.Y.: Whitston Publishing Co., 1975. v, 188 p.

Easily the most complete bibliography of Bryant scholarship and criticism. Divided into chapters on books, periodical articles, book reviews, foreign references, and graduate research. Annotated.

JAMES BRANCH CABELL (1879-1958)

270 Brewer, Frances Joan, ed. JAMES BRANCH CABELL: A BIBLIOGRAPHY OF HIS WRITINGS, BIOGRAPHY, AND CRITICISM. 2 vols. Charlottesville: University Press of Virginia, 1957.

An extensive description of Cabell's published work with an invaluable listing of items about him. Volume 2 contains notes by Matthew J. Bruccoli on the Cabell Collection at the University of Virginia.

271 Davis, Joe Lee. JAMES BRANCH CABELL. TUSAS, no. 21. New York: Twayne, 1962. 174 p. Bibliog.

Attempts a fresh interpretation of Cabell's work. The insights are valuable.

272 Mencken, H.L. JAMES BRANCH CABELL. New York: Robert M. McBride, 1927. 32 p.

Proclaims that Cabell's one aim in life is "to make himself a first-rate artist--and this aim . . . he has come nearer to realizing than any other American of his time."

273 Morley-Mower, Geoffrey. CABELL UNDER FIRE. New York: Revisionist Press, 1975. 29 p.

Four essays printed in a limited edition of two hundred copies. Here a British scholar views Cabell as "one of the minor delights of our era" whose "unique method of remaining sane in a mad world can be applied as well in 1974 as when he sat down to write his books in Richmond-in-Virginia."

274 Rubin, Louis D. NO PLACE ON EARTH. Austin: University of Texas Press, 1959. x, 81 p.

A study of Cabell and Ellen Glasgow and the influence of Richmond, Virginia, on their work.

275 Tarrant, Desmond. JAMES BRANCH CABELL: THE DREAM AND THE REALITY. Norman: University of Oklahoma Press, 1967. xii, 292 p. Bibliog.

A detailed examination of Cabell's voluminous output, which is seen as one of the most ambitious attempts in twentieth-century art to renovate the myth. Cabell, the author holds, saw life "as a pursuit of beauty."

276 Van Doren, Carl. JAMES BRANCH CABELL. New York: Robert M. McBride, 1925. 87 p. Bibliog.

An early essay on Cabell that sees him as a comic poet.

277 Wells, Arvin R. JESTING MOSES: A STUDY IN CABELLIAN COMEDY. Gainesville: University of Florida Press, 1962. ix, 146 p. Bibliog.

Sees Cabell's comedy as approaching tragedy "in its attempt to transcend the whole of the finite predicament and thereby to reconcile man to his role in the scheme of things."

GEORGE WASHINGTON CABLE (1844-1925)

278 Butcher, Philip. GEORGE W. CABLE. TUSAS, no. 24. New York: Twayne, 1962. 189 p. Bibliog.

A critical study of Cable's works set against the background of his life and times, this is the most reliable introduction available to an author not widely known to the general reading public.

279 Ekstrom, Kjell. GEORGE WASHINGTON CABLE: A STUDY OF HIS EARLY LIFE AND WORK. Cambridge, Mass.: Harvard University Press, 1950. vii, 197 p. Bibliog.

An objective study of Cable's early fiction, especially his treatment of Creole life and the reaction of Creoles to it.

280 Rubin, Louis D., Jr. GEORGE W. CABLE; THE LIFE AND TIMES OF A SOUTHERN HERETIC. Pegasus American Authors Series. New York: Pegasus, 1969. ix, 304 p. Bibliog.

A critical biography that centers on Cable and his work in terms of their relationship to the Genteel Tradition and to the long-range direction of southern literature. Makes much of Turner's biography.

281 Turner, Arlin. GEORGE W. CABLE, A BIOGRAPHY. Durham, N.C.: Duke University Press, 1956. xi, 391 p. Bibliog.

Still the definitive work on Cable, with particular emphasis on his campaign in behalf of civil rights for Negroes.

282 ______, ed. CRITICAL ESSAYS ON GEORGE WASHINGTON CABLE. Boston: Twayne, 1980. 251 p. Bibliog.

Includes essays by Lafcadio Hearn, D. Warren Brickell, and Weir Mitchell published for the first time, as well as an extensive introduction by Turner.

ERSKINE CALDWELL (1903--)

283 Korges, James. ERSKINE CALDWELL. UMPAW, no. 78. Minneapolis: University of Minnesota Press, 1969. 48 p. Bibliog.

Sees Caldwell as neglected by academic critics and serious readers, who view him as a writer of merely popular or salacious novels. The essay attempts to redress the balance and place him as one of the most important writers of our time.

284 MacDonald, Scott, ed. CRITICAL ESSAYS ON ERSKINE CALDWELL. Boston: Twayne, 1981. 380 p. Bibliog.

Begins with an overview of Caldwell scholarship by the editor. Features scores of contemporary reviews as well as most of the important critical discussion of Caldwell's work to appear in print. Highlights are Carl Van Doren's "Made in America: Erskine Caldwell," James T. Farrell's "Heavenly Visitation," Kenneth Burke's "Caldwell: Maker of Grotesques," and Malcolm Cowley's "The Two Erskine Caldwells."

WILLA CATHER (1875-1947)

285 Bennett, Mildred R. THE WORLD OF WILLA CATHER. New York: Dodd, Mead, 1951. Reprint with notes and index. Lincoln: University of Nebraska Press, 1961. 285 p.

A close examination of Cather's Nebraska background as used in the stories.

286 Bloom, Edward A., and Bloom, Lillian D. WILLA CATHER'S GIFT OF SYMPATHY. Carbondale: Southern Illinois University Press, 1962. 260 p.

Analyzes Cather's themes and techniques as well as her methods of composition.

287 Brown, E.K., completed by Leon Edel. WILLA CATHER: A CRITICAL BIOGRAPHY. New York: Knopf, 1953. xxiv, 351 p. Bibliog. note.

As close to a definitive biography as we have.

288 Brown, Marion Marsh, and Crone, Ruth. ONLY ONE POINT OF THE COMPASS: WILLA CATHER IN THE NORTHEAST. N.p.: Archer Editions Press, 1980. 136 p. Illus.

An attractively written account of the three "sanctuaries" Willa Cather loved for their beauty and even more for the opportunity they provided her to work undistracted: Jaffrey, New Hampshire, Northeast Harbor, Maine, and Grand Manan, New Brunswick.

289 Daiches, David. WILLA CATHER: A CRITICAL INTRODUCTION. Ithaca, N.Y.: Cornell University Press, 1951. Reprint. New York: Collier Books, 1962. 126 p.

Assesses the fiction as well as Cather's place in American literature. Pays close attention to her style.

290 Edel, Leon. WILLA CATHER, THE PARADOX OF SUCCESS. Washington, D.C.: Library of Congress, Reference Department, 1960. 17 p.

A lecture delivered at the library in 1959 in which Cather's central theme is seen as "that of people who pull themselves up by their bootstraps."

291 Gerber, Philip. WILLA CATHER. TUSAS, no. 258. Boston: Twayne, 1975. 187 p. Bibliog.

Traces the development of the artist. Approaches the novels thematically.

292 Giannone, Richard. MUSIC IN WILLA CATHER'S FICTION. Lincoln: University of Nebraska Press, 1968. ix, 254 p. Bibliog.

The uses of music made by Cather in her stories and novels. Finds such uses pervasive.

293 Lewis, Edith. WILLA CATHER LIVING. New York: Knopf, 1953. 197 p. Illus.

An informal biography by the life-long friend who lived with Cather for many years.

294 Schroeter, James, ed. WILLA CATHER AND HER CRITICS. Ithaca, N.Y.: Cornell University Press, 1967. xiii, 392 p. Bibliog. note.

A useful collection of critical essays by various authors covering the period 1916-65.

295 Sergeant, Elizabeth Shepley. WILLA CATHER: A MEMOIR. Lincoln: University of Nebraska Press, 1963. 303 p. Illus. Bibliog.

Concerns the years 1910-31.

296 Slote, Bernice, ed. THE KINGDOM OF ART: WILLA CATHER'S FIRST PRINCIPLES AND CRITICAL STATEMENTS 1893-1896. Lincoln: University of Nebraska Press, 1966. xiv, 489 p. Bibliog.

The editor prefaces her selection of Cather's critical pieces from the Nebraska years with two essays: "Writer in Nebraska" and "The Kingdom of Art" in which she summarizes the first, elementary principles on which Cather based her art.

297 Slote, Bernice, and Faulkner, Virginia, eds. THE ART OF WILLA CATHER. Lincoln: University of Nebraska Press, 1974. xii, 267 p.

Papers presented at the international seminar on the art of Willa Cather at the University of Nebraska at Lincoln, 25-28 October 1973.

298 Stouck, David. WILLA CATHER'S IMAGINATION. Lincoln: University of Nebraska Press, 1975. viii, 253 p.

Attempts to illustrate "the unusual range and depth of Willa Cather's imagination" through a careful examination of her fiction.

299 Van Ghent, Dorothy. WILLA CATHER. UMPAW, no. 36. Minneapolis: University of Minnesota Press, 1964. 48 p. Bibliog.

Assesses the achievement of Cather and emphasizes the search for self and security.

300 Woodress, James. WILLA CATHER: HER LIFE AND ART. Pegasus American Authors Series. New York: Pegasus, 1970. xvi, 288 p. Bibliog.

A scholarly and very readable study that makes use of material unavailable to Brown and Edel in their earlier biography.

CHARLES W. CHESNUTT (1858-1932)

301 Chesnutt, Helen M. CHARLES WADDELL CHESNUTT: PIONEER OF THE COLOR LINE. Chapel Hill: University of North Carolina Press, 1952. 324 p. Illus.

A straightforward biographical record written by Chesnutt's daughter.

302 Ellison, Curtis W., and Metcalf, E.W., eds. CHARLES W. CHESNUTT: A REFERENCE GUIDE. Boston: G.K. Hall, 1977. vx, 150 p.

The most complete bibliography of Chesnutt extant. It is thoroughly annotated and contains almost every known published writing about him.

303 Heermance, J. Noel. CHARLES W. CHESNUTT: AMERICA'S FIRST GREAT BLACK NOVELIST. Hamden, Conn.: Archon Books, 1974. xiii, 258 p. Bibliog.

A biography that considers the cultural, historical, and literary backgrounds affecting Chesnutt. His art is discussed in terms of themes, techniques, and purpose. The most scholarly book on Chesnutt to date.

304 Keller, Frances Richardson. AN AMERICAN CRUSADE; THE LIFE OF CHARLES WADDELL CHESNUTT. Provo, Utah: Brigham Young University Press, 1978. xvi, 304 p. Bibliog. note.

A not particularly well-written biography that provides few critical insights to Chesnutt's writing.

KATE CHOPIN (1851-1904)

305 Rankin, Daniel S. KATE CHOPIN AND HER CREOLE STORIES. Philadelphia: University of Pennsylvania Press, 1932. viii, 313 p. Bibliog.

The first biography of Kate Chopin, the book retains its value although Father Rankin reveals discomfort over THE AWAKENING, which he dismisses as "exotic in setting, morbid in theme, erotic in motivation."

306 Seyersted, Per. KATE CHOPIN: A CRITICAL BIOGRAPHY. Baton Rouge: Louisiana State University Press, 1969. 246 p. Bibliog.

An excellent portrayal of Mrs. Chopin's life and career, with a perceptive approach to aspects of her realism and her artistic achievement. The discussion of Chopin's masterpiece, THE AWAKENING, is particularly good.

307 Springer, Marlene, ed. EDITH WHARTON AND KATE CHOPIN: A REFERENCE GUIDE. Boston: G.K. Hall, 1976. xiv, 305 p.

An invaluable guide to writings about Chopin and her work. Equally thorough for Wharton. Annotated.

SAMUEL LANGHORNE CLEMENS (MARK TWAIN) (1835-1910)

308 Anderson, Frederick, ed. MARK TWAIN, THE CRITICAL HERITAGE. London: Routledge and Kegan Paul, 1971. xvi, 347 p.

A large collection of reviews, both British and American, of Twain's work from 1869 to his death in 1910.

309 Asselineau, Roger. THE LITERARY REPUTATION OF MARK TWAIN FROM 1910 TO 1950. Paris: Librairie Marcel Didier, 1954. 240 p.

A critical essay and an annotated bibliography of works on Mark Twain. The essay is perceptive.

310 Bellamy, Gladys Carmen. MARK TWAIN AS A LITERARY ARTIST. Norman: University of Oklahoma Press, 1950. xiii, 396 p. Illus. Bibliog.

Evaluates Twain as professional author, craftsman, and literary artist. Finds him much more the conscious craftsman than is generally believed.

311 Benson, Ivan. MARK TWAIN'S WESTERN YEARS. Palo Alto, Calif.: Stanford University Press, 1938. Reprint. New York: Russell and Russell, 1966. x, 218 p. Illus. Bibliog.

Studies the development of Twain as a writer during his five and a half years in Nevada and California, 1861-66.

312 Blair, Walter. MARK TWAIN AND HUCK FINN. Berkeley and Los Angeles: University of California Press, 1960. xvi, 436 p. Bibliog.

An attempt to define the forces that gave ADVENTURES OF HUCKLEBERRY FINN its substance and form.

313 Brooks, Van Wyck. THE ORDEAL OF MARK TWAIN. New York: Dutton, 1920. Rev. ed. 1933. Reprint. New York: AMS Press, 1977. 325 p.

The famous book in which Brooks rocked the literary world by seeing Mark Twain as a kind of man-child, unfulfilled as man or writer, subject to "some deep malady of the soul" and warped by his marriage to the genteel Livy.

314 Carrington, George C., Jr. THE DRAMATIC UNITY OF HUCKLEBERRY FINN. Columbus: Ohio State University Press, 1976. xviii, 201 p.

Contends that the structure of the novel is very carefully and deliberately designed and that, contrary to much critical opinion, the ending is "necessary and right."

315 Clemens, Clara. MY FATHER MARK TWAIN. New York: Harper, 1931. vii, 292 p.

A rather naive memoir by Twain's daughter in which emphasis is on her travels with the family.

316 Covici, Pascal, Jr. MARK TWAIN'S HUMOR, THE IMAGE OF A WORLD. Dallas: Southern Methodist University Press, 1962. xiii, 266 p.

A detailed examination of the origins, method, and effects of Twain's humor.

317 Cox, James M. MARK TWAIN: THE FATE OF HUMOR. Princeton, N.J.: Princeton University Press, 1966. viii, 321 p.

Studies Twain's writing in the light of Freud's analysis of Twain's humor as "a perfect example of the economy of expenditure of affection."

318 DeVoto, Bernard. MARK TWAIN AT WORK. Cambridge, Mass.: Harvard University Press, 1942. ix, 144 p. Illus.

As successor to A.B. Paine as custodian of the Mark Twain Papers, DeVoto studied them exhaustively. This book contains essays on the composition of TOM SAWYER and HUCKLEBERRY FINN and on "The Symbols of Despair," Twain's later manuscripts, from CONNECTICUT YANKEE to MYSTERIOUS STRANGER.

319 ______. MARK TWAIN'S AMERICA. Boston: Little, Brown, 1932. xvi, 353 p. Bibliog.

A biography of Twain against the compelling background of the times and places in which he lived and worked. Contains a frontal attack on Brooks's thesis in THE ORDEAL OF MARK TWAIN.

320 Duckett, Margaret. MARK TWAIN AND BRET HARTE. Norman: University of Oklahoma Press, 1964. xiii, 365 p. Illus. Bibliog.

Examines in detail the "strange and finally painful relationship between two very different human beings."

321 Ferguson, DeLancey. MARK TWAIN: MAN AND LEGEND. Indianapolis: Bobbs-Merrill, 1943. Reprint. New York: Russell and Russell, 1965. 352 p. Bibliog.

Traces in detail Twain's career as a writer, with little or no attention to the many other facets of his life.

322 French, Bryant Morey. MARK TWAIN AND THE GILDED AGE. Dallas: Southern Methodist University Press, 1965. xi, 379 p. Bibliog.

A painstaking study of the origins and composition of "the book that named an era."

323 Gale, Robert L. PLOTS AND CHARACTERS IN THE WORKS OF MARK TWAIN. 2 vols. Hamden, Conn.: Archon Books, 1973. xlix, 1299 p.

Volume 1 contains synopses of the plots; volume 2 places every one of Mark Twain's characters.

324 Ganzel, Dewey. MARK TWAIN ABROAD. Chicago and London: University of Chicago Press, 1968. xiii, 330 p.

The true story of the cruise of the QUAKER CITY to Europe and the Holy Land, out of which grew THE INNOCENTS ABROAD. Shows Clemens as an indefatigable tourist.

325 Geismar, Maxwell. MARK TWAIN, AN AMERICAN PROPHET. Boston: Houghton Mifflin, 1970. 564 p.

A detailed critical study of Twain's literary career in which much use is made of autobiographical material to clarify certain issues of Twain's work.

326 Gribben, Alan, ed. MARK TWAIN'S LIBRARY: A RECONSTRUCTION. 2 vols. Boston: G.K. Hall, 1980. xxv, 958 p.

The annotated catalog of Mark Twain's personal library, as well as documentation of instances when he drew upon the resources of public and private libraries. Reveals him to have been very widely read, contrary to the impression he tried to foster.

327 Hill, Hamlin. MARK TWAIN, GOD'S FOOL. New York: Harper and Row, 1973. xxviii, 308 p.

Studies in detail the last ten years of Twain's life, a decade of almost uninterrupted catastrophe. Hill regards as remarkable the fact that Clemens retained even a spark of humor.

328 Kahn, Sholom J. MARK TWAIN'S MYSTERIOUS STRANGER: A STUDY OF THE MANUSCRIPT TEXTS. Columbia and London: University of Missouri Press, 1978. xix, 252 p.

Finds two distinct works of major importance in the MANUSCRIPTS volume, with No. 44, labeled "Print Shop" by DeVoto, the only true text of THE MYSTERIOUS STRANGER.

329 Kaplan, Justin. MARK TWAIN AND HIS WORLD. London: Michael Joseph, 1974. 224 p. Illus.

Handsomely illustrated, the book traces Twain's life with particular attention to the effect on the writer of the places and times in which he lived.

330 ______. MR. CLEMENS AND MARK TWAIN: A BIOGRAPHY. New York: Simon and Schuster, 1966. 424 p. Illus.

Excellent for the period covered, but begins when Mark Twain was thirty-one-years old. The rationale is that Twain's own accounts of the early years are "incomparably the best possible."

331 Krause, Sydney J. MARK TWAIN AS CRITIC. Baltimore: Johns Hopkins Press, 1967. xi, 308 p. Bibliog.

Discusses Twain as a literary critic, dividing the analysis into three parts: (1) the early criticism, showing the critic as "Muggins" or fool; (2) the later criticism, showing him as "Grumbler" or rebel; and (3) the appreciative criticism, written with the mask of Muggins or Grumbler off.

332 Long, E. Hudson. MARK TWAIN HANDBOOK. New York: Hendricks House, 1958. xxi, 454 p. Bibliog.

Chapters on "The Growth of Twain Bibliography," "Backgrounds," "The Man of Letters," "Mind and Art," "Fundamental Ideas," and "Mark Twain's Place in Literature."

333 Macnaughton, William R. MARK TWAIN'S LAST YEARS AS A WRITER. Columbia and London: University of Missouri Press, 1979. 254 p. Bibliog.

A concentrated study of the work produced in the last thirteen years of Twain's life--1897 to 1910--much of which Macnaughton finds to be of high quality.

334 Masters, Edgar Lee. MARK TWAIN, A PORTRAIT. New York: Scribner, 1938. Reprint. New York: Biblo and Tannen, 1966. 259 p.

An unflattering portrait in which Masters concludes that Twain "did not live and write up to the call that his genius and his country made upon him." Holds that he had no historical insight, no philosophical genius, and was a clown, with a clown's reward in money and popularity.

335 Paine, Albert Bigelow. MARK TWAIN: A BIOGRAPHY. 3 vols. New York: Harper, 1912. 1,719 p. Illus.

The authorized biography, by Twain's literary executor. Although not always reliable in its views of Twain's writing, it remains the fountainhead of information on his life.

336 Regan, Robert. UNPROMISING HEROES: MARK TWAIN AND HIS CHARACTERS. Berkeley and Los Angeles: University of California Press, 1966. xi, 246 p.

Explores the tug of the whole body of folk tales on Twain's sensibilities. For example, the story of the unpromising youngster who, against all odds, wins his way to success is one that recurs frequently in his fiction.

337 Rogers, Franklin R. MARK TWAIN'S BURLESQUE PATTERNS. Dallas: Southern Methodist University Press, 1960. ix, 189 p. Bibliog.

A study of Twain's structural patterns derived from burlesque, as seen in the novels and narratives between 1855 and 1885.

338 Salsbury, Edith Colgate, ed. SUSY AND MARK TWAIN: FAMILY DIALOGUES. New York: Harper and Row, 1965. xvii, 444 p. Bibliog.

The biography of her father begun by Clemens's daughter Susy in 1885 when she was thirteen provides the nucleus for this intimate study of the Clemens family circle.

339 Scott, Arthur L. ON THE POETRY OF MARK TWAIN, WITH SELECTIONS FROM HIS VERSE. Urbana and London: University of Illinois Press, 1966. 132 p.

A survey of Twain's life-long interest in poetry, together with selections by or probably by Twain.

340 ______, ed. MARK TWAIN, SELECTED CRITICISM. Rev. ed. Dallas: Southern Methodist University Press, 1967. xii, 306 p.

Originally published in 1955, Scott's work is a wide-ranging selection of relatively brief critical essays by well-known authors like Harte and Howells, and by eminent Twain scholars.

341 Sloane, David E.E. MARK TWAIN AS A LITERARY COMEDIAN. Baton Rouge and London: Louisiana State University Press, 1979. xi, 221 p. Bibliog.

Contends that Twain, despite his denunciation of literary comedians, owed a great deal to them as well as being one of them; however, in his best work, he transcended them.

342 Smith, Henry Nash. MARK TWAIN, THE DEVELOPMENT OF A WRITER. Cambridge, Mass.: Belknap Press of Harvard University Press, 1962. ix, 212 p.

Beginning with a consideration of the problems of style and structure Twain faced at the outset of his career and the handling of these problems in nine of his principal works, the book progresses to a consideration of "how his writing reveals a conflict between the dominant culture of his day and an emergent attitude associated with the vernacular language of the native American humorists."

343 ______, ed. MARK TWAIN: A COLLECTION OF CRITICAL ESSAYS. Englewood Cliffs, N.J.: Prentice-Hall, 1963. 179 p. Bibliog. note.

Essays on various facets of Twain and his work by well-known scholars. Most appeared originally in scholarly journals or as chapters in books.

344 Stone, Albert E., Jr. THE INNOCENT EYE; CHILDHOOD IN MARK TWAIN'S IMAGINATION. New Haven, Conn.: Yale University Press, 1961. Reprint. Hamden, Conn.: Archon Books, 1970. vii, 289 p.

"To a degree unexcelled by any of the novelists of his generation, he devoted a career to writing about childhood," but he always related the child's world "to the larger adult sphere and to the social and moral problems that are eternal human concerns."

345 Tuckey, John S. MARK TWAIN AND LITTLE SATAN: THE WRITING OF THE MYSTERIOUS STRANGER. Lafayette, Ind.: Purdue University Studies, 1963. Reprint. Westport, Conn.: Greenwood Press, 1972. 100 p. Bibliog.

Demonstrates that THE MYSTERIOUS STRANGER as published does not represent Mark Twain's intention because of the extensive editorial omissions and additions.

346 Wagenknecht, Edward. MARK TWAIN, THE MAN AND HIS WORK. New Haven, Conn.: Yale University Press, 1935. Reprint. 3d ed., rev. Norman: University of Oklahoma Press, 1971. xiii, 302 p. Bibliog.

This is a revision of the original work published as part of the centenary celebration of Twain's birth. Contains a helpful commentary on Twain criticism and scholarship since 1960. The book is highly opinionated.

347 Webster, Samuel Charles, ed. MARK TWAIN, BUSINESS MAN. Boston: Little, Brown, 1946. xii, 409 p. Illus.

The son of Mark Twain's partner in the publishing house of Charles L. Webster and Co. tells the story of the activities of that house, its eventual failure, and Twain's multifarious business ventures, culminating in the fiasco of the Paige Type-Setting Machine.

348 Wecter, Dixon. SAM CLEMENS OF HANNIBAL. Boston: Houghton Mifflin, 1952. ix, 335 p.

This is the first portion of the definitive biography that Wecter, third editor of the Mark Twain Estate, completed before his sudden death in 1950. It follows Twain up to his leaving Hannibal in 1853.

JAMES FENIMORE COOPER (1789-1851)

349 Clavel, Marcel. FENIMORE COOPER AND HIS CRITICS; AMERICAN, BRITISH AND FRENCH CRITICISMS OF THE NOVELISTS'S EARLY WORK. Aix-en-Provence, France.: Imprimerie Universitaire de Provence, 1938. 418 p.

The reviews of Cooper's novels from PRECAUTION to THE LAST OF THE MOHICANS.

350 Dekker, George. JAMES FENIMORE COOPER, THE AMERICAN SCOTT. New York: Barnes and Noble, 1967. xvii, 265 p.

A very good British critical survey of Cooper's fiction that devotes a good deal of attention to Cooper's politics and to "his assimilation and development of the historical novel as first perfected by Sir Walter Scott." Dekker finds Cooper owing an enormous debt to Scott.

351 Dekker, George, and McWilliams, John P., eds. FENIMORE COOPER: THE CRITICAL HERITAGE. Critical Heritage Series. London and Boston: Routledge and Kegan Paul, 1973. xi, 306 p.

Brings together the most important nineteenth-century discussions of Cooper. There is a lengthy introduction.

352 Grossman, James. JAMES FENIMORE COOPER. American Men of Letters Series. New York: William Sloane Associates, 1949. x, 286 p. Bibliog. note.

Combining biography with a nice critical judgment, Grossman has written a very useful introduction to the writer and his works.

353 Lounsbury, Thomas R. JAMES FENIMORE COOPER. Boston: Houghton Mifflin, 1882. Reprint. Gale Library of Lives and Letters, American Writers Series. Detroit: Gale Research Co., 1968. 306 p.

The earliest full-length biography. No analysis of the works.

354 Nevius, Blake. COOPER'S LANDSCAPES: AN ESSAY ON THE PICTURESQUE VISION. Berkeley, Los Angeles, and London: University of California Press, 1976. xii, 127 p. Illus.

On the development of Cooper's visual imagination and the ways in which he made it serve the purposes of narrative.

355 Peck, H. Daniel. A WORLD BY ITSELF: THE PASTORAL MOMENT IN COOPER'S FICTION. New Haven, Conn., and London: Yale University Press, 1977. xiv, 213 p.

Cooper in his fiction gave to the American pastoral a quality of permanence. His unique sensibility had in it "a timeless vision of simplicity and childhood wonder."

356 Philbrick, Thomas. JAMES FENIMORE COOPER AND THE DEVELOPMENT OF AMERICAN SEA FICTION. Cambridge, Mass.: Harvard University Press, 1961. xi, 329 p. Illus. Bibliog.

Centers on the work of Cooper, "the originator of the sea novel and the writer who contributed most to its subsequent development before the appearance of MOBY-DICK."

357 Ringe, Donald A. JAMES FENIMORE COOPER. TUSAS, no. 11. New York: Twayne, 1962. 175 p. Bibliog.

Believes that Cooper has long been undervalued as a writer and regards him as a major American artist. Concentrates on analysis of the work.

358 Spiller, Robert E. FENIMORE COOPER, CRITIC OF HIS TIMES. New York: Minton, Balch, 1931. xiii, 337 p. Illus. Bibliog. note.

Studies in detail Cooper's attitude toward the America of his day as revealed in his work.

359 _____. JAMES FENIMORE COOPER. UMPAW, no. 48. Minneapolis: University of Minnesota Press, 1965. 48 p. Bibliog.

A brief analysis of Cooper's works which concludes that he will be best remembered for the Leather-Stocking tales and for his pioneering in the realistic novel of social purpose.

360 Spiller, Robert E., and Blackburn, Philip C., eds. A DESCRIPTIVE BIBLIOGRAPHY OF THE WRITINGS OF JAMES FENIMORE COOPER. New York: R.R. Bowker, 1934. ix, 259 p.

Useful for Cooper scholars.

361 Walker, Warren S. JAMES FENIMORE COOPER: AN INTRODUCTION AND INTERPRETATION. American Authors and Critics Series. New York: Barnes and Noble, 1962. xv, 142 p. Illus. Bibliog.

Sees Cooper's principal contributions as his portraits of the American frontier and the life of the sea. This is a somewhat underdeveloped volume.

362 _____, ed. PLOTS AND CHARACTERS IN THE FICTION OF JAMES FENIMORE COOPER. Plots and Characters Series. Hamden, Conn.: Archon Books, 1978. xi, 346 p.

Provides plot summaries for all of the novels as well as description and identification of all of the characters.

363 Waples, Dorothy. THE WHIG MYTH OF JAMES FENIMORE COOPER. Yale Studies in English, no. 88. New Haven, Conn.: Yale University Press, 1938. viii, 318 p.

The story of Cooper's association with the Democratic party and of revenges taken upon him by the offended Whigs, revenges misinterpreted by later generations.

JAMES GOULD COZZENS (1903--)

364 Bracher, Frederick. THE NOVELS OF JAMES GOULD COZZENS. New York: Harcourt, Brace, 1959. 306 p. Bibliog.

Judges the eight novels published between 1931 and 1957, the publication date of BY LOVE POSSESSED, to constitute a record of achievement in our time matched only by Faulkner and Hemingway. No detailed analysis, however, of any single novel.

365 Bruccoli, Matthew J., ed. JAMES GOULD COZZENS: NEW ACQUIST OF TRUE EXPERIENCE. Carbondale and Edwardsville: Southern Illinois University Press, 1979. xiii, 145 p.

An excellent collection of critical essays on Cozzens and his work.

366 Hicks, Granville. JAMES GOULD COZZENS. UMPAW, no. 58. Minneapolis: University of Minnesota Press, 1966. 48 p. Bibliog.

A well-balanced view of the writer and his work.

367 Maxwell, D.E.S. COZZENS. Writers and Critics Series. Edinburgh and London: Oliver and Boyd, 1964. 119 p. Bibliog.

A generally sound introduction.

368 Mooney, Harry John, Jr. JAMES GOULD COZZENS, NOVELIST OF INTELLECT. Critical Essays in Modern Literature. Pittsburgh: University of Pittsburgh Press, 1963. 186 p.

Detailed analysis of each of the novels up to and including BY LOVE POSSESSED.

HART CRANE (1899-1932)

369 Brown, Susan Jenkins. ROBBER ROCKS: LETTERS AND MEMORIES OF HART CRANE, 1923-1932. Middletown, Conn.: Wesleyan University Press, 1969. 176 p.

Besides some previously unpublished Crane letters, there are remembrances of Crane by Mrs. Brown, Malcolm Cowley, and Peggy Conklin.

370 Butterfield, R.W. THE BROKEN ARC: A STUDY OF HART CRANE. Edinburgh: Oliver and Boyd, 1969. xii, 276 p. Bibliog.

Sees Crane as "a central and absolutely crucial figure in American cultural and intellectual history." Draws attention to many of the less known poems and examines contradictions within THE BRIDGE. Tries also to isolate the reasons for Crane's poetic and personal disintegration.

371 Horton, Philip. HART CRANE; THE LIFE OF AN AMERICAN POET. New York: Norton, 1937. x, 352 p. Illus.

The first full-length biography of Crane, the book concentrates on the life and attempts little analysis of the poetry.

372 Lane, Gary, ed. A CONCORDANCE TO THE POEMS OF HART CRANE. New York: Haskell House, 1972. 338 p.

Correlated to the Weber COMPLETE POEMS AND SELECTED LETTERS AND PROSE OF HART CRANE.

373 Leibowitz, Herbert A. HART CRANE: AN INTRODUCTION TO THE POETRY. New York and London: Columbia University Press, 1968. 308 p. Bibliog.

Views Crane as "a great synthesizer: a man consciously welding disparate materials into coherent and aesthetically satisfying poems." Studies Crane's diction, imagery, syntax, verse forms, and metrics.

374 Lewis, R.W.B. THE POETRY OF HART CRANE: A CRITICAL STUDY. Princeton, N.J.: Princeton University Press, 1967. xiii, 426 p.

Follows the development of Crane's poetry from the apprentice poems to "The Broken Tower." Concludes that Crane is one of the "dozen-odd major poets in American history."

375 Lohf, Kenneth A., comp. THE LITERARY MANUSCRIPTS OF HART CRANE. Columbus: Ohio State University Press, 1967. xiii, 151 p.

Locates and describes all of the known manuscripts.

376 Perry, Robert L. THE SHARED VISION OF WALDO FRANK AND HART CRANE. Studies: New Series, no. 33. Lincoln: University of Nebraska, May 1966. 73 p. Bibliog.

Explores the nature of Frank's influence on Crane.

377 Quinn, Vincent. HART CRANE. TUSAS, no. 35. New York: Twayne, 1963. 141 p. Bibliog.

A good introduction for undergraduates. Only the major poems are analyzed. Crane is viewed as being in the tradition of visionary poets.

378 Schwartz, Joseph, ed. HART CRANE: AN ANNOTATED CRITICAL BIBLIOGRAPHY. New York: David Lewis, 1970. xi, 276 p.

An inclusive bibliography of books and articles on Crane or which make only brief or passing reference to him.

379 Unterecker, John. VOYAGER; A LIFE OF HART CRANE. New York: Farrar, Straus and Giroux, 1969. xii, 787 p. Illus.

The definitive life of Crane, based on much previously unavailable material, including many interviews with friends of the poet.

380 Uroff, M.D. HART CRANE: THE PATTERNS OF HIS POETRY. Urbana, Chicago, and London: University of Illinois Press, 1974. 236 p.

A thorough exploration of the lyrics, which Uroff feels have been neglected in the critical emphasis on THE BRIDGE. Sees "violence and possession, flight and stasis as the alternating and inextricably intertwined patterns in Crane's poetry."

381 Weber, Brom. HART CRANE: A BIOGRAPHICAL AND CRITICAL STUDY. 1948. Rev. ed. New York: Russell and Russell, 1970. 452 p. Illus. Bibliog.

A corrected edition of the 1948 publication, this intertwines the life and work of the poet, who is regarded as "unquestionably the major poetic talent of twentieth-century America."

STEPHEN CRANE (1871-1900)

382 Baron, Herman, ed. A CONCORDANCE TO "THE POEMS OF STEPHEN CRANE." Boston: G.K. Hall, 1974. xv, 311 p.

Uses the Joseph Katz critical edition of the poems.

383 Beer, Thomas. STEPHEN CRANE; A STUDY IN AMERICAN LETTERS. Introduction by Joseph Conrad. Garden City, N.Y.: Garden City Publishing Co., 1923. 248 p.

The first biography of Crane. Though unreliable, it retains value for the student. The introduction is memorable.

384 Berryman, John. STEPHEN CRANE. American Men of Letters Series. New York: William Sloane Associates, 1950. xv, 347 p. Bibliog.

A relatively brief biography that contains some errors and spends too many pages in psychoanalyzing its subject.

385 Cady, Edwin H. STEPHEN CRANE. Rev. ed. TUSAS, no. 23. Boston: Twayne, 1980. 175 p. Bibliog.

A major revision of the TUSAS edition of 1962, this is the best introductory study of Crane and his work.

386 Cazemajou, Jean. STEPHEN CRANE. UMPAW, no. 76. Minneapolis: University of Minnesota Press, 1969. 47 p. Bibliog.

A somewhat thin introduction to Crane.

387 Crosland, Andrew T., comp. A CONCORDANCE TO THE COMPLETE POETRY OF STEPHEN CRANE. Detroit: Gale Research Co., 1975. xx, 189 p.

Uses the University of Virginia edition of THE WORKS OF STEPHEN CRANE (Charlottesville, 1969-75, 10 vols.).

388 Hoffman, Daniel. THE POETRY OF STEPHEN CRANE. New York and London: Columbia University Press, 1957. xiii, 304 p. Bibliog.

A detailed and scholarly reading of all Crane's verse.

389 Linson, Corwin K. MY STEPHEN CRANE. Edited and introduction by Edwin H. Cady. Syracuse: Syracuse University Press, 1958. xiv, 115 p.

Edited from a typescript composed by Crane's close friend, the American painter Corwin Linson. A fascinating memoir.

390 Stallman, R.W. STEPHEN CRANE: A BIOGRAPHY. New York: Braziller, 1968. xvi, 664 p. Illus.

The fullest account of Crane's life to date, but one which created controversy among Crane scholars.

391 ______, ed. STEPHEN CRANE: A CRITICAL BIBLIOGRAPHY. Ames: Iowa State University Press, 1972. xlii, 642 p.

The most complete annotated bibliography of writings by and about Crane up to 1970.

392 Weatherford, Richard M. STEPHEN CRANE: THE CRITICAL HERITAGE. London and Boston: Routledge and Kegan Paul, 1973. xviii, 343 p.

Reviews of Crane's works from the Hamlin Garland review of MAGGIE in the June 1893 ARENA to Joseph Conrad's critique of THE RED BADGE OF COURAGE in 1926.

See also no. 739.

E.E. CUMMINGS (1894-1962)

393 Baum, S.V., ed. EΣTI: e e c: E.E. CUMMINGS AND THE CRITICS. East Lansing: Michigan State University Press, 1962. xv, 220 p. Bibliog.

A good introductory essay by Baum is followed by twenty-six reviews of, and essays on, Cummings and his work.

394 Dumas, Bethany K. E.E. CUMMINGS: A REMEMBRANCE OF MIRACLES. Barnes and Noble Critical Studies. New York: Barnes and Noble, 1974. 157 p. Bibliog. note.

A general introduction. After a biographical chapter, the book proceeds to discuss the early poetry, the later poetry, the prose, the plays, and Cummings as linguistic radical.

395 Fairley, Irene. E.E. CUMMINGS AND UNGRAMMAR: A STUDY OF SYNTACTIC DEVIANCE IN HIS POEMS. Searingtown, N.Y.: Watermill Publishers, n.d. 202 p.

Originally a Harvard doctoral dissertation, the book is a linguistic study of the irregularities in Cummings's poetic syntax.

396 Friedman, Norman. E.E. CUMMINGS: THE ART OF HIS POETRY. Baltimore: Johns Hopkins Press, 1960. viii, 195 p.

A detailed study of Cummings's vision and technique. Defines the major themes and reveals the growth of the poetry.

397 _____. E.E. CUMMINGS: THE GROWTH OF A WRITER. Carbondale: Southern Illinois University Press, 1964. x, 193 p. Bibliog. note.

Sees Cummings as belonging "with Coleridge and the Romantic tradition in seeing the natural order as superior to man-made orders." The poetry is thoroughly discussed, and Cummings is discerned as a writer who steadily grew.

398 _____, ed. E.E. CUMMINGS: A COLLECTION OF CRITICAL ESSAYS. Englewood Cliffs, N.J.: Prentice-Hall, 1972. vi, 185 p. Bibliog.

Excellent collection, with a sound introductory essay by the editor.

399 Kennedy, Richard S. DREAMS IN THE MIRROR: A BIOGRAPHY OF E.E. CUMMINGS. New York: Liveright Publishing, 1980. xiv, 529 p. Illus., bibliog. essay.

By far the most complete biography of Cummings, it is also helpful in commentary on the poems. Well researched and eminently readable.

400 Kidder, Rushworth M. E.E. CUMMINGS: AN INTRODUCTION TO THE POETRY. Columbia Introductions to 20th Century American Poetry. New York: Columbia University Press, 1979. xxviii, 275 p.

A reader's guide to individual poems. Helpful to teachers and students.

401 Lane, Gary. I AM: A STUDY OF E.E. CUMMINGS' POEMS. Lawrence, Manhattan, and Wichita: University Press of Kansas, 1976. ix, 134 p. Bibliog. note.

Five of Cummings's major themes are examined through analysis of specific poems: seduction, individual heroism, the transcendental unification of life and death, death in life, and love as means to, and end of, transcendence.

402 Marks, Barry A. E.E. CUMMINGS. TUSAS, no. 46. New York: Twayne, 1964. 156 p. Bibliog.

Especially good on the aesthetics of Cummings. Also suggests that he is a religious writer who reveals the virtue of humility.

403 Norman, Charles. E.E. CUMMINGS, THE MAGICMAKER. New York: Macmillan, 1958. Reprint, with new introduction. Boston: Little, Brown, 1972. xv, 365 p. Illus.

A biography of Cummings through 1955 with considerable critical commentary.

404 Rotella, Guy L., ed. E.E. CUMMINGS, A REFERENCE GUIDE. Boston: G.K. Hall, 1979. xxxiv, 212 p.

Thorough annotated bibliography of works about Cummings through 1977.

405 Triem, Eve. E.E. CUMMINGS. UMPAW, no. 87. Minneapolis: University of Minnesota Press, 1969. 48 p. Bibliog.

An appreciative essay that sees Cummings as a transcendentalist. Examines three major themes at length: sensory awareness, the integrity of the individual, and the true meaning of love.

406 Wegner, Robert E. THE POETRY AND PROSE OF E.E. CUMMINGS. New York: Harcourt, Brace and World, 1965. ix, 177 p.

An appreciation of Cummings as poet, and a demonstration that, in Cummings's work, there is a close association between experience and art.

RICHARD HENRY DANA (1815-1882)

407 Adams, Charles Francis. RICHARD HENRY DANA; A BIOGRAPHY. 2 vols. Boston: Houghton Mifflin, 1890. Reprint. Detroit: Gale Research Co., 1968.

A fairly typical nineteenth-century biography, which stresses Dana's cultural aspects. Rather outmoded.

408 Gale, Robert L. RICHARD HENRY DANA, JR. TUSAS, no. 143. New York: Twayne, 1969. 191 p. Bibliog.

The first study to incorporate Dana's biography with an evaluation of his major writings. Chapters 1 to 5 treat the life story, 6 and 7 deal with TWO YEARS BEFORE THE MAST, 8 with Dana's other works, and 9 presents a brief summary.

409 Shapiro, Samuel. RICHARD HENRY DANA, JR.: 1815-1882. East Lansing: Michigan State University Press, 1961. xi, 251 p. Bibliog.

A thorough biography, written from a political historian's viewpoint. Dana is seen as a failure.

EMILY DICKINSON (1830-1886)

410 Agrawal, Abha. EMILY DICKINSON; SEARCH FOR SELF. New Delhi: Young Asia Publications, 1977. ii, 207 p. Bibliog.

Investigates the search for self with particular reference to the poetry. Sees Dickinson's technique as a fit instrument of her meaning and vision.

411 Anderson, Charles R. EMILY DICKINSON'S POETRY: STAIRWAY OF SURPRISE. New York: Holt, Rinehart and Winston, 1960. xviii, 334 p.

Careful readings of approximately one hundred of the poems that Anderson prefers, thematically arranged.

412 Bingham, Millicent Todd. ANCESTORS' BROCADES: THE LITERARY DEBUT OF EMILY DICKINSON. New York and London: Harper, 1945. xi, 464 p. Illus.

Mabel Loomis Todd's daughter tells the story of the first editing of the Dickinson poems, and of the feuding that erupted over publication of the manuscripts.

413 _____. EMILY DICKINSON: A REVELATION. New York: Harper, 1954. 109 p. Illus.

Makes the case that Emily's correspondence with Judge Otis Lord, her dead father's best friend, shows that he was the love of her life and that his emotional tie to her was strong despite his own family bonds.

414 _____, ed. EMILY DICKINSON'S HOME: LETTERS OF EDWARD DICKINSON AND HIS FAMILY, WITH DOCUMENTATION AND COMMENT. New York: Harper, 1955. xvii, 600 p. Bibliog.

An intimate picture of the Dickinson household as derived from letters written to one another by members of the family.

415 Blake, Caesar R., and Wells, Carlton F., eds. THE RECOGNITION OF EMILY DICKINSON: SELECTED CRITICISM SINCE 1890. Ann Arbor: University of Michigan Press, 1964. xvii, 314 p.

Reprinting of a wide range of criticism, mostly periodical, between 1890 and 1960.

416 Buckingham, Willis J., ed. EMILY DICKINSON: AN ANNOTATED BIBLIOGRAPHY. Bloomington and London: Indiana University Press, 1970. xii, 322 p.

The best and fullest bibliography of writings, scholarship, criticism, and ana that we have to date.

417 Capps, Jack L. EMILY DICKINSON'S READING, 1836-1886. Cambridge, Mass.: Harvard University Press, 1966. ix, 230 p. Bibliog.

Finds that a careful examination of Emily's reading reveals that much of her poetry can be related to such external sources.

418 Chase, Richard. EMILY DICKINSON. American Men of Letters Series. New York: William Sloane Associates, 1951. Reprint. Westport, Conn.: Greenwood Press, 1971. xii, 328 p.

A critical biography that closely analyzes several poems to show the psychological acumen that they reveal.

419 Cody, John. AFTER GREAT PAIN: THE INNER LIFE OF EMILY DICKINSON. Cambridge, Mass.: Belknap Press of Harvard University Press, 1971. ix, 538 p.

A biography that employs the psychoanalytic method. Attempts to establish the nature of Emily's psychological imbalance, to detail the phenomenology and dynamics that preceded her breakdown, and to present the processes by which she "entered upon this catastrophe a competent poet and emerged an inspired one."

420 Donoghue, Denis. EMILY DICKINSON. UMPAW, no. 81. Minneapolis: University of Minnesota Press, 1969. 47 p. Bibliog.

A brief essay that sees Dickinson's best poems as those on the moral universals: love, pain, loss, doubt, death.

421 Duncan, Douglas. EMILY DICKINSON. Writers and Critics Series. Edinburgh: Oliver and Boyd, 1965. 110 p. Bibliog.

An introduction to the life and work. Also a chapter on Dickinson's critical reception.

422 Ferlazzo, Paul J. EMILY DICKINSON. TUSAS, no. 280. Boston: Twayne, 1976. 168 p. Bibliog.

Besides providing basic details of Dickinson's life, the book attempts to relate the influences of the time and place in which she lived to the poetry. Interesting final chapters treat her prose and her influence on modern writing.

423 Franklin, R.W. THE EDITING OF EMILY DICKINSON: A RECONSIDERATION. Madison, Milwaukee, and London: University of Wisconsin Press, 1967. xvii, 187 p. Bibliog.

Follows the history of the editing of the Dickinson poems and shows that even the Thomas Johnson three-volume variorum edition (EMILY DICKINSON'S POEMS; INCLUDING VARIANT READINGS [Cambridge, Mass.: Belknap Press of Harvard University Press, 1955]) is not free from error. Sees important work still to be done in the editing of the poetry.

424 Gelpi, Albert J. EMILY DICKINSON: THE MIND OF THE POET. Cambridge, Mass.: Harvard University Press, 1965. xiii, 201 p. Bibliog.

Uses poems and letters to go beyond the biographical data to arrive at "the design of the poet's mind."

425 Griffith, Clark. THE LONG SHADOW: EMILY DICKINSON'S TRAGIC POETRY. Princeton, N.J.: Princeton University Press, 1964. viii, 308 p.

Focuses on Dickinson's fears of change, deprivation, commitment, and masculinity. Much psychoanalytic explication of poems.

426 Jenkins, MacGregor. EMILY DICKINSON, FRIEND AND NEIGHBOR. Boston: Little, Brown, 1930. 150 p.

Childhood impressions of Emily and her family by one who was born across the street from them in 1869.

427 Johnson, Thomas H. EMILY DICKINSON, AN INTERPRETIVE BIOGRAPHY. Cambridge, Mass.: Belknap Press of Harvard University Press, 1966. viii, 276 p. Illus. Bibliog. note.

Although giving many poems a close reading, the editor of the definitive text of Dickinson's poems provides a full picture of Emily in her surroundings.

428 Khan, Salamatulllah. EMILY DICKINSON'S POETRY: THE FLOOD SUBJECTS. New Delhi: Aarti Book Centre, 1969. x, 170 p. Bibliog.

Some interesting insights to the poetry from an Indian perspective.

429 Leyda, Jay. THE YEARS AND HOURS OF EMILY DICKINSON. 2 vols. New Haven, Conn.: Yale University Press, 1960. lxxxi, 928 p.

Attempts to get at the truth of Emily Dickinson by compiling an almost day-by-day log of the documentary evidence transcribed and extracted from manuscript and printed sources.

430 Lindberg-Seyersted, Brita. THE VOICE OF THE POET: ASPECTS OF STYLE IN THE POETRY OF EMILY DICKINSON. Uppsala, Sweden: Almquist and Wiksells, 1968. 290 p. Bibliog.

Detailed exploration of Dickinson's poetic language and of the poetic effects of the poems.

431 Lucas, Dolores Dyer. EMILY DICKINSON AND RIDDLE. DeKalb: Northern Illinois University Press, 1969. 151 p.

Contends that Dickinson consciously exploited the technique of riddle in much of her work as particularly applicable to her love of ambiguity.

432 MacLeish, Archibald; Bogan, Louise; and Wilbur, Richard. EMILY DICKINSON: THREE VIEWS. Amherst, Mass.: Amherst College Press, 1960. 46 p.

Three distinguished poets' papers, delivered at the Bicentennial celebration of the town of Amherst, 23 October 1959.

433 McNaughton, Ruth Flanders. THE IMAGERY OF EMILY DICKINSON. New Series, no. 4. Lincoln: University of Nebraska Studies, 1949. ix, 66 p.

Discusses the sources and the nature of Dickinson's imagery, as well as its appeal to the senses.

434 Miller, Ruth. THE POETRY OF EMILY DICKINSON. Middletown, Conn.: Wesleyan University Press, 1968. x, 480 p. Bibliog.

The thesis here is that much of Dickinson's poetry was the result of her frustration about being unpublished, and her unrequited love for Samuel Bowles.

435 Patterson, Rebecca. EMILY DICKINSON'S IMAGERY. Amherst: University of Massachusetts Press, 1979. xviii, 238 p.

In a book as controversial as her biography of Dickinson, Patterson engages in a sustained and fascinating study of the poet's symbolism and imagery, which she finds to be dominantly sexual. She concludes that "the study of this web of symbolism would suggest treating the work of her major period . . . as one total poem."

436 _____. THE RIDDLE OF EMILY DICKINSON. Boston: Houghton Mifflin, 1951. Reprint. New York: Cooper Square Publishers, 1973. xiii, 434 p. Bibliog.

Studies Dickinson's attachment to Susan Gilbert and to Kate Scott Anthon. The latter is said to be the inspiration of the love poems and the cause of Dickinson's grief in 1861. A lesbian relationship is suggested.

437 Pollitt, Josephine. EMILY DICKINSON: THE HUMAN BACKGROUND OF HER POETRY. New York: Harper, 1930. xii, 350 p. Illus.

The first full-length biography, it proposes that Emily secretly loved Major Edward Hunt, first husband of her friend Helen Hunt Jackson.

438 Porter, David T. THE ART OF EMILY DICKINSON'S EARLY POETRY. Cambridge, Mass.: Harvard University Press, 1966. xiv, 206 p. Bibliog.

Plots the boundary of the developmental period in Dickinson's career, and purports to discover the early stylistic habits that equipped her for the flood of poems let loose in the year 1862 and after.

439 Power, Sister Mary James. IN THE NAME OF THE BEE: THE SIGNIFICANCE OF EMILY DICKINSON. New York: Sheed and Ward, 1943. Reprint. New York: Biblo and Tannen, 1970. xi, 138 p.

The themes of renunciation, death, and immortality in Dickinson's poetry are discussed and interpreted from the viewpoint of Christian mysticism.

440 Sewall, Richard B. THE LIFE OF EMILY DICKINSON. 2 vols. New York: Farrar, Straus and Giroux, 1974. xxvii, 821 p. Bibliog.

The nearest thing to a definitive biography that exists to date. All known facts and all theories and legends about Emily are included.

441 ______, ed. EMILY DICKINSON: A COLLECTION OF CRITICAL ESSAYS. Englewood Cliffs, N.J.: Prentice-Hall, 1963. 183 p.

Reprints sixteen of the best essays on Dickinson published between 1924 and 1961.

442 Sherwood, William R. CIRCUMFERENCE AND CIRCUMSTANCE: STAGES IN THE MIND AND ART OF EMILY DICKINSON. New York and London: Columbia University Press, 1968. xiii, 302 p. Bibliog.

An attempt to describe the development of Dickinson's principal ideas and to characterize the mind that produced those ideas.

443 Taggard, Genevieve. THE LIFE AND MIND OF EMILY DICKINSON. New York: Knopf, 1930. Reprint. New York: Cooper Square Publishers, 1967. xxi, 378 p., vi.

Views Emily's life as forcibly double, and her mind as divided. Thus her eye saw a double reality and "she was ever at work to compose that external contradiction into one. It was this troublesome 'double' that compelled her to be a poet."

444 Thackrey, Donald E. EMILY DICKINSON'S APPROACH TO POETRY. Studies, New Series, no. 13. Lincoln: University of Nebraska, 1954. x, 82 p. Bibliog.

Discusses her attitude toward language, her mystical tendency, and her aesthetic position. Concludes with an examination of an example of her best work, "There's a certain slant of light."

445 Wells, Henry W. INTRODUCTION TO EMILY DICKINSON. Chicago: Hendricks House, 1947. Reprint. New York: Hendricks House, 1959. xvii, 286 p.

Describing his work as "an experiment in critical method," Wells divides the book into three parts: "Representation of Man," "Representation of Men," and "The Poetry in Itself."

446 Whicher, George Frisbie. THIS WAS A POET: A CRITICAL BIOGRAPHY OF EMILY DICKINSON. New York and London: Scribner, 1938. xiii, 337 p. Illus. Bibliog. postscript.

The earliest reliable scholarly biography, it also includes sensitive discussion of Dickinson's poetic method.

JOHN DOS PASSOS (1896-1970)

447 Belkind, Allen, ed. DOS PASSOS, THE CRITICS, AND THE WRITER'S INTENTION. Carbondale and Edwardsville: Southern Illinois University Press, 1971. lxi, 288 p. Bibliog.

A collection of seventeen of the best essays on Dos Passos and his work, preceded by an enlightening introduction by the editor.

448 Brantley, John D. THE FICTION OF JOHN DOS PASSOS. The Hague and Paris: Mouton, 1968. 136 p. Bibliog.

Sees Dos Passos as suggesting a number of patterns of relationship between the individual and the "machine," patterns which determine the structure of the novels. Concludes that Dos Passos "is a better biographer than a poet, a better poet than historian, a better historian than novelist."

449 Colley, Iain. DOS PASSOS AND THE FICTION OF DESPAIR. Totowa, N.J.: Rowman and Littlefield, 1978. viii, 170 p. Bibliog.

Believes that "in renouncing affirmative values such as appear in the writing of his contemporaries (e.g., Hemingway and Fitzgerald) Dos Passos approaches the terminal despair of Samuel Beckett." Examines the novels in depth.

450 Davis, Robert Gorham. JOHN DOS PASSOS. UMPAW, no. 20. Minneapolis: University of Minnesota Press, 1962. 47 p. Bibliog.

Sees Dos Passos as having given us, despite the weaknesses of the later novels, a challenging commentary on the quality of American experience.

450A Ludington, Townsend. JOHN DOS PASSOS: A TWENTIETH CENTURY ODYSSEY. New York: Dutton, 1980. 568 p. Illus.

The authorized biography, by the editor of Dos Passos's diaries and letters, is successful in detailing the development of his thought and work. Of particular interest is the account of his literary influence in South and Central America.

451 Wagner, Linda W. DOS PASSOS: ARTIST AS AMERICAN. Austin and London: University of Texas Press, 1979. xxiv, 220 p. Bibliog.

A close examination of the canon of Dos Passos reveals that "a half century of work focused on the search for country, hero, and self." Audacity, subject matter, and an impressionistic craft that defied age were the essential elements of his art.

452 Wrenn, John H. JOHN DOS PASSOS. TUSAS, no. 9. New York: Twayne, 1961. 208 p. Bibliog.

Attempts a fresh look at Dos Passos's work in the context of his life and times. The life story is ably woven into the discussion of the literary works.

THEODORE DREISER (1871-1945)

453 Atkinson, Hugh C., ed. THEODORE DREISER: A CHECKLIST. Kent, Ohio: Kent State University Press, 1971. 104 p.

Includes books, articles, and reviews about Dreiser.

454 Dreiser, Vera, with Brett Howard. MY UNCLE THEODORE. New York: Nash Publishing, 1976. ix, 238 p. Illus.

Tries to show Dreiser in the family setting out of which he grew, and its influence on him.

455 Dudley, Dorothy. FORGOTTEN FRONTIERS: DREISER AND THE LAND OF THE FREE. New York: Smith and Haas, 1932. Reprint. New York: AMS Press, 1970. 485 p.

An early biography, largely undocumented, and replete with purple passages.

456 Elias, Robert H. THEODORE DREISER: APOSTLE OF NATURE. New York: Knopf, 1949. xii, 354 p. xxi.

The interest of the author is to investigate the contradictions in Dreiser, trace their development, and interpret them in relation to Dreiser's career. Dreiser himself contributed many of the materials for the study.

457 Gerber, Philip L. THEODORE DREISER. TUSAS, no. 52. New York: Twayne, 1964. 220 p. Bibliog.

A sound introduction to the man and his work. Sees Dreiser's reputation steadily in the ascendant despite the frequent clumsiness of his writing.

458 ______, ed. PLOTS AND CHARACTERS IN THE FICTION OF THEODORE DREISER. Archon's Plots and Characters Series. Hamden, Conn.: Archon Books, 1977. xxi, 153 p.

This book outlines the plots of all of Dreiser's novels and shorter fiction as well as providing identification of all characters.

459 Kazin, Alfred, and Shapiro, Charles, eds. THE STATURE OF THEODORE DREISER: A CRITICAL SURVEY OF THE MAN AND HIS WORK. Introduction by Alfred Kazin. Bloomington: Indiana University Press, 1955. 303 p. Bibliog.

Still the best collection of critical essays on Dreiser and his work.

460 Kennell, Ruth Epperson. THEODORE DREISER AND THE SOVIET UNION, 1927-1945: A FIRST-HAND CHRONICLE. New York: International Publishers, 1969. 320 p. Illus.

The story of Dreiser's 1927 tour of the Soviet Union based on the diary of the seventy-seven-day journey kept for him by his American secretary, together with a record of the long-term influence of the tour on Dreiser.

461 Lehan, Richard. THEODORE DREISER: HIS WORLD AND HIS NOVELS. Carbondale and Edwardsville: Southern Illinois University Press, 1969. xiv, 280 p. Bibliog. essay.

A study of the novels, their genesis, evolution, pattern, and meaning. In connection with meaning, the influences that shaped Dreiser's imagination are examined.

462 Lunden, Rolf. DREISER LOOKS AT SCANDINAVIA. Stockholm: Almquist and Wiksell International, 1977. 143 p. Bibliog.

Presents a portrait of the middle-aged Dreiser and outlines the 1920s as they appeared in America and in the Scandinavian countries. Largely based on the unpublished diary kept during his trip to Scandinavia from 22 June to 5 August 1926.

463 Moers, Ellen. TWO DREISERS. New York: Viking, 1969. xvii, 366 p.

The story of Dreiser's two masterworks, SISTER CARRIE and AN AMERICAN TRAGEDY, the book is a fascinating account of how these books were written as well as a profound study of each.

464 Pizer, Donald. THE NOVELS OF THEODORE DREISER: A CRITICAL STUDY. Minneapolis: University of Minnesota Press, 1976. ix, 382 p.

Establishes the facts of the sources and composition of each of Dreiser's eight published novels, and studies the themes and form of each. A valuable book for the student of Dreiser.

465 ______, ed. CRITICAL ESSAYS ON THEODORE DREISER. Boston: Twayne, 1981. 330 p. Bibliog.

Excellent collection, spanning eight decades of Dreiser criticism. Nearly every major critic who has written on his fiction is represented, including Mencken, Lionel Trilling, F.O. Matthiessen, and Alfred Kazin.

466 Salzman, Jack, ed. THEODORE DREISER: THE CRITICAL RECEPTION. New York: David Lewis, 1972. xxxvii, 741 p.

Reprints reviews of Dreiser's work from 1900 through 1947. Introduction by the editor.

467 Shapiro, Charles. THEODORE DREISER: OUR BITTER PATRIOT. Carbondale: Southern Illinois University Press, 1962. xv, 137 p.

Analyzes Dreiser's novels thematically and critically. Sees Dreiser as an artist with a purpose, each of whose novels illustrates a different aspect of the misdirection of America's energies.

468 Swanberg, W.A. DREISER. New York: Scribner's, 1965. xvii, 614 p. Illus.

A full dress portrait of Dreiser studded with numerous anecdotes and observations, but with rather little critical discussion of his works. Still the best biography.

469 Tjader, Marguerite. THEODORE DREISER: A NEW DIMENSION. Norwalk, Conn.: Silvermine Publishers, 1965. x, 244 p.

A series of interesting reminiscences by one of his close friends from 1928 to his death in 1945.

WILLIAM DUNLAP (1766-1839)

470 Canary, Robert H. WILLIAM DUNLAP. TUSAS, no. 164. New York: Twayne, 1970. 162 p. Bibliog.

Chapter 1 treats Dunlap's life, chapter 2 his histories of American arts and the American theater, 3-5 his plays, 6 his minor works, and 7 provides a final evaluation. Dunlap is seen as an excellent playwright for his time, but as even more important for his cultural histories.

471 Coad, Oral Sumner. WILLIAM DUNLAP: A STUDY OF HIS LIFE AND WORKS AND OF HIS PLACE IN CONTEMPORARY CULTURE. New York: Dunlap Society, 1917. xiii, 313 p.

A biography of the playwright and a critical examination of his dramatic writings.

JONATHAN EDWARDS (1703-1758)

472 Aldridge, Alfred Owen. JONATHAN EDWARDS. Great American Thinkers Series. New York: Washington Square Press, 1966. 181 p. Bibliog.

A critical biography that pays much attention to Edwards's writings.

473 Davidson, Edward H. JONATHAN EDWARDS: THE NARRATIVE OF A PURITAN MIND. Cambridge, Mass.: Harvard University Press, 1968. xii, 161 p.

A splendid intellectual biography that should be extremely useful to anyone who has encountered difficulty in understanding Edwards's thought processes. Although a man of his age, he was apart from it in seeing beyond the ordered system of a beneficent God "the dark terror of the human spirit . . . as despairing as it had ever been."

474 Griffin, Edward M. JONATHAN EDWARDS. UMPAW, no. 97. Minneapolis: University of Minnesota Press, 1971. 46 p. Bibliog.

An excellent essay to introduce Edwards to students. The focus is on Edwards as man, spokesman of an era, and symbol.

475 Holbrook, Clyde A. THE ETHICS OF JONATHAN EDWARDS: MORALITY AND AESTHETICS. Ann Arbor: University of Michigan Press, 1973. ix, 227 p. Bibliog.

A detailed examination of Edwards's philosophy.

476 Levin, David, ed. JONATHAN EDWARDS: A PROFILE. New York: Hill and Wang, 1969. xxi, 263 p. Bibliog.

Essays by Samuel Hopkins, Williston Walker, Henry Bamford Parkes, Ola E. Winslow, Perry Miller, John E. Smith, James Carse, Peter Gay, and Robert Lowell. An excellent and varied collection.

477 McGiffert, Arthur Cushman, Jr. JONATHAN EDWARDS. New York: Harper, 1932. 225 p.

A straightforward biography that pays scant attention to Edwards's gifts as a poetic writer.

478 Miller, Perry. JONATHAN EDWARDS. American Men of Letters Series. New York: William Sloane Associates, 1949. xv, 348 p.

A biography that focuses on the life of the mind. Edwards is seen as one of America's five or six major artists, "who happened to work with ideas instead of with poems or novels." Edwards, however, remains, in the final analysis, an enigma.

479 Parkes, Henry Bamford. JONATHAN EDWARDS, THE FIERY PURITAN. New York: Minton, Balch, 1930. 271 p. Illus., bibliog.

This biography, by a noted historian, is divided into three sections: "The Student," "The Parish Minister," and "The Exile." Very little discussion of Edwards's writing as literature.

480 Scheick, William J., ed. CRITICAL ESSAYS ON JONATHAN EDWARDS. Boston: Twayne, 1980. 310 p. Bibliog.

An excellent collection of twenty-six items.

481 Tracy, Patricia J. JONATHAN EDWARDS: RELIGION AND SOCIETY IN EIGHTEENTH-CENTURY NORTHAMPTON. New York: Hill and Wang, 1980. viii, 270 p.

A splendid new study of Edwards's critical years as pastor to the Northampton congregation.

482 Winslow, Ola E. JONATHAN EDWARDS, 1703-1758; A BIOGRAPHY. New York: Macmillan, 1940. xii, 406 p. Bibliog.

A reliable biography, dealing well with the known facts of Edwards's life.

T.S. ELIOT (1888-1965)

483 Ali, Ahmed. MR. ELIOT'S PENNY WORLD OF DREAMS. London: P.A. King and Staples, 1942. x, 138 p. Bibliog.

Sees a progressive decline in Eliot's poetry after THE WASTE LAND and "The Hollow Men." Regrets his decision to write plays. Believes Eliot refused to discuss the "real evils of our industrial-mechanical civilization" and erred in insisting on religion as the way out.

484 Bantock, G.H. T.S. ELIOT AND EDUCATION. New York: Random House, 1969. 117 p.

In a book intended primarily for undergraduates, Eliot is said to have seen education as "both creative and uncreative restriction, as offering both freedom and oppression in accordance with its suitability for the pupil."

485 Bergonzi, Bernard. T.S. ELIOT. Masters of World Literature Series. New York: Macmillan, 1972. xiv, 208 p. Bibliog.

A very good brief biographical and critical introduction.

486 Bolgan, Anne C. WHAT THE THUNDER REALLY SAID: A RETROSPECTIVE ESSAY ON THE MAKING OF THE WASTE LAND. Montreal and London: McGill-Queen's University Press, 1973. xvi, 184 p.

Reinterpretation of Eliot's most famous poem.

487 Bradbrook, M.C. T.S. ELIOT: THE MAKING OF THE WASTE LAND. Harlow, Essex: Longman Group, 1972. 38 p. Bibliog.

Deals with the lost manuscript of THE WASTE LAND, with Eliot's interpretation of the poem, and with the roles of Pound and Quinn in its composition and publication.

488 Cattani, Georges. T.S. ELIOT. Translated by Claire Pace and Jean Stewart. London: Merlin Press, 1966. x, 128 p. Bibliog.

A French introduction to the life and works of Eliot. Attempts to define Eliot's philosophy.

489 Drew, Elizabeth. T.S. ELIOT: THE DESIGN OF HIS POETRY. New York: Scribner's, 1949. 215 p. Bibliog.

Stimulating analysis of the poetry through FOUR QUARTETS. Finds an interesting parallel in symbolic content between dream symbols described by Jung and some of those in Eliot's poetry.

490 Frye, Northrop. T.S. ELIOT. Edinburgh: Oliver and Boyd, 1963. Reprint. New York: Barnes and Noble, 1966. 106 p. Bibliog.

An elementary handbook that contends that "a thorough knowledge of Eliot is compulsory for anyone interested in contemporary literature."

491 Gardner, Helen. THE ART OF T.S. ELIOT. New York: Dutton, 1950. 186 p.

In the belief that FOUR QUARTETS is Eliot's masterpiece, Gardner begins and ends her book with discussion of it. She views Eliot as a visionary poet and also pays a great deal of attention to the musical quality of his language and rhythms. This is one of the best books about his work.

492 Headings, Philip R. T.S. ELIOT. TUSAS, no. 57. Boston: Twayne, 1964. 191 p. Bibliog.

A good overview to introduce students to the poetry and drama. Also contains a biographical sketch. Sees Dante's influence on Eliot as most important.

493 Hoskot, S.S. T.S. ELIOT: HIS MIND AND PERSONALITY. Bombay: University of Bombay, 1961. 297 p. Bibliog.

An interesting attempt by an Indian scholar who, at the time of writing, had never been in either England or New England, to determine the extent to which Eliot's intellectual and emotional outlook were conditioned by his New England background and experience. The book also assesses the relevance and value of Eliot's criticism to modern western life.

494 Howarth, Herbert. NOTES ON SOME FIGURES BEHIND T.S. ELIOT. Boston: Houghton Mifflin, 1964. xii, 396 p.

A helpful biographical-critical study of the man and the poet.

495 Jones, Genesius. APPROACH TO THE PURPOSE: A STUDY OF THE POETRY OF T.S. ELIOT. London: Hodder and Stoughton, 1964. 351 p. Bibliog.

Father Jones's lengthy study is divided into two parts: "The Ground of the Approach" and "Ways of Approach."

496 Kenner, Hugh. THE INVISIBLE POET: T.S. ELIOT. New York: McDowell, Obolensky, 1959. 346 p.

Commentary on the poetry through FOUR QUARTETS with a final brief chapter on Eliot as playwright.

497 Kirk, Russell. ELIOT AND HIS AGE: T.S. ELIOT'S MORAL IMAGINATION IN THE TWENTIETH CENTURY. New York: Random House, 1971. xii, 462 p.

A leading conservative's encomium of Eliot. Sees him as a poet confronting hard reality with "the armed vision," as a dramatist reinvigorating the verse play, as a literary critic rescuing the critic's art from personal impressionism, and as a critic of society stripping the follies of the age.

498 Kojecky, Roger. T.S. ELIOT'S SOCIAL CRITICISM. London: Faber and Faber, 1971. 255 p.

In an expository and biographical approach, the author traces the course of Eliot's ideas on society.

499 Levy, William Turner, and Scherle, Victor. AFFECTIONATELY, T.S. ELIOT; THE STORY OF A FRIENDSHIP: 1947-1965. Philadelphia and New York: Lippincott, 1968. 148 p.

A delightful record of the friendship between Mr. Levy, an Episcopalian priest, and Eliot, based on Levy's records of their many meetings and on the more than seventy letters he received from Eliot.

500 Lucy, Sean. T.S. ELIOT AND THE IDEA OF TRADITION. New York: Barnes and Noble, 1960. xiii, 222 p.

Concentrates on Eliot's critical writings and tries to show that the theme of tradition is central both to the criticism and to the creative work.

501 Margolis, John D. T.S. ELIOT'S INTELLECTUAL DEVELOPMENT, 1922-1939. Chicago and London: University of Chicago Press, 1972. xix, 226 p.

An excellent study of Eliot's ideas on literature as they developed during the critical years involved.

502 Masao, Hirai, and Tomlin, E.W.F., eds. T.S. ELIOT: A TRIBUTE FROM JAPAN. Tokyo: Kenkyusha, 1966. ix, 207 p. Bibliog.

Essays by a group of Japanese and English scholars, the latter being, or having been, teachers in Japan.

503 Matthews, T.S. GREAT TOM: NOTES TOWARDS THE DEFINITION OF T.S. ELIOT. New York: Harper and Row, 1974. xix, 219 p. Illus. Bibliog.

An "unauthorized" biography of Eliot, the book raises more questions about him than it answers. Matthews acknowledges that his work is far from definitive; nonetheless it holds one's interest.

504 Matthiessen, F.O. THE ACHIEVEMENT OF T.S. ELIOT: AN ESSAY ON THE NATURE OF POETRY. Rev. and enl. New York: Oxford University Press, 1958. xv, 248 p. Originally published in 1935; rev. and enl. in 1947.

An early but perceptive evaluation of Eliot's method and achievement as an artist.

505 Misra, K.S. THE PLAYS OF T.S. ELIOT: A CRITICAL STUDY. New Delhi: Sana's University Publications, 1977. x, 175 p. Bibliog.

Analysis by an Indian professor of the literary aspects of the plays, such as character portrayal, structure, and versification.

506 Montgomery, Marion. ELIOT'S REFLECTIVE JOURNEY TO THE GARDEN. Troy, N.Y.: Whitston Publishing Co., 1979. 170 p. Bibliog.

An attempt to probe the mind of Eliot as it is revealed in THE WASTE LAND.

507 Mowbray, Allan. T.S. ELIOT'S IMPERSONAL THEORY OF POETRY. Lewisburg, Pa.: Bucknell University Press, 1974. 189 p. Bibliog.

An extended analysis of Eliot's critical thought.

508 Ricks, Beatrice, comp. T.S. ELIOT: A BIBLIOGRAPHY OF SECONDARY WORKS. Metuchen, N.J., and London: Scarecrow Press, 1980. xxiii, 366 p.

The most complete, up-to-date bibliography available. Unfortunately, most items are not annotated. Where annotations exist, they are spare.

509 Robbins, Rossell Hope. THE T.S. ELIOT MYTH. New York: Henry Schuman, 1951. 226 p.

A blistering attack on Eliot as man and writer. Seeks to disentangle the actual Eliot, "a poet of minor achievement, emotionally sterile and with a mind coarsened by snobbery and constricted by bigotry, from the myth which has exalted him into a great poet and an advanced cultural leader." The critics have created the myth, Robbins holds.

510 Sarkar, Subhas. T.S. ELIOT THE DRAMATIST. Calcutta: Minerva Associates, 1972. x, 313 p. Bibliog.

After an analysis of Eliot's theory of drama the author proceeds to a thorough examination of all of Eliot's plays.

511 Schneider, Elisabeth. T.S. ELIOT: THE PATTERN IN THE CARPET. Berkeley, Los Angeles, and London: University of California Press, 1975. ix, 226 p.

A careful critical analysis of the entire corpus of Eliot's poetry.

512 Sencourt, Robert. T.S. ELIOT: A MEMOIR. Edited by Donald Adamson. New York: Dodd, Mead, 1971. xiv, 266 p. Illus.

The unfinished memoir that Sencourt, Eliot's friend for thirty-seven years, left in typescript on his death in 1969. It is a record of his recollections and impressions of the man and the writer.

513 Smidt, Kristian. POETRY AND BELIEF IN THE WORKS OF T.S. ELIOT. Oslo: Norwegian Academy of Science and Letters, 1949. Reprint. Rev. ed. New York: Humanities Press, 1961. xiii, 258 p.

Treats background and influences, criticism, poetic beliefs, point of view, technique, appearance and reality in Eliot's poetry.

514 Smith, Grover. T.S. ELIOT'S POETRY AND PLAYS. Chicago and London: University of Chicago Press, 1950. xii, 342 p.

Analyzes both poems and plays, and examines their sources insofar as they are identifiable.

515 Spender, Stephen. T.S. ELIOT. Modern Masters Series. New York: Viking, 1976. xiii, 269 p. Bibliog.

An excellent examination of the poetry, the plays, and the criticism against the background of Eliot's life and personality. Spender sees great difference between the work of the early, middle, and late periods. An aim running through both poetry and criticism is to escape from the subjective self into a world of objective values. Eliot is defined as a "ritualist."

516 Tate, Allen, ed. T.S. ELIOT: THE MEN AND HIS WORK. New York: Delacorte, 1966. vi, 400 p.

A critical evaluation by twenty-six well-known poets and critics.

517 Traversi, Derek. T.S. ELIOT: THE LONGER POEMS. New York and London: Harcourt Brace Jovanovich, 1976. 238 p. Bibliog.

Intensive discussion of THE WASTE LAND, "Ash Wednesday," and FOUR QUARTETS.

518 Unger, Leonard. T.S. ELIOT. UMPAW, no. 8. Minneapolis: University of Minnesota Press, 1961. 48 p. Bibliog.

As brief introductory essays go, this is one of the best.

519 _____, ed. T.S. ELIOT: A SELECTED CRITIQUE. New York: Rinehart, 1948. Reprint. New York: Russell and Russell, 1966. xix, 478 p. Bibliog.

An early but still useful collection of critical essays by well-known scholars and poets.

520 Weinberg, Kerry. T.S. ELIOT AND CHARLES BAUDELAIRE. The Hague and Paris: Mouton, 1969. 84 p. Bibliog.

Interesting comparative study, pointing out many similarities in phrasing and substance between Eliot and the earlier French poet.

521 Williamson, George. A READER'S GUIDE TO T.S. ELIOT: A POEM-BY-POEM ANALYSIS. 2d ed. with epilogue titled "T.S. Eliot, 1888-1965." New York: Farrar, Straus and Giroux, 1966. Reprint. New York: Octagon Books, 1974. 270 p. Bibliog. note.

Particularly useful to undergraduate students.

See also no. 1373.

RALPH WALDO EMERSON (1803-1882)

522 Anderson, John Q. THE LIBERATING GODS: EMERSON ON POETS AND POETRY. Coral Gables, Fla.: University of Miami Press, 1971. 128 p. Bibliog.

Treats Emerson's theory of poetry, his idea of the ideal poet, his view of his contemporaries, and his contribution to poetic theory.

523 Bishop, Jonathan. EMERSON ON THE SOUL. Cambridge, Mass.: Harvard University Press, 1964. xi, 248 p.

A detailed and valuable explication of Emerson's understanding of the central action of experiencing, which he calls the Soul.

524 Bode, Carl, ed. RALPH WALDO EMERSON: A PROFILE. American Profile Series. New York: Hill and Wang, 1968. xvi, 201 p. Bibliog.

A collection of essays intended to portray Emerson the man, introduced by a biographical sketch composed by the editor.

525 Boswell, Jeanetta, ed. RALPH WALDO EMERSON AND THE CRITICS: A CHECKLIST OF CRITICISM, 1900-1977. Scarecrow Author Bibliographies, no. 39. Metuchen, N.J., and London: Scarecrow Press, 1979. xi, 198 p.

Lists alphabetically all books and articles written in English on Emerson and his works since about 1900, and published in America. Largely unannotated.

526 Brooks, Van Wyck. THE LIFE OF EMERSON. New York: Dutton, 1932. 315 p.

A highly readable, if not always reliable, biography.

527 Cabot, James Elliot. A MEMOIR OF RALPH WALDO EMERSON. 2 vols. London and New York: Macmillan, 1887. vii, 810 p.

The "authorized" biography, by Emerson's literary executor.

528 Carpenter, Frederic Ives. EMERSON AND ASIA. Cambridge, Mass.: Harvard University Press, 1930. xiii, 282 p. Bibliog.

Projects the influence of Asian thought on Emerson. Beginning with Greek Neoplatonism, the study moves to the influences of Brahmin wisdom, Persian poetry, Arabian literature and the Koran, the Zoroastrian forgeries, and Confucius and China.

529 ______. EMERSON HANDBOOK. New York: Hendricks House, 1953. xiv, 268 p. Bibliog.

Useful as an introduction to Emerson and as an aid to research.

530 Cowan, Michael H. CITY OF THE WEST: EMERSON, AMERICA, AND URBAN METAPHOR. Yale Publications in American Studies. New Haven, Conn., and London: Yale University Press, 1967. xiv, 284 p. Bibliog. note.

A specialized study intended to reveal the ways in which Emerson treated urban material. His use of urban metaphor is found to be as "varied as his own fertile mind."

531 Duncan, Jeffrey L. THE POWER AND FORM OF EMERSON'S THOUGHT. Charlottesville: University Press of Virginia, 1973. xiv, 105 p.

Describes and analyzes the significance of polarity in Emerson's examinations of nature, society, and the individual; also evaluates his optimism.

532 Emerson, Edward Waldo. EMERSON IN CONCORD. Boston and New York: Houghton Mifflin, 1888. 266 p.

A memoir by Emerson's son, written primarily for his father's neighbors and close friends.

533 Francis, Elamanamadathil V. EMERSON AND HINDU SCRIPTURES. Cochin, India: Academic Publications, 1972. 189 p. Bibliog.

An Indian professor shows the similarities between Emerson's ideas and the major tenets of Hindu philosophy. The influence of Hindu scriptures on Emerson's intellectual development is also studied.

534 Harding, Walter, ed. EMERSON'S LIBRARY. Charlottesville: University Press of Virginia, 1967. x, 338 p.

A descriptive catalog of Emerson's personal library. Valuable as evidence of Emerson's wide reading.

535 Harrison, John S. THE TEACHERS OF EMERSON. New York: Sturgis and Walton, 1910. 325 p. Bibliog.

An invaluable work for students of Emerson. Its aim is to show the essentially Platonic quality of Emerson's thought. Greek thought rather than German romantic philosophy or Oriental mysticism is seen as the most important element in his intellectual development.

536 Holmes, Oliver Wendell. RALPH WALDO EMERSON. Boston and New York: Houghton Mifflin, 1884. vii, 441 p.

The earliest full-scale biography of Emerson by a famous contemporary who knew him well.

537 Konvitz, Milton R., ed. THE RECOGNITION OF RALPH WALDO EMERSON: SELECTED CRITICISM SINCE 1837. Ann Arbor: University of Michigan Press, 1972. xvi, 224 p.

The book is divided into four parts: contemporaneous criticism, 1837-82; 1883-1900; 1901-25; and 1926-71. The selections are generally excellent.

538 Levin, David, ed. EMERSON: PROPHECY, METAMORPHOSIS, AND INFLUENCE. Selected Papers from the English Institute. New York and London: Columbia University Press, 1975. vii, 181 p.

Seven scholarly essays on Emerson's influence and development.

539 Michaud, Regis. EMERSON, THE ENRAPTURED YANKEE. Translated from French by George Boas. New York: Harper, 1930. xvii, 444 p.

An uncritical biography, much of which is highly speculative.

540 Miles, Josephine. RALPH WALDO EMERSON. UMPAW, no. 41. Minneapolis: University of Minnesota Press, 1964. 48 p. Bibliog.

An adequate introduction to the man and his writings.

541 Nicoloff, Philip L. EMERSON ON RACE AND HISTORY: AN EXAMINATION OF ENGLISH TRAITS. New York: Columbia University Press, 1961. x, 315 p. Bibliog.

Emerson's historical theory closely examined through the medium of his volume ENGLISH TRAITS.

542 Perry, Bliss. EMERSON TODAY. Princeton, N.J.: Princeton University Press, 1931. Reprint. New York: Archon Books, 1969. v, 140 p.

Based on a lecture series given at Princeton, the book attempts to reevaluate Emerson for our time.

543 Pommer, Henry F. EMERSON'S FIRST MARRIAGE. Carbondale and Edwardsville: Southern Illinois University Press, 1967. vi, 126 p. Illus.

The story of Emerson's brief marriage to Ellen Tucker, who died before she was twenty, and its effect on him.

544 Porte, Joel. REPRESENTATIVE MAN: RALPH WALDO EMERSON IN HIS TIME. New York: Oxford University Press, 1979. xxvi, 361 p.

Difficult to categorize, the book is a kind of intellectual biography organized according to the seasons of the year: "Rites of Spring," the young Emerson; "A Summer of Discontent: Emerson in 1838," the year of the crucial Divinity School Address; "The Fall of Man," Emerson from the time he acknowledged man as sinful; and "A Winter's Tale: the Elder Emerson."

545 Porter, David. EMERSON AND LITERARY CHANGE. Cambridge, Mass., and London: Harvard University Press, 1978. xiii, 232 p.

A study that seeks the aesthetic figuration whereby Emerson meant to accomplish his primary aim: "to invite men drenched in time to recover themselves and come out of time, and taste their native immortal air."

546 Reaver, J. Russell. EMERSON AS MYTHMAKER. Gainesville: University of Florida Press, 1954. ix, 106 p. Bibliog.

Tries to illustrate Emerson's belief that "man's imagination springs from ultimately reliable intuitive sources existing constantly in human nature."

547 Rusk, Ralph L. THE LIFE OF RALPH WALDO EMERSON. New York: Scribner, 1949. ix, 592 p. Bibliog.

Remains the fullest and most authoritative biography.

548 Russell, Phillips. EMERSON, THE WISEST AMERICAN. New York: Brentano's, 1929. 320 p. Illus.

A popularized rather than scholarly biography. Devoid of documentation.

549 Scheick, William J. THE SLENDER HUMAN WORD: EMERSON'S ARTISTRY IN PROSE. Knoxville: University of Tennessee Press, 1978. xiv, 162 p.

"Emerson's understanding of imagery lies at the core of his literary practice, of his artistry in prose." Several essays are explicated in order to show the function of the image as Emerson used it.

550 Sowder, William J. EMERSON'S REVIEWERS AND COMMENTATORS. Hartford, Conn.: Transcendental Books, 1968. 64 p.

A biographical and bibliographical analysis of nineteenth-century periodical criticism with a detailed index.

551 Wagenknecht, Edward. RALPH WALDO EMERSON: PORTRAIT OF A BALANCED SOUL. New York: Oxford University Press, 1974. 307 p. Bibliog.

The primary concern here is the character and personality of Emerson rather than his ideas or his writing as literature. The method used is "psychography."

552 Waggoner, Hyatt. EMERSON AS POET. Princeton, N.J.: Princeton University Press, 1974. xiii, 211 p.

A competent study of Emerson's theory and practice of poetry.

553 Whicher, Stephen E. FREEDOM AND FATE: AN INNER LIFE OF RALPH WALDO EMERSON. Philadelphia: University of Pennsylvania Press, 1953. xvi, 203 p. Bibliog.

The attempt is to project the drama of ideas to be found in Emerson's writings, particularly his journals. Thus Whicher hopes to complement Rusk's biography, which, he feels, does not take us very far into the life of Emerson's mind.

554 Wynkoop, William H. THREE CHILDREN OF THE UNIVERSE: EMERSON'S VIEW OF SHAKESPEARE, BACON, AND MILTON. London, The Hague, and Paris: Mouton, 1966. 199 p. Bibliog.

The aim is to demonstrate that Emerson habitually regarded Shakespeare, Bacon, and Milton as the men most representative in the English Renaissance of "the three stages of growth reflecting the divine trinity he found reappearing 'under different names in every system of thought.'"

555 Yoder, R.A. EMERSON AND THE ORPHIC POET IN AMERICA. Berkeley, Los Angeles, and London: University of California Press, 1978. xvi, 240 p.

The book falls into three parts: (1) a study of Emerson's Orphic aspirations as they relate to his predecessors and as they are shaped in the development of his prose; (2) the poems growing out of Emerson's heightened conviction in 1839 that his thought demanded a more dramatic form; and (3) an assessment of the distinguishing features of his legacy in American poetry.

JAMES T. FARRELL (1904-1979)

556 Branch, Edgar. JAMES T. FARRELL. TUSAS, no. 185. New York: Twayne, 1971. 192 p. Bibliog.

The best general study of Farrell available.

557 ______, ed. A BIBLIOGRAPHY OF JAMES T. FARRELL'S WRITINGS, 1921-1957. Philadelphia: University of Pennsylvania Press, 1959. xix, 142 p.

The bibliography is descriptive and has been updated by Branch in supplements published in the AMERICAN BOOK COLLECTOR issues of Summer 1961, May 1967, and March-April 1971.

558 Wald, Alan M. JAMES T. FARRELL: THE REVOLUTIONARY SOCIALIST YEARS. New York: New York University Press, 1978. xx, 190 p. Illus. Bibliog.

A literary, political, and intellectual portrait of Farrell during his revolutionary Socialist years--from the late 1920s to the late 1940s. Demonstrates the importance of his involvement with Trotskyism to his intellectual development.

WILLIAM FAULKNER (1897-1962)

559 Adams, Richard P. FAULKNER: MYTH AND MOTION. Princeton, N.J.: Princeton University Press, 1968. xiv, 260 p.

Traces Faulkner's developing aesthetic from the early poetry through the major fiction, linking it to his mythic method. Bases the study on Faulkner's theory that life is motion and the writer's goal is to arrest it.

560 Bassett, John, ed. WILLIAM FAULKNER: AN ANNOTATED CHECKLIST OF CRITICISM. New York: David Lewis, 1972. xiii, 551 p.

The most complete work of its kind up to 1972. Lists books on Faulkner, studies of individual novels, studies of short stories, poetry and miscellaneous writings, topical studies, and other materials.

561 ______. WILLIAM FAULKNER: THE CRITICAL HERITAGE. Critical Heritage Series. London and Boston: Routledge and Kegan Paul, 1975. xvi, 422 p. Bibliog.

Reprints reviews of Faulkner's works from 1924 to 1954.

562 Beck, Warren. MAN IN MOTION: FAULKNER'S TRILOGY. Madison: University of Wisconsin Press, 1961. xi, 203 p.

Detailed analysis of the trilogy SNOPES--composed of THE HAMLET, THE TOWN, and THE MANSION. Beck sees the trilogy revealing at its height Faulkner's commitment to human verities and the range of realistic awareness, "gathered up as a superb sweep of sheer creative power."

563 Blotner, Joseph. FAULKNER: A BIOGRAPHY. 2 vols. New York: Random House, 1974. Vol. 1, xv, 909 p. and 127 p. Notes: Vol. 2, ix, 937 p. and 142 p. notes and index.

To date this is the definitive biography. The approach is critical as well as biographical, and the amount of factual detail is staggering.

564 Brooks, Cleanth. WILLIAM FAULKNER: THE YOKNAPATAWPHA COUNTRY. New Haven, Conn., and London: Yale University Press, 1963. xiv, 499 p.

Detailed analysis of all the fiction dealing with Faulkner's mythical county. Also contains a helpful descriptive index of all the characters to be found there. An important book in Faulkner scholarship.

565 ______. WILLIAM FAULKNER: TOWARD YOKNAPATAWPHA AND BEYOND. New Haven: Yale University Press, 1978. 445 p.

The sequel to THE YOKNAPATAWPHA COUNTRY, it deals with the non-Yoknapatawpha novels and stories as well as with Faulkner's youthful romantic poetry. The first five chapters treat his early literary development.

566 Brown, Calvin S. A GLOSSARY OF FAULKNER'S SOUTH. New Haven, Conn. and London: Yale University Press, 1976. 241 p.

An invaluable aid, especially for Faulkner readers unfamiliar with southern vocabulary and dialects.

567 Coughlan, Robert. THE PRIVATE WORLD OF WILLIAM FAULKNER. New York: Harper, 1954. 151 p. Illus.

A brief, undocumented, biocritical look at Faulkner and his career.

568 Cowley, Malcolm. THE FAULKNER-COWLEY FILE: LETTERS AND MEMORIES, 1944-1962. New York: Viking, 1966. 184 p.

Interesting reminiscences and some previously unpublished correspondence.

569 Cullen, John B., in collaboration with Floyd C. Watkins. OLD TIMES IN THE FAULKNER COUNTRY. Chapel Hill: University of North Carolina Press, 1961. xvi, 132 p.

A friend of Faulkner since boyhood describes him in his native environment and tells how he used the home county's locations and characters in his fiction.

570 Dain, Martin J. FAULKNER'S COUNTY: YOKNAPATAWPHA. New York: Random House, 1964. 159 p.

A book of photographs of the places and types of people appearing in Faulkner's fiction about his native Lafayette County.

571 Falkner, Murry C. THE FALKNERS OF MISSISSIPPI: A MEMOIR. Baton Rouge: Louisiana State University Press, 1967. xxv, 205 p. Illus.

One of Faulkner's brothers tells the story of the four Falkner brothers and their growing up in Oxford, Mississippi. Helpful to the student of Yoknapatawpha.

572 Faulkner, John. MY BROTHER BILL; AN AFFECTIONATE REMINISCENCE. New York: Trident Press, 1963. 277 p.

Published shortly after his brother's death, this is a warm portrayal of William by the writing brother who himself died in the year of its publication.

573 Ford, Margaret P., and Kincaid, Suzanne, eds. WHO'S WHO IN FAULKNER. Baton Rouge: Louisiana State University Press, 1963. vii, 120 p. Bibliog.

A character index, with brief identification of the people in Faulkner's fiction. Also contains a biographical sketch.

574 Goldman, Arnold, ed. TWENTIETH CENTURY INTERPRETATIONS OF ABSALOM, ABSALOM! Twentieth Century Interpretation Series. Englewood Cliffs, N.J.: Prentice-Hall, 1971. iii, 120 p. Bibliog.

Goldman presents five essays on Faulkner's famous novel, by Richard Poirier, John Paterson, Michael Millgate, Melvin Backman, and James Guetti.

575 Guttenberg, Barnett, ed. FAULKNER STUDIES: AN ANNUAL OF RESEARCH, CRITICISM, AND REVIEWS, I. Coral Gables: University of Miami, 1980. v, 189 p.

The inaugural volume of an annual publication "designed to provide a home" for work on Faulkner. Contains thirteen new essays by both eminent and promising scholars, and thirteen reviews of recent books on Faulkner and his work.

576 Harrington, Evans, and Abadie, Ann J., eds. FAULKNER, MODERNISM, AND FILM: FAULKNER AND YOKNAPATAWPHA, 1978. Jackson: University of Mississippi Press, 1979. xv, 199 p.

The edited papers presented at the 1978 University of Mississippi Conference.

577 _____. THE SOUTH AND FAULKNER'S YOKNAPATAWPHA: THE ACTUAL AND THE APOCRYPHAL. Jackson: University Press of Mississippi, 1977. 212 p.

Edited versions of papers presented at the 1974-76 Faulkner and Yoknapatawpha Conferences at the University of Mississippi.

578 Hunt, John W. WILLIAM FAULKNER: ART IN THEOLOGICAL TENSION. Syracuse, N.Y.: Syracuse University Press, 1965. Reprint. New York: Haskell House, 1973. xv, 184 p.

Attempts to show, through a study of THE SOUND AND THE FURY, ABSALOM, ABSALOM! and "The Bear" that Faulkner employs strategies implying a complex theological vision.

579 Hunter, Edwin R. WILLIAM FAULKNER: NARRATIVE PRACTICE AND PROSE STYLE. Washington, D.C., and Lothian, Md.: Windhover Press, 1973. xv, 267 p.

Studies the Faulkner novels to determine the narrative methods and the elements of style that are distinctively Faulknerian.

580 Irwin, John T. DOUBLING AND INCEST/REPETITION AND REVENGE: A SPECULATIVE READING OF FAULKNER. Baltimore: Johns Hopkins University Press, 1975. 183 p.

Freudian commentary on the Faulkner novels, especially THE SOUND AND THE FURY and ABSALOM, ABSALOM! particularly the parts dealing with Quentin Compson.

581 Jehlen, Myra. CLASS AND CHARACTER IN FAULKNER'S SOUTH. New York: Columbia University Press, 1976. 181 p.

Contends that the central ideological issue of Faulkner's work is his class consciousness, which is also the source of his literary greatness.

582 Kawin, Bruce. FAULKNER AND FILM. New York: Frederick Ungar, 1977. 194 p.

Faulkner's use of cinematic techniques in his fiction, the movie adaptations of his novels and stories, his own screenwriting, and his influence on later film history are all discussed. A valuable contribution.

583 Kerr, Elizabeth M. WILLIAM FAULKNER'S GOTHIC DOMAIN. Literary Criticism Series, National University Publications. Port Washington, N.Y., and London: Kennikat Press, 1979. 264 p. Bibliog.

A close examination of what the author terms "the pervasive Gothic elements" in the Yoknapatawpha novels.

584 ______. YOKNAPATAWPHA: FAULKNER'S "LITTLE POSTAGE STAMP OF NATIVE SOIL." New York: Fordham University Press, 1969. 284 p. Bibliog.

Charts the historical, geographical, economic, and social development of Yoknapatawpha County and attempts to relate it to the reality of Lafayette County.

585 Kirk, Robert W., with Marvin Klotz. FAULKNER'S PEOPLE: A COMPLETE GUIDE AND INDEX TO CHARACTERS IN THE FICTION OF WILLIAM FAULKNER. Berkeley and Los Angeles: University of California Press, 1963. xvi, 354 p.

Indispensable.

586 Levins, Lynn Gartrell. FAULKNER'S HEROIC DESIGN: THE YOKNAPATAWPHA NOVELS. Athens: University of Georgia Press, 1976. x, 202 p.

Treats the major Yoknapatawpha novels from SARTORIS to THE REIVERS. The "heroic design" is Faulkner's juxtaposition of the events of his rural community against scenes from, and echoes of, myths, classic drama, epic poetry, and chivalric and historical romance.

587 Malin, Irving. WILLIAM FAULKNER: AN INTERPRETATION. Stanford, Calif.: Stanford University Press, 1957. viii, 99 p.

An early psychoanalytic study.

588 Millgate, Michael. THE ACHIEVEMENT OF WILLIAM FAULKNER. London: Constable, 1966. xii , 344 p.

A valuable critical review, by an English critic, of Faulkner's overall achievement, with independent analyses of each novel and each book of short stories. Each book is placed in the context of the career as a whole. There is also an extended account of those aspects of Faulkner's life that seem relevant to an understanding of his work.

589 Mottram, Eric. WILLIAM FAULKNER. Profiles in Literature Series. London: Routledge and Kegan Paul, 1971. ix, 110 p. Bibliog.

An introduction to Faulkner, his life and works. Only a few of the major novels are considered in detail.

590 O'Connor, William Van. THE TANGLED FIRE OF WILLIAM FAULKNER. Minneapolis: University of Minnesota Press, 1954. Reprint. New York: Gordian Press, 1968. xv, 182 p.

Tries to offset the limitations in the criticism that centers attention on the "Southern Myth." Much of the earlier criticism is viewed as "shockingly wrong-headed." Faulkner is seen as a great but very uneven writer.

591 ______. WILLIAM FAULKNER. Rev. ed. UMPAW, no. 3. Minneapolis: University of Minnesota Press, 1964. 47 p. Bibliog. Originally published in 1959.

A good brief introduction to Faulkner's work.

592 Page, Sally R. FAULKNER'S WOMEN: CHARACTERIZATION AND MEANING. Deland, Fla.: Everett and Edwards, 1972. xxix, 233 p. Bibliog.

An in-depth study that concludes that, in Faulkner's fiction, "the earth and woman are symbolic of the nature of the human condition, and they embody both its limitations and its potentialities."

593 Peavy, Charles D. GO SLOW NOW: FAULKNER AND THE RACE QUESTION. Eugene: University of Oregon Books, 1971. 105 p. Bibliog.

Discusses Faulkner's nonfiction statements on racial equality and contends that if some of them seem to be in conflict with his treatment of the Negro in fiction it is because in fiction he is suggesting the ideal, while in nonfiction he is delineating the real.

594 Richardson, H. Edward. WILLIAM FAULKNER: THE JOURNEY TO SELF-DISCOVERY. Columbia: University of Missouri Press, 1969. xii, 258 p. Bibliog.

On Faulkner's apprentice period. Tries to show a pattern of self-discovery that reached its apex in SARTORIS.

595 Richardson, Kenneth E. FORCE AND FAITH IN THE NOVELS OF WILLIAM FAULKNER. Studies in American Literature, vol. 7. The Hague and Paris: Mouton, 1967. 187 p. Bibliog.

The novels are analyzed in terms of a relationship between the forces that operate in Faulkner's fictional world and what is referred to as "Faulkner's faith."

596 Robb, Mary Cooper. WILLIAM FAULKNER: AN ESTIMATE OF HIS CONTRIBUTION TO THE MODERN AMERICAN NOVEL. Critical Essays in English and American Literature, no. 1. Pittsburgh: University of Pittsburgh Press, 1957. 70 p. Bibliog.

A somewhat plodding monograph that concludes that Faulkner is an original in spite of his literary debts.

597 Runyan, Harry, ed. A FAULKNER GLOSSARY. New York: Citadel Press, 1964. 310 p.

Besides the glossary, included are appendixes: a biographical sketch, poetry, nonfiction prose, fiction, histories of the principal families of Yoknapatawpha County, geography of the county, and the documents of the county.

598 Schoenberg, Estella. OLD TALES AND TALKING: QUENTIN COMPSON IN WILLIAM FAULKNER'S ABSALOM, ABSALOM! AND RELATED WORKS. Jackson: University Press of Mississippi, 1977. xi, 156 p.

"A developing fictionalist, apprentice to the mastercraftsman William Faulkner, Quentin forces unity upon the 'ragtag and bob-ends of old tales and talking' by forcing them into the mold of his own experience."

599 Smart, George K. RELIGIOUS ELEMENTS IN FAULKNER'S EARLY NOVELS: A SELECTIVE CONCORDANCE. Coral Gables: University of Miami Press, 1965. ix, 144 p.

SOLDIERS' PAY, MOSQUITOES, and SARTORIS are the novels. In his introduction Smart suggests that the Christian tradition and values are central in Faulkner's creative synthesis.

600 Volpe, Edmond L. A READER'S GUIDE TO WILLIAM FAULKNER. New York: Farrar, Straus, 1964. Reprint. New York: Octagon Books, 1974. xiii, 427 p. Bibliog.

The guide is divided into three sections: (1) introduction, an attempt to describe the dominant patterns in the fiction; (2) novels, offers interpretations of all nineteen; and (3) appendix, notes, and bibliography. The appendix offers a chronology of scenes and events in several novels.

601 Waggoner, Hyatt H. WILLIAM FAULKNER: FROM JEFFERSON TO THE WORLD. Lexington: University of Kentucky Press, 1959. vi, 279 p.

Explores the fiction, both long and short, from the beginnings through A FABLE.

602 Warren, Robert Penn, ed. FAULKNER: A COLLECTION OF CRITICAL ESSAYS. Twentieth Century Views Series. Englewood Cliffs, N.J.: Prentice-Hall, 1966. 311 p. Bibliog.

An excellent collection of twenty-four essays, including the editor's fine introduction.

603 Wilde, Meta Carpenter, and Borsten, Orin. A LOVING GENTLEMAN: THE LOVE STORY OF WILLIAM FAULKNER AND META CARPENTER. New York: Simon and Schuster, 1976. 334 p. Illus.

The undocumented account of the love affair between Faulkner and his Hollywood script girl.

604 Williams, David. FAULKNER'S WOMEN: THE MYTH AND THE MUSE. Montreal: McGill-Queen's University Press, 1977. 284 p.

Examines Faulkner's female characters and suggests that from first to last "the vision he most frequently reverts to is the archetype of woman in man."

F. SCOTT FITZGERALD (1896-1940)

605 Bruccoli, Matthew J. THE COMPOSITION OF TENDER IS THE NIGHT: A STUDY OF THE MANUSCRIPTS. Pittsburgh: University of Pittsburgh Press, 1963. xxv, 252 p.

Attempts to take an inventory of the manuscripts of TENDER and to interpret the purpose and meaning of the novel. Shows Fitzgerald as an unmethodical worker.

606 _____. "THE LAST OF THE NOVELISTS": F. SCOTT FITZGERALD AND THE LAST TYCOON. Carbondale and Edwardsville: Southern Illinois University Press, 1977. ix, 163 p.

Shows, through close examination of the manuscripts and notes for THE LAST TYCOON that Edmund Wilson's published text of the "unfinished novel" is misleading because it presents Fitzgerald's working drafts in a finished form. The work should be regarded only as "material toward a novel."

607 _____. SCOTT AND ERNEST: THE AUTHORITY OF FAILURE AND THE AUTHORITY OF SUCCESS. New York: Random House, 1978. xv, 168 p. Illus.

Examines the Fitzgerald-Hemingway relationship and tries to set the record straight; thus this documentary reconstruction of their friendship and estrangement.

608 _____, ed. F. SCOTT FITZGERALD; A DESCRIPTIVE BIBLIOGRAPHY. Pittsburgh Series in Bibliography. Pittsburgh: University of Pittsburgh Press, 1972. xxiii, 369 p.

609 Bruccoli, Matthew J., and Layman, Richard, eds. FITZGERALD/HEMINGWAY ANNUAL 1979. Detroit: Gale Research Co., 1980. 530 p.

The latest in the series of annuals begun in 1969. Contains many items on both authors as well as reviews of recent books about them, together with checklists.

610 Bruccoli, Matthew J., et al., eds. THE ROMANTIC EGOISTS. New York: Scribner, 1974. x, 246 p. Illus.

A pictorial biography of Scott and Zelda, done with the editorial assistance of their daughter, Scottie Fitzgerald Smith, and Joan P. Kerr.

611 Bryer, Jackson R., ed. F. SCOTT FITZGERALD: THE CRITICAL RECEPTION. American Critical Tradition Series, no. 5. New York: Burt Franklin, 1978. xxx, 386 p.

Presents a representative and sizable selection of reviews of Fitzgerald's books during his lifetime.

612 Buttitta, Tony. AFTER THE GOOD GAY TIMES: ASHEVILLE--SUMMER OF '35, A SEASON WITH F. SCOTT FITZGERALD. New York: Viking, 1974. xii, 173 p.

The account of the author's brief relationship with Fitzgerald at the lowest point of the latter's career. The memoir was written from notes jotted down at the time, and provides a vivid portrait of Fitzgerald.

613 Eble, Kenneth E. F. SCOTT FITZGERALD. TUSAS, no. 36. New York: Twayne, 1977. 187 p. Bibliog.

A reliable introduction to the life and works.

614 ______, ed. F. SCOTT FITZGERALD; A COLLECTION OF CRITICISM. Contemporary Studies in Literature. New York: McGraw-Hill, 1973. vii, 152 p. Bibliog.

One of the better collections.

615 Fahey, William A. F. SCOTT FITZGERALD AND THE AMERICAN DREAM. Twentieth Century American Writers Series. New York: Crowell, 1973. 177 p. Bibliog.

Examines Fitzgerald's fiction as an expression of the myth of two families, "the royal and the humble." Fahey contends that Fitzgerald continued, "with at least one part of his mind, to believe that he was the son of a king who ruled the world and that he would never die like other people." The belief is viewed as part of his strength as a writer.

616 Gallo, Rose Adrienne. F. SCOTT FITZGERALD. Modern Literature Monographs. New York: Frederick Ungar, 1978. ix, 166 p. Bibliog.

A generally reliable brief account of Fitzgerald's life and work that adds little that is new. A chapter is devoted to each of the novels, with one to the short stories, and another to his work on stage and screen.

617 Graham, Sheilah. COLLEGE OF ONE. New York: Viking, 1967. viii, 245 p.

The story of Graham's education as devised by Fitzgerald during his Hollywood period. Includes reproduction of the typed curriculum that he drew up.

618 ______. THE REAL F. SCOTT FITZGERALD, THIRTY-FIVE YEARS LATER. New York: Grosset and Dunlap, 1976. 287 p. Illus.

Fitzgerald's intimate companion, a Hollywood columnist, pictures him as a Jekyll-Hyde personality. One Scott is kind, the other cruel; one is mature, the other a child; and so on. The story of their relationship as remembered by Graham.

619 Graham, Sheilah, with Gerold Frank. BELOVED INFIDEL; THE EDUCATION OF A WOMAN. New York: Holt, 1958. 338 p. Illus.

Autobiography of Sheilah Graham, with strong emphasis on the relationship with Fitzgerald.

620 Higgins, John A. F. SCOTT FITZGERALD: A STUDY OF THE STORIES. Jamaica, N.Y.: St. John's University Press, 1971. xiii, 212 p. Bibliog.

Analysis of the short fiction.

621 Kazin, Alfred, ed. F. SCOTT FITZGERALD: THE MAN AND HIS WORK. Cleveland: World Publishing Co., 1951. Reprint. New York: Collier Books, 1962. 221 p.

Pieces by various hands, with an introduction by Kazin.

622 Lehan, Richard D. F. SCOTT FITZGERALD AND THE CRAFT OF FICTION. Crosscurrents/Modern Critiques. Carbondale and Edwardsville: Southern Illinois University Press, 1966. xv, 206 p. Bibliog.

Attempts to reconcile biography and criticism by concerning itself primarily with the quality of Fitzgerald's developing imagination. A very useful volume.

623 Milford, Nancy. ZELDA: A BIOGRAPHY. New York, Evanston, Ill., and London: Harper and Row, 1970. xiv, 424 p.

Although primarily a biography of Zelda Fitzgerald, the book is virtually a biography of Scott as well. The insights are acute.

624 Miller, James E., Jr. F. SCOTT FITZGERALD: HIS ART AND TECHNIQUE. New York: New York University Press, 1964. xiv, 173 p. Bibliog.

An expansion of Miller's 1957 study, THE FICTIONAL TECHNIQUE OF SCOTT FITZGERALD. Whereas the earlier volume ended with THE GREAT GATSBY, this one includes discussion of TENDER IS THE NIGHT and THE LAST TYCOON.

625 Mizener, Arthur. THE FAR SIDE OF PARADISE: A BIOGRAPHY OF F. SCOTT FITZGERALD. Boston: Houghton Mifflin, 1951. xx, 362 p.

A balanced treatment of the man, his writings, and his relation to his time. The best biography to date.

626 ______. SCOTT FITZGERALD AND HIS WORLD. London: Thames and Hudson, 1972. 128 p. Bibliog.

A book of remarkable photographs of Fitzgerald, his family, his friends and acquaintances, and the places he lived in. Accompanied by text.

627 Piper, Henry Dan. F. SCOTT FITZGERALD: A CRITICAL PORTRAIT. New York, Chicago, and San Francisco: Holt, Rinehart and Winston, 1965. xi, 334 p.

Attempts to separate myth from fact and to tell the story of Fitzgerald's life as a writer more fully than it had been told before. The focus is entirely on his career as writer and artist.

628 Shain, Charles E. SCOTT FITZGERALD. UMPAW, no. 15. Minneapolis: University of Minnesota Press, 1961. 48 p. Bibliog.

A competent introduction.

629 Sklar, Robert. F. SCOTT FITZGERALD: THE LAST LAOCOÖN. New York: Oxford University Press, 1967. 376 p.

A study of Fitzgerald's mind and art from his early fiction through THE LAST TYCOON. Attempts to prove that Fitzgerald had not only great literary talent but also profound critical intelligence.

630 Stavola, Thomas J. SCOTT FITZGERALD; CRISIS IN AN AMERICAN IDENTITY. New York: Barnes and Noble, 1979. 176 p. Bibliog.

A psychoanalytical interpretation of Fitzgerald and his work.

631 Stern, Milton R. THE GOLDEN MOMENT: THE NOVELS OF F. SCOTT FITZGERALD. Urbana, Chicago, and London: University of Illinois Press, 1970. xiii, 462 p.

Uses Fitzgerald's life to illuminate his fiction. Stern presents extensive and perceptive analysis of THIS SIDE OF PARADISE, THE BEAUTIFUL AND DAMNED, THE GREAT GATSBY, and TENDER IS THE NIGHT.

632 Turnbull, Andrew. SCOTT FITZGERALD. New York: Scribner, 1962. xi, 364 p.

The focus here is almost exclusively on the man.

JOHN GOULD FLETCHER (1886-1950)

633 de Chasca, Edmund S. JOHN GOULD FLETCHER AND IMAGISM. Columbia and London: University of Missouri Press, 1978. v, 242 p. Bibliog.

Clears up the question of Fletcher's relationship to imagism and the imagists in order to view his poetry free of "a confusing and encumbering label." Fletcher's critical theory and his poetry are compared with strict imagist theory and practice, and his relations with Ezra Pound, Amy Lowell and other contemporaries are recounted in detail.

634 Morton, Bruce, ed. JOHN GOULD FLETCHER: A BIBLIOGRAPHY. Serif Series, no. 37. Kent, Ohio: Kent State University Press, 1979. xv, 203 p.

A very useful annotated bibliography of works by and about the subject.

635 Simon, Charlie May. JOHNSWOOD. New York: Dutton, 1953. 249 p.

Fletcher's wife offers a biographical reminiscence of their life together.

636 Stephens, Edna B. JOHN GOULD FLETCHER. TUSAS, no. 118. New York: Twayne, 1967. 160 p. Bibliog.

The best introduction available although the biographical information is sketchy. Explication and analysis of the poetry indicate the poet's method and the direction of his thought. Sees Fletcher's imagist label as a deterrent to his recognition as a fine poet, and regards him as significant as a modern poet-mystic. He is also viewed as a stylist and fine critic.

HAROLD FREDERIC (1856-1898)

637 Briggs, Austin, Jr. THE NOVELS OF HAROLD FREDERIC. Ithaca, N.Y., and London: Cornell University Press, 1969. x, 234 p. Bibliog.

The first book-length study of Frederic's fiction, it describes and analyzes the novels in detail, correcting many errors in earlier evaluations of Frederic and his work.

638 Garner, Stanton. HAROLD FREDERIC. UMPAW, no. 83. Minneapolis: University of Minnesota Press, 1969. 48 p. Bibliog.

A good brief introduction to the writer and his work.

639 O'Donnell, Thomas F., and Franchere, Hoyt C. HAROLD FREDERIC. TUSAS, no. 3. New York: Twayne, 1961. 186 p. Bibliog.

Gives a quite full portrait of Frederic both in New York and London, assays his best-known works of fiction, devoting an entire chapter to THE DAMNATION OF THERON WARE, and attempts generally to rescue him from an undeserved obscurity.

640 O'Donnell, Thomas F., et al., eds. A BIBLIOGRAPHY OF WRITINGS BY AND ABOUT HAROLD FREDERIC. Research Bibliographies in American Literature, no. 4. Boston: G.K. Hall, 1975. xi, 342 p.

A comprehensive bibliography, not descriptive, but containing many helpful annotations.

641 Polk, Noel, ed. THE LITERARY MANUSCRIPTS OF HAROLD FREDERIC: A CATALOGUE. New York and London: Garland Publishing Co., 1979. xvii, 123 p.

The extant manuscripts, described in this catalog, show Frederic to have been a disciplined, methodical worker and an unusually meticulous craftsman.

MARY WILKINS FREEMAN (1852-1930)

642 Foster, Edward. MARY E. WILKINS FREEMAN. New York: Hendricks House, 1956. ix, 229 p. Bibliog.

The only full-length biography, it does an excellent job in presenting Mrs. Freeman's life as writer, woman, and symbol of latter-day New England. There is also keen analysis of some of the better short stories and novels.

643 Westbrook, Perry D. MARY WILKINS FREEMAN. TUSAS, no. 122. New York: Twayne, 1967. 191 p. Bibliog.

Considers only Freeman's fiction for adults. Sees her greatest strength as lying in her insights to the post-Calvinist psyche of back-country New England at the close of the nineteenth century. The book is the best introduction to Freeman and her work readily available.

PHILIP FRENEAU (1752-1832)

644 Adkins, Nelson F. PHILIP FRENEAU AND THE COSMIC ENIGMA: THE RELIGIOUS AND PHILOSOPHICAL SPECULATIONS OF AN AMERICAN POET. New York: New York University Press, 1949. 84 p.

A detailed analysis of a facet of Freneau not treated before in any depth.

645 Austin, Mary S. PHILIP FRENEAU; THE POET OF THE REVOLUTION: A HISTORY OF HIS LIFE AND TIMES. New York: A. Wessels, 1901. x, 285 p. Illus.

The first full-length biography of Freneau, it is far from reliable and is hampered by a cliche-ridden style.

646 Bowden, Mary Weatherspoon. PHILIP FRENEAU. TUSAS, no. 260. Boston: Twayne, 1976. 194 p. Bibliog.

An excellent study of Freneau, which views him as reflecting the Enlightenment most strongly in the variety of his interests. His importance as a transitional poet is stressed, as is the broad scope of his work. A chapter each is devoted to his heritage, his occasional poetry, his prose, and his poetry for art's sake.

647 Leary, Lewis. THAT RASCAL FRENEAU: A STUDY IN LITERARY FAILURE. New Brunswick, N.J.: Rutgers University Press, 1941. x, 501 p. Bibliog.

The fullest and most scholarly biography of Freneau, containing also the best bibliography of his writing. Later biographers, such as Marsh, question Leary's major premise: that Freneau "failed in almost everything he attempted."

648 Marsh, Philip M. PHILIP FRENEAU: POET AND JOURNALIST. Minneapolis, Minn.: Dillon Press, 1967. v, 444 p. Bibliog.

A more readable biography than Leary's (see no. 647), with less emphasis on criticism, is attempted here. Freneau is regarded as "basic to a full understanding of our political, historical, and literary genesis." He is seen as the best American poet of his time.

649 ______. THE WORKS OF PHILIP FRENEAU: A CRITICAL STUDY. Metuchen, N.J.: Scarecrow Press, 1968. v, 197 p. Bibliog.

Includes a good biographical sketch as prelude to the description, interpretation, and evaluation of the poetry and prose.

ROBERT FROST (1874-1963)

650 Barry, Elaine. ROBERT FROST. Modern Literature Monographs. New York: Frederick Ungar, 1973. ix, 145 p. Bibliog.

This provocative study sees Frost not as a great poet but as a very good one; he falls short of greatness because he is not a believer. There are chapters on "The Lyric Voice," the "Dramatic Narrative," "Frost and the Sonnet Form," and the "Meditative Voice."

651 Cox, James M., ed. ROBERT FROST: A COLLECTION OF CRITICAL ESSAYS. Twentieth Century Views. Englewood Cliffs, N.J.: Prentice-Hall, 1962. 205 p. Bibliog.

A nicely balanced collection of eleven essays by, among others, Lawrance Thompson, Malcolm Cowley, Yvor Winters, Randall Jarrell, Lionel Trilling, and George W. Nitchie. Cox's introduction describes the main themes of the poems.

652 Cox, Sidney. A SWINGER OF BIRCHES: A PORTRAIT OF ROBERT FROST. New York: New York University Press, 1957. xi, 177 p.

Cox, a close friend of Frost for forty years, records his impressions of the man he deems the wisest he has ever known.

653 Frost, Lesley. NEW HAMPSHIRE'S CHILD; THE DERRY JOURNALS OF LESLEY FROST. Notes and index by Lawrance Thompson and Arnold Grade. Albany: State University of New York Press, 1969. Unpaged.

Reproduces the journals Frost's daughter began to keep when she was five years old, and which she continued for four years. There is a good introduction by Ms. Frost.

654 Jennings, Elizabeth. FROST. Writers and Critics Series. Edinburgh and London: Oliver and Boyd, 1964. 119 p.

An overview of Frost's career, a discussion of some of the poetry, and a section on his critical reception.

655 Karki, Mohan Singh. ROBERT FROST: THEORY AND PRACTICE OF THE COLLOQUIAL AND SOUND OF SENSE. Aligarh, India: Granthayan, 1979. iv, 151 p.

Restricted to an estimate of Frost as poet, with special reference to his theory of the colloquial and sound of sense.

656 Kemp, John C. ROBERT FROST AND NEW ENGLAND: THE POET AS REGIONALIST. Princeton, N.J.: Princeton University Press, 1979. xiii, 273 p.

An in-depth study of Frost's ambiguous relationship with New England. Frost is seen as not a regional poet in the usual sense. Indeed, "Frost's best New England poems transcend the limitations of local-color writing and attain a complexity and universality not inherently regional."

657 Lentricchia, Frank. ROBERT FROST: MODERN POETICS AND THE LANDSCAPES OF SELF. Durham, N.C.: Duke University Press, 1975. xiii, 200 p.

An analysis in depth of Frost's poetry. He is viewed as "an ironist in the profoundest sense who teaches us that the dreaded antifictive--the real thing--is often to be preferred to what we make, in the imagination, because the fictive 'world elsewhere' may be a place of madness."

658 Lentricchia, Frank, and Lentricchia, Melissa Christensen, comps. ROBERT FROST: A BIBLIOGRAPHY, 1913-1974. Metuchen, N.J.: Scarecrow Press, 1976. viii, 238 p.

The most complete bibliography of primary and secondary materials to date. Unannotated.

659 Lynen, John F. THE PASTORAL ART OF ROBERT FROST. New Haven, Conn.: Yale University Press, 1960. xii, 208 p. Bibliog.

A study of Frost's poetic form that carefully analyzes many of the poems. Frost is seen as always stopping short of being a completely personal poet, for his individualism is justified by "a system of values which lies beyond the individual."

660 Munson, Gorham B. ROBERT FROST: A STUDY IN SENSIBILITY AND GOOD SENSE. New York: George H. Doran, 1928. Reprint. New York: Haskell House, 1973. 135 p.

An early study about half devoted to biographical data and the remainder to Frost's poetic techniques.

661 Poirier, Richard. ROBERT FROST, THE WORK OF KNOWING. New York: Oxford University Press, 1977. xvii, 322 p.

Perceptive interpretations of many of the poems. Very helpful to students of the poetry.

662 Reeve, F.D. ROBERT FROST IN RUSSIA. Boston and Toronto: Little, Brown, 1964. 135 p.

A day-by-day account of Frost's visit in 1962.

663 Sergeant, Elizabeth Shepley. ROBERT FROST: THE TRIAL BY EXISTENCE. New York: Holt, Rinehart and Winston, 1960. xxvii, 451 p.

An extended and somewhat idealized portrait of Frost based largely on a series of interviews with the poet.

664 Squires, Radcliffe. THE MAJOR THEMES OF ROBERT FROST. Ann Arbor: University of Michigan Press, 1963. 119 p. Bibliog.

Concerned with those aspects of Frost's work which make it valuable: "its legality of language, its relevance to life, and above all its truth and honor of concept."

665 Thompson, Lawrance. FIRE AND ICE: THE ART AND THOUGHT OF ROBERT FROST. New York: Holt, 1942. xiii, 241 p. Reprint. New York: Russell and Russell, 1961.

A penetrating analysis of Frost's theory of poetry, practice of poetry, and attitude toward life.

666 _____. ROBERT FROST. UMPAW, no. 2. Minneapolis: University of Minnesota Press, 1959. 43 p. Bibliog.

A very useful brief introduction to the poet and the poetry.

667 _____. ROBERT FROST: THE EARLY YEARS, 1874-1915. New York, Chicago, and San Francisco: Holt, Rinehart and Winston, 1966. xxvi, 641 p. Illus.

_____. ROBERT FROST: THE YEARS OF TRIUMPH, 1915-1938. New York, Chicago, and San Francisco: Holt, Rinehart and Winston, 1970. xxii, 744 p. Illus.

_____. ROBERT FROST: THE LATER YEARS, 1938-1963. With R.H. Winnick. New York, Chicago, and San Francisco: Holt, Rinehart and Winston, 1976. xxiii, 468 p. Illus.

The three volumes comprise the authorized biography of Frost, an impressive work of dedicated scholarship which leaves few stones unturned. It has been a somewhat controversial book because of what many readers conceived to be an overly candid and revealing portrait of the poet which does not show him as being always lovable or inevitably admirable.

668 Van Egmond, Peter, ed. THE CRITICAL RECEPTION OF ROBERT FROST. Research Bibliographies in American Literature, no. 1. Boston: G.K. Hall, 1974. xiv, 319 p.

Ten sections cover: reviews; interviews and talks; letters; news items; bibliographies and checklists; books, pamphlets, criticism of books; articles; anthologies; poems to or about Frost; doctoral dissertations; foreign criticism. Annotated.

MARGARET FULLER (1810-1850)

669 Allen, Margaret Vanderhaar. THE ACHIEVEMENT OF MARGARET FULLER. University Park and London: Pennsylvania State University Press, 1979. xiii, 212 p. Bibliog.

Not primarily a biography, the book is concerned with Fuller's ideas and with where they led her. The influence of Emerson and Goethe is explored in depth, and each aspect of her manifold accomplishment is examined. Praises her lavishly.

670 Anthony, Katharine. MARGARET FULLER, A PSYCHOLOGICAL BIOGRAPHY. New York: Harcourt, Brace and Howe, 1920. v, 223 p. Bibliog.

Offers no new facts, but interprets Fuller as "a modern woman who died in 1850." Her legend "was created mainly by unemancipated men." Attempts to analyze the emotional values of Fuller's life, and her social transformation. Written by a champion of feminism.

671 Blanshard, Paula. MARGARET FULLER: FROM TRANSCENDENTALISM TO REVOLUTION. Radcliffe Biography Series. New York: Delacorte Press and Seymour Lawrence, 1978. xii, 370 p. Illus. Bibliog.

A scholarly full-scale biography that tries to correct the myths which have made a true picture of Fuller difficult to achieve. The bias here is feminist.

672 Braun, Frederick Augustus. MARGARET FULLER AND GOETHE. New York: Holt, 1910. vii, 271 p.

Attempts to trace the inner development of Fuller's powerful personality. Sees Goethe as the prime source of her intellectual growth and her concept of life. Her role in encouraging knowledge of German literature in America is also stressed.

673 Brown, Arthur W. MARGARET FULLER. TUSAS, no. 48. New York: Twayne, 1964. 159 p. Bibliog.

Combining biography with generally sound evaluation of Fuller's work, this is the best introduction available. An important aim of the book is "to wipe out the impression that Margaret Fuller belonged to a kind of third sex because she dared to use her mind and to speak on topics upon which there was a conspiracy of silence."

674 Chipperfield, Faith. IN QUEST OF LOVE: THE LIFE AND DEATH OF

MARGARET FULLER. New York: Coward-McCann, 1957. 320 p. Bibliog. notes.

A somewhat dramatized biography, which frequently employs imaginary conversations. Not well documented.

675 Deiss, Joseph Jay. THE ROMAN YEARS OF MARGARET FULLER. New York: Crowell, 1969. xiii, 338 p. Illus., bibliog.

The story of Margaret Fuller in Italy, her life with Ossoli, and their tragic death off Fire Island.

676 Durning, Russell E. MARGARET FULLER, CITIZEN OF THE WORLD. Heidelberg, Germany: Carl Winter, 1969. 144 p. Bibliog.

Fuller is viewed in this erudite study as "an intermediary between European and American literatures." The five chapters are: (1) "Margaret Fuller: Critic, Translator, Feminist, and Traveler"; (2) "Margaret Fuller, Teacher and Conversationalist"; (3) "Margaret Fuller and France, Italy, and Spain"; (4) "Margaret Fuller and Germany"; (5) "The Achievement of Margaret Fuller."

677 Emerson, R.W., et al., eds. MEMOIRS OF MARGARET FULLER OSSOLI. 2 vols. Boston: Phillips, Sampson, 1852. Unpaged.

Along with W.H. Channing and J.F. Clarke, Emerson edited this first biography of Fuller, which is a compilation of comments about her by contemporaries, with selections from her letters and journals. The picture of an egocentric, intellectually aloof individualist emerges.

678 Higginson, Thomas Wentworth. MARGARET FULLER OSSOLI. Boston: Houghton Mifflin, 1890. Reprint. New York: Greenwood Press, 1968. 323 p.

A sympathetic biography by one who knew her and valued her. Her life is seen as a triumphant rather than a sad one.

679 Howe, Julia Ward. MARGARET FULLER (MARCHESA OSSOLI). Boston: Roberts Brothers, 1883. Reprint. Westport, Conn.: Greenwood Press, 1970. x, 298 p.

A flattering portrait by a friend who attempts to capture Fuller's personality rather than to add to factual information about her life or to provide criticism of her work.

680 Myerson, Joel, ed. CRITICAL ESSAYS ON MARGARET FULLER. Boston: Twayne, 1980. 289 p. Bibliog.

Presents more than fifty critical pieces from 1840 to 1980 with a good introduction by the editor.

681 ______. MARGARET FULLER: AN ANNOTATED SECONDARY BIBLIOGRAPHY. New York: Burt Franklin, 1977. xix, 272 p.

An excellent starting point for the study of Fuller.

682 Stern, Madeleine B. THE LIFE OF MARGARET FULLER. New York: Dutton, 1942. xvi, 549 p. Illus., bibliog.

Although the author professes that her biography is entirely factual, she succumbs to the temptation to overdramatize, to tell us that "Margaret turned in her sleep" and so on. However, her book is most readable and contains a very full bibliography.

683 Wade, Mason. MARGARET FULLER: WHETSTONE OF GENIUS. New York: Viking, 1940. xvi, 304 p. Bibliog. note.

One of the best biographies of Fuller. It is well researched, ably written, and not given to flights of fancy.

HAMLIN GARLAND (1860-1940)

684 Bryer, Jackson R., and Harding, Eugene, eds., with Robert A. Rees. HAMLIN GARLAND AND THE CRITICS: AN ANNOTATED BIBLIOGRAPHY. Troy, N.Y.: Whitston Publishing Co., 1973. v, 282 p.

Contains annotated lists of reviews of books by Garland, periodical articles about Garland, books and parts of books about him, author and subject indexes, and an index to works by Garland.

685 Gish, Robert. HAMLIN GARLAND: THE FAR WEST. BSU Western Writers Series, no. 24. Boise, Idaho: Boise State University, 1976. 48 p. Bibliog.

Focuses on Garland's middle period and his far western writing, in which he nourished the myth of the West as the land of success and the good life, at least in his Rocky Mountain romances.

686 McCullough, Joseph B. HAMLIN GARLAND. TUSAS, no. 299. Boston: Twayne, 1978. 143 p. Bibliog.

A good general introduction to the life and work. The aspects of Garland's life that influenced his writing are stressed, and his literary achievement is examined in relation to his social and literary ideas. Major writings of each of the three phases are discussed (middle border fiction, Rocky Mountain romance, and literary autobiography).

687 Pizer, Donald. HAMLIN GARLAND'S EARLY WORK AND CAREER. University of California English Studies, 22. Berkeley and Los Angeles: University of California Press, 1960. ix, 220 p. Bibliog.

In-depth study of Garland's life and work from 1884 to 1895.

688 Silet, Charles L.P., ed. HENRY BLAKE FULLER AND HAMLIN GARLAND: A REFERENCE GUIDE. Boston: G.K. Hall, 1977. xiii, 148 p.

An annotated list of published writings on Garland occupies about half the book.

Note: Unfortunately the two most extensive books on Garland are in French and German respectively: Robert Mane's HAMLIN GARLAND, L'HOMME ET L'OEUVRE (1860-1940), 1968, and Hans Borchers's HAMLIN GARLAND, DIE ENTWICKLUNG EINES AMERIKANISCHEN REALISTEN, 1975.

ALLEN GINSBERG (1926--)

689 Kramer, Jane. ALLEN GINSBERG IN AMERICA. New York: Random House, 1969. xix, 202 p.

A lively journalistic portrait of Ginsberg and his environment.

690 Kraus, Michelle P., ed. ALLEN GINSBERG: AN ANNOTATED BIBLIOGRAPHY, 1969-1977. Metuchen, N.J., and London: Scarecrow Press, 1980. xxx, 328 p. Illus.

A valuable book for those interested in Ginsberg's work, it is divided into two main sections: primary works and secondary works. The annotations are quite helpful. 1,419 items are included, 817 of which are secondary.

691 Merrill, Thomas F. ALLEN GINSBERG. TUSAS, no. 161. New York: Twayne, 1969. 183 p. Bibliog.

The first book-length attempt to come to grips with Ginsberg and to answer the question: is he a real poet or a personality "posing as the bard of the 1950's and 1960's"? After two chapters that discuss Ginsberg and the Beat Attitude, there is a chapter each on EMPTY MIRROR, HOWL AND OTHER POEMS, KADDISH, and REALITY SANDWICHES AND LATER POEMS. The final chapter, which was supposed to answer the question whether Ginsberg is a poet appears to duck the issue and is content to say that he "achieves energy in his poetry through two modes: the tightness of his catalogues and his meter."

692 Portuges, Paul. THE VISIONARY POETICS OF ALLEN GINSBERG. Santa Barbara, Calif.: Ross-Erikson, 1978. xiv, 181 p. Bibliog.

The book is divided into two parts: (1) "Allen Ginsberg's William Blake and the Poetics of Vision, 1948-1963," the primary purpose of which is to explain what happened to Ginsberg during an eventful week in 1948 "while he was under the spell of the poet William Blake's apparitional voice," and the far-reaching effects of these visions on his poetry and poetics; and (2) "The Visionary Poetics, 1945-1976: Conversations with Ginsberg on Drugs, Mantras, and Tibetan Buddhism."

ELLEN GLASGOW (1874-1945)

693 Auchincloss, Louis. ELLEN GLASGOW. UMPAW, no. 33. Minneapolis: University of Minnesota Press, 1964. 48 p. Bibliog.

An incisive analysis of Glasgow's work. Sees her as a bridge, and a necessary one, between the world of Thomas Nelson Page and the world of Faulkner, Katherine Anne Porter, Eudora Welty, and Tennessee Williams.

694 Ekman, Barbro. THE END OF A LEGEND: ELLEN GLASGOW'S HISTORY OF SOUTHERN WOMEN. Stockholm: Almquist and Wiksell, 1979. 171 p. Bibliog.

A doctoral dissertation at Uppsala University. Attempts to trace the history of the southern woman from the years just before the Civil War up to World War II both historically and as seen through Glasgow's eyes. "Her importance lies in the fact that . . . she covers the entire period of the feminist movement."

695 Field, Louise Maunsell. ELLEN GLASGOW: NOVELIST OF THE OLD AND THE NEW SOUTH. Garden City, N.Y.: Doubleday, Page, 1923. Reprint. Folcroft, Pa.: Folcroft Press, 1970. 20 p.

An overblown "appreciation" of the writer together with a reprinted essay from THE BOOKMAN by Frederic Taber Cooper on Glasgow's technique.

696 Godbold, E. Stanly, Jr. ELLEN GLASGOW AND THE WOMAN WITHIN. Baton Rouge: Louisiana State University Press, 1972. xiii, 322 p. Illus., bibliog.

The fullest biography of Glasgow, it engages in comparatively little critical analysis of her work.

697 Inge, M. Thomas, ed. ELLEN GLASGOW: CENTENNIAL ESSAYS. Charlottesville: University Press of Virginia, 1976. vii, 232 p.

Essays on Glasgow the woman, on her novels, and on her ideas by leading Glasgow scholars such as Howard Mumford Jones, Frederick P.W. McDowell, Blair Rouse, and C. Hugh Holman.

698 McDowell, Frederick P.W. ELLEN GLASGOW AND THE IRONIC ART OF FICTION. Madison: University of Wisconsin Press, 1960. xi, 292 p. Bibliog.

The first full-length study of Glasgow and her work. McDowell believes Glasgow to have been underestimated. He sees her as the social historian of Virginia from 1850 to 1939 and analyzes her novels in depth. He concludes that "an ironic detachment from experience, in conjunction with an idealistic commitment to a flexible but strongly apprehended spiritual principle . . . helped give her books their authentic quality."

699 Myer, Elizabeth Gallup. THE SOCIAL SITUATION OF WOMEN IN THE NOVELS OF ELLEN GLASGOW. Hicksville, N.Y.: Exposition Press, 1978. 80 p. Bibliog.

Written from the feminist point of view, this brief study emphasizes the theme that "in accomplishing so much for the Southern gentlewoman, Miss Glasgow stated the case for women everywhere, who have known a defeat in life through restricted opportunity."

700 Raper, Julius Rowan. FROM THE SUNKEN GARDEN: THE FICTION OF ELLEN GLASGOW, 1916-1945. Southern Literary Studies Series. Baton Rouge and London: Louisiana State University Press, 1980. xiii, 220 p. Bibliog.

Focuses on Raper's discovery of the psychological technique Glasgow developed "for exploring the invisible hemisphere of man's reality," a technique that avoids Freudian symbolism and "permits her to create characters arguably more complex than the tripartite figures of the Freudians."

701 ______. WITHOUT SHELTER: THE EARLY CAREER OF ELLEN GLASGOW. Baton Rouge: Louisiana State University Press, 1971. xii, 273 p. Bibliog.

The central concern here is to follow Glasgow's "use of the complex realism associated with Darwin as a critical tool to strip away the veneers of southern ideology." Treats the novels through 1906.

702 Richards, Marion K. ELLEN GLASGOW'S DEVELOPMENT AS A NOVELIST. Studies in American Literature. The Hague and Paris: Mouton, 1971. 203 p. Bibliog.

Although marred by faulty proofreading (e.g., "Frank Morris and Theodore Drieser), the book offers a clear view of Glasgow's entire career; there is, however, little that is new.

703 Rouse, Blair. ELLEN GLASGOW. TUSAS, no. 26. New York: Twayne, 1962. 160 p. Bibliog.

The best brief introduction to the life and works. Traces the development of Glasgow's theory and practice of the art of fiction, and discusses each of her novels, providing summaries of the plots. Ends with a survey of her critical reception.

704 Santas, Joan Foster. ELLEN GLASGOW'S AMERICAN DREAM. Charlottesville: University Press of Virginia, 1965. 248 p. Bibliog.

A penetrating analysis of the novels. More and more Glasgow is seen to lament what she saw as the mounting surrender of order and design to violence and horror in our life and literature. Her literary career was dedicated "to preserving from futility the American dream and those who would realize it."

See also no. 274.

JOEL CHANDLER HARRIS (1848-1908)

705 Bickley, R. Bruce, Jr. JOEL CHANDLER HARRIS. TUSAS, no. 308. Boston: Twayne, 1978. 174 p. Bibliog.

An excellent introduction to the life and work of Harris. Examines critically the entire Harris canon and finds him a more complex and contradictory personality than his contemporaries realized.

706 Bickley, R. Bruce, Jr., ed., with Karen L. Bickley and Thomas H. English. JOEL CHANDLER HARRIS: A REFERENCE GUIDE. Boston: G.K. Hall, 1978. xxi, 360 p.

Annotated list of writings about Harris from 1862 through 1976. Very helpful to students interested in sources for the study of Harris.

707 Cousins, Paul M. JOEL CHANDLER HARRIS: A BIOGRAPHY. Southern

Literary Studies Series. Baton Rouge: Louisiana State University Press, 1968. xiv, 237 p. Illus., bibliog.

The only scholarly full-length biography of Harris, it is detailed, reliable, and interesting.

708 Harris, Julia Collier. THE LIFE AND LETTERS OF JOEL CHANDLER HARRIS. Boston and New York: Houghton Mifflin, 1918. x, 621 p. Bibliog.

An adulatory biography by Harris's daughter-in-law. Contains valuable reminiscences of family and friends.

BRET HARTE (1836-1902)

709 Barnett, Linda Diz, ed. BRET HARTE: A REFERENCE GUIDE. Boston: G.K. Hall, 1980. xix, 427 p.

Includes 2,350 articles and books about Harte from 1865 to 1977. Annotated.

710 Harlow, Alvin F. BRET HARTE OF THE OLD WEST. New York: Julian Messner, 1943. 316 p.

Overdramatized and inaccurate, with very little criticism of Harte's work.

711 Morrow, Patrick. BRET HARTE. BSC Western Writers Series, no. 5. Boise, Idaho: Boise State College, 1972. 51 p. Bibliog.

A brief analysis of Harte's major works and an overview of the author.

712 O'Connor, Richard. BRET HARTE: A BIOGRAPHY. Boston and Toronto: Little, Brown, 1966. 331 p. Bibliog.

A popularized biography that employs much undocumented material.

713 Pemberton, T. Edgar. THE LIFE OF BRET HARTE. London: C. Arthur Pearson, 1903. vii, 358 p. Illus., bibliog.

Published shortly after Harte's death, the book is a tribute to Harte by an English friend more than it is a reliable biography. Contains little objective criticism.

714 Stewart, George R., Jr. BRET HARTE, ARGONAUT AND EXILE. Boston and New York: Houghton Mifflin, 1931. Reprint. New York: AMS Press, 1979. xii, 385 p. Illus.

Remains the best and most scholarly biography of Harte. The focus is on the life rather than on the literary production.

NATHANIEL HAWTHORNE (1804-1864)

715 Abele, Rudolph von. THE DEATH OF THE ARTIST: A STUDY OF HAWTHORNE'S DISINTEGRATION. The Hague: Martinus Nijhoff, 1955. 111 p.

A close reading of "Egotism, Or the Bosom Serpent," "The Artist of the Beautiful," and the four major romances leads to the conclusion that Hawthorne was a failure as a writer, "crippled in the development of his artistic powers by a pseudoplatonism . . . and inhibited as well by a profound unease with respect to his position as a coterie artist in a blatantly democratic culture."

716 Axelsson, Arne. THE LINKS IN THE CHAIN: ISOLATION AND INTERDEPENDENCE IN NATHANIEL HAWTHORNE'S FICTIONAL CHARACTERS. Uppsala, Swed.: Uppsala University, 1974. 190 p. Bibliog.

A Swedish doctoral dissertation that argues that "through the isolation-interdependence theme it is possible to arrive at a synthesis of all Hawthorne's fiction."

717 Bassan, Maurice. HAWTHORNE'S SON: THE LIFE AND LITERARY CAREER OF JULIAN HAWTHORNE. Columbus: Ohio State University Press, 1970. xix, 284 p. Bibliog.

Although the emphasis here is, naturally, on the life of Hawthorne's son, the chapters treating the relationship of father and son are valuable to the Hawthorne scholar.

718 Baym, Nina. THE SHAPE OF HAWTHORNE'S CAREER. Ithaca, N.Y., and London: Cornell University Press, 1976. 283 p.

A detailed examination of Hawthorne's literary development from FANSHAWE through the unfinished romances. Sees Hawthorne as changing from a "commonsensical, even antiromantic" writer to one with an underlying romantic vision.

719 Bell, Michael Davitt. HAWTHORNE AND THE HISTORICAL ROMANCE OF NEW ENGLAND. Princeton, N.J.: Princeton University Press, 1971. xii, 253 p. Bibliog.

An inquiry into the treatment of the Puritan past in Hawthorne's fiction.

720 Bridge, Horatio. PERSONAL RECOLLECTIONS OF NATHANIEL HAWTHORNE. New York: Harper, 1893. ix, 200 p. Illus.

The emphasis is on Hawthorne's college days.

721 Brodhead, Richard H. HAWTHORNE, MELVILLE, AND THE NOVEL. Chicago and London: University of Chicago Press, 1976. viii, 216 p.

Contends that both Hawthorne and Melville possessed imaginations that were "in a fundamental way hostile to the kind of formal procedure that the novel's organization requires."

722 Cameron, Kenneth Walter, ed. HAWTHORNE AMONG HIS CONTEMPORARIES: A HARVEST OF ESTIMATES, INSIGHTS, AND ANECDOTES FROM THE VICTORIAN LITERARY WORLD AND AN INDEX. Hartford, Conn.: Transcendental Books, 1968. 560 p.

Reprints from a wide variety of sources.

723 Cantwell, Robert. NATHANIEL HAWTHORNE, THE AMERICAN YEARS. New York and Toronto: Rinehart, 1948. xiv, 499 p. Illus., bibliog.

A very readable biography which, however, is extremely limited in discussion of Hawthorne's writing. It is also limited to Hawthorne's life in America before the European period, which Cantwell intended to cover in a second volume.

724 Carlson, Patricia Ann. HAWTHORNE'S FUNCTIONAL SETTINGS: A STUDY OF ARTISTIC METHOD. Amsterdam: Rodopi, 1977. 208 p.

Contends that setting and scenic elements play a major role in many of Hawthorne's works, and that identifiable patterns of the use of setting are apparent throughout the canon.

725 Clark, C.E. Frazer, Jr., ed. NATHANIEL HAWTHORNE: A DESCRIPTIVE BIBLIOGRAPHY. Pittsburgh Series in Bibliography. Pittsburgh: University of Pittsburgh Press, 1978. xxi, 478 p.

The most complete descriptive bibliography of Hawthorne's works yet published. An indispensable aid.

726 Cohen, B. Bernard, ed. THE RECOGNITION OF NATHANIEL HAWTHORNE: SELECTED CRITICISM SINCE 1828. Ann Arbor: University of Michigan Press, 1969. xx, 300 p.

Reprints important critical essays through 1966. Divided into three periods: 1828-64, 1865-1910, and 1911-66.

727 Crews, Frederick C. THE SINS OF THE FATHERS: HAWTHORNE'S PSYCHOLOGICAL THEMES. New York: Oxford University Press, 1966. viii, 279 p.

Asserts that Hawthorne was "emotionally engaged in his fiction, and the emotions he displays are those of a self-divided, self-tormented man." A provocative book.

728 Crowley, J. Donald. NATHANIEL HAWTHORNE. Profiles in Literature Series. London: Routledge and Kegan Paul, 1971. x, 101 p. Bibliog.

A good brief introduction to the life and works. There are sections on Hawthorne's discovery of a basic subject matter, point of view, plot and structure, setting and description, character-portrayal, allegory and symbol, and theme.

729 ______, ed. HAWTHORNE: THE CRITICAL HERITAGE. Critical Heritage Series. New York: Barnes and Noble, 1970. xvi, 532 p.

Reprints reviews and essays from 1828 through 1879.

730 ______. NATHANIEL HAWTHORNE: A COLLECTION OF CRITICISM. New York: McGraw-Hill, 1975. x, 149 p. Bibliog.

Ten reprinted essays on various facets of Hawthorne's work by respected Hawthorne scholars.

731 Dauber, Kenneth. REDISCOVERING HAWTHORNE. Princeton, N.J.: Princeton University Press, 1977. xii, 235 p.

An important new study that attempts to present an abstraction of Hawthorne's art. The fiction is elaborated into a theory of the novel. Dauber sees his book as "the poetics that Hawthorne might have written." The short stories as well as the major novels are examined with an eye to uncovering a cohesive theory of fiction underlying the work.

732 Dryden, Edgar A. NATHANIEL HAWTHORNE: THE POETICS OF ENCHANTMENT. Ithaca, N.Y., and London: Cornell University Press, 1977. 182 p. Bibliog.

Examining the entire canon, Dryden finds the themes of enchantment and disenchantment to be central. He believes that "an alternating movement between enchanted realms and the cold hillside is the dominating force in Hawthorne's work."

733 Elder, Marjorie J. NATHANIEL HAWTHORNE, TRANSCENDENTAL SYMBOLIST. Athens: Ohio University Press, 1969. vii, 215 p. Bibliog.

Shows that, although Hawthorne did not consider himself a transcendentalist, transcendentalism exerted a strong influence upon him and his aesthetic theory. As artist "he was always concerned . . . with man's relation to God." Concludes that in the romances, as in the tales, his artistry in all its phases evidences the transcendental aesthetic.

734 Fogle, Richard Harter. HAWTHORNE'S FICTION: THE LIGHT AND THE DARK. Norman: University of Oklahoma Press, 1952. ix, 219 p. Bibliog.

Sees Hawthorne "as a unique and wonderful combination of light and darkness." The light is clarity of design. The darkness is his tragic complexity. Hawthorne's works are examined accordingly.

735 _____. HAWTHORNE'S IMAGERY: THE "PROPER LIGHT AND SHADOW" IN THE MAJOR ROMANCES. Norman: University of Oklahoma Press, 1969. xv, 178 p.

Supplements Fogle's earlier volume, but narrower in focus in order to demonstrate fully the light and dark patterns in the four major romances.

736 Fossum, Robert H. HAWTHORNE'S INVIOLABLE CIRCLE: THE PROBLEM OF TIME. Deland, Fla.: Everett and Edwards, 1972. xiii, 188 p. Bibliog. note.

Sees much of Hawthorne's work as centering on "the ways in which time, especially the past, affects man's psychological state, his sense of identity, his relations with other men--in short, the conditions of his existence."

737 Gollin, Rita K. NATHANIEL HAWTHORNE AND THE TRUTH OF DREAMS. Baton Rouge and London: Louisiana State University Press, 1979. 235 p. Bibliog.

A thorough exploration of the role of dreams in Hawthorne's fiction.

738 Gorman, Herbert. HAWTHORNE, A STUDY IN SOLITUDE. New York: George H. Doran, 1927. 179 p.

The view of Hawthorne as a melancholy, solitary figure presented here has been fairly well exploded by much modern scholarship.

739 Gross, Theodore L., and Wertheim, Stanley, eds. HAWTHORNE, MELVILLE, STEPHEN CRANE: A CRITICAL BIBLIOGRAPHY. New York: Free Press, 1971. viii, 301 p.

The Hawthorne and Melville bibliographies are by Gross; the Crane by Wertheim. The aim of this tremendously valuable book is to present the most important scholarship on the three writers with extensive critical commentary.

740 Hawthorne, Hildegarde. ROMANTIC REBEL: THE STORY OF NATHANIEL HAWTHORNE. New York and London: Century Co., 1932. xv, 231 p. Illus.

The life of Hawthorne simply told for young readers by a granddaughter.

741 Hawthorne, Julian. HAWTHORNE AND HIS CIRCLE. New York and London: Harper, 1903. xxi, 372 p. Illus.

The story of Hawthorne's friendships and acquaintances as related by his son.

742 ______. NATHANIEL HAWTHORNE AND HIS WIFE: A BIOGRAPHY. 2 vols. Cambridge, Mass.: Osgood, 1884. vi, 970 p. Illus.

The biography by Hawthorne's son which has been the original fount of information about him.

743 Hoeltje, Hubert H. INWARD SKY: THE MIND AND HEART OF NATHANIEL HAWTHORNE. Durham, N.C.: Duke University Press, 1962. 579 p. Illus., bibliog. essay.

A strenuous attempt, by studying the entire range of Hawthorne's writing, to discover the pattern of his thought and to correlate it with the facts of the outer life and thereby disclose, as far as possible, the whole man.

744 James, Henry. HAWTHORNE. 1887. Reprint. English Men of Letters Series. New York: AMS Press, n.d. vi, 183 p.

This famous monograph reveals James's affinity with Hawthorne. It remains a staple of Hawthorne criticism. Originally published in 1879 (London, Macmillan).

745 Jones, Buford, ed. A CHECKLIST OF HAWTHORNE CRITICISM, 1951-1966. Hartford, Conn.: Transcendental Books, 1967. 91 p.

Thoroughly annotated. Includes bibliographies, critical introductions, books, monographs and pamphlets, essays in books, articles, doctoral dissertations, foreign-language criticism, and indexes of authors and of Hawthorne's works.

746 Kaul, A.N., ed. HAWTHORNE: A COLLECTION OF CRITICAL ESSAYS. Englewood Cliffs, N.J.: Prentice-Hall, 1966. 182 p. Bibliog.

Reprints twelve appraisals of individual novels and tales.

747 Lathrop, George Parsons. A STUDY OF HAWTHORNE. Boston: Houghton Mifflin, 1876. Reprint. New York: AMS Press, 1969. 350 p.

This study is one of the earliest portraits of Hawthorne. Lathrop never knew Hawthorne personally, but was guided in his study of the author by intuition. The emphasis is on the early life. Contains some analysis of the work.

748 Lathrop, Rose Hawthorne. MEMORIES OF HAWTHORNE. Boston: Houghton Mifflin, 1897. Reprint. New York: AMS Press, 1969. xii, 482 p.

A Hawthorne daughter presents a portrait of her father as derived principally from letters written by her mother, Sophia.

749 Loggins, Vernon. THE HAWTHORNES: THE STORY OF SEVEN GENERATIONS OF AN AMERICAN FAMILY. New York: Columbia University Press, 1951. 365 p. Bibliog. note.

Fascinating history of the Hawthorne family from 1607 to 1949, when Julian's widow died.

750 McPherson, Hugo. HAWTHORNE AS MYTH-MAKER: A STUDY IN IMAGINATION. Toronto: University of Toronto Press, 1969. xi, 256 p.

Concerns itself with "the myth-making nature of Hawthorne's imagination."

751 Male, Roy R. HAWTHORNE'S TRAGIC VISION. Austin: University of Texas Press, 1957. ix, 187 p.

Analyzes the organic relation of Hawthorne's major works and the details of his essentially tragic view of life.

752 Martin, Terence. NATHANIEL HAWTHORNE. TUSAS, no. 75. New York: Twayne, 1965. 205 p. Bibliog.

General introduction to Hawthorne's life and literary career.

753 Mather, Edward. NATHANIEL HAWTHORNE, A MODEST MAN. New York: Crowell, 1940. viii, 356 p. Illus. Bibliog.

The stress here is on the man rather than on his work. Mather, an Englishman, is especially interested in Hawthorne's English years and in his "violent opinions" concerning the English.

754 Mellow, James R. NATHANIEL HAWTHORNE IN HIS TIMES. Boston: Houghton Mifflin, 1980. xiii, 684 p. Illus., bibliog.

This new biography is the first volume of a quartet, with biographies of Margaret Fuller, Thoreau, and Emerson to follow. The result of indefatigable research, it presents Hawthorne against a richly woven tapestry of the people and events of his "times." Much the fullest account to date.

755 Morris, Lloyd. THE REBELLIOUS PURITAN: PORTRAIT OF MR. HAWTHORNE. New York: Harcourt, Brace, 1927. 368 p. Illus.

A popularized biography that adds little to what Julian Hawthorne had already published.

756 Newman, Lea Bertain Vozar, ed. A READER'S GUIDE TO THE SHORT STORIES OF NATHANIEL HAWTHORNE. Boston: G.K. Hall, 1979. xvii, 380 p.

A compendium of historical and critical data for each of Hawthorne's fifty-four short stories. It is a valuable guide for general readers and a review and research tool for those with a special interest in Hawthorne's fiction. A chapter is devoted to each story. Publication history, circumstances of composition, sources and influences, relationship with other Hawthorne works, and interpretations and criticism are indicated.

757 Normand, Jean. NATHANIEL HAWTHORNE: AN APPROACH TO AN ANALYSIS OF ARTISTIC CREATION. Translated by Derek Coltman. Cleveland, Ohio, and London: Press of Case Western Reserve University, 1970. xxxvi, 474 p. Bibliog.

This is an excellent translation of the 1964 French edition of a French psychologist's analytical study of Hawthorne's creative processes.

758 O'Connor, Evangeline M., ed. AN ANALYTICAL INDEX TO THE WORKS OF NATHANIEL HAWTHORNE, WITH A SKETCH OF HIS LIFE. Boston: Houghton Mifflin, 1882. 294 p. Reprint. Detroit: Gale Research Co., 1967.

The index includes proper names and topics and remains a useful tool for the Hawthorne scholar.

759 Ricks, Beatrice, et al., eds. NATHANIEL HAWTHORNE: A REFERENCE BIBLIOGRAPHY, 1900-1971. Boston: G.K. Hall, 1972. v, 337 p.

Contains also important selected nineteenth-century materials. Indispensable although, with a few exceptions, the bibliography is not annotated.

760 Sanborn, F.B. HAWTHORNE AND HIS FRIENDS: REMINISCENCES AND TRIBUTE. Cedar Rapids, Iowa: Torch Press, 1908. 84 p.

A Concord, Massachusetts, neighbor reminisces on Hawthorne and his relationships in Concord and elsewhere in New England.

761 Stein, William Bysshe. HAWTHORNE'S FAUST: A STUDY OF THE DEVIL ARCHETYPE. Gainesville: University of Florida Press, 1953. Bibliog. Reprint. New York: Archon Books, 1968. vii, 172 p.

> Contends that the purpose of Hawthorne's art is to illustrate that the dualism of nature (and of human experience) is the basis of harmony in the universe. Thus the myth of the devil is the necessary evil in the equation of human destiny. God and the devil must contest for the integrity of man's soul.

762 Stewart, Randall. NATHANIEL HAWTHORNE, A BIOGRAPHY. New Haven, Conn.: Yale University Press, 1948. v, 279 p.

> A clearly written, generally reliable account of Hawthorne's life, the best until the Mellow and Turner biographies of 1980. Contains relatively little criticism of Hawthorne's work.

763 Taylor, J. Golden. HAWTHORNE'S AMBIVALENCE TOWARD PURITANISM. Monograph Series, vol. 12, no. 1. Logan: Utah State University Press, July 1965. 69 p.

> Discusses Hawthorne's use of his Puritan materials and closely analyzes "The Maypole of Merry Mount" and "The Gentle Boy" as best reflecting his ambivalence.

764 Tharpe, Jac. NATHANIEL HAWTHORNE, IDENTITY AND KNOWLEDGE. Crosscurrents/Modern Critiques Series. Carbondale and Edwardsville: Southern Illinois University Press, 1967. ix, 180 p. Bibliog.

> Views and reinterprets Hawthorne's work within the context of western literature. Sees him as being influenced by, and as exerting influence on, European writers.

765 Ticknor, Caroline. HAWTHORNE AND HIS PUBLISHER. Boston and New York: Houghton Mifflin, 1913. 339 p. Illus.

> The interesting story of Hawthorne's relations with William D. Ticknor.

766 Turner, Arlin. NATHANIEL HAWTHORNE: A BIOGRAPHY. New York and Oxford, Engl.: Oxford University Press, 1980. xii, 457 p. Illus.

> Attempts to present "the rich variety of Hawthorne's personality, and the individuality and complexity of his thought." Also places his works within the context of his life. Lacking, however, in the rich background of Mellow's biography (see no. 754).

767 Wagenknecht, Edward. NATHANIEL HAWTHORNE: MAN AND WRITER. New York: Oxford University Press, 1961. x, 233 p. Bibliog.

The method used here is "psychography." Thus, it is a study of Hawthorne's character and personality based on his writings, letters, and journals, as well as on much that has been written about him.

768 Waggoner, Hyatt H. HAWTHORNE, A CRITICAL STUDY. Rev. ed. Cambridge, Mass.: Belknap Press of Harvard University Press, 1963. 278 p. Originally published in 1955.

Close readings of the tales, the four major romances, and the incomplete late romances. Finds Hawthorne "first and last a realist, unwilling to deny any part of his experience." A new chapter on THE MARBLE FAUN sees the book in a more favorable light.

769 ______. THE PRESENCE OF HAWTHORNE. Baton Rouge and London: Louisiana State University Press, 1979. xiii, 166 p.

A reprinting, with revisions, of seven previously published essays together with a new one bearing the volume's title. It is concerned with the feeling of Hawthorne's "presence" in the writing of Henry James, Faulkner, and Robert Penn Warren.

LAFCADIO HEARN (1850-1904)

770 Bisland, Elizabeth, ed. LIFE AND LETTERS OF LAFCADIO HEARN. 4 vols. Boston and New York: Houghton Mifflin, 1923. vol. 1, viii, 377 p.

The first volume contains the first biography of Hearn, written by his devoted admirer, Mrs. Elizabeth Bisland Wetmore, and first published in 1906, two years after his death.

771 Frost, O.W. YOUNG HEARN. Tokyo: Hokuseido Press, 1958. iv, 222 p.

Gives the first adequate account of Hearn's first twenty-eight years (1850-78). The European period and the full story of Hearn's journalistic career in Cincinnati are covered in detail.

772 Kennard, Nina H. LAFCADIO HEARN. New York: Appleton, 1912. x, 356 p.

Contains basic biographical information, but also some inaccuracies and serious biases.

773 Koizumi, Kazuo. FATHER AND I; MEMORIES OF LAFCADIO HEARN. Boston and New York: Houghton Mifflin, 1935. viii, 208 p.

Recollections of Hearn's eldest son.

774 Koizumi, Setsuko. REMINISCENCES OF LAFCADIO HEARN. Translated by Paul K. Hisada and Frederick Johnson. Boston and New York: Houghton Mifflin, 1918. viii, 87 p.

As Hearn's wife remembers him.

775 Kunst, Arthur E. LAFCADIO HEARN. TUSAS, no. 158. New York: Twayne, 1969. 146 p. Bibliog.

The best introduction to Hearn's life and work. His literary output and his development as a creative writer from the early days in Cincinnati to the last days in Japan are traced.

776 McWilliams, Vera. LAFCADIO HEARN. Boston: Houghton Mifflin, 1946. x, 464 p. Bibliog.

A popularized biography that continues some of the errors of earlier biographers.

777 Mordell, Albert, ed. DISCOVERIES: ESSAYS ON LAFCADIO HEARN. Tokyo: Orient/West, 1964. xiv, 240 p.

A collection of scholarship on Hearn.

778 Perkins, P.D., and Perkins, Ione, eds. LAFCADIO HEARN: A BIBLIOGRAPHY OF HIS WRITINGS. Boston: Houghton Mifflin, 1934. Reprint. New York: B. Franklin, 1968. xvii, 444 p.

The most complete Hearn bibliography.

779 Stevenson, Elizabeth. LAFCADIO HEARN. New York: Macmillan, 1961. xvi, 362 p. Bibliog.

The best biography of Hearn.

780 Tinker, Edward L. LAFCADIO HEARN'S AMERICAN DAYS. New York: Dodd, Mead, 1924. xiv, 374 p. Illus.

Contains valuable information on Hearn in New Orleans.

781 Yu, Beongcheon. AN APE OF GODS: THE ART AND THOUGHT OF LAFCADIO HEARN. Detroit: Wayne State University Press, 1964. xiv, 346 p. Bibliog.

A critical examination of Hearn's achievement in its entirety. Three major phases are considered: art, criticism, and philosophy. The book is a valuable contribution to the understanding of Hearn and his work.

ERNEST HEMINGWAY (1899-1961)

782 Arnold, Lloyd R. HIGH ON THE WILD WITH HEMINGWAY. Caldwell, Id.: Caxton Printers, 1968. xiv, 343 p. Illus.

Memoir of Hemingway in his Ketchum, Idaho, days.

783 Asselineau, Roger, ed. THE LITERARY REPUTATION OF HEMINGWAY IN EUROPE. New York: New York University Press, 1965. 212 p.

A collection of essays, largely by European scholars, from a symposium on the critical reception of Hemingway's work held in Italy in 1960.

784 Atkins, John. THE ART OF ERNEST HEMINGWAY: HIS WORK AND PERSONALITY. London: Peter Nevill, 1952. viii, 245 p. Rev. ed. London: Spring Books, 1964. x, 258 p. Illus.

An English critic discusses the significant events in Hemingway's life, and how his work reflects them and reveals his personality.

785 Baker, Carlos. ERNEST HEMINGWAY; A LIFE STORY. New York: Scribner's, 1969. xvi, 697 p. Illus.

The authorized biography, it contains more factual information about Hemingway than can be found in any other work. Unfortunately, the biographer seems at times to be repelled by the personality of his subject.

786 ______. HEMINGWAY: THE WRITER AS ARTIST. Princeton, N.J.: Princeton University Press, 1952. xx, 322 p. 3d ed. enl., 1963. xx, 379 p. 4th ed. enl., 1972.

A study of Hemingway as literary artist, stylist, and craftsman. Analyzes and evaluates the work from 1920. The third edition includes a new final chapter on the last ten years of Hemingway's life and work. The fourth edition includes nearly 25 percent new material.

787 ______, ed. ERNEST HEMINGWAY: CRITIQUES OF FOUR MAJOR NOVELS. New York: Scribner's, 1962. xx, 204 p.

Reprints critical commentaries by various hands on THE SUN ALSO RISES, A FAREWELL TO ARMS, FOR WHOM THE BELL TOLLS, and THE OLD MAN AND THE SEA.

788 ______. HEMINGWAY AND HIS CRITICS: AN INTERNATIONAL ANTHOLOGY. New York: Hill and Wang, 1961. xiv, 298 p.

Reprints eighteen essays by American, French, English, Italian, Russian, Spanish, German, and Japanese critics, with an introduction by the editor. A rewarding selection.

789 Baker, Sheridan. ERNEST HEMINGWAY: AN INTRODUCTION AND INTERPRETATION. New York: Holt, Rinehart and Winston, 1967. ix, 150 p. Bibliog.

Studies the entire fiction chronologically. Finds that by the 1950s Hemingway's "despair" had turned to "existential courage."

790 Benson, Jackson J. HEMINGWAY: THE WRITER'S ART OF SELF DEFENSE. Minneapolis: University of Minnesota Press, 1969. x, 202 p.

Focuses on Hemingway's use of irony and analyzes all the major fiction with emphasis on its use.

791 Benson, Jackson J., and Astro, Richard, eds. HEMINGWAY IN OUR TIME. Corvallis: Oregon State University Press, 1974. 214 p.

A collection of previously unpublished essays by Hemingway scholars.

792 Broer, Lawrence R. HEMINGWAY'S SPANISH TRAGEDY. University: University of Alabama Press, 1973. xii, 131 p. Illus., bibliog.

Claims that Hemingway felt at home in Spain, and explores the reasons why.

793 Burgess, Anthony. ERNEST HEMINGWAY AND HIS WORLD. New York: Scribner's, 1978. 128 p. Illus., bibliog.

By means of word and picture Burgess relates Hemingway to the times and places he knew and used in his fiction.

794 Castillo-Puche, Jose Luis. HEMINGWAY IN SPAIN: A PERSONAL REMINISCENCE OF HEMINGWAY'S YEARS IN SPAIN BY HIS FRIEND. Translated by Helen R. Lane. Garden City, N.Y.: Doubleday, 1974. xv, 388 p. Illus.

A fascinating account of the Spanish author's friendship with Hemingway beginning in 1954. Hemingway is viewed as the best observer of Spain in the modern era, and as a man both "pathetically lonely" and "pathologically devious." The Spanish writer's respect for him and his work is enormous.

795 Farrington, S. Kip, Jr. FISHING WITH HEMINGWAY AND GLASSEL. New York: David McKay, 1971. ix, 118 p. Illus.

Makes clear that Hemingway was indeed an expert fisherman.

796 Fenton, Charles A. THE APPRENTICESHIP OF ERNEST HEMINGWAY: THE EARLY YEARS. New York: Farrar, Straus and Young, 1954. xi, 302 p.

Attempts to define the process whereby Hemingway "transposed a conventional talent into an artistic skill." Studies Hemingway and his work closely from 1916 to 1924 when "the principal instrument of his literary apprenticeship was journalism."

797 Grebstein, Sheldon N. HEMINGWAY'S CRAFT. Carbondale: Southern Illinois University Press, 1973. xvii, 245 p. Bibliog.

Tries to find terms for elements of Hemingway's craft: dialogue, sentence rhythm, paragraphing, imagery.

798 Gurko, Leo. ERNEST HEMINGWAY AND THE PURSUIT OF HEROISM. New York: Crowell, 1968. 247 p. Bibliog.

A long biographical chapter is followed by discussion of each major novel, the nonfiction, and the short stories, the concept of "heroism" being the unifying theme.

799 Hanneman, Audre, ed. ERNEST HEMINGWAY: A COMPREHENSIVE BIBLIOGRAPHY. Princeton, N.J.: Princeton University Press, 1967. xiv, 568 p. Supplement published in 1975 with additions to the original listing through 1973.

Indispensable for Hemingway scholars. In three parts: (1) a descriptive and enumerative bibliography of Hemingway's work; (2) an enumerative biobibliography, including books on Hemingway, books in which he is significantly discussed, and periodical and newspaper items on him; and (3) an appendix, listing place of publication of newspapers and periodicals cited.

800 Hemingway, Gregory. PAPA: A PERSONAL MEMOIR. Boston: Houghton Mifflin, 1976. xv, 119 p. Illus.

Hemingway's physician son reveals some intimate family details in questionable taste.

801 Hemingway, Leicester. MY BROTHER, ERNEST HEMINGWAY. Cleveland, Ohio: World, 1962. 283 p. Illus.

This biography first appeared in installments in the December

1961 and January, February, and March 1962 issues of PLAYBOY. Based on many conversations between the brothers, it offers important insights to the man and the artist.

802 Hemingway, Mary Welsh. HOW IT WAS. New York: Knopf, 1976. vi, 537 p., xi. Illus.

The autobiography of Hemingway's widow, with, of course, a major portion devoted to the marriage with Hemingway, the events leading up to it, and very little following the death of Hemingway. Mrs. Hemingway manages to keep the spotlight on herself.

803 Hotchner, A.E. PAPA HEMINGWAY: A PERSONAL MEMOIR. New York: Random House, 1966. 304 p. Illus.

Recounts the author's close association with Hemingway from 1949 to 1961. Gives a detailed account of Hemingway's last illness and his death.

804 Hovey, Richard B. HEMINGWAY: THE INWARD TERRAIN. Seattle: University of Washington Press, 1968. xxiii, 248 p. Bibliog. note.

A Freudian analysis.

805 Joost, Nicholas. ERNEST HEMINGWAY AND THE LITTLE MAGAZINES: THE PARIS YEARS. Barre, Mass.: Barre Publishers, 1968. 186 p.

Hemingway's dealings with THE DOUBLE-DEALER, TRANSATLANTIC REVIEW, LITTLE REVIEW, and others.

806 Kiley, Jed. HEMINGWAY: AN OLD FRIEND REMEMBERS. New York: Hawthorn Books, 1965. 198 p. Illus.

Reminiscences about Hemingway in Paris in the 1920s, and then in Bimini and Key West. First appeared in eight installments in PLAYBOY, September 1956 to September 1957.

807 Killinger, John. HEMINGWAY AND THE DEAD GODS: A STUDY IN EXISTENTIALISM. Lexington: University of Kentucky Press, 1960. x, 114 p.

Relates the fictional world created by Hemingway to the world view of existentialism.

808 Kvam, Wayne E. HEMINGWAY IN GERMANY: THE FICTION, THE LEGEND, AND THE CRITICS. Athens: Ohio University Press, 1973. x, 214 p. Bibliog.

Analysis of Hemingway's reputation in Germany, particularly

since World War II. Sees German readers responding to Hemingway as "fellow sufferer" and "model for living."

809 Lewis, Robert W., Jr. HEMINGWAY ON LOVE. Austin and London: University of Texas Press, 1965. 252 p. Bibliog.

The study considers "the subject of love as treated by Hemingway in major and representative works."

810 McCaffery, John K.M., ed. ERNEST HEMINGWAY: THE MAN AND HIS WORK. Cleveland, Ohio, and New York: World, 1950. 352 p.

Early collection of essays, both pro and con, on various facets of Hemingway and his work.

811 McLendon, James. PAPA: HEMINGWAY IN KEY WEST. Mimai, Fla.: E.A. Seemann, 1972. 222 p. Illus., bibliog.

Concentrates on the years 1928 to 1940, which the author regards as the most important years of Hemingway's life and the ones about which the least is known. The picture of Hemingway is based largely on interviews with those who knew him in Key West.

812 Miller, Madelaine Hemingway. ERNIE: HEMINGWAY'S SISTER "SUNNY" REMEMBERS. New York: Crown, 1975. ix, 149 p. Illus.

The more than 130 personal photographs are the most important part of this somewhat worshipful series of reminiscences. The accent is on the early years.

813 Montgomery, Constance Cappel. HEMINGWAY IN MICHIGAN. New York: Fleet Publishing, 1966. 224 p. Illus., bibliog.

Identifies and describes all places used by Hemingway in his Michigan stories. Also identifies the originals of the characters employed. Reprints three short stories he wrote for the Oak Park High School literary magazine.

814 Nahal, Chaman. THE NARRATIVE PATTERN IN ERNEST HEMINGWAY'S FICTION. Rutherford, N.J.: Fairleigh Dickinson University Press, 1971. 245 p. Bibliog.

Sees a systolic-diastolic pattern in the movement of Hemingway's fiction.

815 Peterson, Richard K. HEMINGWAY: DIRECT AND OBLIQUE. The Hague: Mouton, 1969. 231 p. Bibliog.

The concentration is on patterns of word usage, symbols, and syntax, aimed at a study of style.

816 Ross, Lillian. PORTRAIT OF HEMINGWAY. New York: Simon and Schuster, 1961. 66 p.

A redoing, with minor revisions, of the notorious profile in the NEW YORKER of 13 May 1950. The profile was scarcely complimentary to Hemingway.

817 Rovit, Earl. ERNEST HEMINGWAY. TUSAS, no. 41. New York: Twayne, 1963. 192 p. Bibliog.

Analyzes Hemingway's work and his significance in American literary history.

818 Sanderson, Stewart F. ERNEST HEMINGWAY. Writers and Critics Series, no. 7. Edinburgh and London: Oliver and Boyd, 1961. 120 p. Bibliog.

A critical introduction to Hemingway's work.

819 Sanford, Marcelline Hemingway. AT THE HEMINGWAYS: A FAMILY PORTRAIT. Boston: Atlantic, Little, Brown, 1962. viii, 244 p. Illus.

An inside view by Hemingway's older sister of growing up in Oak Park, of the summer vacations in northern Michigan, of Hemingway's return from the First World War, and of the family's view of his writing.

820 Seward, William. MY FRIEND ERNEST HEMINGWAY: AN AFFECTIONATE REMINISCENCE. New York: A.S. Barnes, 1969. 69 p. Illus.

Considerable attention is paid to Hemingway's writing.

821 Sokoloff, Alice Hunt. HADLEY, THE FIRST MRS. HEMINGWAY. New York: Dodd, Mead, 1973. 111 p. Illus.

Based on many interviews with Hadley Hemingway Mowrer, the book tells the story of Hadley's life with the author up through the divorce.

822 Stephens, Robert O. HEMINGWAY'S NON-FICTION: THE PUBLIC VOICE. Chapel Hill: University of North Carolina Press, 1968. xi, 391 p.

The nonfiction analyzed in regard to its ideas, its revelation of Hemingway's self, its relation to the fiction, and its artistry.

823 Wagner, Linda Welshimer, ed. ERNEST HEMINGWAY: A REFERENCE GUIDE. Reference Guides in Literature, no. 13. Boston: G.K. Hall, 1977. xix, 363 p.

A valuable annotated guide to writings about Hemingway from 1923 through 1975.

824 _____, ed. ERNEST HEMINGWAY: FIVE DECADES OF CRITICISM. East Lansing: Michigan State University Press, 1974. vii, 328 p.

Reprints reviews and critical essays.

825 Waldhorn, Arthur. A READER'S GUIDE TO ERNEST HEMINGWAY. New York: Farrar, Straus and Giroux, 1972. xiv, 284 p. Bibliog.

Helpful study of Hemingway's life, style, and themes, with readings of the major fiction, and chapters on the Nick Adams stories and on Hemingway as poet, dramatist, journalist, and satirist.

826 Watts, Emily Stipes. ERNEST HEMINGWAY AND THE ARTS. Urbana: University of Illinois Press, 1971. xvi, 243 p. Illus.

Thorough study of Hemingway's interest in and use of painting, sculpture, and architecture in his fiction.

827 Weeks, Robert P., ed. HEMINGWAY: A COLLECTION OF CRITICAL ESSAYS. Twentieth Century Views Series. Englewood Cliffs, N.J.: Prentice-Hall, 1962. 180 p. Bibliog.

Sixteen reprinted essays on the man and his work, with an introduction by the editor.

828 Young, Philip. ERNEST HEMINGWAY: A RECONSIDERATION. Rev. ed. with new foreword and an afterword. University Park and London: Pennsylvania State University Press, 1966. x, 298 p. Originally published as ERNEST HEMINGWAY. New York and Toronto: Rinehart, 1952. xii, 244 p. Bibliog. notes.

A keen, critical analysis of Hemingway's work. Psychological approach.

829 _____. ERNEST HEMINGWAY. UMPAW, no. 1. Minneapolis: University of Minnesota Press, 1959. 44 p. Bibliog.

The best brief critical and biographical introduction.

JAMES A. HERNE (1839-1901)

830 Edwards, Herbert J., and Herne, Julie A. JAMES A. HERNE: THE RISE OF REALISM IN THE AMERICAN DRAMA. University of Maine Studies, Second Series, no. 80. Orono: University of Maine Press, 1964. vi, 182 p. Illus., bibliog.

The basis of this study is an unpublished biography of her father written by Julie Herne, who died in 1955. Accounts of Herne's best plays are provided. The book provides the fullest account of Herne's work yet published.

831 Perry, John. JAMES A. HERNE, THE AMERICAN IBSEN. Chicago: Nelson-Hall, 1978. x, 343 p. Bibliog. refs.

Concentrates on Herne's life as actor and playwright. There is, however, not much critical analysis of his plays.

JOSEPH HERGESHEIMER (1880-1954)

832 Jones, Llewellyn. JOSEPH HERGESHEIMER, THE MAN AND HIS BOOKS. New York: Knopf, 1920. 32 p.

A cursory introduction to a writer who was becoming popular at the time.

833 Martin, Ronald E. THE FICTION OF JOSEPH HERGESHEIMER. Philadelphia: University of Pennsylvania Press, 1965. 288 p. Bibliog.

The most thorough analysis and evaluation of Hergesheimer's fiction. He is viewed as a minor novelist who, nevertheless, wrote some very good fiction that deserves study.

ROBERT HERRICK (1868-1938)

834 Budd, Louis J. ROBERT HERRICK. TUSAS, no. 178. New York: Twayne, 1971. 142 p. Bibliog.

A chronological account of Herrick's fiction which can serve as an excellent introduction to the work of a writer whose talent fell just short of being major.

835 Nevius, Blake. ROBERT HERRICK: THE DEVELOPMENT OF A NOVELIST. Berkeley and Los Angeles: University of California Press, 1962. xviii, 364 p. Illus., bibliog.

Not a formal biography, the book nonetheless presents a quite full account of Herrick's life and personality. A large part of it, however, is a close study of the novels. To date, the definitive work on Herrick.

OLIVER WENDELL HOLMES (1809-1894)

836 Carpenter, Wesley M., ed. PROCEEDINGS AT THE DINNER GIVEN BY THE MEDICAL PROFESSION OF THE CITY OF NEW YORK, APRIL 12, 1883, TO OLIVER WENDELL HOLMES, M.D., LL.D. New York: Putnam, 1883. 61 p. Illus.

Dr. Carpenter provides an interesting record of the testimonial dinner, complete with names of guests and with transcripts of toasts and speeches made.

837 Howe, Mark Anthony DeWolfe. HOLMES OF THE BREAKFAST-TABLE. New York: Oxford University Press, 1939. vi, 172 p.

A gracefully written appreciation of Holmes and his work.

838 Hoyt, Edwin P. THE IMPROPER BOSTONIAN: DR. OLIVER WENDELL HOLMES. New York: William Morrow, 1979. 319 p. Bibliog. notes.

A very readable and straightforward biography which makes good use of its materials.

839 Morse, John T., Jr. LIFE AND LETTERS OF OLIVER WENDELL HOLMES. 2 vols. Boston and New York: Houghton Mifflin, 1896. Illus.

The biography is written largely through commentary on the letters. Lacks objective evaluation and analysis, but contains much intimate detail not to be found elsewhere.

840 Oberndorf, Clarence P. THE PSYCHIATRIC NOVELS OF OLIVER WENDELL HOLMES. New York: Columbia University Press, 1943. viii, 268 p.

Dr. Oberndorf abridges the novels ELSIE VENNER, THE GUARDIAN ANGEL, and A MORTAL ANTIPATHY in order to study their psychiatric content. Finds it often anticipatory, far sighted, cogent and valid in respect to modern psychiatric thinking.

841 Small, Miriam Rossiter. OLIVER WENDELL HOLMES. TUSAS, no. 29. Boston: Twayne, 1962. 176 p. Bibliog.

A very good biographical sketch precedes a sound analysis of the fiction and poetry.

842 Tilton, Eleanor M. AMIABLE AUTOCRAT: A BIOGRAPHY OF DR. OLIVER WENDELL HOLMES. New York: Henry Schuman, 1947. xi, 470 p. Illus.

The most reliable and scholarly biography of Holmes.

E.W. HOWE (1853-1937)

843 Bucco, Martin. E.W. HOWE. Western Writers Series, no. 26. Boise, Idaho: Boise State University, 1977. 48 p. Bibliog.

Sketches the reputation, western life, achievement, and

status of the author of THE STORY OF A COUNTRY TOWN. Uses the psychological principle of repetition-compulsion to analyze the problem of unity and organic form in the novel.

844 Pickett, Calder M. ED HOWE: COUNTRY TOWN PHILOSOPHER. Lawrence: University Press of Kansas, 1968. ix, 401 p. Illus., bibliog.

An excellent biographical study that includes evaluation of Howe's journalistic work as well as of his fiction.

845 Sackett, S.J. E.W. HOWE. TUSAS, no. 195. New York: Twayne, 1972. 189 p. Bibliog.

Supplies a good biographical sketch, followed by two chapters on the fiction, a chapter on Howe as common-sense philosopher and aphorist, and a final chapter on his travel books and autobiography. Howe's excellence is seen as deriving from his fidelity to his own experience.

WILLIAM DEAN HOWELLS (1837-1920)

846 Bennett, George N. THE REALISM OF WILLIAM DEAN HOWELLS, 1889-1920. Nashville: Vanderbilt University Press, 1973. x, 254 p.

Sees Howells as a humorist, a meliorist, a sceptical rationalist, and a hopeful agnostic. In short, he was a realist.

847 ______. WILLIAM DEAN HOWELLS: THE DEVELOPMENT OF A NOVELIST. Norman: University of Oklahoma Press, 1959. 220 p. Illus.

The major novels are analyzed as artistic achievements rather than as social documents.

848 Brenni, Vito J., comp. WILLIAM DEAN HOWELLS: A BIBLIOGRAPHY. Metuchen, N.J.: Scarecrow Press, 1973. 212 p.

The most complete bibliography to date.

849 Brooks, Van Wyck. HOWELLS, HIS LIFE AND WORLD. New York: Dutton, 1959. viii, 296 p.

A perceptive and reliable biography written with Brooks's usual flair.

850 Cady, Edwin. THE ROAD TO REALISM: THE EARLY YEARS, 1837-1885, OF WILLIAM DEAN HOWELLS. Syracuse, N.Y.: Syracuse University Press, 1958. x, 283 p. Bibliog. notes.

851 ______. THE REALIST AT WAR; THE MATURE YEARS, 1885-1920, OF WILLIAM DEAN HOWELLS. Syracuse, N.Y.: Syracuse University Press, 1958. ix, 299 p. Bibliog. notes.

The two volumes, taken together, comprise the definitive biography of Howells to date. Excellent analysis of the novels.

852 Carrington, George C., Jr., and Carrington, Ildiko de Papp, eds. PLOTS AND CHARACTERS IN THE FICTION OF WILLIAM DEAN HOWELLS. Plots and Characters Series. Hamden, Conn.: Archon Books, 1976. xxiii, 306 p.

A Howells chronology and a chronological list of his fiction precede the plot summaries and the list of character identifications.

853 Carter, Everett. HOWELLS AND THE AGE OF REALISM. Philadelphia: Lippincott, 1950. 307 p. Reprint. Hamden, Conn.: Archon Books, 1966.

Intended as a study of a man's sensibility rather than as his biography. The five chapters bear the titles "Background," "The Attack on the Sentimental," "Towards a Philosophy of Literary Realism," "Critical Realism," and "Naturalism and Introspection."

854 Cooke, Delmar Gross. WILLIAM DEAN HOWELLS: A CRITICAL STUDY. New York: Dutton, 1922. 279 p. Bibliog.

Published two years after Howells's death, this is a broadly based study of the man, his concept of criticism, his ideals of literature, his literary method, his poetry and travels, and his fiction.

855 Dean, James L. HOWELLS' TRAVELS TOWARD ART. Albuquerque: University of New Mexico Press, 1970. 145 p.

A careful study of Howells's travel books. Dean contends that they "reveal how much his travels were a part of his search for the real."

856 Eble, Kenneth E., ed. HOWELLS; A CENTURY OF CRITICISM. Dallas: Southern Methodist University Press, 1962. xii, 247 p.

A valuable selection of critical writings.

857 Eichelberger, Clayton L., ed. PUBLISHED COMMENT ON WILLIAM DEAN HOWELLS THROUGH 1920: A RESEARCH BIBLIOGRAPHY. Boston: G.K. Hall, 1976. xii, 330 p.

The most complete annotated bibliography of secondary sources through the year of Howells's death.

858 Firkins, Oscar W. WILLIAM DEAN HOWELLS; A STUDY. Cambridge, Mass.: Harvard University Press, 1924. viii, 356 p.

An early scholarly biography which remains useful.

859 Fryckstedt, Olov W. IN QUEST OF AMERICA: A STUDY OF HOWELLS' EARLY DEVELOPMENT AS A NOVELIST. New York: Russell and Russell, 1971. 287 p. Bibliog.

A reissue of a book first published in 1958, this study deals with the development of Howells up to 1882. Concentrates on the slow growth of his ability to portray America from "the first vague sketches of suburban Cambridge to the powerful novel, A MODERN INSTANCE."

860 Gibson, William M. WILLIAM DEAN HOWELLS. UMPAW, no. 63. Minneapolis: University of Minnesota Press, 1967. 48 p. Bibliog.

A lucid introduction to the man and his work.

861 Hough, Robert L. THE QUIET REBEL, WILLIAM DEAN HOWELLS AS SOCIAL COMMENTATOR. Lincoln: University of Nebraska Press, 1959. 137 p. Bibliog.

Howells's impact on social thought in America.

862 Kirk, Clara M. W.D. HOWELLS, AND ART IN HIS TIME. New Brunswick, N.J.: Rutgers University Press, 1965. xvi, 336 p. Bibliog.

Studies Howells's knowledge of, and relation to, the visual arts.

863 _____. W.D. HOWELLS, TRAVELER FROM ALTRURIA, 1889-1894. New Brunswick, N.J.: Rutgers University Press, 1962. xi, 148 p.

Interprets Howells's view of the American scene in the years of the Utopian novels.

864 Kirk, Clara M., and Kirk, Rudolf. WILLIAM DEAN HOWELLS. TUSAS, no. 16. New York: Twayne, 1962. 223 p. Bibliog.

The Kirks provide an excellent introduction to Howells and his work. They see him as belonging to the objective, classical school of Goldsmith and Jane Austen.

865 Lynn, Kenneth S. WILLIAM DEAN HOWELLS; AN AMERICAN LIFE. New York: Harcourt Brace Jovanovich, 1971. 372 p. Illus., bibliog.

A solid critical biography, but it contributes little that is new.

866 Vanderbilt, Kermit. THE ACHIEVEMENT OF WILLIAM DEAN HOWELLS: A REINTERPRETATION. Princeton, N.J.: Princeton University Press, 1968. ix, 226 p. Bibliog. comment.

An excellent study, in which a chapter apiece is devoted to explication and reinterpretation of four novels of the 1880s: THE UNDISCOVERED COUNTRY, A MODERN INSTANCE, THE RISE OF SILAS LAPHAM, and A HAZARD OF NEW FORTUNES.

867 Wagenknecht, Edward. WILLIAM DEAN HOWELLS: THE FRIENDLY EYE. New York: Oxford University Press, 1969. x, 340 p. Bibliog.

Uses Wagenknecht's familiar psychographic approach. The man and his work are both studied in detail. Expresses great admiration for both.

LANGSTON HUGHES (1902-1967)

868 Barksdale, Richard K. LANGSTON HUGHES, THE POET AND HIS CRITICS. Chicago: American Library Association, 1977. xii, 155 p. Bibliog.

A study assessing the critics of Hughes's poetry. The method used is chronological and covers the forty-seven years of the poet's career. Barksdale also provides his own critical introductions to Hughes's poetry in each chapter before presenting the reactions of the critics.

869 Dickinson, Donald C. A BIO-BIBLIOGRAPHY OF LANGSTON HUGHES, 1902-1967. 2d ed., rev. Hamden, Conn.: Archon Books, 1972. xiii, 273 p.

Basically the same as the 1964 first edition except that secondary entries are updated to 1969. The book is in two parts: (1) a biography that is the most reliable to date, and (2) a complete bibliography of works by Hughes through 1965, with a brief bibliography of works about Hughes.

870 Emanuel, James A. LANGSTON HUGHES. TUSAS, no. 123. Boston: Twayne, 1967. 192 p. Bibliog.

The first major study of Hughes, it remains among the best. The chapters are arranged to present, first, a comprehensive biographical and literary survey of Hughes to 1960; subsequent chapters present analysis in depth of the better poems and short stories; the final chapter treats the works of the 1960s.

871 Jemie, Onwuchekwa. LANGSTON HUGHES: AN INTRODUCTION TO THE POETRY. Columbia Introductions to Twentieth-Century American Poetry. New York: Columbia University Press, 1976. xxxii, 234 p. Bibliog.

Limited to Hughes's collected poems, with a brief look at his prose fiction. A chronology and biographical sketch are included. Hughes is seen as primarily a social poet, but also as a lyricist of the first order.

872 Mandelik, Peter, and Schatt, Stanley, comps. A CONCORDANCE TO THE POETRY OF LANGSTON HUGHES. Detroit: Gale Research Co., 1975. xv, 296 p.

A very helpful computerized concordance that reveals a corpus of 48,490 words.

873 Meltzer, Milton. LANGSTON HUGHES: A BIOGRAPHY. New York: Crowell, 1968. xiii, 281 p. Bibliog.

Maintains that Hughes believed that good writing must come out of one's own life. The biography is based almost entirely on Hughes's two autobiographies, THE BIG SEA (1940) and I WONDER AS I WANDER (1956).

874 Miller, R. Baxter, ed. LANGSTON HUGHES AND GWENDOLYN BROOKS: A REFERENCE GUIDE. Boston: G.K. Hall, 1978. xxxiii, 149 p.

Major writings by Hughes are listed; writings about him, both books and shorter pieces, are listed by year with quite full annotations.

875 Myers, Elizabeth P. LANGSTON HUGHES: POET OF HIS PEOPLE. Champaign, Ill.: Garrard Publishing Co., 1970. 144 p.

Asserts that Paul Laurence Dunbar and Carl Sandburg were Hughes's poetic models.

876 O'Daniel, Therman B., ed. LANGSTON HUGHES: BLACK GENIUS. New York: Morrow, 1971. 241 p. Bibliog.

Reprints fourteen essays by Hughes scholars.

877 Rollins, Charlemae H. BLACK TROUBADOR: LANGSTON HUGHES. New York: Rand McNally, 1970. 143 p. Illus.

Says Sandburg, Vachel Lindsay, and Amy Lowell were primary literary influences. Contends that Hughes's work broke down racial barriers.

WASHINGTON IRVING (1783-1859)

878 Bowers, Claude G. THE SPANISH ADVENTURES OF WASHINGTON IRVING. Boston: Houghton Mifflin, 1940. xvii, 306 p. Illus.

The American ambassador to Spain from 1933 to 1939 tells the story of following the trail of Irving through Spain in the days when he was American minister there. The result is a fascinating book.

879 Cracroft, Richard H. WASHINGTON IRVING: THE WESTERN WORKS. Western Writers Series, no. 14. Boise, Idaho: Boise State University, 1974. 48 p. Bibliog.

Irving's enchantment with the American West lasted from 1829 to 1838 and coincided with his defection from the Federalist party. A TOUR ON THE PRAIRIES, ASTORIA, and THE ADVENTURES OF CAPTAIN BONNEVILLE, U.S.A., IN THE ROCKY MOUNTAINS AND THE FAR WEST are discussed.

880 Ellsworth, Henry Leavitt. WASHINGTON IRVING ON THE PRAIRIE OR A NARRATIVE OF A TOUR OF THE SOUTHWEST IN THE YEAR 1832. Edited by Stanley T. Williams and Barbara D. Simison. New York: American Book Co., 1937. xviii, 152 p.

Written as a letter to his wife, this narrative, now in print for the first time, throws much light on unknown aspects of Irving's personality as he traveled in frontier country with his friend, a newly appointed U.S. commissioner.

881 Hedges, William L. WASHINGTON IRVING: AN AMERICAN STUDY, 1802-1832. Baltimore: Johns Hopkins Press, 1965. xiv, 274 p.

In this extended essay on the relevance of Irving, the author confines himself to the period of Irving's major works. He defines Irving's principal contributions as a writer and tries to work out in detail his relation to his intellectual environment. The method is that of literary analysis and comparison.

882 Irving, Pierre M. THE LIFE AND LETTERS OF WASHINGTON IRVING. 4 vols. New York: Putnam, 1862. 1,808 p.

The indispensable first biography of Irving, written by his nephew, who drew largely on his uncle's voluminous correspondence and journals. The book is, as might be expected, highly laudatory of its subject.

883 Johnston, Johanna. THE HEART THAT WOULD NOT HOLD: A BIOGRAPHY OF WASHINGTON IRVING. New York: M. Evans, 1971. viii, 376 p. Bibliog.

A dramatized biography that pays scant attention to Irving's literary production.

884 Langfeld, William R., comp., with assistance of Philip C. Blackburn. WASHINGTON IRVING; A BIBLIOGRAPHY. New York: New York Public Library, 1933. ix, 90 p. Illus.

Valuable descriptive bibliography of Irving's works.

885 Leary, Lewis. WASHINGTON IRVING. UMPAW, no. 25. Minneapolis: University of Minnesota Press, 1963. 48 p. Bibliog.

An introduction to Irving whose tone is set by the opening sentence: "Few writers have successfully stretched a small talent farther than Washington Irving."

886 McClary, Ben Harris. WASHINGTON IRVING AND THE HOUSE OF MURRAY: GEOFFREY CRAYON CHARMS THE BRITISH, 1817-1856. Knoxville: University of Tennessee Press, 1969. xlv, 242 p. Illus., bibliog.

A study of the close relationship between Irving and his British publisher, John Murray II, based on their correspondence, which is here reproduced.

887 McFarland, Philip. SOJOURNERS. New York: Atheneum, 1979. xvii, 587 p. Illus.

An extremely interesting recreation of the worlds through which Irving moved in the United States, Britain, Germany, France, and Spain. The interweaving of his life with the lives of Aaron Burr, Walter Scott, Mary Shelley, John Jacob Astor, and particularly John Brown, the abolitionist, is very well handled.

888 Myers, Andrew B., ed. A CENTURY OF COMMENTARY ON THE WORKS OF WASHINGTON IRVING. Tarrytown, N.Y.: Sleepy Hollow Restorations, 1976. xxxviii, 504 p. Illus.

Reprints commentary from Bryant's "A Discourse" in 1860 to Springer's introduction to the 1974 edition of RIP VAN WINKLE AND THE LEGEND OF SLEEPY HOLLOW.

889 _____. THE WORLDS OF WASHINGTON IRVING, 1783-1859. Tarrytown, N.Y.: Sleepy Hollow Restorations, 1974. ix, 134 p.

The materials here reproduced were selected and annotated

by Myers from an exhibition of rare book and manuscript materials in the Special Collections of the New York Public Library, which houses the largest collection of Irving manuscripts in existence.

890 _____. WASHINGTON IRVING, A TRIBUTE. Tarrytown, N.Y.: Sleepy Hollow Restorations, 1972. x, 86 p. Illus.

Prints the papers read at a symposium in 1970. Among Irving scholars included are Haskell Springer, William L. Hedges, Herbert L. Kleinfield, and Myers.

891 Reichart, Walter A. WASHINGTON IRVING AND GERMANY. University of Michigan Publications in Language and Literature, vol. 28. Ann Arbor: University of Michigan Press, 1957. 212 p.

Retraces Irving's footsteps in Dresden, Germany, where Irving spent half a year, and shows that both "Rip Van Winkle" and "The Legend of Sleepy Hollow" are indebted to German literature for much of their substance. Tabulates Irving's extensive contacts with German literature, provides a list of German titles recorded in his notebooks, and a catalogue of the German books in his library at Sunnyside.

892 Roth, Martin. COMEDY AND AMERICA: THE LOST WORLD OF WASHINGTON IRVING. Port Washington, N.Y., and London: Kennikat Press, 1976. xiv, 205 p.

Attempts to show that "under the tutelage of Sterne and Rabelais, Irving finally settled on a mode of the comic that has never been properly defined . . . I refer to it as BURLESQUE COMEDY." THE HISTORY OF NEW YORK is the prime example studied.

893 Springer, Haskell, ed. WASHINGTON IRVING: A REFERENCE GUIDE. Reference Guides in Literature, no. 6. Boston: G.K. Hall, 1976. xi, 235 p.

The most up-to-date bibliography of writings about Irving, arranged by years from 1807 through 1974. Annotated.

894 Wagenknecht, Edward. WASHINGTON IRVING: MODERATION DISPLAYED. New York: Oxford University Press, 1962. x, 223 p. Bibliog.

The author describes his book as a portrait rather than a biography. The life of Irving is briefly sketched in part 1; aspects of the man are explored in part 2; part 3 is devoted to a relatively brief examination of Irving's work.

895 Warner, Charles Dudley. WASHINGTON IRVING. American Men of Letters Series. Boston: Houghton Mifflin, 1881. vi, 304 p.

A conventional early portrait of Irving and his career.

896 Williams, Stanley T. THE LIFE OF WASHINGTON IRVING. 2 vols. New York: Oxford University Press, 1935. Vol. 1, xxi, 501 p. Illus. Vol. 2, viii, 445 p. Illus., bibliog notes.

Remains the definitive biography. Williams believes that Irving's fame as a writer was "inseparably joined with his roles of journalist, politician, diplomat." He sees Irving as "never deeply creative" but always a sharp-eyed observer of contemporary life. The bibliographical notes are lengthy and helpful.

HENRY JAMES (1843-1916)

897 Anderson, Charles R. PERSON, PLACE, AND THING IN HENRY JAMES'S NOVELS. Durham, N.C.: Duke University Press, 1977. ix, 308 p.

Examines RODERICK HUDSON, THE AMERICAN, PORTRAIT OF A LADY, THE PRINCESS CASAMASSIMA, THE WINGS OF THE DOVE, and THE AMBASSADORS from the viewpoint of James as literary impressionist.

898 Anderson, Quentin. THE AMERICAN HENRY JAMES. New Brunswick, N.J.: Rutgers University Press, 1957. xiii, 369 p.

The thesis here is that "Emblems derived or borrowed from his father's system of universal analogies must be identified for an understanding of THE GOLDEN BOWL and much of James's earlier work."

899 Babiiha, Thaddeo K. THE JAMES-HAWTHORNE RELATION: BIBLIOGRAPHICAL ESSAYS. Boston: G.K. Hall, 1980. xiv, 313 p. Bibliog.

Contains six essays. The first considers forty-one items of James's reference to Hawthorne and/or his works; the second reviews those works in English that have considered, in whole or in part, the general relationship between the two writers and their fiction; the four others evaluate those items that have focused on the specific influence of, respectively, THE SCARLET LETTER, THE BLITHEDALE ROMANCE, THE MARBLE FAUN, and Hawthorne's other works, on James's novels and tales.

900 Beach, Joseph Warren. THE METHOD OF HENRY JAMES. New Haven, Conn.: Yale University Press, 1918. Reprint. Enl. and corr. ed.

Philadelphia: Albert Saifer, 1954. cxiv, 289 p. Bibliog. note.

The enlarged edition contains a long introduction by Beach which updates his earlier version and reviews the body of critical work published since its appearance. Although an early study, it remains valuable.

901 Blackall, Jean Frantz. JAMESIAN AMBIGUITY AND "THE SACRED FOUNT." Ithaca, N.Y.: Cornell University Press, 1965. ix, 191 p. Bibliog.

Detailed examination and explication of James's story.

902 Brooks, Van Wyck. THE PILGRIMAGE OF HENRY JAMES. New York: Dutton, 1925. vii, 170 p.

Holds that, for James, America was a chamber of horrors and Europe remained forever a fairyland. Written with the usual Brooks psychological probing and touch of the dramatic.

903 Buitenhuis, Peter. THE GRASPING IMAGINATION: THE AMERICAN WRITINGS OF HENRY JAMES. Toronto: University of Toronto Press, 1970. xii, 288 p.

Concentrates on the fiction that is set entirely in the United States. Some of the stories set partly in the United States are also considered. Detailed analysis of the texts.

904 Chatman, Seymour. THE LATER STYLE OF HENRY JAMES. Language and Style Series, no. 2. Oxford, Engl.: Basil Blackwell, 1972. 135 p.

Studies the elements of the style in great detail.

905 Dupee, F.W. HENRY JAMES. American Men of Letters Series. New York: William Sloane Associates, 1951. Reprint. Westport, Conn.: Greenwood Press, 1973. xiii, 301 p.

A good general biographical and critical introduction.

906 _____, ed. THE QUESTION OF HENRY JAMES: A COLLECTION OF CRITICAL ESSAYS. New York: Holt, Rinehart and Winston, 1945. Reprint. New York: Octagon Books, 1973. xxii, 302 p. Bibliog.

Twenty-six well-chosen essays by well-known writers and scholars, such as Howells, Max Beerbohm, Conrad, Ford, T.S. Eliot, Spender, Auden, Gide, Joseph W. Beach, Van Wyck Brooks, V.L. Parrington, Edmund Wilson, R. P. Blackmur, F.O. Matthiessen, and Philip Rahv.

907 Edel, Leon. HENRY JAMES. UMPAW, no. 4. Minneapolis: University of Minnesota Press, 1960. 48 p. Bibliog.

The best short introduction to James and his work.

908 ______, ed. HENRY JAMES: A COLLECTION OF CRITICAL ESSAYS. Englewood Cliffs, N.J.: Prentice-Hall, 1963. 186 p. Bibliog.

Eighteen essays by well-known authors and critics.

909 ______. HENRY JAMES, 1843-1870, THE UNTRIED YEARS. Philadelphia and New York: Lippincott, 1953. 350 p. Illus.

______. HENRY JAMES, 1870-1881, THE CONQUEST OF LONDON. Philadelphia and New York: Lippincott, 1962. 465 p. Illus.

______. HENRY JAMES, 1882-1895, THE MIDDLE YEARS. Philadelphia and New York: Lippincott, 1962. 408 p. Illus.

______. HENRY JAMES, 1895-1901, THE TREACHEROUS YEARS. Philadelphia and New York: Lippincott, 1969. 381 p. Illus.

______. HENRY JAMES, 1901-1916, THE MASTER. Philadelphia and New York: Lippincott, 1972. 591 p. Illus. Bibliog.

Edel's monumental biography is now the take-off point for much James scholarship. The fourth volume is of particular interest, focusing as it does on James's "spiritual illness" between 1895 and the beginning of a new century, and describing how he rids himself of his private demons by writing about them.

910 Edgar, Pelham. HENRY JAMES: MAN AND AUTHOR. Boston and New York: Houghton Mifflin, 1927. Reprint. New York: Russell and Russell, 1964. 351 p. Illus.

Takes issue with Van Wyck Brooks's derogatory view of the works of James's later period, and, through analysis, attempts to show a definite progress upward.

911 Egan, Michael. HENRY JAMES: THE IBSEN YEARS. London: Vision, 1972. 154 p. Bibliog.

Contends that James's encounter with the work of Ibsen was primarily responsible for his use of dramatic approaches in the work from 1895 on.

912 Gale, Robert L., ed. PLOTS AND CHARACTERS IN THE FICTION OF HENRY JAMES. Plots and Characters Series. Hamden, Conn.: Archon Books, 1965. xxi, 207 p.

Useful plot summaries of all the novels and tales, as well as identification of all characters.

913 Geismar, Maxwell. HENRY JAMES AND THE JACOBITES. Boston: Houghton Mifflin, 1963. 463 p.

Following Brooks's lead, Geismar contends that James was not a major writer because of the narrow range of his work and because the area of his art was "completely artificial and fanciful." Expresses the belief that he is the figurehead of "a dominant, and powerful, and fearsome literary establishment."

914 Goode, John, ed. THE AIR OF REALITY: NEW ESSAYS ON HENRY JAMES. London: Methuen, 1972. 368 p.

Nine essays by British scholars on THE AMERICAN, WASHINGTON SQUARE, THE BOSTONIANS, THE TRAGIC MUSE, WHAT MAISIE KNEW, THE AWKWARD AGE, THE AMBASSADORS AND THE SACRED FOUNT, THE WINGS OF THE DOVE, and THE GOLDEN BOWL.

915 Graham, Kenneth. HENRY JAMES: THE DRAMA OF FULFILMENT, AN APPROACH TO THE NOVELS. Oxford, Engl.: Clarendon Press, 1975. xvi, 234 p.

Close readings of "Mme de Mauves," DAISY MILLER, RODERICK HUDSON, THE ASPERN PAPERS, THE TRAGIC MUSE, THE SPOILS OF POYNTON, and THE WINGS OF THE DOVE, featuring Graham's own direct response to them.

916 Grattan, C. Hartley. THE THREE JAMESES: HENRY JAMES, SR., WILLIAM JAMES, HENRY JAMES. London, New York, and Toronto: Longmans, Green, 1932. xi, 376 p. Illus., bibliog. notes.

An interesting study of the father and his two famous sons that contends that Henry James, Sr., forms the intellectual background out of which his sons grew. All were psychologists, each in his own way.

917 Grover, Philip. HENRY JAMES AND THE FRENCH NOVEL: A STUDY IN INSPIRATION. Novelists and Their World Series. London: Paul Elek, 1973. 221 p.

Examines the abiding interest of James in French literature, and studies three strong influences on him: Balzac, Flaubert, and the "Art for Art's Sake" movement.

918 Hoffman, Charles G. THE SHORT NOVELS OF HENRY JAMES. New York: Bookman Associates, 1957. 143 p. Bibliog.

The best of James's short novels are analyzed: DAISY MILLER, WASHINGTON SQUARE, THE SPOILS OF POYNTON, THE TURN OF THE SCREW, THE BEAST IN THE JUNGLE, and THE BENCH OF DESOLATION.

919 Holland, Laurence Bedwell. THE EXPENSE OF VISION: ESSAYS ON THE CRAFT OF HENRY JAMES. Princeton, N.J.: Princeton University Press, 1964. xii, 414 p.

Essays on PORTRAIT, SPOILS, ASPERN, SACRED FOUNT, AMBASSADORS, WINGS, and GOLDEN BOWL.

920 Hyde, H. Montgomery. HENRY JAMES AT HOME. London: Methuen, 1969. xiv, 322 p. Illus.

An interesting account of James's life in England.

921 Isle, Walter. EXPERIMENTS IN FORM: HENRY JAMES'S NOVELS, 1896-1901. Cambridge, Mass.: Harvard University Press, 1968. xii, 251 p.

Analyzes THE OTHER HOUSE, THE SPOILS OF POYNTON, WHAT MAISIE KNEW, THE AWKWARD AGE, and THE SACRED FOUNT.

922 Kraft, James. THE EARLY TALES OF HENRY JAMES. Crosscurrents/Modern Critiques. Carbondale and Edwardsville: Southern Illinois University Press, 1969. xvi, 143 p. Bibliog.

Discusses the thirty-seven tales published between 1864 and 1879.

923 Laitinen, Tuomo. ASPECTS OF HENRY JAMES'S STYLE. Helsinki: Suomalainen Tiedeakatemia, 1975. 150 p. Bibliog.

After a general consideration of aspects of James's style, the author studies style in PORTRAIT, ASPERN, SPOILS, and AMBASSADORS.

924 Lebowitz, Naomi. THE IMAGINATION OF LOVING: HENRY JAMES'S LEGACY TO THE NOVEL. Detroit: Wayne State University Press, 1965. 183 p.

The morality of relationship is seen as the heart of the James novel. THE PORTRAIT OF A LADY, THE WINGS OF THE DOVE, THE AMBASSADORS, and THE GOLDEN BOWL are studied intensively.

925 Lee, Brian. THE NOVELS OF HENRY JAMES: A STUDY OF CULTURE AND CONSCIOUSNESS. New York: St. Martin's Press, 1978. ix, 123 p.

Examines novels from early to late, but contends that it is in "the late novels, if anywhere, that James lays claim to be the foremost novelist and the most radical innovator of his age," a body of work that Lee describes as "the first great fiction of the modern era."

926 Leyburn, Ellen Douglass. STRANGE ALLOY: THE RELATION OF COMEDY TO TRAGEDY IN THE FICTION OF HENRY JAMES. Chapel Hill: University of North Carolina Press, 1968. xviii, 180 p.

Examines the fiction to show the dextrous blending of the tragic and comic elements.

927 Matthiessen, F.O. HENRY JAMES: THE MAJOR PHASE. New York: Oxford University Press, 1944. xvi, 190 p.

Shrewd critical analysis of THE AMBASSADORS, THE WINGS OF THE DOVE, THE GOLDEN BOWL, and THE IVORY TOWER.

928 Maves, Carl. SENSUOUS PESSIMISM: ITALY IN THE WORK OF HENRY JAMES. Bloomington and London: Indiana University Press, 1973. xvi, 169 p.

The focus is the precise nature of James's response to Italy, primarily as shown in his fiction. One large reason for James's fascination with Italy is, the author says, that it was the one European country he discovered for himself.

929 Moore, Harry T. HENRY JAMES AND HIS WORLD. London: Thames and Hudson, 1974. 128 p. Illus.

A sketch of the people and places James knew, with numerous interesting photographs.

930 Mordell, Albert, comp. and ed. DISCOVERY OF A GENIUS: WILLIAM DEAN HOWELLS AND HENRY JAMES. New York: Twayne, 1961.

The first collection of the published articles and book reviews written by Howells about James's publications.

931 Mull, Donald L. HENRY JAMES'S 'SUBLIME ECONOMY': MONEY AS SYMBOLIC CENTER IN THE FICTION. Middletown, Conn.: Wesleyan University Press, 1973. x, 195 p. Bibliog.

An inquiry into James's concern with money in his fiction. Sees a tension in his mind "between his sense of money as the source of potential imaginative experience and his sense of it as the mere hard cash by which one had to live." Early tales, THE PORTRAIT OF A LADY, THE GOLDEN BOWL, and THE IVORY TOWER are examined.

932 Nettels, Elsa. JAMES AND CONRAD. Athens: University of Georgia Press, 1977. xi, 289 p. Bibliog.

Studies the fiction and criticism of the two writers and analyzes their relationship and that of their work.

933 O'Neill, John P. WORKABLE DESIGN: ACTION AND SITUATION IN THE FICTION OF HENRY JAMES. Port Washington, N.Y., and London: Kennikat Press, 1973. 152 p. Bibliog.

Examines THE PORTRAIT OF A LADY, THE PRINCESS CASAMASSIMA, THE SPOILS OF POYNTON, THE AWKWARD AGE, and THE WINGS OF THE DOVE in the light of James's use of polar design.

934 Perosa, Sergio. HENRY JAMES AND THE EXPERIMENTAL NOVEL. Charlottesville: University Press of Virginia, 1978. vii, 219 p.

Examines the novels of James's middle period from the point of view of their experimental aspects.

935 Peterson, Dale E. THE CLEMENT VISION: POETIC REALISM IN TURGENEV AND JAMES. Port Washington and London: Kennikat Press, 1975. 157 p. Bibliog.

Seeks to establish the influence of Turgenev on James. Sees formal and temperamental affinities linking the two in the practice of realism.

936 Pirie, Gordon. HENRY JAMES. Totowa, N.J.: Rowman and Littlefield, 1974. 152 p. Bibliog.

A critical introduction to James's life and work, with analysis of THE EUROPEANS, WASHINGTON SQUARE, THE PORTRAIT OF A LADY, THE BOSTONIANS, WHAT MAISIE KNEW, and some of the tales.

937 Poirier, Richard. THE COMIC SENSE OF HENRY JAMES: A STUDY OF THE EARLY NOVELS. New York: Oxford University Press, 1960. Reprint. New York: Oxford University Press, Galaxy, 1967. 260 p.

The 1967 Galaxy edition has an additional preface. The study examines RODERICK HUDSON, THE AMERICAN, THE EUROPEANS, CONFIDENCE, WASHINGTON SQUARE, and THE PORTRAIT OF A LADY as illustrative of the strong sense of the comic in James.

938 Powers, Lyall H. HENRY JAMES AND THE NATURALIST MOVEMENT. East Lansing: Michigan State University Press, 1971. 200 p.

Contends that, at the age of forty, James saw his career take a new turn. Powers attributes it to the influence of a group of European realist and naturalist writers to whom he was introduced in 1875: Flaubert, de Goncourt, Turgenev, Zola, Daudet, and Maupassant.

939 Putt, S. Gorley. HENRY JAMES: A READER'S GUIDE. Ithaca, N.Y.: Cornell University Press, 1966. 432 p. Bibliog. note.

A knowledgeable survey of James's fiction designed to provide the largely uninitiated reader with a kind of roadmap of the territory open for travel.

940 Ricks, Beatrice, comp. HENRY JAMES: A BIBLIOGRAPHY OF SECONDARY WORKS. Scarecrow Author Bibliographies, no. 24. Metuchen, N.J.: Scarecrow Press, 1975. xxii, 461 p.

More than forty-six hundred items are listed. The bibliography is divided into the following sections: biography, critical studies of specific works, general criticism, bibliography, topical index, index of authors. Valuable as an aid to serious research.

941 Samuels, Charles Thomas. THE AMBIGUITY OF HENRY JAMES. Urbana, Chicago, and London: University of Illinois Press, 1971. x, 235 p. Bibliog. notes.

Tries to demonstrate that not all of James's famed ambiguities are that; some are confusions and others are complexities.

942 Schneider, Daniel J. THE CRYSTAL CAGE: ADVENTURES OF THE IMAGINATION IN THE FICTION OF HENRY JAMES. Lawrence: Regents Press of Kansas, 1978. vii, 189 p. Bibliog.

Stresses "the unity of James's imagery, its derivation from a single imaginative center and a consolidated sense of life."

943 Sears, Sallie. THE NEGATIVE IMAGINATION: FORM AND PERSPECTIVE IN THE NOVELS OF HENRY JAMES. Ithaca, N.Y.: Cornell University Press, 1963. xiii, 231 p. Bibliog.

Contends that the relationship between an obsession with defeat and renunciation, attended by a yearning for almost utopian gratification, became extremely complex in James's middle and late works. Analyzes THE EUROPEANS, WHAT MAISIE KNEW, THE WINGS OF THE DOVE, THE AMBASSADORS, and THE GOLDEN BOWL in pursuit of the thesis.

944 Stafford, William T., ed. A NAME, TITLE, AND PLACE INDEX TO THE CRITICAL WRITINGS OF HENRY JAMES. Englewood, Colo.: Microcard Editions Books, 1975. 270 p.

The only index extant that provides the references indicated for all of James's nonfiction except his letters.

945 Tanner, Tony, ed. HENRY JAMES: MODERN JUDGMENTS. Modern Judgments Series. Nashville and London: Aurora Publishers, 1969. 351 p. Bibliog.

Twenty recent essays by important James scholars.

946 Veeder, William. HENRY JAMES--THE LESSONS OF THE MASTER: POPULAR FICTION AND PERSONAL STYLE IN THE NINETEENTH CENTURY. Chicago and London: University of Chicago Press, 1975. xiii, 287 p.

Studies the impact of the popular fiction of his time on James's own writing, as well as his on it.

947 Wallace, Ronald. HENRY JAMES AND THE COMIC FORM. Ann Arbor: University of Michigan Press, 1975. 202 p. Bibliog.

While submitting that James's novels "are a curious mixture of elements," Wallace asserts that "comedy informs the structure, character, and vision of many of his major works." The comedy is seen as a serious high comedy of reflection and irony.

948 Ward, J.A. THE IMAGINATION OF DISASTER: EVIL IN THE FICTION OF HENRY JAMES. Lincoln: University of Nebraska Press, 1961. xi, 185 p.

For James "evil is stasis, or restriction of development." Much of the fiction is examined in this light.

949 ______. THE SEARCH FOR FORM: STUDIES IN THE STRUCTURE OF JAMES'S FICTION. Chapel Hill: University of North Carolina Press, 1967. xiv, 228 p.

Studies James's structure through close analysis of WATCH AND WARD, "Madame de Mauves," THE EUROPEANS, THE PRINCESS CASAMASSIMA, WHAT MAISIE KNEW, THE WINGS OF THE DOVE, and THE GOLDEN BOWL.

950 Weinstein, Philip M. HENRY JAMES AND THE REQUIREMENTS OF THE IMAGINATION. Cambridge, Mass.: Harvard University Press, 1971. 207 p.

The conflict between imagination and experience as viewed in RODERICK HUDSON, THE PORTRAIT OF A LADY, WHAT MAISIE KNEW, THE SACRED FOUNT, THE AMBASSADORS, and THE GOLDEN BOWL.

951 Winner, Viola Hopkins. HENRY JAMES AND THE VISUAL ARTS. Charlottesville: University Press of Virginia, 1970. 201 p.

Shows the diverse ways in which James's cultivation of the art of seeing found expression in his practice and conception of the art of fiction. His lifelong interest in painting, sculpture, and architecture is well documented, as is their relation to his fiction.

952 Yeazell, Ruth Bernard. LANGUAGE AND KNOWLEDGE IN THE LATE NOVELS OF HENRY JAMES. Chicago and London: University of Chicago Press, 1976. vii, 143 p.

The chapter headings well reflect the content: (1) "Translations into Late James" (the need for the reader to translate the convolutions of James's late period into his own language), (2) "The Syntax of Knowing," (3) "The Imagination of Metaphor," (4) "Talking in James," and (5) "The Difficulty of Ending" (Maggie Verver in THE GOLDEN BOWL).

See also no. 1679.

RANDALL JARRELL (1914-1965)

953 Lowell, Robert, et al., eds. RANDALL JARRELL, 1914-1965. New York: Farrar, Straus and Giroux, 1967. xii, 308 p.

Lowell, Peter Taylor, and Robert Penn Warren collaborated in editing this book of essays in memory of Jarrell. There are offerings by Hannah Arendt, John Berryman, Elizabeth Bishop, Philip Booth, Cleanth Brooks, James Dickey, Denis Donoghue, Leslie Fiedler, Robert Fitzgerald, R.W. Flint, Alfred Kazin, Stanley Kunitz, Lowell, William Merideth, Marianne Moore, Robert Phelps, Sr. Bernetta Quinn, John Crowe Ransom, Adrienne Rich, Delmore Schwartz, Maurice Sendak, Karl Shapiro, Allen Tate, Eleanor Ross Taylor, Peter Taylor, P.L. Travers, Robert Watson, Mrs. Randall Jarrell, and Jarrell himself.

ROBINSON JEFFERS (1887-1962)

954 Adamic, Louis. ROBINSON JEFFERS: A PORTRAIT. Seattle: University of Washington Book Store, 1929. 35 p.

A chapbook that paints its subject larger than life.

955 Alberts, Sydney Seymour, ed. A BIBLIOGRAPHY OF THE WORKS OF ROBINSON JEFFERS. New York: Random House, 1933. Reprint. Burt Franklin, n.d. xvi, 262 p. Illus.

The standard primary and secondary bibliography.

956 Antoninus, Brother (William Oliver Everson). ROBINSON JEFFERS: FRAGMENTS OF AN OLDER FURY. Berkeley, Calif.: Oyez, 1968. xv, 173 p.

Seven essays and an elegy by a long-time disciple of Jeffers, whom he calls his "old master." Explains Jeffers's philosophy and defends him against the charge of being a Fascist.

957 Beilke, Marlan. SHINING CLARITY: GOD AND MAN IN THE WORKS OF ROBINSON JEFFERS. Amador City, Calif., and Moonah, Australia, 1977. lvi, 294 p. Illus.

Contends that Jeffers's major ideas are openly and plainly stated and that, if they are not understood, it is the fault of the reader. Sees Jeffers as having had a life-long interest in theology, derived from his father. Attempts a chronological study of his ideas on God and man. Several heretofore unpublished photographs of Jeffers.

958 Bennett, Melba Berry. ROBINSON JEFFERS AND THE SEA. San Francisco: Gelber, Lilienthal, 1936. Reprint. Folcroft, Pa.: Folcroft Press, 1969. xiv, 174 p.

Biographical. Includes sea passages from the poetry. Contributes little.

959 ______. THE STONE MASON OF TOR HOUSE: THE LIFE AND WORK OF ROBINSON JEFFERS. Los Angeles: Ward Ritchie Press, 1966. xvi, 264 p. Illus., bibliog.

Written by a personal friend, the biography is subjective and fragmented. The personality of Jeffers is never established. Criticism of the work is shallow, but a brief analysis of each book is provided.

960 Brophy, Robert J. ROBINSON JEFFERS. Western Writers Series, no. 19. Boise, Idaho: Boise State University, 1975. 50 p. Bibliog.

A good brief introduction to Jeffers and his poetry.

961 ______. ROBINSON JEFFERS: MYTH, RITUAL, AND SYMBOL IN HIS NARRATIVE POEMS. Cleveland, Ohio, and London: Press of Case Western Reserve University, 1973. xviii, 321 p. Illus., bibliog. notes.

A major contribution to Jeffers scholarship. Brophy, using a contextual approach, analyzes TAMAR, ROAN STALLION, THE TOWER BEYOND TRAGEDY, CAWDOR, AT THE BIRTH OF AN AGE, and the lyric poem "Apology for Bad Dreams."

962 Carpenter, Frederic I. ROBINSON JEFFERS. TUSAS, no. 22. New York: Twayne, 1962. 159 p. Bibliog.

An excellent introduction to the life and poetry that appeared shortly after Jeffers's death. The narrative and lyric poems are considered together with Jeffers's philosophy and his critical reception. Jeffers's greatest strength as a poet is said to be his power of pure expression.

963 Coffin, Arthur B. ROBINSON JEFFERS: POET OF INHUMANISM. Madison, Milwaukee, and London: University of Wisconsin Press, 1971. xxiv, 300 p. Bibliog.

Asserts that Jeffers's poetry, "which often appears to be a monotonous litany of doom, reveals upon close study a remarkably dynamic quest for satisfactory answers." Special reference is made to the influence of Nietzsche and Lucretius. Traces the development of Jeffers's doctrine of Inhumanism.

964 Luhan, Mabel Dodge. UNA AND ROBIN. Edited and foreword by Mark Schorer. Berkeley: Friends of the Bancroft Library, University of California, 1976. xii, 36 p. Illus.

A memoir by a close friend of the Jefferses, which centers on the relationship of husband and wife.

965 Nolte, William H. ROCK AND HAWK: ROBINSON JEFFERS AND THE ROMANTIC AGONY. Athens: University of Georgia Press, 1978. ix, 212 p.

Provides a brilliant reading of the poetry. Sees Jeffers as a great poet, unapproached by any other American poet in the ability to endow character with life. He has done what all great writers have done: provided insight to the human condition.

966 Powell, Lawrence Clark. ROBINSON JEFFERS: THE MAN AND HIS WORK. Foreword by Robinson Jeffers. Pasadena, Calif.: San Pasqual Press, 1940. Reprint. New York: Haskell House, 1970. xvii, 222 p. Illus., bibliog.

An updated version of AN INTRODUCTION TO ROBINSON JEFFERS, first published in 1932 in France, and revised in 1934. A good general introduction for readers unfamiliar with Jeffers and his work.

967 Squires, Radcliffe. THE LOYALTIES OF ROBINSON JEFFERS. Ann Arbor: University of Michigan Press, 1956. Ann Arbor, Mich.: Ann Arbor Paperback, 1963. x, 202 p. Bibliog.

Very good discussion of Jeffers's poetry which attempts to

construct a cosmography from both the poetry and the intellectual background. Also examines the relation of the poetry to Jeffers's temperament, to philosophy and science, and to the work of other writers such as D.H. Lawrence and Whitman.

968 Vardamis, Alex A., ed. THE CRITICAL RECEPTION OF ROBINSON JEFFERS: A BIBLIOGRAPHICAL STUDY. Hamden, Conn.: Archon Books, 1972. x, 317 p.

Consists of three sections: (1) reviews of Jeffers's books and critiques of major productions of his plays; (2) periodical articles, more extensive critical studies, and reviews of minor productions of the plays; and (3) books and portions of books about Jeffers. Includes a very good introduction.

SARAH ORNE JEWETT (1849-1909)

969 Buchan, A.M. "OUR DEAR SARAH": AN ESSAY ON SARAH ORNE JEWETT. Studies, New Series Language and Literature, no. 24. St. Louis, Mo.: Washington University, 1953. 48 p.

Sees Jewett as, above all, a lady. Her work, Buchan maintains, was "uniquely feminine."

970 Cary, Richard. SARAH ORNE JEWETT. TUSAS, no. 19. New York: Twayne, 1962. 175 p. Bibliog.

An attempt "to bring back to light the buried excellences of Miss Jewett." After a biographical sketch, Cary proceeds to six chapters of analysis of her materials, methods, and forms. Each sketch, short story, and novel is examined.

971 _____, ed. APPRECIATION OF SARAH ORNE JEWETT: 29 INTERPRETIVE ESSAYS. Waterville, Maine: Colby College Press, 1973. 305 p.

Reprints the essays with a foreword which traces the history of Jewett scholarship.

972 Matthiessen, Francis Otto. SARAH ORNE JEWETT. Boston and New York: Houghton Mifflin, 1929. 160 p. Illus.

A biography that concentrates on the personality rather than on the work. Matthiessen, however, places Jewett with Emily Dickinson as "the two principal women writers America has had."

973 Nagel, Gwen L., and Nagel, James, eds. SARAH ORNE JEWETT: A REFERENCE GUIDE. Boston: G.K. Hall, 1978. xxii, 178 p.

An indispensable guide to the study of Jewett. Includes a well-annotated list of writings about her from 1873 through 1976.

974 Thorp, Margaret Farrand. SARAH ORNE JEWETT. UMPAW, no. 61. Minneapolis: University of Minnesota Press, 1966. 48 p. Bibliog.

A good overview in which the belief is expressed that THE COUNTRY OF THE POINTED FIRS is the proper starting point for the reading of Jewett.

JOHN PENDLETON KENNEDY (1795-1870)

975 Bohner, Charles H. JOHN PENDLETON KENNEDY: GENTLEMAN FROM BALTIMORE. Baltimore: Johns Hopkins Press, 1961. xi, 266 p.

A scholarly biography based on the abundant Kennedy Papers in the Peabody Institute in Baltimore, it emphasizes Kennedy as a public figure.

976 Gwathmey, Edward M. JOHN PENDLETON KENNEDY. New York: Thomas Nelson and Sons, 1931. ix, 193 p.

Pays more attention to Kennedy the author than to Kennedy the public man. The relations with Thackeray and Poe are given complete chapters. The biographical detail is based on Tuckerman's earlier biography, but there are some serious inaccuracies.

977 Ridgely, J.V. JOHN PENDLETON KENNEDY. TUSAS, no. 102. New York: Twayne, 1966. 156 p. Bibliog.

This very good introduction to the work of Kennedy is concerned with him only as a literary figure. Concludes that he is to be remembered primarily for his contributions "as a maker of national legend and for his presentation of the baffling social and cultural problems" existent in America by the 1830s.

978 Tuckerman, Henry T. THE LIFE OF JOHN PENDLETON KENNEDY. New York: Putnam, 1871. 489 p.

The "official" biography, written by Kennedy's literary executor. Although there are chapters on his fiction, the emphasis is on his career as a public figure.

SIDNEY LANIER (1842-1881)

979 DeBellis, Jack. SIDNEY LANIER. TUSAS, no. 205. New York: Twayne, 1972. 169 p. Bibliog.

The most objective study of Lanier to date. Examines the aesthetic and moral complexity of his work and finds his position in American letters to be solid. Lanier's major themes and symbols are identified, and his use of chivalry and his maturing social consciousness are examined. The chief poems are interpreted with lucidity.

980 _____. SIDNEY LANIER, HENRY TIMROD, AND PAUL HAMILTON HAYNE; A REFERENCE GUIDE. Boston: G.K. Hall, 1978. 213 p.

The most complete guide to secondary materials on Lanier. Thoroughly annotated. Includes publications through 1976.

981 Graham, Philip, and Jones, Joseph. A CONCORDANCE TO THE POEMS OF SIDNEY LANIER. Austin: University of Texas Press, 1939. vi, 447 p.

Lists in alphabetical order every word occurring in the poems.

982 Mims, Edwin. SIDNEY LANIER. Boston: Houghton Mifflin, 1905. Reprint. Port Washington, N.Y.: Kennikat Press, 1968. vii, 386 p.

A biography rather than a critical study. Relies heavily on Lanier's letters. Stresses the early career and Lanier's relation to the South.

983 Parks, Edd Winfield. SIDNEY LANIER: THE MAN, THE POET, THE CRITIC. Athens: University of Georgia Press, 1968. x, 108 p.

Based on three lectures given at Wesleyan College, Macon, Georgia, in 1968. "The Man" updates Lanier's biography. "The Poet" treats obstacles that kept Lanier from becoming a "great" poet. "The Critic" contends that Lanier was not a logical or a consistent critic.

984 Starke, Aubrey. SIDNEY LANIER: A BIOGRAPHICAL AND CRITICAL STUDY. Chapel Hill: University of North Carolina Press, 1933. Reprint. New York: Russell and Russell, 1964. 525 p. Bibliog.

Sees Lanier as a forerunner of the Fugitive-Agrarian school. Interprets all of Lanier's work against the background of his life.

RING LARDNER (1885-1933)

985 Bruccoli, Matthew J., and Layman, Richard, comps. RING W. LARDNER; A DESCRIPTIVE BIBLIOGRAPHY. Pittsburgh Series in Bibliography. Pittsburgh: University of Pittsburgh Press, 1976. xxi, 424 p. Illus.

The most thorough bibliography of Lardner's works.

986 Elder, Donald. RING LARDNER; A BIOGRAPHY. Garden City, N.Y.: Doubleday, 1956. 409 p.

The definitive biography to date, based on manuscripts, letters, and family documents. It is, however, lacking in close analysis of the literary output.

987 Evans, Elizabeth. RING LARDNER. Modern Literature Monograph Series. New York: Frederick Ungar, 1979. 150 p. Bibliog.

Portrays Lardner as a "natural" who was "a superb humorist, an effective satirist, and a gifted short story writer." Although he did not achieve greatness, "as a spokesman of the twenties he showed how many people lived, . . . displaying their foibles, pettiness, misguided ambition, misplaced values."

988 Friedrich, Otto. RING LARDNER. UMPAW, no. 49. Minneapolis: University of Minnesota Press, 1965. 48 p. Bibliog.

An extremely perceptive analysis of Lardner and his work. Sees the best of Lardner's stories as repeatedly expressing "a deep hatred for the whole world in which he lived."

989 Geismar, Maxwell. RING LARDNER AND THE PORTRAIT OF FOLLY. New York: Crowell, 1972. 166 p. Bibliog.

Perceives Lardner as the "special historian" of the American middle class "who rose to quick success and power on the easy money of the twenties, which followed the slippery and often illegal profit of the First World War." Geismar believes that Lardner's "extraordinary sense of innocence about life" and his Puritan morality were violated by the materialistic aspects of American society; thus the bitterness and despair beneath the satire.

990 Lardner, Ring, Jr. THE LARDNERS: MY FAMILY REMEMBERED. New York: Harper and Row, 1976. viii, 371 p. Illus.

A family biography that sheds interesting light on the senior Ring.

991 Patrick, Walton R. RING LARDNER. TUSAS, no. 32. New York: Twayne, 1963. 175 p. Bibliog.

The study aims to describe and evaluate Lardner's literary achievement. He is seen as a master of the American short story who was "an acutely sensitive idealist disturbed by the deviations of the real world . . . from a better or more ideal world that might be possible if human beings were less prone . . . to self-delusion, pretentiousness, and hypocrisy."

992 Yardley, Jonathan. RING: A BIOGRAPHY OF RING LARDNER. New York: Random House, 1977. 415 p. Illus., bibliog.

Yardley includes more commentary on Lardner's literary output than had earlier biographers.

SINCLAIR LEWIS (1885-1951)

993 Dooley, D.J. THE ART OF SINCLAIR LEWIS. Lincoln: University of Nebraska Press, 1967. xvi, 286 p. Bibliog.

The best extended introduction to Lewis's work, it makes good use of the critical literature on the writer.

994 Grebstein, Sheldon Norman. SINCLAIR LEWIS. TUSAS, no. 14. New York: Twayne, 1962. 192 p. Bibliog.

Argues convincingly against the injustice of Lewis's current status "in which his good books are lumped together with the bad." The study focuses on his successes and failures as writer and social critic. The decade 1920-29 is studied in particular depth.

995 Lewis, Grace Hegger. WITH LOVE FROM GRACIE: SINCLAIR LEWIS, 1912-1925. New York: Harcourt, Brace, 1955. ix, 335 p. Illus.

The engagingly written story of a marriage, by Lewis's first wife. The picture of Lewis that emerges is a strikingly human portrait, with strengths and weaknesses well limned.

996 Light, Martin. THE QUIXOTIC VISION OF SINCLAIR LEWIS. West Lafayette, Ind.: Purdue University Press, 1975. xiii, 162 p. Bibliog.

Sees the conflict in Lewis between romance and realism as

"an expression of quixotism." Lewis is said to be "quixotic in his approach to life and recreated in his fiction the stories of significant quixotic heroes." MAIN STREET, BABBITT, ARROWSMITH, MANTRAP, ELMER GANTRY, and DODSWORTH are analyzed, each in detail.

997 Lundquist, James. SINCLAIR LEWIS. Modern Literature Monographs. New York: Frederick Ungar, 1973. ix, 150 p. Bibliog.

A brilliant review of Lewis's work that concludes with the observation that his reputation "most likely will continue to rest on his notoriety as a polemicist." Finds that the loose structure of his novels has given them the "peculiar and lasting effect that they have."

998 O'Connor, Richard. SINCLAIR LEWIS. Foreword by Mark Schorer. New York: McGraw-Hill, 1971. 144 p. Bibliog.

The best and most readable brief biography. It starkly reveals the failure of Lewis's personal life.

999 Schorer, Mark. SINCLAIR LEWIS. UMPAW, no. 27. Minneapolis: University of Minnesota Press, 1963. 47 p. Bibliog.

The best brief introduction to Lewis, somewhat more charitable than Schorer's monumental biography. Concludes that, in a strict literary sense, Lewis was not a great writer, "but without his writing one cannot imagine modern American literature."

1000 ______. SINCLAIR LEWIS: AN AMERICAN LIFE. New York: McGraw-Hill, 1961. xiii, 867 p. Illus., checklist.

The authorized biography, nine years in the making. In regard to the facts of Lewis's life, it is not likely to be superseded; however, Schorer's final judgment that he "was one of the worst writers in modern American literature" is certainly questionable.

1001 ______, ed. SINCLAIR LEWIS: A COLLECTION OF CRITICAL ESSAYS. Englewood Cliffs, N.J.: Prentice-Hall, 1962. x, 174 p. Bibliog.

Twenty-four essays by well-known scholars and writers, including Mencken, Geismar, Rebecca West, Sherwood Anderson, Joseph Wood Krutch, V.L. Parrington, E.M. Forster, Ford Madox Ford, Lewis Mumford, Edmund Wilson, Malcolm Cowley, and Schorer.

1002 Sheean, Vincent. DOROTHY AND RED. Boston: Houghton Mifflin, 1963. xii, 363 p. Illus.

A somewhat sensational depiction of "the tangled romance" of Lewis and his second wife, the columnist Dorothy Thompson.

VACHEL LINDSAY (1879-1931)

1003 Hallwas, John E., and Reader, Dennis J., eds. THE VISION OF THIS LAND: STUDIES OF VACHEL LINDSAY, EDGAR LEE MASTERS, AND CARL SANDBURG. [Macomb]: Western Illinois University, 1976. 129 p. Illus.

Contains two essays on Lindsay: Dennis Q. McInerny's "Vachel Lindsay: A Reappraisal" and Marc Chenetier's "Vachel Lindsay's American Mythocracy and Some Unpublished Sources." Also contains a bibliography of biographical and critical works on Lindsay through 1975.

1004 Harris, Mark. CITY OF DISCONTENT: AN INTERPRETIVE BIOGRAPHY OF VACHEL LINDSAY. Indianapolis and New York: Bobbs-Merrill, 1952. 403 p.

Also the story of Springfield, Illinois, and of Lindsay's love for it, for the state of Illinois, and for the nation, this is perhaps the book that best captures the essence of Lindsay despite the use of the techniques of the novelist.

1005 Massa, Ann. VACHEL LINDSAY, FIELDWORKER FOR THE AMERICAN DREAM. Bloomington and London: Indiana University Press, 1970. x, 310 p. Bibliog.

Studies the entire output of Lindsay and concludes that his works "form a coherent whole, bound together by an intellectual and artistic commitment to improving America." He is seen as "a field worker for the American democracy in its physical, artistic, and spiritual dimensions."

1006 Masters, Edgar Lee. VACHEL LINDSAY, A POET IN AMERICA. New York and London: Scribner's, 1935. ix, 392 p. Illus.

The official critical biography, which, however, is unreliable and reveals more about Masters than it does about Lindsay. Masters's bigoted opposition to Christianity, Lincoln, and racial equality makes him seem unsympathetic to his subject.

1007 Ruggles, Eleanor. THE WEST-GOING HEART: A LIFE OF VACHEL LINDSAY. New York: Norton, 1959. 448 p. Illus.

There is much valuable primary material in this biography, but the work is marred by an excessive sentimentality about its subject.

1008 Trombly, Albert Edmund. VACHEL LINDSAY, ADVENTURER. Columbia, Mo.: Lucas Bros., 1929. xii, 164 p. Illus., bibliog.

After an opening chapter of biography, the author attempts cursory analysis of Lindsay's prose and verse.

JACK LONDON (1876-1916)

1009 Barltrop, Robert. JACK LONDON, THE MAN, THE WRITER, THE REBEL. London: Pluto Press, 1976. vii, 206 p. Illus.

A British biography, it contributes little that is new and is not particularly well written.

1010 Day, A. Grove. JACK LONDON IN THE SOUTH SEAS. New York: Four Winds Press, 1971. xiii, 167 p. vii. Illus.

Traces London's cruise aboard his yacht SNARK as well as the events involved in the building of the boat. The text is marred by atrocious proofreading.

1011 Franchere, Ruth. JACK LONDON: THE PURSUIT OF A DREAM. New York: Crowell, 1962. 264 p.

Written at a juvenile level, it adds nothing new.

1012 Labor, Earle. JACK LONDON. TUSAS, no. 230. New York: Twayne, 1974. 179 p. Bibliog.

Although confined by the limitations imposed by this series, this may well be the best all-around study of London. It shows the enormous extent of London's work, probes the mystery of his creative genius, and analyzes closely a number of his works that represent major thematic concerns. Concludes that London should be recognized as a major American writer.

1013 London, Charmian [Kittredge]. THE BOOK OF JACK LONDON. 2 vols. New York: Century, 1921. 841 p. Illus., bibliog.

A one-sided portrait by London's second wife that excludes what she wished to exclude and slants other material. However; there is a large amount of basic material not before available.

1014 ______. THE LOG OF THE SNARK. New York: Macmillan, 1915. 496 p. Illus.

First-hand account of the voyage of London's yacht from 25 April 1907 to 15 October 1908.

1015 London, Joan. JACK LONDON AND HIS TIMES: AN UNCONVENTIONAL BIOGRAPHY. New York: Doubleday, 1939. 391 p. Reprint. with new introduction by the author. Seattle: University of Washington Press, 1968, 1974.

Written by a daughter of his first marriage, the book is more about his "times" than about Jack. Nonetheless, it includes valuable material.

1016 McClintock, James I. WHITE LOGIC: JACK LONDON'S SHORT STORIES. Grand Rapids, Mich.: Wolf House Books, 1975. 222 p.

Analyzes many of the stories and attempts to show the influences at work in London's writing of them.

1017 O'Connor, Richard. JACK LONDON: A BIOGRAPHY. Boston and Toronto: Little, Brown, 1964. x, 430 p. Illus.

Without adding anything particularly new, O'Connor repeats most of the fictions about London recorded in Stone's novelistic biography.

1018 Sherman, Joan R., ed. JACK LONDON: A REFERENCE GUIDE. Boston: G.K. Hall, 1977. xxviii, 323 p.

Includes a list of works by Jack London, an extensive annotated bibliography of writings about him from 1900 through 1976, lists of poems about him and master's theses on him, and a description of manuscript collections. Invaluable for London scholars.

1019 Sinclair, Andrew. JACK: A BIOGRAPHY OF JACK LONDON. New York: Harper and Row, 1977. xv, 297 p. Illus., bibliog.

Based on the extensive family papers only recently made available, the biography is the first to present more fact than fiction about its subject.

1020 Stone, Irving. JACK LONDON, SAILOR ON HORSEBACK: THE BIOGRAPHY OF JACK LONDON. Cambridge, Mass.: Houghton Mifflin, 1938. 338 p. Reprint. JACK LONDON, SAILOR ON HORSEBACK: A BIOGRAPHICAL NOVEL. New York: Pocket Books, 1960. 314 p.

The most popular of London biographies, it is also one of the least trustworthy.

1021 Walcutt, Charles Child. JACK LONDON. UMPAW, no. 57. Minneapolis: University of Minnesota Press, 1966. 48 p. Bibliog. Rpt. 1974.

A summary of London's life and writings. Provides plot digests and analyses of several novels and short stories. Sees London as belonging to the naturalistic movement.

1022 Walker, Dale L. THE ALIEN WORLDS OF JACK LONDON. Grand Rapids, Mich.: Wolf House Books, 1973. 47 p.

A pioneering study of London's "fantasy fiction."

1023 Walker, Dale L., comp., with James E. Sisson III. THE FICTION OF JACK LONDON: A CHRONOLOGICAL BIBLIOGRAPHY. El Paso: Texas Western Press, 1972. xv, 40 p. Illus.

The first London bibliography to concentrate solely on the fiction, as well as the first full-length annotated London bibliography.

1024 Walker, Franklin. JACK LONDON AND THE KLONDIKE: THE GENESIS OF AN AMERICAN WRITER. San Marino, Calif.: Huntington Library, 1966. 288 p.

A detailed look at London's year in the Klondike (1897-98) and the use he made of it in his fiction. Scholarly and reliable.

1025 Woodbridge, Hensley C., et al., comps. JACK LONDON: A BIBLIOGRAPHY. Georgetown, Calif.: Talisman Press, 1966. 423 p. Reprint. Rev. and enl. Millwood, N.Y.: Kraus Reprint, 1973. 554 p.

The only extended London bibliography, with over four thousand entries in English and seventy foreign languages. Writings by and about London are included.

HENRY WADSWORTH LONGFELLOW (1807-1882)

1026 Arvin, Newton. LONGFELLOW: HIS LIFE AND WORK. Boston: Little, Brown, 1963. 338 p. Illus.

Contains the most detailed critical examination of Longfellow's poems yet to appear in print. Although classifying Longfellow as "a minor writer," Arvin seems ambivalent on the subject.

1027 Clarke, Helen Archibald. LONGFELLOW'S COUNTRY. New York: Baker and Taylor, 1909. 252 p. Illus.

The author visits and describes places that inspired many of Longfellow's poems, such as the New England coast and Nova Scotia.

1028 Crowninshield, Clara. THE DIARY OF CLARA CROWNINSHIELD: A EUROPEAN TOUR WITH LONGFELLOW, 1835-1836. Edited by Andrew Hilen. Seattle: University of Washington Press, 1956. xxxv, 304 p. Illus.

The interesting record of the eighteen months a young New England woman spent touring Europe with Longfellow and his wife Mary. Sheds light on the poet as traveler.

1029 Gorman, Herbert S. A VICTORIAN AMERICAN, HENRY WADSWORTH LONGFELLOW. New York: Doran, 1926. xv, 363 p. Illus.

In a biography written entirely from secondary sources, Gorman presents a highly unfavorable portrait of Longfellow as an American Victoria full of "didactic obsessions," insisting on the purities of living, abstaining out of congenital necessity from passion of any sort, and writing a steady stream of poetry that contained "many demerits and few virtues."

1030 Hatfield, James Taft. NEW LIGHT ON LONGFELLOW, WITH SPECIAL REFERENCE TO HIS RELATIONS TO GERMANY. Boston and New York: Houghton Mifflin, 1933. viii, 187 p. Illus., bibliog.

A study of Longfellow's life, with emphasis on his days in Germany as student and traveler, his knowledge and use of German language and literature, and his German connections. Appendixes include a list of his German friends and correspondents, and a list of his German studies and reading.

1031 Hawthorne, Hildegarde. THE POET OF CRAIGIE HOUSE: THE STORY OF HENRY WADSWORTH LONGFELLOW. New York and London: Appleton-Century, 1936. xiii, 238 p. Illus.

A popularized biography that presents an idealized picture of the man and his poetry.

1032 Hilen, Andrew. LONGFELLOW AND SCANDINAVIA: A STUDY OF THE POET'S RELATIONSHIP WITH THE NORTHERN LANGUAGES AND LITERATURE. Yale Studies in English, vol. 107. New Haven, Conn.: Yale University Press, 1947. vii, 190 p. Bibliog.

Shows that, although Longfellow did much to bring Scandinavia into the American consciousness, his research was directed entirely "toward substantiating his romantic dreams." Thus, his picture of the north was an enlargement on popular fallacies.

1033 Hirsh, Edward. HENRY WADSWORTH LONGFELLOW. UMPAW, no. 35. Minneapolis: University of Minnesota Press, 1964. 48 p. Bibliog.

Very helpful evaluation of the poetry.

1034 Johnson, Carl L. PROFESSOR LONGFELLOW OF HARVARD. Studies in Literature and Philology, no. 5. Eugene: University of Oregon Monographs, 1944. xii, 112 p.

Based on personal letters and official documents, this is an account of Longfellow's years as Smith Professor of Modern Languages at Harvard, a post he resigned in 1854.

1035 Longfellow, Samuel, ed. LIFE OF HENRY WADSWORTH LONGFELLOW. 2 vols. Boston: Ticknor and Co., 1886. Vol. 1, viii, 433 p. Vol. 2, vi, 481 p.

Still the fundamental biographical source, this life by Longfellow's younger brother was done from letters and journals as well as from personal reminiscence. The picture drawn is, expectedly, highly favorable. The poet's own words are allowed to tell most of the story.

1036 Skinner, Henrietta Dana. AN ECHO FROM PARNASSUS: BEING GIRLHOOD MEMORIES OF LONGFELLOW AND HIS FRIENDS. New York: J.H. Sears, 1928. xi, 275 p.

The daughter of Richard Henry Dana, who as a child went to school daily with the Longfellow children in Craigie House under the Longfellows' English governess, reminisces about the poet and some of his friends whom she met there.

1037 Thompson, Lawrance. YOUNG LONGFELLOW (1807-1843). New York: Macmillan, 1938. xxiv, 443 p. Illus.

A strictly biographical study of Longfellow's development based on an examination of original sources. Seeks to correct inaccurate notions of him and to visualize him as "his early friends saw him, in the formative, vigorous years." He is seen as a man attracted, not by the present, but by the past of poetry, chivalry, and romance.

1038 Wagenknecht, Edward. HENRY WADSWORTH LONGFELLOW: PORTRAIT OF AN AMERICAN HUMANIST. New York: Oxford University Press, 1966. xi, 252 p. Bibliog.

The book contains the essence of Wagenknecht's earlier LONGFELLOW: A FULL-LENGTH PORTRAIT (see no. 1039) with additional materials. There is less quoted matter, and the organization of the book is superior to that of the earlier volume.

1039 ______. LONGFELLOW: A FULL-LENGTH PORTRAIT. New York, London, and Toronto: Longmans, Green, 1955. xiii, 370 p. Bibliog.

The first full-scale scholarly biography to appear in the

twentieth century, this is still one of the best. Longfellow is viewed as scholar, teacher, and man of letters. His social relationships are carefully examined, and attempt is made to get at "the essential Longfellow," that is, the core of the man. The bibliography is excellent.

1040 Whitman, Iris Lilian. LONGFELLOW AND SPAIN. New York: Instituto de las Espanas, 1927. ix, 249 p. Bibliog.

A scholarly study of Spain's part in Longfellow's life and work. It reveals his knowledge of the country and its customs, language and literature, as well as his teaching of Spanish at Bowdoin and Harvard. The use of this knowledge in his poetry is also assessed.

1041 Williams, Cecil B. HENRY WADSWORTH LONGFELLOW. TUSAS, no. 68. New York: Twayne, 1964. 221 p. Bibliog.

A more than adequate introduction to Longfellow's life and work, the book is about equally divided into two parts: (1) the life and, (2) the works.

AMY LOWELL (1874-1925)

1042 Damon, S. Foster. AMY LOWELL: A CHRONICLE WITH EXTRACTS FROM HER CORRESPONDENCE. Boston and New York: Houghton Mifflin, 1935. xxi, 773 p. Illus.

A biography based largely on the files of Lowell's correspondence, it provides the fullest picture we have of her, as well as a considerable analysis of her work.

1043 Gregory, Horace. AMY LOWELL: PORTRAIT OF THE POET IN HER TIME. New York, Edinburgh, and Toronto: Thomas Nelson and Sons, 1958. ix, 213 p. Illus.

The emphasis here is on the personality of Amy Lowell. Relatively little analysis of her work is provided.

1044 Wood, Clement. AMY LOWELL. New York: Harold Vinal, 1926. 185 p.

A tempered judgment that finds Amy Lowell to be neither a distinguished poet nor a great critic, but decidedly herself, a part she played well.

JAMES RUSSELL LOWELL (1819-1891)

1045 Beatty, Richmond Croom. JAMES RUSSELL LOWELL. Nashville: University of Tennessee Press, 1942. xviii, 316 p. Illus., bibliog. note.

Severely critical of Lowell's poetical and literary attitudes and judgments.

1046 Cooke, George Willis, comp. A BIBLIOGRAPHY OF JAMES RUSSELL LOWELL. Boston and New York: Houghton Mifflin, 1906. 208 p.

A valuable work that has not been entirely supplanted.

1047 Duberman, Martin. JAMES RUSSELL LOWELL. Boston: Houghton Mifflin, 1966. xxii, 516 p. Illus., bibliog.

The definitive modern biography, based largely on manuscript materials. Finds Lowell to be a tremendously appealing man, a person of utter integrity and charm, much more interesting than the work he accomplished.

1048 Greenslet, Ferris. JAMES RUSSELL LOWELL, HIS LIFE AND WORK. Boston: Houghton Mifflin, 1905. x, 309 p.

Very readable and adequate in scholarship, but superseded by Duberman's work.

1049 Howard, Leon. A VICTORIAN KNIGHT ERRANT, A STUDY OF THE EARLY CAREER OF JAMES RUSSELL LOWELL. Berkeley and Los Angeles: University of California Press, 1952. x, 388 p.

Valuable analytical study of the early work.

1050 McGlinchee, Claire. JAMES RUSSELL LOWELL. TUSAS, no. 120. New York: Twayne, 1967. 143 p. Bibliog.

An adequate introduction to Lowell's life and work which provides a biographical sketch, an analysis of his poetry early and late, an evaluation of his criticism, and a discussion of his career as a professor and as a diplomat in Spain and England.

1051 Scudder, Horace Elisha. JAMES RUSSELL LOWELL, A BIOGRAPHY. 2 vols. Boston and New York: Houghton Mifflin, 1901. ix, 937 p. Illus.

A formal biography that is scholarly and thorough. The standard life.

1052 Stewart, Charles Oran. LOWELL AND FRANCE. Nashville: Vanderbilt University Press, 1951. xiii, 136 p. Bibliog.

A careful study of those works of Lowell that sprang from French inspiration and sources.

1053 Wagenknecht, Edward. JAMES RUSSELL LOWELL: PORTRAIT OF A MANY-SIDED MAN. New York: Oxford University Press, 1971. ix, 276 p. Bibliog.

Using his familiar psychographic approach, Wagenknecht does a character portrait of Lowell as a man of virtually catholic interests.

ROBERT LOWELL (1917-1977)

1054 Axelrod, Steven G. ROBERT LOWELL: LIFE OF ART. Princeton, N.J.: Princeton University Press, 1978. xiii, 286 p. Illus.

The most recent full-length study of Lowell and his work.

1055 Cooper, Philip. THE AUTOBIOGRAPHICAL MYTH OF ROBERT LOWELL. Chapel Hill: University of North Carolina Press, 1970. ix, 170 p. Bibliog.

Explores the coherence of Lowell's poetry as a single body. Sees his confessional mode as the principle of poetry itself. The personal touches are viewed as archetypal, becoming autobiographical myth.

1056 Cosgrave, Patrick. THE PUBLIC POETRY OF ROBERT LOWELL. New York: Taplinger Publishing Co., 1972. 222 p. Bibliog.

Examines the poetry from POEMS 1938-49 through NEAR THE OCEAN (1967) using the moral and absolutist theory of poetry advocated by Yvor Winters, on which Cosgrave believes English literature is founded.

1057 Crick, John. ROBERT LOWELL. Modern Writers Series. Edinburgh: Oliver and Boyd, 1974. 166 p. Bibliog.

One of the better brief introductions to the poet and his work.

1058 Fein, Richard J. ROBERT LOWELL. TUSAS, no. 176. New York: Twayne, 1970. 173 p. Bibliog.

A minimum of biographical material is followed by sensitive critical analysis of the poetry from LORD WEARY'S CASTLE (1946) through NEAR THE OCEAN (1967).

1059 Martin, Jay. ROBERT LOWELL. UMPAW, no. 92. Minneapolis: University of Minnesota Press, 1970. 48 p. Bibliog.

In an able essay Martin stresses Lowell's characteristic approach to the present as through the perspective of the past.

1060 Mazzaro, Jerome. THE POETIC THEMES OF ROBERT LOWELL. Ann Arbor: University of Michigan Press, 1965. ix, 145 p. Bibliog.

A useful chronological study of the basic themes of the poetry from LAND OF UNLIKENESS (1944) through FOR THE UNION DEAD (1964). Emphasis is placed on Lowell's Roman Catholicism.

1061 ______, ed. THE ACHIEVEMENT OF ROBERT LOWELL: 1939-1959. Detroit: University of Detroit Press, 1960. 41 p.

A bibliography divided into four parts: (1) books by Lowell, (2) books containing contributions by Lowell not contained in his own volumes, (3) individual works of Lowell, and (4) materials on Lowell.

1062 Meiners, R.K. EVERYTHING TO BE ENDURED: AN ESSAY ON ROBERT LOWELL AND MODERN POETRY. Columbia: University of Missouri Press, 1970. 89 p.

The basis of the essay is the shared vision of Lowell and Allen Tate. "Both Lowell and Tate do share the catastrophic, apocalyptic imagination."

1063 Parkinson, Thomas, ed. ROBERT LOWELL: A COLLECTION OF CRITICAL ESSAYS. Twentieth Century Views. Englewood Cliffs, N.J.: Prentice-Hall, 1968. xii, 176 p. Bibliog.

Contains nineteen of the best essays on Lowell and his work, including two by the editor, as well as others by Allen Tate, R.P. Blackmur, Randall Jarrell, Richard Eberhart, Hugh B. Staples, William Carlos Williams, Stephen Spender, M.L. Rosenthal, John Berryman, and others, Lowell among them.

1064 Perloff, Marjorie G. THE POETIC ART OF ROBERT LOWELL. Ithaca, N.Y., and London: Cornell University Press, 1973. xiii, 209 p.

Describes and evaluates Lowell's lyric poetry in regard to imagery, genre, convention, syntax, and tone. The aim is to discriminate "between what is permanently valuable in Lowell's poetry and what is second-rate." Sees his work as extremely uneven in technical execution.

1065 Smith, Vivian. THE POETRY OF ROBERT LOWELL. Sydney Studies in Literature. Sydney: Sydney University Press, 1974. 124 p. Bibliog.

An Australian study designed to introduce Lowell's poetry to new readers. A reader's guide to the poetry, it contains much interpretation and explication.

1066 Staples, Hugh B. ROBERT LOWELL, THE FIRST TWENTY YEARS. New York: Farrar, Straus and Cudahy, 1962. 121 p. Bibliog.

This is the first book-length study of Lowell's poetry. The detailed notes to the poems and the bibliography of Lowell's poems are very helpful. A good part of the difficulty in interpreting his poetry is seen as arising "out of his characteristic ambivalence towards his subject."

1067 Williamson, Alan. PITY THE MONSTERS: THE POLITICAL VISION OF ROBERT LOWELL. New Haven, Conn., and London: Yale University Press, 1974. xi, 221 p.

Valuable study that sees Lowell as "the best, the most inclusive, the most deeply intelligent American public poet of his time." Examines closely a wide range of the poetry and perceives Lowell as always scrupulously honest and true to his vision of reality.

1068 Yenser, Stephen. CIRCLE TO CIRCLE: THE POETRY OF ROBERT LOWELL. Berkeley, Los Angeles, and London: University of California Press, 1975. xii, 370 p. Bibliog.

Close analysis of the poetry from LAND OF UNLIKENESS (1944) through HISTORY (1973). The book "moves from discussion of Lowell's methods of organization at the level of the individual poem, through an examination of his structures at the levels of the sequence and the volume, toward a consideration of the unity of his work as a whole."

Note: Two books that deal with the Lowell family in general and the three poets in particular follow.

1069 Greenslet, Ferris. THE LOWELLS AND THEIR SEVEN WORLDS. Boston: Houghton Mifflin, 1946. xi, 442 p. Illus.

A fascinating account, genealogically oriented, of the family in America. Contains a skeletonized genealogical chart of the Boston Lowells in direct descent for eleven generations from Percival Lowle, who settled in New England in 1639.

1070 Heymann, C. David. AMERICAN ARISTOCRACY: THE LIVES AND TIMES OF JAMES RUSSELL, AMY, AND ROBERT LOWELL. New York: Dodd, Mead, 1980. xiii, 561 p.

After a chapter on family background, the book devotes a chapter to each of the writing Lowells, with Robert receiving the most attention. "They were conservative by birthright, individualistic, formal, and ceremonious. But they were also excruciatingly honest, educated, urbane, sensitive, and uncompromisingly dedicated to the cause of serious literature."

CARSON McCULLERS (1917-1967)

1071 Carr, Virginia Spencer. THE LONELY HUNTER: A BIOGRAPHY OF CARSON McCULLERS. Garden City, N.Y.: Doubleday, 1975. xix, 600 p. Illus., bibliog.

As close to the definitive biography as we are likely to get. Thoroughly researched and well written, it presents a reliable picture of McCullers and a detailed account of all stages of her life. Comparatively little analysis of her writing.

1072 Cook, Richard M. CARSON McCULLERS. Modern Literature Monographs. New York: Frederick Ungar, 1975. x, 150 p. Bibliog.

Provides a clear summary and helpful commentary on each major work, as well as a biographical sketch. McCullers is seen as speaking "for people, who, in their trapped inwardness, could not speak for themselves, who loved without hope of being loved."

1073 Edmonds, Dale. CARSON McCULLERS. Southern Writers Series, no. 6. Austin, Tex.: Steck-Vaughn, 1969. 43 p. Bibliog.

A short but helpful introduction to the life and work.

1074 Evans, Oliver. THE BALLAD OF CARSON McCULLERS: A BIOGRAPHY. New York: Coward-McCann, 1966. 220 p. Illus.

A biography that concentrates on the fiction rather more than on the author's life, it fails to have the scope and authority of the Carr biography. However, the commentary on McCullers's writing is frequently sensitive and perceptive.

1075 Graver, Lawrence. CARSON McCULLERS. UMPAW, no. 84. Minneapolis: University of Minnesota Press, 1969. 48 p. Bibliog.

After a brief biographical sketch, this summary discusses each major work with considerable insight. McCullers is seen as comparable with Eudora Welty, Katherine Anne Porter, and Flannery O'Connor, and perhaps as first among them.

1076 McDowell, Margaret B. CARSON McCULLERS. TUSAS, no. 354. Boston: Twayne, 1980. 158 p. Bibliog.

The best relatively brief introduction to McCullers's life and work, this new volume devotes a chapter to her development as a writer and to her theory of fiction, a chapter each to THE HEART IS A LONELY HUNTER, REFLECTIONS IN A GOLDEN EYE, THE BALLAD OF THE SAD CAFE, THE MEMBER OF THE WEDDING, CLOCK WITH HANDS, and the short stories, poems, and a second play. A final chapter, entitled "Perspectives," suggests that, had she lived longer, "she might finally have become a genius of the stature of George Eliot or Jane Austen or Edith Wharton."

See also no. 1352.

ARCHIBALD MacLEISH (1892--)

1077 Falk, Signi Lenea. ARCHIBALD MacLEISH. TUSAS, no. 93. New York: Twayne, 1965. 189 p. Bibliog.

The only full-length study.

1078 Mullaly, Edward J., ed. ARCHIBALD MacLEISH: A CHECKLIST. Kent, Ohio: Kent State University Press, 1973. xiv, 95 p.

Divided into works by MacLeish and works by others about MacLeish, this is the most complete bibliography available. The second section is annotated.

NORMAN MAILER (1923--)

1079 Adams, Laura. EXISTENTIAL BATTLES: THE GROWTH OF NORMAN MAILER. Athens: Ohio University Press, 1976. vii, 192 p. Bibliog.

Traces Mailer's career and analyzes his fiction in detail.

1080 ______, comp. NORMAN MAILER: A COMPREHENSIVE BIBLIOGRAPHY. Scarecrow Author Bibliographies, no. 20. Metuchen, N.J.: Scarecrow Press, 1974. xix, 131 p.

Indispensable for research on Mailer, the volume is divided into primary sources and secondary sources, the latter including reviews and articles, books on Mailer, theses and dissertations, research in progress, unpublished work, interviews, nonprint media, and bibliographies.

1081 _____, ed. WILL THE REAL NORMAN MAILER PLEASE STAND UP? Port Washington, N.Y.: Kennikat Press, 1974. 274 p. Bibliog.

Fourteen essays with an introduction by the editor. Does not repeat the Lucid collection (see no. 1090).

1082 Bailey, Jennifer. NORMAN MAILER--QUICK CHANGE ARTIST. New York: Barnes and Noble, 1979. ix, 160 p. Bibliog.

Sees Mailer as somewhat of a literary opportunist.

1083 Braudy, Leo, ed. NORMAN MAILER: A COLLECTION OF CRITICAL ESSAYS. Twentieth Century Views. Englewood Cliffs, N.J.: Prentice-Hall, 1972. v, 185 p.

A dozen essays and an introduction by the editor. Repeats a few essays included in Lucid's book (see no. 1090).

1084 Bufithis, Philip H. NORMAN MAILER. Modern Literature Monographs. New York: Frederick Ungar, 1978. xi, 147 p. Bibliog.

A good introduction to Mailer and his work. Following a biographical sketch, each of Mailer's books through 1976 is examined in turn. Concludes that the moral power of his writing "derives from his depiction of human will and human imagination battling against the forces of constraint."

1085 Cohen, Sandy. NORMAN MAILER'S NOVELS. Costerus Essays in English and American Language and Literature, New Series, vol. 20. Amsterdam: Rodopi, 1979. 133 p.

Although the writing is often awkward, the author's discussions of THE NAKED AND THE DEAD, BARBARY SHORE, THE DEER PARK, AN AMERICAN DREAM, ARMIES OF THE NIGHT, WHY ARE WE IN VIETNAM? and MARILYN are descriptive of these books.

1086 Ehrlich, Robert. NORMAN MAILER: THE RADICAL AS HIPSTER. Metuchen, N.J., and London: Scarecrow Press, 1978. ix, 234 p. Bibliog.

Attempts to show that Mailer's "development as a novelist, journalist, and essayist can be understood as an outgrowth of his 'philosophy of Hip.'" His work is critically examined in the light of this thesis.

1087 Foster, Richard. NORMAN MAILER. UMPAW, no. 73. Minneapolis: University of Minnesota Press, 1968. 46 p. Bibliog.

Sees Mailer as a "true intellectual--acute, sophisticated, and dead serious in his probing criticisms of the life of his time" and as "an extraordinary prose stylist in the big-voiced American tradition of Melville and Faulkner."

1088 Kaufmann, Donald L. NORMAN MAILER: THE COUNTDOWN: THE FIRST TWENTY YEARS. Carbondale: Southern Illinois University Press, 1969. xvi, 190 p. Bibliog.

A probing analysis of Mailer's work through the first two decades of his career.

1089 Leeds, Barry H. THE STRUCTURED VISION OF NORMAN MAILER. New York: New York University Press, 1969. xv, 270 p. Bibliog.

Sees Mailer as a tightly disciplined writer.

1090 Lucid, Robert F., ed. NORMAN MAILER: THE MAN AND HIS WORK. Boston and Toronto: Little, Brown, 1971. vii, 310 p.

An excellent collection of essays with a sound introduction by the editor. Some of the critics represented are Alfred Kazin, Gore Vidal, Elizabeth Hardwick, Tom Wolfe, Richard Poirier, Dwight Macdonald, and James Baldwin.

1091 Merrill, Robert. NORMAN MAILER. TUSAS, no. 322. Boston: Twayne, 1978. 169 p. Bibliog.

A useful introduction to the life and work.

1092 Poirier, Richard. NORMAN MAILER. Modern Masters Series. New York: Viking, 1972. xiv, 176 p. Bibliog.

Another useful introduction to the writer and his work.

1093 Radford, Jean. NORMAN MAILER: A CRITICAL STUDY. London: Macmillan, 1975. ix, 203 p. Bibliog.

Concentrates on the period from 1948 to 1968 although the later work is also discussed. Believes that the later work is a repetition or recapitulation of earlier efforts. Thematic and political trends in Mailer's work are examined, and his style is thoroughly analyzed.

1094 Solotaroff, Robert. DOWN MAILER'S WAY. Urbana: University of Illinois Press, 1974. x, 289 p. Bibliog.

Attempts to analyze what makes Mailer "tick" as a writer. A useful study.

BERNARD MALAMUD (1914--)

1095 Astro, Richard, and Benson, Jackson J., eds. THE FICTION OF BERNARD MALAMUD. American Authors Series. Corvallis: Oregon State University Press, 1977. 190 p.

Contains essays by Benson, Ihab Hassan, W.J. Handy, Peter L. Hays, Leslie Field, Ben Siegel, Leslie Fiedler, and provides a comprehensive checklist of Malamud criticism compiled by Donald Risty.

1096 Ducharme, Robert. ART AND IDEA IN THE NOVELS OF BERNARD MALAMUD: TOWARD THE FIXER. The Hague and Paris: Mouton, 1974. vi, 151 p. Bibliog.

Close analysis of THE NATURAL, THE ASSISTANT, A NEW LIFE, and THE FIXER. Attempts to show that, in the theme of suffering, the four novels "display a gradually changing attitude" that fully emerges only in the last one. Malamud's method throughout is viewed as mythic.

1097 Field, Leslie A., and Field, Joyce W., eds. BERNARD MALAMUD: A COLLECTION OF CRITICAL ESSAYS. Twentieth Century Views. Englewood Cliffs, N.J.: Prentice-Hall, 1975. 179 p. Bibliog.

The best collection of essays available. Contains eleven essays plus an introduction.

1098 ______. BERNARD MALAMUD AND THE CRITICS. New York: New York University Press, 1970. xxvi, 353 p. Bibliog.

A valuable collection divided into four parts: (1) "In the Jewish Tradition?" (2) "Myth, Ritual, Folklore"; (3) "Varied Approaches"; (4) "Specific Novels and Stories."

1099 Hershinow, Sheldon J. BERNARD MALAMUD. Modern Literature Monographs. New York: Frederick Ungar, 1980. viii, 165 p. Bibliog.

This excellent introduction to Malamud and his works has the advantage of being up to date, treating, as it does, all of Malamud's important work through DUBIN'S LIVES of 1979. In a perceptive concluding chapter on Malamud's moral and artistic vision, the point is emphasized that "his vision has its roots in the Old Testament, while the Christian idea of Salvation derives from the New Testament."

1100 Meeter, Glenn. PHILIP ROTH AND BERNARD MALAMUD: A CRITICAL ESSAY. Contemporary Writers in Christian Perspective. Grand Rapids, Mich.: William B. Eerdmans, 1968. 48 p. Bibliog.

Compares and contrasts these two "Jewish romantics." Malamud is seen as more given to symbolism, Roth to a realistic approach. Malamud is viewed as the more powerful of the two.

1101 Richman, Sidney. BERNARD MALAMUD. TUSAS, no. 109. Boston: Twayne, 1966. 160 p. Bibliog.

A novel-by-novel, story-by-story analysis of Malamud's fiction. After a biographical sketch there are chapters on THE NATURAL, THE ASSISTANT, A NEW LIFE, and the short stories. In a concluding chapter, Malamud's literary progress is measured.

J.P. MARQUAND (1893-1960)

1102 Bell, Millicent. MARQUAND, AN AMERICAN LIFE. Boston and Toronto: Little, Brown, 1979. xv, 537 p. Illus.

The definitive biography, written with insight and skill. Contains a helpful listing of Marquand's works.

1103 Birmingham, Stephen. THE LATE JOHN MARQUAND, A BIOGRAPHY. Philadelphia and New York: Lippincott, 1972. xiii, 322 p. Illus.

The emphasis in this somewhat fragmentary biography is on Marquand's failed second marriage and his love for Carol Brandt, who seems to have provided much of the material to the biographer, a young friend of Marquand and a novelist himself. The style is more that of a work of fiction than of fact.

1104 Holman, C. Hugh. J.P. MARQUAND. UMPAW, no. 46. Minneapolis: University of Minnesota Press, 1965. 45 p. Bibliog.

An excellent introduction to the novelist and his work.

EDGAR LEE MASTERS (1869-1950)

1105 Flanagan, John T. EDGAR LEE MASTERS: THE SPOON RIVER POET AND HIS CRITICS. Metuchen, N.J.: Scarecrow Press, 1974. viii, 175 p.

A survey of the critical reception of Masters's poetry and prose, together with a biographical sketch.

1106 Masters, Hardin Wallace. EDGAR LEE MASTERS: A BIOGRAPHICAL SKETCHBOOK ABOUT A FAMOUS AMERICAN AUTHOR. Rutherford,

Madison, and Teaneck, N.J.: Fairleigh Dickinson University Press, 1978. 181 p. Illus., bibliog.

A valuable series of sketches written by Masters's son and close companion for twenty years.

See also no. 1003.

HERMAN MELVILLE (1819-1891)

1107 Allen, Gay Wilson. MELVILLE AND HIS WORLD. New York: Viking, 1971. 144 p. Illus.

An account of Melville's connection with the places he used as settings for his stories, and of the world he knew. Generously illustrated.

1108 Anderson, Charles Roberts. MELVILLE IN THE SOUTH SEAS. New York: Columbia University Press, 1939. Reprint. New York: Dover, 1966. 514 p.

The first full study of Melville's four years in the South Seas: his voyage on a whaler, his adventures among Polynesian primitives, and his return home on an American man-of-war.

1109 Arvin, Newton. HERMAN MELVILLE. American Men of Letters Series. New York: William Sloane Associates, 1950. xiii, 316 p. Bibliog. note.

An interestingly written but often unreliable account of Melville's life, with highly impressionistic analyses of his works, many of which seem to be undervalued by Arvin.

1110 Bernstein, John. PACIFISM AND REBELLION IN THE WRITINGS OF HERMAN MELVILLE. London, The Hague, and Paris: Mouton, 1964. 232 p. Bibliog.

Studies all of the fiction and poetry and concludes that pacifism or rebellion appear as constant themes, emerging as polarities in the major works. Contends that a study of Melville's attitudes towards them is a key to understanding his concept of the universe.

1111 Berthoff, Warner. THE EXAMPLE OF MELVILLE. Princeton, N.J.: Princeton University Press, 1962. 218 p.

Concerned with the example Melville presents as a writer. His use of setting, characters, narrators; the art of his story-telling; his use of words, sentences, paragraphs, and chapters are all examined. He is found to be a master of prose style second only to Emerson.

1112 Bowen, James K., and Vanderbeets, Richard, eds. A CRITICAL GUIDE TO HERMAN MELVILLE: ABSTRACTS OF FORTY YEARS OF CRITICISM. Glenview, Ill., and London: Scott, Foresman, 1971. 139 p. Bibliog.

Summaries of over one hundred critical essays published between 1928 and 1969 bearing on the interpretation and analysis of Melville's novels, tales, and poetry.

1113 Branch, Watson G., ed. MELVILLE, THE CRITICAL HERITAGE. Critical Heritage Series. London and Boston: Routledge and Kegan Paul, 1974. xix, 444 p.

Reprints 163 items from 1846 to 1892, presenting a broad and accurate picture of contemporary critical response to Melville's work.

1114 Bredahl, A. Carl, Jr. MELVILLE'S ANGLES OF VISION. University of Florida Humanities Monographs, no. 37. Gainesville: University of Florida Press, 1972. vii, 74 p.

Discusses the function and uses of perspective in Melville's art, using TYPEE, REDBURN, WHITE JACKET, PIERRE, ISRAEL POTTER, THE CONFIDENCE MAN, and BILLY BUDD, SAILOR for close study.

1115 Brodtkorb, Paul, Jr. ISHMAEL'S WHITE WORLD: A PHENOMENOLOGICAL READING OF MOBY DICK. New Haven, Conn., and London: Yale University Press, 1965. vii, 170 p.

Tries to explain Melville's great novel by use of a twentieth-century methodology, phenomenology, which assumes that arrangements of letters on a page express states of mind and thereby make manifest states of being.

1116 Canaday, Nicholas, Jr. MELVILLE AND AUTHORITY. University of Florida Humanities Monographs, no. 28. Gainesville: University of Florida Press, 1968. 61 p.

Studies the extent to which the theme of authority appears in Melville's works through 1851.

1117 Chase, Richard. HERMAN MELVILLE, A CRITICAL STUDY. New York: Macmillan, 1949. Reprint. New York: Hafner Publishing Co., 1971. xi, 305 p.

Suggests that, in refusing to accept a facile idea of progress, Melville accepted a tragic view of life. Chase tends to analyze the author and his works through the glasses of modern psychoanalysis. He is also concerned with exposing the "progressive" critics' blindness to what he sees as one of the central intellectual facts about Melville: "that he was a profound and prophetic critic of liberal-progressivism."

1118 Dillingham, William B. AN ARTIST IN THE RIGGING: THE EARLY WORK OF HERMAN MELVILLE. Athens: University of Georgia Press, 1972. xi, 157 p.

A study of the five books that preceded MOBY-DICK: TYPEE, OMOO, MARDI, REDBURN, and WHITE-JACKET. Melville's own disparaging remarks about them are refuted, and they are seen as infinitely more than apprentice work for his monumental novel.

1119 _____. MELVILLE'S SHORT FICTION, 1853-1856. Athens: University of Georgia Press, 1977. 390 p.

Imaginative readings of the short fiction, in which Melville is seen as studying closely two opposing ways of life, one dominated by fear, the other by anger--the emotions he saw as strongest and most compelling. The third character type, the ironist, reflects his own middle position.

1120 Finkelstein, Dorothee Metlitsky. MELVILLE'S ORIENDA. New Haven, Conn. and London: Yale University Press, 1961. xiii, 317 p. Illus. Bibliog.

Examines Melville's interest in the Near East to show how it affected his work. The study is limited to a consideration of the non-Christian elements in his use of the history, creeds, and mythologies of the Islamic Orient.

1121 Fisher, Marvin. GOING UNDER: MELVILLE'S SHORT FICTION AND THE AMERICAN 1850S. Baton Rouge: Louisiana State University Press, 1977. xii, 216 p.

A thematic approach to the fifteen stories written between 1853 and 1856. They are seen as exploring a series of social, intellectual, and spiritual crises that confronted mid nineteenth-century America. "They suggest apocalyptically that the social and political ideas of American life . . . were going under."

1122 Flibbert, Joseph. MELVILLE AND THE ART OF BURLESQUE. Amsterdam: Rodopi N.V., 1974. 163 p.

Studies Melville's use of burlesque in TYPEE, OMOO, MARDI, MOBY-DICK, PIERRE, ISRAEL POTTER, and THE CONFIDENCE MAN.

1123 Fogle, Richard Harter. MELVILLE'S SHORTER TALES. Norman: University of Oklahoma Press, 1960. ix, 150 p.

Examines the stories in some detail and finds them very uneven in quality, with "Benito Cereno" the only complete artistic triumph. Believes Melville to be "too heavy for the delicate fabric of the kind of tale he is trying to write."

1124 Franklin, H. Bruce. THE WAKE OF THE GODS: MELVILLE'S MYTHOLOGY. Stanford, Calif.: Stanford University Press, 1963. xii, 236 p.

Discusses Melville's use of myth and mythology in much of his work.

1125 Freeman, John. HERMAN MELVILLE. London: Macmillan, 1926. Reprint. Folcroft, Pa.: Folcroft Press, 1970. x, 200 p. Bibliog. note.

The first book on Melville to be published in England, it is divided into a brief biography, dependent largely on Weaver's book (see no. 1162), and a somewhat superficial discussion of the writer's works, prose, and poetry.

1126 Gilman, William H. MELVILLE'S EARLY LIFE AND REDBURN. New York: New York University Press, 1951. ix, 378 p.

A detailed examination of Melville's life up to 1841 which results in the conclusion that REDBURN is not so much barely disguised autobiography as had been asserted by earlier critics. Analyzes the novel as a work of art.

1127 Hetherington, Hugh W. MELVILLE'S REVIEWERS, BRITISH AND AMERICAN, 1846-1891. Chapel Hill: University of North Carolina Press, 1961. x, 304 p.

Identifies and discusses the reviews and reviewers of TYPEE, OMOO, MARDI, REDBURN, WHITE JACKET, MOBY-DICK, and the later tales.

1128 Higgins, Brian, ed. HERMAN MELVILLE: AN ANNOTATED BIBLIOGRAPHY. Vol. 1: 1846-1930. Boston: G.K. Hall, 1979. xxiii, 397 p.

The first volume of what will be, when completed, an indispensable reference tool.

1129 Hillway, Tyrus. HERMAN MELVILLE. Rev. ed. Boston: Twayne, 1979. 177 p. Bibliog.

A generally reliable introduction to Melville's life and works. Discussion of his books is accomplished through grouping: the novels of maritime adventure; the philosophical works; the remainder, including the poetry; and a chapter on BILLY BUDD.

1130 Hillway, Tyrus, and Mansfield, Luther S., eds. MOBY-DICK: CENTENNIAL ESSAYS. Dallas: Southern Methodist University Press, 1953. xiv, 182 p.

Attempts by a number of scholars including Hillway, Walter Bezanson, Henry Nash Smith, Ernest Leisy, Hugh Hetherington, Perry Miller, and Randall Stewart to interpret for the modern reader the nature and meaning of Melville's great novel, and to cast light on the mind of its author.

1131 Howard, Leon. HERMAN MELVILLE. UMPAW, no. 13. Minneapolis: University of Minnesota Press, 1961. 48 p. Bibliog.

The student will find this to be a reliable, if all too brief, introduction to the writer and his work.

1132 _____. HERMAN MELVILLE: A BIOGRAPHY. Berkeley and Los Angeles: University of California Press, 1967. xi, 354 p.

A narrative biography planned to complement Jay Leyda's MELVILLE LOG (see no. 1136), which provided both the source material and the documentation for it. The result is a very readable and remarkably well grounded story of a fascinating life.

1133 Humphreys, A.R. HERMAN MELVILLE. Edinburgh: Oliver and Boyd; New York: Grove Press, 1962. 120 p. Bibliog..

A sketch for students of Melville's life and fiction. Includes discussion of the novels and tales.

1134 James, C.L.R. MARINERS, RENEGADES AND CASTAWAYS: THE STORY OF HERMAN MELVILLE AND THE WORLD WE LIVE IN. New York: C.L.R. James, 1953. x, 203 p.

The author, a Trotskyite denied citizenship by the United States, sees Melville as "the most representative writer of modern civilization," who towers above his countrymen as "the unsurpassed interpreter of the age in which we live, its past, its present and its uncertain future." Scarcely a balanced judgment of Melville and his work.

1135 Lebowitz, Alan. PROGRESS INTO SILENCE: A STUDY OF MELVILLE'S HEROES. Bloomington and London: Indiana University Press, 1970. xii, 240 p.

Examines Melville's nine novels in relation to what is perceived as their dominant concern: the complex relation between "the Promethean hero and the young aspiring neophyte who gains important education from him." Contends that Melville had only two characters--Ishmael and Ahab--and one story, repeated in various guises.

1136 Leyda, Jay. THE MELVILLE LOG: A DOCUMENTARY LIFE OF HERMAN MELVILLE 1819-1891. 2 vols. New York: Harcourt, Brace and World, 1951. Reprint. with additional material. New York: Gordian Press, 1969. xxiii, 965 p. Illus.

A day-by-day record of Melville's life as retrieved from documentary sources. Invaluable as a starting point for all further study of Melville.

1137 Mailloux, Steve, and Parker, Hershel, eds. CHECKLIST OF MELVILLE REVIEWS. N.p.: Melville Society, 1975. ix, 90 p.

Includes all known reviews through 1876.

1138 Maxwell, D.E.S. HERMAN MELVILLE. Profiles in Literature. London: Routledge and Kegan Paul; New York: Humanities Press, 1968. x, 101 p. Bibliog.

Provides a brief biographical sketch followed by discussion of elements of Melville's fiction as represented in some of the novels and tales, with illustrative extracts from these works.

1139 Metcalf, Eleanor Melville. HERMAN MELVILLE: CYCLE AND EPICYCLE. Cambridge, Mass.: Harvard University Press, 1953. xvii, 311 p. Illus.

Letters by, to, and about Melville, with commentary by his granddaughter. Contains many interesting family reminiscences.

1140 Miller, Edwin Haviland. MELVILLE. New York: Braziller, 1975. xiv, 382 p. Illus. Bibliog.

A rather unconvincing study of Melville's life and works that suggests a strong strain of homosexuality in Melville. Hawthorne is viewed as his ideal love, and the suggestion is made that Hawthorne broke off his relationship with Melville because he was being made increasingly uncomfortable by the younger man's worshipful attentions.

1141 Miller, James E., Jr. A READER'S GUIDE TO HERMAN MELVILLE. New York: Farrar, Straus, and Cudahy, 1962. Reprint. New York: Octagon Books, 1973. xv, 266 p. Bibliog.

The book is limited in that, except for CLAREL, it omits discussion of Melville's poetry. The discussion of the novels and tales is adequate if not inspired.

1142 Moore, Maxine. THAT LONELY GAME: MELVILLE, "MARDI," AND THE ALMANAC. Columbia: University of Missouri Press, 1975. xxv, 281 p. Illus., bibliog.

Applies astromythology to MARDI by using a map of the Pacific Ocean, an atlas of the heavens, a sky map calendar, and a specific almanac. So approached, "the reading of MARDI reveals a tumultuous undertow of unexpected metaphors and meanings, linked together by one hidden and subtle figure--Neptune."

1143 Mumford, Lewis. HERMAN MELVILLE. New York: Harcourt, Brace, 1929. 377 p.

An early biography, very well written, that seeks to explore Melville's spirituality. Mumford regards Melville as a realist "in the sense that the great religious teachers are realists." A weakness of the book is Mumford's almost total acceptance of Melville's writing as autobiographical.

1144 Myerson, Joel, and Miller, Arthur H., Jr., eds. MELVILLE DISSERTATIONS: AN ANNOTATED DIRECTORY. N.p.: Compiled for the Melville Society of America, 1972. vi, 57 p.

Chronological listing of 248 doctoral dissertations completed on Melville by December of 1971.

1144A Olson, Charles. CALL ME ISHMAEL. New York: Harcourt, Brace, 1947. New York: Grove Press, 1958. 119 p.

An opinionated and free-wheeling discussion of Melville's mind, the influence of Shakespeare on him, and the writing of MOBY-DICK. Interesting, but far from objective.

1145 Parker, Hershel, ed. THE RECOGNITION OF HERMAN MELVILLE: SELECTED CRITICISM SINCE 1846. Ann Arbor: University of Michigan Press, 1967. xvii, 364 p.

Reprints a selection of reviews and critical essays through 1966. Very helpful in providing a sense of the reaction to Melville's various books.

1146 Pommer, Henry F. MILTON AND MELVILLE. Pittsburgh: University of Pittsburgh Press, 1950. xi, 172 p. Illus., bibliog.

Attempts to demonstrate the influence on Melville of Milton both in his minor works and more particularly in PARADISE LOST.

1147 Pops, Martin Leonard. THE MELVILLE ARCHETYPE. Kent, Ohio: Kent State University Press, 1970. xi, 287 p.

Approaches Melville as a religious artist in quest of the Sacred. The quest, Pops claims, "carried his heroes outside the boundaries of formal worship" toward the "archetypal experience C.G. Jung called individuation." The Melville texts are examined within this framework.

1148 Pullin, Faith, ed. NEW PERSPECTIVES ON MELVILLE. Kent, Ohio: Kent State University Press, 1978. xii, 314 p.

Interesting collection of scholarly essays designed to present a specifically Anglo-American view of Melville. Six of the essayists represented are British, six American. The predominant concern is Melville's attitudes toward society and toward language.

1149 Ricks, Beatrice, and Adams, Joseph D., comps. HERMAN MELVILLE: A REFERENCE BIBLIOGRAPHY, 1900-1972 WITH SELECTED NINETEENTH CENTURY MATERIALS. Boston: G.K. Hall, 1973. xxii, 332 p.

Covering about thirty-five hundred items, the bibliography is in two parts: a master list of items, alphabetically arranged and consecutively numbered; and an index in which references are numerically listed under works and various topics. Annotations are brief and uncritical.

1150 Robillard, Douglas, ed. SYMPOSIUM: MELVILLE THE POET. Essays in Arts and Sciences, vol. 5, no. 2. New Haven, Conn.: University of New Haven, July 1976, pp. 83-206.

Participants in the symposium discuss many aspects of Melville's poetry.

1151 Rosenberry, Edward H. MELVILLE. London, Henley, and Boston: Routledge and Kegan Paul, 1979. xii, 170 p. Bibliog.

A new account of Melville's work in which the author and his books are seen against their background of time and place. All of the novels, as well as the tales, sketches, and poetry, are considered. A helpful book for undergraduate students.

1152 Sealts, Merton M., Jr. THE EARLY LIVES OF MELVILLE: NINETEENTH-CENTURY BIOGRAPHICAL SKETCHES & THEIR AUTHORS. Madison: University of Wisconsin Press, 1974. xiii, 280 p. Illus.

Surveys the basis and authority of the most important nineteenth-century biographical sketches of Melville, written either while he was alive or shortly after his death by persons who knew him. Reprints and comments on short articles from four contemporary reference works published between 1852 and 1890, and six retrospective essays of 1891-92; presents reminiscences of Melville by his wife and two by his granddaughters.

1153 Sedgwick, William Ellery. HERMAN MELVILLE: THE TRAGEDY OF MIND. Cambridge, Mass.: Harvard University Press, 1944. Reprint. New York: Russell and Russell, 1962. 255 p.

Melville's books seen as the record of the unfolding of inward vision, "a vision not so much of life as of what it is to be alive, and alive as a complete human being." TYPEE, MARDI, REDBURN, WHITE JACKET, MOBY-DICK, PIERRE, CLAREL, BILLY BUDD examined at length.

1154 Seelye, John. MELVILLE: THE IRONIC DIAGRAM. Evanston, Ill.: Northwestern University Press, 1970. xiv, 177 p. Bibliog. note.

Studies the range of Melville's work and tries to show that his structures "involve a planetary balance of forces, in which the narrative thrust--the forward movement of a quest--is countered by a system of paradoxical contrasts." The diagram is one of ironic contrasts that persist throughout his artistic development.

1155 Sherrill, Rowland A. THE PROPHETIC MELVILLE: EXPERIENCE, TRANSCENDENCE, AND TRAGEDY. Athens: University of Georgia Press, 1979. xii, 269 p.

Attempts to isolate and define the ways in which TYPEE, REDBURN, and WHITE-JACKET each contributed to Melville's progress toward an idea of the transcendent, and to assess the genesis, emergence, and shape of this idea as most fully expressed in MOBY-DICK, and finally to discern in PIERRE and BILLY BUDD how this idea became a controlling factor in Melville's mature view of life.

1156 Shurr, William H. THE MYSTERY OF INIQUITY: MELVILLE AS POET, 1857-1891. Lexington: University Press of Kentucky, 1972. ix, 283 p. Bibliog.

The most thorough study of Melville's achievement as poet, the book also shows the importance of the poetry in shedding light on BILLY BUDD. Melville is seen as a much finer poet than he has usually been credited with being.

1157 Stafford, William T., ed. MELVILLE'S BILLY BUDD AND THE CRITICS. Wadsworth Guides to Literary Study. San Francisco: Wadsworth, 1961. x, 180 p. Bibliog.

A study guide that reprints the views of various critics on various facets of Melville's posthumously published story.

1158 Sweeney, Gerard M. MELVILLE'S USE OF CLASSICAL MYTHOLOGY. Amsterdam: Rodopi, N.V., 1975. 169 p.

Attempts to show in detail Melville's use of classic mythology in MOBY-DICK, PIERRE, and some of the later stories.

1159 Thompson, Lawrance. MELVILLE'S QUARREL WITH GOD. Princeton, N.J.: Princeton University Press, 1952. 474 p.

Analyzes and interprets Melville's art and thought, and concludes that Melville came to hate the Calvinistic concept of God, and "then proceeded to hate God." Like Captain Ahab, he remained a defiant rebel even in the face of death.

1160 Vincent, Howard P. THE TRYING-OUT OF MOBY-DICK. Boston: Houghton Mifflin, 1949. xvi, 400 p. Illus.

The story of the writing of MOBY-DICK, with extended comment and analysis of the novel.

1161 Way, Brian. HERMAN MELVILLE: MOBY DICK. Studies in English Literature, no. 69. London: Edward Arnold, 1978. 64 p. Bibliog.

An interpretation of the novel based on the idea that Melville was a writer of his own time with a strong affinity with the Shakespeare of the great tragedies. He is seen as deriving "enormous creative energies from his imaginative feeling for antiquity" and should not be judged by the standards of modern criticism.

1162 Weaver, Raymond M. HERMAN MELVILLE, MARINER AND MYSTIC. Introduction by Mark Van Doren. New York: George H. Doran, 1921. Reprint. New York: Cooper Square Publishers, 1968. 399 p. Illus. Bibliog.

The first full-length biography, which began the revival of interest in Melville and his work. The book is now outdated in the light of such biographies as Leyda's and Howard's (see nos. 1136 and 1132).

1163 Wright, Nathalia. MELVILLE'S USE OF THE BIBLE. Durham, N.C.: Duke University Press, 1949. Reprint. With new appendix. New York: Octagon Books, 1969. 209 p.

Sees the Bible and Shakespeare as the two major influences on Melville's writing and believes that "the common denominator he found between them illuminates his own pervasive moral purpose."

1164 Zoellner, Robert. THE SALT-SEA MASTODON: A READING OF MOBY-DICK. Berkeley, Los Angeles, and London: University of California Press, 1973. xii, 288 p.

Undertakes a systematic analysis of the text "in the hope of locating, delimiting, and understanding the sources of the incandescent emotional intensity with which Ishmael invests his story." Concludes that "MOBY-DICK, at the deepest level, is a vision--a way of seeing things--and this may be its ultimate significance for a technological world now sick unto death."

See also nos. 721 and 739.

H.L. MENCKEN (1880-1956)

1165 Bode, Carl. MENCKEN. Carbondale and Edwardsville: Southern Illinois University Press, 1969. ix, 452 p. Illus.

The definitive biography, which must include every known fact about its subject.

1166 ______, ed. THE YOUNG MENCKEN: THE BEST OF HIS WORK. New York: Dial Press, 1973. xxxii, 576 p.

Reprints, with an introductory essay and commentary, the best of Mencken from 1896 through 1917. Bode's commentary is enlightening and occupies much of the space.

1167 Boyd, Ernest. H.L. MENCKEN. New York: Robert M. McBride, 1927. Reprint. Folcroft, Pa.: Folcroft Press, 1969. 89 p. Bibliog.

Despite its years, this remains one of the most searching analyses of the man and his work--by an Irish critic who knew Mencken well.

1168 Douglas, George H. H.L. MENCKEN: CRITIC OF AMERICAN LIFE. Hamden, Conn.: Archon Books, 1978. 248 p. Bibliog. essay.

Mainly concerned with Mencken's creative work of the middle and late twenties as revealed in the later volumes of the PREJUDICES, in his NOTES ON DEMOCRACY, and in his editorship of AMERICAN MERCURY.

1169 Fecher, Charles A. MENCKEN, A STUDY OF HIS THOUGHT. New York: Knopf, 1978. xxi, 391 p. Bibliog. note.

A penetrating analysis of Mencken's ideas and attitudes in which the thesis is that his influence was all to the good. He is seen as having had an immense impact on his time, an impact that "puts him among the giants in our cultural history."

1170 Goldberg, Isaac. THE MAN MENCKEN: A BIOGRAPHICAL AND CRITICAL SURVEY. New York: Simon and Schuster, 1925. Reprint. New York: AMS Press, 1968. xiv, 388 p. Illus.

A highly impressionistic and rather poorly written book that fails to do justice to its subject.

1171 Hobson, Fred C., Jr. SERPENT IN EDEN: H.L. MENCKEN AND THE SOUTH. Chapel Hill: University of North Carolina Press, 1974. xv, 242 p. Bibliog.

A scholarly consideration of Mencken's role in southern literary and intellectual life of the 1920s. He is seen as a catalyst--"the truth-telling serpent in a self-deluded Eden, and the forbidden fruit he offered was a knowledge of the South's inadequacies."

1172 Kemler, Edgar. THE IRREVERENT MR. MENCKEN. Boston: Little, Brown, 1950. x, 317 p. Illus.

Written with the knowledge and assistance of Mencken, who placed his papers at Kemler's disposal and wrote long autobiographical memoranda for him, this is a biography that paints him as "a skeptic of the first rank--an American Rabelais, Swift or Shaw--who has somehow abused his gifts." THE AMERICAN LANGUAGE and the DAYS books are seen as the only works likely to endure.

1173 Mayfield, Sara. THE CONSTANT CIRCLE: H.L. MENCKEN AND HIS FRIENDS. New York: Delacorte, 1968. 397 p.

One of the close circle of Mencken's friends, the author has written a delightful book in which Mencken's personality is captured through reminiscence, observation, and the use of unpublished letters, diaries, and notes in the University of Alabama's Mayfield Collection.

1174 Nolte, William H. H.L. MENCKEN, LITERARY CRITIC. Middletown, Conn.: Wesleyan University Press, 1966. xiii, 282 p.

Finds the vast amount of literary criticism Mencken wrote between 1905 and 1925 to be astonishingly sound.

1175 Stenerson, Douglas C. H.L. MENCKEN, ICONOCLAST FROM BALTIMORE. Chicago and London: University of Chicago Press, 1971. xv, 287 p. Illus.

Traces the genesis and development of Mencken's ideas and attitudes, and of the forceful style that became his trademark. Also evaluates the significance that his views and his manner of presenting them had for American culture. However, Stenerson scarcely ventures beyond 1920.

1176 Williams, W.H.A. H.L. MENCKEN. TUSAS, no. 297. Boston: Twayne, 1977. 179 p. Bibliog.

Tries, on the whole successfully, to interpret Mencken through the interaction of the man and his times.

EDNA ST. VINCENT MILLAY (1890-1950)

1177 Atkins, Elizabeth. EDNA ST. VINCENT MILLAY AND HER TIMES. Chicago: University of Chicago Press, 1936. xiii, 266 p.

The emphasis here is on appreciation of Millay's poems, many of which are discussed in detail and against a background of firm familiarity with English verse.

1178 Brittin, Norman A. EDNA ST. VINCENT MILLAY. TUSAS, no. 116. New York: Twayne, 1967. 192 p. Bibliog.

A competently written introduction to the poet and her poems.

1179 Cheney, Anne. MILLAY IN GREENWICH VILLAGE. University: University of Alabama Press, 1975. xi, 160 p. Bibliog.

The author describes her book as a "psychological portrait of Millay at her finest, after the repressions of her childhood and youth and before the stifling bonds of her marriage." The psychology, however, is somewhat superficial. Most of the book is concerned with a sketchy recital of Millay's affairs with a number of men during her Village period.

1180 Gould, Jean. THE POET AND HER BOOK: A BIOGRAPHY OF EDNA ST. VINCENT MILLAY. New York: Dodd, Mead, 1969. xii, 308 p. Illus., bibliog.

The fullest biography to date, it is ably written and well researched. The bibliography is helpful.

1181 Gray, James. EDNA ST. VINCENT MILLAY. UMPAW, no. 64. Minneapolis: University of Minnesota Press, 1967. 48 p. Bibliog.

A useful brief introduction.

1182 Gurko, Miriam. RESTLESS SPIRIT: THE LIFE OF EDNA ST. VINCENT MILLAY. New York: Crowell, 1962. xii, 271 p. Bibliog.

A quite readable and reliable biography that also pays considerable attention to the poetry without attempting critical analysis.

1183 Sheean, Vincent. THE INDIGO BUNTING: A MEMOIR OF EDNA ST. VINCENT MILLAY. New York: Harper, 1951. 131 p.

A warm account of the poet by a friend who knew her well and admired her both as person and poet.

ARTHUR MILLER (1915--)

1184 Corrigan, Robert W., ed. ARTHUR MILLER: A COLLECTION OF CRITICAL ESSAYS. Twentieth Century Views. Englewood Cliffs, N.J.: Prentice-Hall, 1969. vii, 176 p. Bibliog.

Ten well-selected essays on various facets of the man and his work.

1185 Ferres, John H., ed. ARTHUR MILLER: A REFERENCE GUIDE. Boston: G.K. Hall, 1979. xvi, 225 p.

An annotated bibliography that includes a listing of Miller's major writings; books, pamphlets, dissertations, reviews, and articles in English dealing wholly or in part with Miller; and interviews, biographical sketches, and accounts of his involvement in public affairs, through 1977. Invaluable for the serious student of Miller.

1186 Hayashi, Tetsumaro, ed. AN INDEX TO ARTHUR MILLER CRITICISM. 2d ed. rev. Scarecrow Author Bibliographies, no. 3. Metuchen, N.J.: Scarecrow Press, 1976. xiv, 151 p.

An updating and revision of a 1969 publication. Part 1 includes a list of Miller's published works: plays, fiction, and nonfiction. Part 2 lists secondary sources, both published and unpublished. Unannotated.

1187 Hayman, Ronald. ARTHUR MILLER. New York: Frederick Ungar, 1972. vii, 141 p. Illus., bibliog.

Contains an interview with Miller and analyses of ALL MY

SONS, DEATH OF A SALESMAN, THE CRUCIBLE, A MEMORY OF TWO MONDAYS, A VIEW FROM THE BRIDGE, AFTER THE FALL, INCIDENT AT VICHY, and THE PRICE. Includes cast lists of original productions.

1188 Hogan, Robert. ARTHUR MILLER. UMPAW, no. 40. Minneapolis: University of Minnesota Press, 1964. 48 p. Bibliog.

Briefly discusses the plays up to INCIDENT AT VICHY, and concludes that Miller's position in twentieth-century drama is a lofty one.

1189 Martine, James J., ed. CRITICAL ESSAYS ON ARTHUR MILLER. Critical Essays on American Literature. Boston: G.K. Hall, 1979. xxii, 217 p.

Reprints reviews and critical essays on the various plays from THE MAN WHO HAD ALL THE LUCK (1944) through THE CREATION OF THE WORLD AND OTHER BUSINESS (1974), preceded by a good introduction by the editor.

1190 Moss, Leonard. ARTHUR MILLER. Rev. ed. TUSAS, no. 115. Boston: Twayne, 1980. 182 p. Bibliog.

An excellent introduction to Miller and his plays. Rather than viewing Miller as a social or political propagandist, Moss sees him as a dramatist whose forte is "to visualize the causal complexities and the intensity of deeply personal motives." After a good biographical sketch, the book centers on Miller's technical resources--dialogue styles, narrative conventions, symbolic devices, structural principles--and evaluates his performance.

1191 Nelson, Benjamin. ARTHUR MILLER: PORTRAIT OF A PLAYWRIGHT. New York: David McKay, 1970. 336 p. Bibliog.

Attempts to examine and evaluate the impact of Miller's plays by studying his theater in depth, observing it in the context of his life and times, and analyzing his relationship to the world which he has dramatized. There is considerable biographical information here, but the emphasis is on the plays.

1192 Welland, Dennis. MILLER: A STUDY OF HIS PLAYS. London: Eyre Methuen, 1979. 159 p. Illus., bibliog. note.

Supersedes Welland's earlier (1961) ARTHUR MILLER. Discusses the full range of Miller's plays in considerable depth and with objective critical judgment.

HENRY MILLER (1891-1978)

1193 ART AND OUTRAGE: A CORRESPONDENCE ABOUT HENRY MILLER BETWEEN LAWRENCE DURRELL AND ALFRED PERLES WITH INTERMISSIONS BY HENRY MILLER. New York: Dutton, 1961. 63 p.

An interesting exchange of letters about the mystery of Miller.

1194 Manning, Hugo. THE IT AND THE ODYSSEY OF HENRY MILLER. London: Enitharmon Press, 1972. 30 p.

A somewhat rambling pamphlet on Miller, whom the author regards as "a man of joy rather than as a happy man."

1195 Martin, Jay. ALWAYS MERRY AND BRIGHT: THE LIFE OF HENRY MILLER; AN UNAUTHORIZED BIOGRAPHY. Santa Barbara, Calif.: Capra Press, 1978. xi, 560 p. Illus.

Although not officially blessed by Miller, this book comes as close to being a definitive biography as is likely to be written, based as it is on the examination of over 100,000 pages of relevant manuscript material that Miller permitted Martin to see. The fascinating story is told with an objective eye.

1196 Mathieu, Bertrand. ORPHEUS IN BROOKLYN: ORPHISM, RIMBAUD, AND HENRY MILLER. The Hague and Paris: Mouton, 1976. xii, 230 p. Bibliog.

Miller is seen as an avatar of Rimbaud. The Orpheus figure, Mathieu contends, stands behind both writers. Both Rimbaud and Miller are perceived as rare visionaries and prophets who communicate with God without involving themselves with religious rituals.

1197 Nelson, Jane A. FORM AND IMAGE IN THE FICTION OF HENRY MILLER. Detroit: Wayne State University Press, 1970. 229 p.

An analysis based on Jungian psychology. Maintains that "any final evaluation of his achievement as a writer should begin with the recognition that his work dramatizes a psychic process and that his images reveal the nature of an inner world."

1198 Shifreen, Lawrence J., ed. HENRY MILLER: A BIBLIOGRAPHY OF SECONDARY SOURCES. Scarecrow Author Bibliographies, no. 38. Metuchen, N.J., and London: Scarecrow Press, 1979. xvii, 477 p.

Indispensable, it is by all odds the most complete bibliography of writings on Miller. It is divided into: books about Miller, chapters, prefaces and introductions about Miller, books with significant references to Miller, dissertations about Miller, and articles and reviews on Miller. An index of his works is included. Brief descriptive annotations.

MARIANNE MOORE (1887-1972)

1199 Abbott, Craig S., ed. MARIANNE MOORE: A REFERENCE GUIDE. Boston: G.K. Hall, 1978. xvi, 153 p.

Contains a list of principal works by Moore and a chronological annotated list of writings about her from 1916 through 1976.

1200 Engel, Bernard F. MARIANNE MOORE. TUSAS, no. 54. New York: Twayne, 1964. 176 p. Bibliog.

Contains a biographical sketch and fairly extensive commentary on the poetry. The poems are seen as typically asserting "in a fairly direct manner an opinion on ethics; they usually also are suffused throughout with attitudes of approval or distaste reinforcing that point." Her values are viewed as conventional.

1201 Garrigue, Jean. MARIANNE MOORE. UMPAW, no. 50. Minneapolis: University of Minnesota Press, 1965. 48 p. Bibliog.

Interesting analysis of the poet and her poems. She is perceived as "ironist, moralist, fantasist." She is also seen as a constant experimenter with new modes or aspects of a form.

1202 Hall, Donald. MARIANNE MOORE: THE CAGE AND THE ANIMAL. New York: Pegasus, 1970. x, 199 p.

An introduction to the poet and her poetry through the publication of COMPLETE POEMS. The criticism tends to be more appreciative than incisive.

1203 Lane, Grey, ed. A CONCORDANCE TO THE POEMS OF MARIANNE MOORE. New York: Haskell House, 1972. x, 526 p.

Keyed to COMPLETE POEMS. Three parts: list of words and their occurrence, list of hyphenated compounds, and list of word frequencies.

1204 Nitchie, George W. MARIANNE MOORE: AN INTRODUCTION TO THE POETRY. New York and London: Columbia University Press, 1969. x, 205 p.

One of the best studies of Moore's poetry. The criticism is descriptive, analytical, and evaluative.

1205 Sheehy, Eugene P., and Lohf, Kenneth A., eds. THE ACHIEVEMENT OF MARIANNE MOORE: A BIBLIOGRAPHY, 1907-1957. New York: New York Public Library, 1958. 43 p.

Important bibliography of works by and about Moore.

1206 Therese, Sister, S.D.S. MARIANNE MOORE: A CRITICAL ESSAY. Contemporary Writers in Christian Perspective. Grand Rapids, Mich.: William B. Eerdmans, 1969. 48 p. Bibliog.

Finds Moore's poetry to be implicitly religious, and written from a Christian perspective. Sees Moore as reflecting a love of the world and a sense of its unity.

1207 Tomlinson, Charles, ed. MARIANNE MOORE: A COLLECTION OF CRITICAL ESSAYS. Englewood Cliffs, N.J.: Prentice-Hall, 1969. vi, 185 p. Bibliog.

Reprints essays by poets Ezra Pound, T.S. Eliot, William Carlos Williams, John Crowe Ransom, Wallace Stevens, Randall Jarrell, and critics, including R.P. Blackmur, Kenneth Burke, Howard Nemerov, Hugh Kenner, Dennis Donoghue, and Roy Harvey Pearce.

1208 Weatherhead, A. Kingsley. THE EDGE OF THE IMAGE: MARIANNE MOORE, WILLIAM CARLOS WILLIAMS AND SOME OTHER POETS. Seattle and London: University of Washington Press, 1967. xi, 251 p.

Primarily about Moore and Williams, whose most important common feature "is that they represent objects and scenes clearly and preserve the hard contours of these representations against the kind of blurring and softening that they suffer in other kinds of poetry."

ANNA CORA MOWATT. See ANNA CORA MOWATT RITCHIE.

FRANK NORRIS (1870-1902)

1209 Ahnebrink, Lars. THE INFLUENCE OF EMILE ZOLA ON FRANK NORRIS. Uppsala, Sweden: Almquist and Wiksells, 1947. 68 p. Bibliog.

Tries to show that Norris modelled some of his novels as regards plot or details on Zola's work. McTEAGUE, VANDOVER AND THE BRUTE, THE OCTOPUS, and THE PIT are all seen as being strongly influenced by Zola's example.

1210 Crisler, Jesse S., and McElrath, Joseph R., Jr., comps. FRANK NORRIS: A REFERENCE GUIDE. Boston: G.K. Hall, 1974. xv, 131 p.

Includes published writings in English about Norris through 1973. Annotated. Also lists doctoral dissertations and works in foreign languages, without notation.

1211 Dillingham, William B. FRANK NORRIS: INSTINCT AND ART. Lincoln: University of Nebraska Press, 1969. ix, 179 p. Bibliog.

Divided into three parts: "Life and Career," "Themes," and "Form and Style." Believes that the principles of art that Norris learned from the French academicians during his stay in Paris helped to shape the kind of writer he became. However, Dillingham sees Norris's nature as alien to a philosophy of art and life that advocates strict adherence to form and style.

1212 French, Warren. FRANK NORRIS. TUSAS, no. 25. New York: Twayne, 1962. 160 p. Bibliog.

An able introduction to the life and works. Holds that Norris's closest link "is not with the imported naturalistic tradition but with the transcendentalist tradition" of Emerson and Whitman. The novels are viewed as resembling temperance tracts, with the author seeking to reform not specific institutions but human nature itself.

1213 Gaer, Joseph, ed. FRANK NORRIS: BIBLIOGRAPHY AND BIOGRAPHICAL DATA. California Literary Research Project, Monograph 3, 1934. Reprint. New York: Burt Franklin, 1970. 50 p.

Contains a listing of Norris's writings, an unannotated bibliography of criticism, and some sketchy biographical data and estimates of Norris's work.

1214 Graham, Don. THE FICTION OF FRANK NORRIS: THE AESTHETIC CONTEXT. Columbia and London: University of Missouri Press, 1978. 172 p. Bibliog.

An attempt, generally successful, to define and set forth the best of Norris, and to understand "what is valuable about his fictional world and what is artistically successful in his presentation of that world." He is seen as having "the aesthetic habit of mind." VANDOVER AND THE BRUTE, McTEAGUE, THE OCTOPUS, and THE PIT are subjected to intensive analysis.

1215 ______, ed. CRITICAL ESSAYS ON FRANK NORRIS. Boston: Twayne, 1980. 288 p. Bibliog.

Twenty-eight essays by contemporaries like Howells and Garland and modern critics like Warren French and William B. Dillingham that present a revisionist image of Norris as a complex, many-faceted writer.

1216 Marchand, Ernest. FRANK NORRIS, A STUDY. Palo Alto, Calif.: Stanford University Press, 1942. ix, 258 p. Bibliog.

Places Norris in the context of American naturalism. Finds him ranking among the greatest American writers in observation of detail, of evoking a scene, and of creating the illusion of life.

1217 Pizer, Donald. THE NOVELS OF FRANK NORRIS. Bloomington: Indiana University Press, 1966. Reprint. New York: Haskell House, 1973. xiii, 209 p. Bibliog.

The first attempt to interpret fully the nature and quality of each of Norris's novels. Pizer opposes the view that Norris was a disciple of Zola; rather, he believes that his best novels "arise out of a coherent conception of man, nature, and God." A valuable study.

1218 Walker, Franklin. FRANK NORRIS: A BIOGRAPHY. Garden City, N.Y.: Doubleday, Doran, 1932. Reprint. New York: Russell and Russell, 1963. xv, 317 p.

The only full-scale biography of Norris, it presents his life in an interesting yet factual manner. Shows that Norris introduced much autobiography into his fiction.

JOYCE CAROL OATES (1938--)

1219 Creighton, Joanne V. JOYCE CAROL OATES. TUSAS, no. 321. Boston: Twayne, 1979. 173 p. Bibliog.

After a biographical sketch, this sensitive study is limited to the volumes of fiction published from 1963 through 1976. Poetry, drama, and uncollected fiction are excluded. Oates is seen as "one of the most serious and intellectual of contemporary writers, whose distinctive blend of compelling hallucinatory realism with 'complex propositions about the nature of personality' places great demands on the reader." Creighton deplores the categorizing of her as a "popular" writer.

1220 Grant, Mary Kathryn, R.S.M. THE TRAGIC VISION OF JOYCE CAROL OATES. Durham, N.C.: Duke University Press, 1978. xiv, 167 p. Bibliog.

The focus of this perceptive study is on Oates's thematic concern with violence and the loss of community, as well as on her use of aesthetic and rhetorical violence.

1221 Wagner, Linda W., ed. CRITICAL ESSAYS ON JOYCE CAROL OATES. Boston: Twayne, 1979. 180 p. Bibliog.

This first collection of criticism on Oates contains pieces by Irving Malin, Ellen Friedman, Eileen T. Bender, Peter Stevens, and G.F. Waller among others.

1222 Waller, G.F. DREAMING AMERICA: OBSESSION AND TRANSCENDENCE IN THE FICTION OF JOYCE CAROL OATES. Baton Rouge and London: Louisiana State University Press, 1979. xii, 224 p. Bibliog.

A penetrating reading of the range of Oates's fiction. "For Oates," Waller concludes, "a peculiarity of contemporary American experience is that insight seems overwhelmingly to arise through paradox, contraries, and extremity of feeling. Confrontations of dream and reality, spirit and material, therefore dominate her fiction."

FLANNERY O'CONNOR (1925-1964)

1223 Browning, Preston M., Jr. FLANNERY O'CONNOR. Crosscurrents/ Modern Critiques. Carbondale and Edwardsville: Southern Illinois University Press, 1974. x, 143 p. Bibliog.

A many-faceted volume that deals with O'Connor's beliefs, her craftsmanship, and all of her published fiction. Notice is also taken of prior criticism of her work. All in all, a very good introduction to O'Connor.

1224 Coles, Robert. FLANNERY O'CONNOR'S SOUTH. Baton Rouge and London: Louisiana State University Press, 1980. xxx, 166 p. Ref. note.

A close and extremely rewarding examination of Flannery O'Connor the woman and of her relationship with the South, or at least that part of Georgia she lived in. The book is divided into three long chapters: (1) "The Social Scene," (2) "Hard, Hard Religion," and (3) "A Southern Intellectual." O'Connor is seen as "a Southern intellectual, a writer with few peers in the recent American past, and a writer, also of enormous promise, taken from us far too soon." "A soul blinded by faith, she was thus uncannily endowed with sight," Coles says.

1225 Drake, Robert. FLANNERY O'CONNOR: A CRITICAL ESSAY. Contemporary Writers in Christian Perspective. Grand Rapids, Mich.: William B. Eerdmans, 1966. 48 p. Bibliog.

Sees Jesus Christ as the principal character in all of

O'Connor's fiction, her major theme being that "the Christian religion is a very shocking, indeed a scandalous business . . . and that its Savior is an offense and a stumbling block . . . to many." Because "He revolutionizes the whole Creation and turns the whole world upside down . . . to the scandal of those who believe that they don't need any outside help (a savior) because they're doing all right by themselves."

1226 Driskell, Leon V., and Brittain, Joan T. THE ETERNAL CROSSROADS: THE ART OF FLANNERY O'CONNOR. Lexington: University Press of Kentucky, 1971. xiv, 175 p. Bibliog.

Interprets and evaluates the whole of O'Connor's fiction, and establishes her acceptance of the optimistic and idealistic Christology of the French writer Pierre Teilhard de Chardin. Demonstrates also that the French novelist Francois Mauriac provided her with ideas and images that she made peculiarly her own. Her works are seen as "remarkably uniform in quality."

1227 Eggenschwiler, David. THE CHRISTIAN HUMANISM OF FLANNERY O'CONNOR. Detroit: Wayne State University Press, 1972. 138 p.

Tries to show that the Christian humanism O'Connor held in common with many Catholic and Protestant theologians largely disproves the charge that her view of life was religiously, psychologically, and socially provincial. Indeed, she is seen as exploring in her fiction problems that are central to modern humanism.

1228 Feeley, Sister Kathleen, S.S.N.D. FLANNERY O'CONNOR: VOICE OF THE PEACOCK. New Brunswick, N.J.: Rutgers University Press, 1972. xii, 198 p. Bibliog.

An extended examination of the theological background of O'Connor's work. As the first fiction writer of great talent to view the rural South through the eyes of Roman Catholic orthodoxy, O'Connor is seen as having a secure niche in American letters.

1229 Hendin, Josephine. THE WORLD OF FLANNERY O'CONNOR. ington and London: Indiana University Press, 1970. xi, 177 p. Bibliog.

Different from most other critiques of O'Connor's work in that it avoids the heavily theological and philosophical approach and concentrates on the psychopathological elements in the fiction. Hendin sees Faulkner and Styron expanding the scale of human passion, Capote claiming to reflect it, and O'Connor usually reducing it. "O'Connor made fiction out of their (her heroes) emptiness, tragedies out of the ice in their blood."

1230 Hyman, Stanley Edgar. FLANNERY O'CONNOR. UMPAW, no. 54. Minneapolis: University of Minnesota Press, 1966. 48 p. Bibliog.

An appreciative and almost lyrical essay on the writer and her work.

1231 McFarland, Dorothy Tuck. FLANNERY O'CONNOR. Modern Literature Monographs. New York: Frederick Ungar, 1976. x, 132 p. Bibliog.

Contains a chapter each on A GOOD MAN IS HARD TO FIND, EVERYTHING THAT RISES MUST CONVERGE, WISE BLOOD, and THE VIOLENT BEAR IT AWAY. Concludes that O'Connor does not hate the natural world as some critics have said, but "sees it as a manifestation of divine power, and both its austere beauty and its indifference to the pragmatic concerns of men are signs of its relationship to the divine."

1232 Martin, Carter W. THE TRUE COUNTRY: THEMES IN THE FICTION OF FLANNERY O'CONNOR. Nashville, Tenn.: Vanderbilt University Press, 1969. ix, 253 p. Bibliog.

A thematic study that analyzes O'Connor's meanings by cutting across chronological and generic lines in order to isolate and define the themes in her work as a whole. Her sacramental vision is stressed.

1233 May, John R. THE PRUNING WORD: THE PARABLES OF FLANNERY O'CONNOR. Notre Dame, Ind., and London: University of Notre Dame Press, 1976. xxv, 178 p. Bibliog. of textual analysis.

Contends that O'Connor's fiction "achieves its distinctive dramatic impact through the power of language to interpret its listener rather than through its need to be interpreted by him. The word of revelation spoken or the gesture of judgment seen constitutes the dramatic core of O'Connor's narratives and articulates their meaning for the reader."

1234 Muller, Gilbert H. NIGHTMARES AND VISIONS: FLANNERY O'CONNOR AND THE CATHOLIC GROTESQUE. Athens: University of Georgia Press, 1972. viii, 125 p.

Maintains that O'Connor used the Catholic grotesque as vision and technique, and that its exaggeration lies at the heart of her method with its emphasis on distortion, melodrama, caricature, and fusion.

1235 Orvell, Miles. INVISIBLE PARADE: THE FICTION OF FLANNERY O'CONNOR. Philadelphia: Temple University Press, 1972. xiv, 232 p. Bibliog.

A close reading of the two novels and all of the short stories, based on three aims: (1) to define their chief qualities and to "place" the stories therein, (2) to elucidate them, and (3) to evaluate them.

1236 Shloss, Carol. FLANNERY O'CONNOR'S DARK COMEDIES: THE LIMITS OF INFERENCE. Southern Literary Studies. Baton Rouge and London: Louisiana State University Press, 1980. ix, 159 p. Bibliog.

The concern here is not biography or the themes of the stories, but rather the narrative methods of embodying a point of view. Tries to locate and discuss O'Connor's methods of embodying spiritual meanings, and to examine the ways in which readers encounter these rhetorical devices and use them as a basis for inferring secondary levels of implication in a text.

1237 Walters, Dorothy. FLANNERY O'CONNOR. TUSAS, no. 216. Boston: Twayne, 1973. 172 p. Bibliog.

After a look at O'Connor's life as the source of much of her art, there is a discussion of her method and perspective. Each of the nineteen early collected stories is treated individually, and the two novels, WISE BLOOD and THE VIOLENT BEAR IT AWAY, are discussed in separate chapters. Her Catholic heritage is seen as providing a stable moral perspective from which she consistently views her subjects.

CLIFFORD ODETS (1906-1963)

1238 Cantor, Harold. CLIFFORD ODETS: PLAYWRIGHT: POET. Metuchen, N.J., and London: Scarecrow Press, 1978. viii, 235 p. Bibliog.

Attempts to rescue Odets from what Cantor regards as the "distortions and improper emphases of the legend which surrounds him." The approach used is to examine Odets's plays as a unified body of work rather than through chronology. Believes that he became "a poetic playwright and myth-maker for middle-class ethics and aspirations and the dilemmas they produce."

1239 Mendelsohn, Michael J. CLIFFORD ODETS: HUMANE DRAMATIST. Deland, Fla.: Everett and Edwards, 1969. xviii, 138 p. Bibliog.

"Odets was a humanitarian by inclination and a radical by accident" is the theme of this book, which appraises the playwright's work in considerable detail. The humaneness is seen as the dominant quality.

1240 Murray, Edward. CLIFFORD ODETS: THE THIRTIES AND AFTER. New York: Frederick Ungar, 1968. ix, 229 p.

Analyzes eight plays in respect to structure, character, language, and theme, with the objective of revealing Odets's mastery of form and stimulating appreciation of his artistry. WAITING FOR LEFTY, TILL THE DAY I DIE, and PARADISE LOST are ignored as efforts that add no luster to Odets's critical reputation.

1241 Shuman, R. Baird. CLIFFORD ODETS. TUSAS, no. 30. New York: Twayne, 1962. 160 p. Bibliog.

The first full-length study of Odets and his plays. A biographical sketch is followed by examination of the eleven plays produced, and their critical reception.

1242 Weales, Gerald. CLIFFORD ODETS, PLAYWRIGHT. Pegasus American Authors Series. New York: Pegasus, 1971. ix, 295 p. Bibliog. note.

The fullest analysis of Odets's work to be published to date concludes with the unequivocal judgment that he was one of our most talented playwrights. The Hollywood scripts are considered as well as the stage plays.

JOHN O'HARA (1905-1970)

1243 Bruccoli, Matthew J. THE O'HARA CONCERN: A BIOGRAPHY OF JOHN O'HARA. New York: Random House, 1975. xxix, 417 p. Illus., bibliog.

A critical biography that tries to establish O'Hara's stature through an account of his life and work. Bruccoli writes from the conviction that O'Hara was a major author who was underrated by the critical-academic axis. Relies heavily on O'Hara's letters.

1244 ______, comp. JOHN O'HARA: A CHECKLIST. New York: Random House, 1972. xxi, 136 p.

The first attempt to compile a comprehensive list of O'Hara's published work. Also includes a previously unpublished speech by O'Hara.

1245 ______, ed. JOHN O'HARA: A DESCRIPTIVE BIBLIOGRAPHY. Pittsburgh Series in Bibliography. Pittsburgh: University of Pittsburgh Press, 1978. xv, 324 p.

Indispensable tool for O'Hara scholars.

1246 Carson, Edward Russell. THE FICTION OF JOHN O'HARA. Pittsburgh: University of Pittsburgh Press, 1961. 73 p. Bibliog.

Devotes a chapter to the novels and another to the short stories in this brief but valuable study.

1247 Farr, Finis. O'HARA: A BIOGRAPHY. Boston and Toronto: Little, Brown, 1973. 300 p.

Concentrates on the author's life rather than on analysis of his writing. The story of that life is well and interestingly told.

1248 Grebstein, Sheldon Norman. JOHN O'HARA. TUSAS, no. 103. New York: Twayne, 1966. 175 p. Bibliog.

The first full-scale study of O'Hara presents a balanced judgment of his work that provides a good introduction to the writer, his excellences, and his defects.

1249 MacShane, Frank. THE LIFE OF JOHN O'HARA. New York: Dutton, 1980. xii, 274 p. Bibliog. refs.

This new biography is the best to date. As well as telling the life story with skillful use of information, MacShane exhibits critical acumen in his commentary on O'Hara's fiction.

1250 Walcutt, Charles Child. JOHN O'HARA. UMPAW, no. 80. Minneapolis: University of Minnesota Press, 1969. 48 p. Bibliog.

Sees O'Hara as an extraordinarily good writer of short stories and as an inferior novelist.

EUGENE O'NEILL (1888-1953)

1251 Alexander, Doris. THE TEMPERING OF EUGENE O'NEILL. New York: Harcourt, Brace and World, 1962. xvii, 301 p.

A well-researched biography up to 1920, intended as "a portrait of the artist as a young man."

1252 Bogard, Travis. CONTOUR IN TIME: THE PLAYS OF EUGENE O'NEILL. New York: Oxford University Press, 1972. xx, 491 p. Bibliog. notes.

A thorough study of the development of O'Neill's art. The criticism is profound and genuinely sympathetic.

1253 Boulton, Agnes. PART OF A LONG STORY. Garden City, N.Y.: Doubleday, 1958. 331 p.

A highly personal and readable account of the relationship of O'Neill and his second wife, by her. The early years, 1917-19, are particularly stressed.

1254 Bowen, Croswell. THE CURSE OF THE MISBEGOTTEN. New York: McGraw-Hill, 1959. xviii, 384 p.

Done with the aid of Shane O'Neill, this is a lively but uncritical account of O'Neill's life and times. Undocumented, its reliability as biography is questionable.

1255 Cargill, Oscar, et al., eds. O'NEILL AND HIS PLAYS, FOUR DECADES OF CRITICISM. New York: New York University Press, 1961. xi, 528 p. Bibliog.

An excellent collection of essays on O'Neill the man and his work, with a large number of reviews of individual plays by influential critics. N. Bryllion Fagin and William J. Fisher coedited the book.

1256 Carpenter, Frederic I. EUGENE O'NEILL. Rev. ed. TUSAS, no. 66. Boston: Twayne, 1979. 192 p. Bibliog.

This revision of the 1964 original takes cognizance of new information and new critical insights, as well as updating the bibliography. It is a sound introduction to the dramatist's life and works, which also takes into account the chief criticisms of the work. O'Neill's theory of tragedy is also outlined.

1257 Chabrowe, Leonard. RITUAL AND PATHOS--THE THEATER OF O'NEILL. Lewisburg, Pa.: Bucknell University Press, 1976. xxiii, 226 p. Illus., bibliog.

Contends that O'Neill "achieved nothing less than a renaissance of an art form [tragedy] long thought dead." The book discusses the development of his powers in that form.

1258 Clark, Barrett H. EUGENE O'NEILL, THE MAN AND HIS PLAYS. Originally published as EUGENE O'NEILL. New York: McBride, 1926. Reprint. McBride's Modern American Writers Series, vol. 5. New York: Dover, 1947. ix, 182 p. Bibliog.

The last edition of a book first published in 1925, it is a much enlarged version of the earlier work. Both biographical and critical, it contains much valuable information supplied by O'Neill, as well as letters and interviews.

1259 Engel, Edwin A. THE HAUNTED HEROES OF EUGENE O'NEILL. Cambridge, Mass.: Harvard University Press, 1953. x, 310 p.

This critical study of a wide range of O'Neill's work prefers such early plays as THE EMPEROR JONES and DESIRE UNDER THE ELMS to any of the later plays. O'Neill's heroes are viewed as suffering from excessive self-consciousness and, being at odds with society, from seeking "the remoteness of the cosmos, the privacy of the womb, and the anonymity of the grave."

1260 Falk, Doris V. EUGENE O'NEILL AND THE TRAGIC TENSION: AN INTERPRETIVE STUDY OF THE PLAYS. New Brunswick, N.J.: Rutgers University Press, 1958. xii, 211 p.

The plays are interpreted from the psychological viewpoint that one theme unites all O'Neill's work, a theme "rooted in O'Neill's own personal need," and which represents "an attempt at once to express and to assuage the lifelong torment of a mind in conflict."

1261 Floyd, Virginia, ed. EUGENE O'NEILL, A WORLD VIEW. New York: Frederick Ungar, 1979. ix, 309 p.

A book of essays by various writers, divided into three parts: (1) "A European Perspective," (2) "An American Perspective," and (3) "Performers on O'Neill."

1262 Frazer, Winifred L., ed. E.G. AND E.G.O.: EMMA GOLDMAN AND THE ICEMAN COMETH. University of Florida Humanities Monograph, no. 43. Gainesville: University Presses of Florida, 1974. 105 p.

Demonstrates that the anarchist Emma Goldman was the inspiration for the off-stage character of Rosa Parritt and for the betrayer coplot of O'Neill's ICEMAN.

1263 Frenz, Horst. EUGENE O'NEILL. Translated from German by Helen Sebba. Modern Literary Monographs Series. New York: Frederick Ungar, 1971. 121 p. Bibliog. notes.

A German critique which contends that O'Neill was often a weak thinker, unreliable and superficial, but a frequently successful experimenter in dramatic form whose best plays are "genuine and powerful expressions of--spiritual anguish, helplessness, lies, and mutual human destruction."

1264 Gassner, John. EUGENE O'NEILL. UMPAW, no. 45. Minneapolis: University of Minnesota Press, 1965. 48 p. Bibliog.

The brevity of this series' format permits Gassner to discuss only a few plays and to present an extremely truncated biographical sketch.

1265 ______, ed. O'NEILL: A COLLECTION OF CRITICAL ESSAYS. Englewood Cliffs, N.J.: Prentice-Hall, 1964. 189 p. Bibliog.

Fifteen well-selected essays that range widely over the life and work.

1266 Gelb, Arthur, and Gelb, Barbara. O'NEILL. New York and Evanston, Ill.: Harper and Row, 1962. xx, 970 p. Illus.

An attempt at a comprehensive life and study of O'Neill and his work that is largely undocumented and seemingly unselective. Mr. Gelb, a member of the NEW YORK TIMES news staff, seems almost to have emptied the voluminous TIMES O'Neill file onto the printed page. However, many interviews with O'Neill friends and associates yielded valuable reminiscences.

1267 Goyal, Bhagwat S. THE STRATEGY OF SURVIVAL: HUMAN SIGNIFICANCE OF O'NEILL'S PLAYS. Ghaziabad, India: Vimal Prakashan, 1975. viii, 244 p. Bibliog.

Discussion by an Indian scholar of all of O'Neill's plays, which are seen as dealing with the fundamental problem of human survival in an indifferent universe. Man-made institutions add to the misery of troubled humanity, and O'Neill is thought to advocate the abolition of the institution of private property to enable man to grow spiritually.

1268 Griffin, Ernest G., ed. EUGENE O'NEILL: A COLLECTION OF CRITICISM. New York: McGraw-Hill, 1976. viii, 151 p. Bibliog.

A dozen essays by O'Neill scholars, with an introduction to O'Neill's life and career by the editor.

1269 Long, Chester Clayton. THE ROLE OF NEMESIS IN THE STRUCTURE OF SELECTED PLAYS BY EUGENE O'NEILL. The Hague and Paris: Mouton, 1968. 231 p. Bibliog.

The selected plays are ABORTION, THIRST, THE MOON OF THE CARIBBEES, THE HAIRY APE, DESIRE UNDER THE ELMS, MOURNING BECOMES ELECTRA, THE ICEMAN COMETH, and LONG DAY'S JOURNEY INTO NIGHT. Nemesis is defined as "the personification of an idea, the idea of justice."

1270 Miller, Jordan Y., ed. EUGENE O'NEILL AND THE AMERICAN CRITIC: A SUMMARY AND BIBLIOGRAPHICAL CHECKLIST. 2d ed. rev. Hamden, Conn., and London: Archon Books, 1973. viii, 513 p.

In the revised version of the 1962 original we have the most complete bibliography of books and articles about

O'Neill published prior to 1972. About two thousand items, annotated.

1271 _____. PLAYWRIGHT'S PROGRESS: O'NEILL AND THE CRITICS. Chicago: Scott, Foresman, 1965. 184 p. Bibliog.

Many contemporary reviews of O'Neill's plays are here reprinted as well as a few "general" critiques.

1272 Raghavacharyulu, D.V.K. EUGENE O'NEILL: A STUDY. Bombay: Popular Prakashan, 1965. xv, 232 p. Bibliog.

The growth, change, and conflict in O'Neill's work is seen as a cyclical progression of the artistic consciousness. It is examined through the glasses of Hindu religious philosophy.

1273 Reaver, J. Russell, ed. AN O'NEILL CONCORDANCE. 3 vols. Detroit: Gale Research Co., 1969. 1,846 p.

Based on the standard Random House edition of O'Neill in three volumes, the Random House edition of A MOON FOR THE MISBEGOTTEN, and on the individual plays as published by Yale University Press. Several early plays not included in the Random House edition are omitted.

1274 Scheibler, Rolf. THE LATE PLAYS OF EUGENE O'NEILL. Cooper Monographs on English and American Language and Literature, no. 15. Bern: Francke Verlag, 1970. 222 p. Bibliog.

Examines in detail A TOUCH OF THE POET, THE ICEMAN COMETH, LONG DAY'S JOURNEY INTO NIGHT, and A MOON FOR THE MISBEGOTTEN and finds that they differ from the earlier plays in that in them O'Neill employed Ibsen's naturalistic style and analytical method. Scheibler tries to show that O'Neill's ideas about modern society and life are clear and clearly presented, and also that a "strange light of comfort emerges out of [his] desolate dramatic world."

1275 Shastri, Srimati Aruna. O'NEILL'S TRAGIC VISION. Mysore, India: Bharati Publications, 1972. viii, 104 p. Bibliog.

Attempts to analyze the various aspects of the tragic vision as revealed in the plays, and to present an integrated view of O'Neill's approach to life.

1276 Sheaffer, Louis. O'NEILL, SON AND ARTIST. Boston and Toronto: Little, Brown, 1973. xviii, 750 p. Illus. Bibliog.

The second and final volume of the Sheaffer biography, it

covers O'Neill's career from 1920 until his death. Besides a minute account of his life, there is considerable commentary on the plays.

1277 ______. O'NEILL, SON AND PLAYWRIGHT. Boston and Toronto: Little, Brown, 1968. xx, 543 p. Illus., bibliog.

The first volume of Sheaffer's indispensable biography, it ends in 1920 with the production of BEYOND THE HORIZON on Broadway. Much hitherto unknown material on O'Neill's family and early life is brought to light, and his relations with his parents and his predominant feelings toward each are stressed.

1278 Skinner, Richard Dane. EUGENE O'NEILL: A POET'S QUEST. New York and Toronto: Longmans, Green, 1935. Reprint. New York: Russell and Russell, 1964. xiv, 242 p.

A critic for THE COMMONWEAL discusses O'Neill's plays from the earliest through DAYS WITHOUT END from a distinctly Catholic point of view.

1279 Tornquist, Egil. A DRAMA OF SOULS: STUDIES IN O'NEILL'S SUPER-NATURALISTIC TECHNIQUE. Uppsala, Sweden: Almquist and Wiksells, 1968. 284 p. Bibliog.

Aims to shed light on a problem of central importance to O'Neill: how to express, in a dramatically and theatrically arresting way, the depths of personality and the inscrutable forces acting upon life. O'Neill, in trying to dramatize these "hidden" phenomena, tried to transcend the limitations imposed on drama "by the naturalistic demands for a verisimilitude of appearances."

THOMAS NELSON PAGE (1853-1922)

1280 Gross, Theodore L. THOMAS NELSON PAGE. TUSAS, no. 111. New York: Twayne, 1967. 175 p. Bibliog.

The first full-length study of Page and his work to be published. The first three chapters treat the development of Page's tragedy of the South, with analysis of IN OLE VIRGINIA, the essays on race, and the novel RED ROCK. The last three chapters deal with Page's attempt to emerge from his southern past to judge the contemporary problems arising from a growing industrialism.

1281 Longest, George C., ed. THREE VIRGINIA WRITERS; MARY JOHNSTON, THOMAS NELSON PAGE and AMELIE RIVES TROUBETZKOY: A REFERENCE GUIDE. Boston: G.K. Hall, 1978. xv, 206 p.

Pages 67-148 deal with writings about Page. The bibliography is annotated and includes items from 1886 through 1976.

1282 Page, Rosewell. THOMAS NELSON PAGE: A MEMOIR OF A VIRGINIA GENTLEMAN. New York: Scribner's, 1923. 210 p.

The only published biography of Page, written by his brother, who tends to eulogize his more celebrated sibling. In no sense scholarly.

THEODORE PARKER (1810-1860)

1283 Albrecht, Robert C. THEODORE PARKER. TUSAS, no. 179. New York: Twayne, 1971. 160 p. Bibliog.

A critical study of Parker's work that is concerned with those of his writings that most clearly show his religious, social, political, and moral positions.

1284 Chadwick, John White. THEODORE PARKER: PREACHER AND REFORMER. Boston and New York: Houghton Mifflin, 1901. xx, 422 p. Bibliog.

A sympathetic biography that stresses Parker's position in the theological struggles he was involved in.

1285 Commager, Henry Steele. THEODORE PARKER. Boston: Little, Brown, 1936. ix, 339 p. Bibliog.

A scholarly and highly readable biography with an excellent bibliography of both primary and secondary materials.

1286 Dirks, John Edward. THE CRITICAL THEOLOGY OF THEODORE PARKER. New York: Columbia University Press, 1948. Reprint. Westport, Conn.: Greenwood Press, 1970. viii, 173 p. Bibliog.

Analyzes the extent to which Parker embraced New England transcendentalism and finds him standing "near, but not within" it.

1287 Frothingham, Octavius Brooks. THEODORE PARKER: A BIOGRAPHY. Boston: James R. Osgood, 1874. viii, 588 p.

Although old, this may still be the best biography of Parker. Its author knew him well and presents details about him which provide basic information for Parker scholarship.

1288 Weiss, John. LIFE AND CORRESPONDENCE OF THEODORE PARKER. 2 vols. New York: Appleton, 1864. Reprint. New York: Negro Universities Press, 1969, and New York: Da Capo Press, 1970. Vol. 1, xi, 478 p. Vol. 2, vi, 530 p. Illus.

Invaluable for the study of Parker and his work, but difficult to use because of faulty organization.

FRANCIS PARKMAN (1823-1893)

1289 Doughty, Howard. FRANCIS PARKMAN. New York: Macmillan, 1962. vii, 414 p. Bibliog. note.

Written by a nonhistorian, this penetrating biocritical study analyzes Parkman's major works and provides proof of his modernity.

1290 Farnham, Charles Haight. A LIFE OF FRANCIS PARKMAN. Boston: Little, Brown, 1903. xv, 394 p. Reprint. New York: Haskell House, 1968.

The first full-scale biography, written by Parkman's secretary. Provides valuable details but presents an inaccurate picture of Parkman as a solitary and often pathetic figure.

1291 Gale, Robert L. FRANCIS PARKMAN. TUSAS, no. 220. New York: Twayne, 1973. 204 p. Bibliog.

An excellent introduction to the life and work. The first three chapters are biographical, the next three deal with the works, and the final chapter assesses Parkman's status, concluding that "he was a great historian, a fine nineteenth-century literary artist, and a brave man."

1292 Sedgwick, Henry Dwight. FRANCIS PARKMAN. American Men of Letters. Boston and New York: Houghton Mifflin, 1904. x, 345 p.

An early biography that emphasizes Parkman's character and his professional stature.

1293 Wade, Mason. FRANCIS PARKMAN, HEROIC HISTORIAN. New York: Viking, 1942. xiii, 466 p. Illus., bibliog. note.

A very readable life which makes excellent use of Parkman's letters and journals. He is seen not only as a great historian, but as the best writer among nineteenth-century American historians, including Henry Adams.

EDGAR ALLAN POE (1809-1849)

1294 Alexander, Jean, ed. AFFIDAVITS OF GENIUS: EDGAR ALLAN POE & THE FRENCH CRITICS, 1847-1924. National Universities Publications Series on Literary Criticism. Port Washington, N.Y., and London: Kennikat Press, 1971. 246 p.

Presents a wide range of French criticism in English translation from E.D. Forgues and Charles Baudelaire through Delacroix and Mallarmé to Remy de Gourmont and Paul Valery, preceded by a lengthy introduction by Alexander.

1295 Allen, Hervey. ISRAFEL: THE LIFE AND TIMES OF EDGAR ALLAN POE. 2 vols. New York: Doran, 1926. Vol. 1, xx, 408 p.; vol. 2, viii, 524 p. Illus.

The story of Poe as told by a popular novelist who disregarded the findings of all other biographers before him and depended totally on source material drawn from contemporary documents, letters, and reminiscences of those who knew the man. The result is highly readable, but not so reliable as A.H. Quinn's life.

1296 Allen, Michael. POE AND THE BRITISH MAGAZINE TRADITION. New York: Oxford University Press, 1969. x, 255 p.

Examines Poe's attitude toward British literary magazines during his career as a journalist from 1835 to 1849.

1297 Alterton, Margaret. ORIGINS OF POE'S CRITICAL THEORY. Humanistic Studies Series, vol. 2, no. 3. Iowa City: University of Iowa Studies, 1925. 191 p. Bibliog.

Attempts to show that Poe's ideas on critical theory had a long period of growth, that they began in the early days of his study of British periodicals, and that they passed through other influences--law, the drama and fine arts, philosophy, science--each of which added depth of meaning.

1298 Anderson, Carl L. POE IN NORTHLIGHT: THE SCANDINAVIAN RESPONSE TO HIS LIFE AND WORK. Durham, N.C.: Duke University Press, 1973. viii, 228 p.

Studies the interest in Poe in Denmark, Norway, and Sweden, with chapters on the impact of the American on Ola Hansson and on Strindberg. Contends that Scandinavian interest in Poe was rooted in his genius for rational analysis of the irrational, but that it did not produce the profound effects on Scandinavian literature that it did on French literature.

1299 Asselineau, Roger. EDGAR ALLAN POE. UMPAW, no. 89. Minneapolis: University of Minnesota Press, 1970. 48 p. Bibliog.

A somewhat stale account of Poe's life and character, with a brief resume of his philosophy of composition and of some of the major works.

1300 Benton, Richard P., ed. NEW APPROACHES TO POE: A SYMPOSIUM. Hartford, Conn.: Transcendental Books, 1970. 91 p.

Fourteen essays that do not altogether sustain the promise of the symposium's title.

1301 _____. POE AS LITERARY COSMOLOGER: STUDIES ON EUREKA, A SYMPOSIUM. Hartford, Conn.: Transcendental Books, 1975. 77 p.

Ten essays by Poe scholars on various aspects of EUREKA.

1302 Bittner, William. POE: A BIOGRAPHY. Boston and Toronto: Little, Brown, 1962. x, 306 p. Bibliog.

An attempt to present Poe's life from Poe's viewpoint.

1303 Bonaparte, Marie. THE LIFE AND WORKS OF EDGAR ALLAN POE: A PSYCHO-ANALYTIC INTERPRETATION. Translated from French by John Rodker. London: Imago Publishing Co., 1949. xi, 749 p. Illus., bibliog.

This highly controversial study of Poe and his works by a pupil of Freud, who wrote a laudatory foreword to it, attempts to show that Poe's works were conditioned by his personality, which derived from intense emotional fixations and painful infantile experiences.

1304 Bondurant, Agnes M. POE'S RICHMOND. Richmond: Garrett and Massie, 1942. vii, 264 p. Illus.

Tries to present the city as it was in Poe's time there, and to demonstrate Poe's connection with it.

1305 Booth, Bradford A., and Jones, Claude E., comps. A CONCORDANCE OF THE POETICAL WORKS OF EDGAR ALLAN POE. Baltimore: Johns Hopkins Press, 1941. Reprint. Gloucester, Mass.: Peter Smith, 1967. xiv, 211 p.

The text used is the excellent THE POEMS OF EDGAR ALLAN POE, edited by Killis Campbell.

1306 Buranelli, Vincent. EDGAR ALLAN POE. TUSAS, no. 4. 2d ed. Boston: Twayne, 1977. 166 p. Bibliog.

A critical study that employs biography to explain Poe's works and defend Poe against the severe judgments of adverse critics.

1307 Dameron, J. Lasley, and Cauthen, Irby B., Jr., comps. EDGAR ALLAN POE: A BIBLIOGRAPHY OF CRITICISM 1827-1967. Charlottesville: University Press of Virginia, 1974. xvi, 386 p.

Comprises a briefly annotated checklist of Poe criticism in English and an unannotated checklist of Poe criticism in foreign languages.

1308 Davidson, Edward H. POE: A CRITICAL STUDY. Cambridge, Mass.: Belknap Press of Harvard University Press, 1957. x, 296 p.

One of the best books of Poe criticism, this is a philosophic inquiry into the mind and writings of Poe, approached primarily through the critical and metaphysical theories of Coleridge. The poetry and the fiction are discussed in some detail, but the critical writing is not.

1309 Davis, Richard Beale, ed. CHIVERS' "LIFE OF POE". New York: Dutton, 1952. 127 p.

Prints the formerly unpublished biography by Poe's friend together with an explanatory introduction.

1310 Englekirk, John Eugene. EDGAR ALLAN POE IN HISPANIC LITERATURE. New York: Instituto de las Espanas en los Estados Unidos, 1934. 504 p. Bibliog.

Treats in detail Poe's influence in Spain and in Spanish America; also surveys biographical and critical studies of him in those regions.

1311 Evans, May Garrettson. MUSIC AND EDGAR ALLAN POE: A BIBLIOGRAPHICAL STUDY. Baltimore: Johns Hopkins Press, 1939. 97 p.

An essay on Poe's verse and tales set to music, with bibliographical lists of musical settings of Poe texts, of Poe texts in order of number of musical settings, of changes in original versions, and a summary of settings and composers.

1312 Fagin, N. Bryllion. THE HISTRIONIC MR. POE. Baltimore: Johns Hopkins Press, 1949. xiii, 289 p. Bibliog.

Presents the thesis that Poe was consciously an actor on the stage of his own life and that "many of his poems, stories, and essays are quite clearly theatrical performances."

1313 Fletcher, Richard M. THE STYLISTIC DEVELOPMENT OF EDGAR ALLAN POE. The Hague and Paris: Mouton, 1973. 192 p. Bibliog.

After a detailed examination of Poe's style in fiction and poetry, Fletcher concludes that "Poe is forever using a set, if subtly employed, body of tools in a seemingly endless variety of ways and with a generally consummate mastery of technique and style. Ultimately one sees through his tricks, since a virtuoso artist Poe is . . . and virtuosity is the hallmark . . . and the deficiency alike of his art."

1314 Grossman, Joan Delaney. EDGAR ALLAN POE IN RUSSIA: A STUDY IN LEGEND AND LITERARY INFLUENCE. Würzburg: Jal-Verlag, 1973. 245 p. Bibliog.

Fascinating study of Poe's influence on Russian literature from 1847 to the present.

1315 Harrison, James A. LIFE AND LETTERS OF EDGAR ALLAN POE. 2 vols. New York: Crowell, 1903. Vol. 1, xi, 430 p. Vol. 2, x, 478 p. Illus.

Volume 1 contains the life and volume 2 the letters. The biography is one of the earliest scholarly attempts, and the volume of letters is surpassed only by John Ward Ostrom's volumes published many decades later.

1316 Hoffman, Daniel. POE POE POE POE POE POE POE. Garden City, N.Y.: Doubleday, 1972. xvi, 339 p.

A highly subjective critique of Poe and his works, the theme being that "one side of Poe is devoted to the Enlightenment's faith in reason, while the doppelganger of this rationalist is incessantly undermining that faith with his recourses to the gothic machinery of horror and his appropriation of the explorer's tale, which he turns into the exploration of a psychic soulscape."

1317 Hyneman, Esther F., comp. EDGAR ALLAN POE: AN ANNOTATED BIBLIOGRAPHY OF BOOKS AND ARTICLES IN ENGLISH, 1827-1973. Boston: G.K. Hall, 1974. xv, 335 p.

An invaluable tool for the Poe scholar. The material is first organized into broad chronological categories: 1827-50, 1851-99, and 1900-1973. The twentieth-century section is further organized according to subject, except for the subsection that comprises a list of full-length books on Poe.

1318 Ingram, John H. EDGAR ALLAN POE: HIS LIFE, LETTERS, AND OPINIONS. 2 vols. London: J. Hagg, 1886. Bibliog. Reprint. 2 vols. in 1. New York: AMS Press, 1965. viii, 488 p.

One of the earliest serious efforts to redeem Poe's reputation following the attacks of Griswold and other members of the "literary establishment."

1319 Jacobs, Robert D. POE, JOURNALIST AND CRITIC. Baton Rouge: Louisiana State University Press, 1969. xii, 464 p.

Poe's career as book reviewer. As critic he is seen as having "something of the schizoid condition the characters of his fiction exhibited," not because of mental disorder but because "of the necessity of accommodation to two kinds of truth, the kind apprehended by the imagination and the kind necessary for conducting the business of life."

1320 Krutch, Joseph Wood. EDGAR ALLAN POE, A STUDY IN GENIUS. New York: Knopf, 1926. x, 244 p. Illus.

A Freudian interpretation of Poe. Krutch contends that "his whole life was a struggle . . . against a realization of the psychic impotence of his sexual nature . . . [and] a struggle also against a realization of the mental instability to which the first gave rise."

1321 Lauvrière, Emile. THE STRANGE LIFE AND STRANGE LOVES OF EDGAR ALLAN POE. English version by Edwin G. Rich. Philadelphia and London: Lippincott, 1935. 413 p. Illus.

A French biography that sees Poe as a madman, a pathological case induced by hereditary weakness.

1322 Lloyd, J.A.T. THE MURDER OF EDGAR ALLAN POE. London: Stanley Paul, 1928. 288 p. Illus.

An ingenious attempt to unravel the web of hostility to Poe which was, Lloyd holds, the creation of the diabolical Rufus Griswold, who was responsible, as he sees it, for the early deaths of the poet and Virginia, and for the subsequent murder of Poe's reputation.

1323 Miller, John Carl. BUILDING POE BIOGRAPHY. Baton Rouge and London: Louisiana State University Press, 1977. xix, 269 p. Illus., bibliog.

Working with the John Ingram collection of Poe materials in the University of Virginia Library, Miller studies the methods used by Poe's English biographer in constructing his famous biography of 1880. This volume, the first of a projected four-volume study, presents, with editorial commentary, the more important letters used by Ingram to build his biographies of Poe.

1324 _____, ed. POE'S HELEN REMEMBERS. Charlottesville: University Press of Virginia, 1979. xxviii, 528 p. Illus.

The second volume of Miller's study of Ingram's building of his Poe biographies (see no. 1318) consists of the publication with brief notes of Ingram's seventy-one letters and three postcards to Mrs. Sarah Helen Whitman and her ninety-four replies.

1325 Moss, Sidney P. POE'S LITERARY BATTLES: THE CRITIC IN THE CONTEXT OF HIS LITERARY MILIEU. Durham, N.C.: Duke University Press, 1963. xi, 266 p.

An extremely valuable book which presents in detail Poe's struggle with the literary establishment of New England and New York; Moss shows that Poe ranged himself on the side of the artist; that he called for support of worthy authors; that he urged a free, outspoken, and responsible criticism; and that he fought to provide an audience for deserving works. The price he paid, Moss says, "was enormous--poverty for the most part and defamation for the rest."

1326 Nakamura, Junichi. EDGAR ALLAN POE'S RELATIONS WITH NEW ENGLAND. Tokyo: Hokuseido Press, 1957. 176 p.

Superseded by Moss (see no. 1325).

1327 Parks, Edd Winfield. EDGAR ALLAN POE AS LITERARY CRITIC. Athens: University of Georgia Press, 1964. xii, 114 p.

Holds that Poe was the first important critic to develop and refine his critical theories through the media of book reviews and magazine articles.

1328 Phillips, Mary E. EDGAR ALLAN POE THE MAN. 2 vols. Chicago, Philadelphia, and Toronto: Winston, 1926. lii, 1,685 p. Illus.

Prior to A.H. Quinn's (see no. 1332), this is the most fact-packed biography. It is not, however, easy to read because of its labored organization and its flat prose style.

1329 Pollin, Burton R. POE, CREATOR OF WORDS. Baltimore: Enoch Pratt Free Library, the Edgar Allan Poe Society, and the Library of the University of Baltimore, 1974. 85 p.

Publication of a lecture on Poe as a coiner of words, together with a list of over nine hundred words either coined by him or ascribed to him as first instances in print.

1330 _____, ed. DICTIONARY OF NAMES & TITLES IN POE'S COLLECTED WORKS. New York: Da Capo Press, 1968. xl, 212 p.

Names, titles, and fictional characters in Poe's works are listed in computerized indexes as are titles of Poe's poems and tales, of his articles, and of his reviews.

1331 Pope-Hennessy, Una. EDGAR ALLAN POE, 1809-1849: A CRITICAL BIOGRAPHY. London: Macmillan, 1934. xii, 343 p. Bibliog.

Written by a well-known and scholarly British biographer, this is a useful work although the author repeats such dubious cliches as that Poe was outside the life of America. Believes that Poe's writing was largely shaped by his reading and that Coleridge was his first and most influential master.

1332 Quinn, Arthur Hobson. EDGAR ALLAN POE: A CRITICAL BIOGRAPHY. New York and London: Appleton-Century, 1942. Reprint. New York: Cooper Square Publishers, 1969. xvi, 804 p. Illus., bibliog.

This remains the definitive biography although the criticism of Poe's work tends to be more descriptive than evaluative.

1333 Quinn, Patrick F. THE FRENCH FACE OF EDGAR POE. Carbondale: Southern Illinois University Press, 1957. 310 p. Bibliog.

Tries to show that, by participating in the French critical response to Poe, it becomes possible to achieve a new and enlarged understanding of him as a writer.

1334 Rans, Geoffrey. EDGAR ALLAN POE. Writers and Critics Series. Edinburgh and London: Oliver and Boyd, 1965. 119 p. Bibliog.

A brief biographical sketch is followed by a chapter on EUREKA and Poe's literary criticism, another on the poetry, one on the fiction, and a final chapter on Poe's multifarious critics. A generally sound introduction.

1335 Ransome, Arthur. EDGAR ALLAN POE, A CRITICAL STUDY. London: Methuen, 1915. Reprint. New York: Haskell House, 1972. xiii, 237 p.

Sees Poe's thought as more stimulating than his art, and believes that throughout his life he sought but did not find a philosophy of beauty that should also be a philosophy of life. Traces Poe's thought by discussing his various activities or groups of ideas.

1336 Regan, Robert, ed. POE: A COLLECTION OF CRITICAL ESSAYS. Twentieth Century Views. Englewood Cliffs, N.J.: Prentice-Hall, 1967. 183 p. Bibliog.

Excellent and well-balanced collection.

1337 Robertson, John W., M.D., ed. BIBLIOGRAPHY OF THE WRITINGS OF EDGAR A. POE. San Francisco: Russian Hill Private Press, 1934. 227 p. Illus.

A basic bibliography, with much description, it is in four sections: (1) a chronological list of Poe's writings; (2) Poe publications in book form; (3) magazines and periodicals edited by Poe or contributed to by him; and (4) gift books and annuals contributed to by Poe.

1338 ______. COMMENTARY ON THE BIBLIOGRAPHY OF EDGAR A. POE. San Francisco: Russian Hill Press, 1934. 300 p. Index. Illus.

Companion volume to the preceding, it indicates the constant changes and emendations adopted by Poe for his definitive edition of 1845.

1339 Sinclair, David. EDGAR ALLAN POE. Totowa, N.J.: Rowman and Littlefield, 1977. 272 p. Illus., bibliog.

An opinionated attempt to understand Poe the man more than Poe the artist. Concludes that, rather than being mad, alcoholic or addicted to drugs, he was ill, weak, and often foolish.

1340 Stanard, Mary Newton. THE DREAMER: A ROMANTIC RENDERING OF THE LIFE-STORY OF EDGAR ALLAN POE. Rev. and enl. ed. Philadelphia and London: Lippincott, 1925. 382 p.

The revised and enlarged edition of the original 1909 limited edition. The author presents an idealized portrait of Poe in prose steeped in purple.

1341 Stovall, Floyd. EDGAR POE THE POET: ESSAYS NEW AND OLD ON THE MAN AND HIS WORK. Charlottesville: University Press of Virginia, 1969. vii, 273 p.

Reprints several previously published essays along with new ones on Poe's career, a new Poe discovery, and Poe's poetic theories.

1342 Thompson, G.R. POE'S FICTION: ROMANTIC IRONY IN THE GOTHIC TALES. Madison: University of Wisconsin Press, 1973. xv, 254 p.

Thompson contends that Poe was at once a Romantic idealist devoted to transcendental vision and also a satirist, "the preeminent American follower of the European 'Romantic Ironists' whose influence was once felt around the world in the larger Romantic Movement emanating from Germany."

1343 Ticknor, Caroline. POE'S HELEN. New York: Scribner's, 1916. x, 292 p. Illus.

A memoir of Sarah Helen Whitman that includes some of her previously unpublished letters and stresses her relations with Poe.

1344 Wagenknecht, Edward. EDGAR ALLAN POE: THE MAN BEHIND THE LEGEND. New York: Oxford University Press, 1963. 276 p. Bibliog.

Studies the character and personality of Poe with little attention to his work. Reviews the principal Poe scholarship on his life in the attempt to disentangle fact from fiction.

1345 Whitman, Sarah Helen. EDGAR POE AND HIS CRITICS. New York: Rudd and Carleton, 1860. 59 p. Reprint. Introduction and notes by Oral S. Coad. New Brunswick, N.J.: Rutgers University Press, 1949. 105 p.

A strong defense of Poe against the attacks of Griswold and others by the woman who had once been engaged to Poe.

1346 Winwar, Frances. THE HAUNTED PALACE: A LIFE OF EDGAR ALLAN POE. New York: Harper, 1959. viii, 408 p. Illus., bibliog.

An overdramatized biography that is as much fiction as fact.

1347 Woodberry, George E. THE LIFE OF EDGAR ALLAN POE, PERSONAL AND LITERARY, WITH HIS CHIEF CORRESPONDENCE WITH MEN OF LETTERS. 2 vols. Boston and New York: Houghton Mifflin, 1909. Vol. 1, xii, 383 p. Vol. 2, viii, 481 p. Illus.

For many years the standard biography, it has been superseded by the work of A.H. Quinn and other more modern scholars.

KATHERINE ANNE PORTER (1890-1980)

1348 Emmons, Winfred S. KATHERINE ANNE PORTER: THE REGIONAL STORIES. Southwest Writers Series, no. 6. Austin, Tex.: Steck-Vaughn, 1967. 43 p. Bibliog.

Deals with the stories that have a southern background.

1349 Hardy, John Edward. KATHERINE ANNE PORTER. Modern Literature Monographs. New York: Frederick Ungar, 1973. xi, 160 p. Bibliog.

A biographical essay prefaces discussion of Porter's stories.

1350 Hartley, Lodwick, and Core, George eds. KATHERINE ANNE PORTER: A CRITICAL SYMPOSIUM. Athens: University of Georgia Press, 1969. xxii, 242 p. Bibliog.

A series of essays which investigate the craft and genius of Porter. They range from Barbara Thompson's PARIS REVIEW interview and Glenway Wescott's personal reminiscences to Robert Penn Warren's "Irony with a Center." There are pieces by noted authors and critics like Eudora Welty, Cleanth Brooks, Robert B. Heilman, John W. Aldridge, and Ray B. West, Jr., as well as studies by Porter specialists like Hartley and Core.

1351 Hendrick, George. KATHERINE ANNE PORTER. TUSAS, no. 90. Boston: Twayne, 1965. 176 p. Bibliog.

After a biographical sketch, the book proceeds to a careful explication of all of Porter's stories and also comments on her nonfiction. She is viewed as a conscious artist in the mold of James and Joyce.

1352 Kiernan, Robert F., ed. KATHERINE ANNE PORTER AND CARSON McCULLERS: A REFERENCE GUIDE. Boston: G.K. Hall, 1976. xiv, 194 p.

An annotated chronological listing of works about Porter from 1924-74.

1353 Krishnamurthi, M.G. KATHERINE ANNE PORTER: A STUDY. Mysore, India: Rao and Raghavan, 1971. 215 p. Bibliog.

Considers the fiction through SHIP OF FOOLS and views the stories as complex structures in which Porter makes a sustained attempt to understand the stresses on modern man and the causes of his failures.

1354 Liberman, M.M. KATHERINE ANNE PORTER'S FICTION. Detroit: Wayne State University Press, 1971. 115 p.

Claims that critics who have disparaged Porter's fiction have not understood it and have failed to see that she is a "classical modern artist."

1355 Nance, William L. KATHERINE ANNE PORTER AND THE ART OF REJECTION. Chapel Hill: University of North Carolina Press, 1964. x, 258 p. Bibliog.

Sees Porter's work as unified by a "rejection" theme. Although not always explicit, it always governs the emotional effects of the stories.

1356 West, Ray B., Jr. KATHERINE ANNE PORTER. UMPAW, no. 28. Minneapolis: University of Minnesota Press, 1963. 48 p. Bibliog.

A very good introduction to Porter and her work. West believes that "there is probably no other writer of fiction in America who has maintained so consistently high a level."

WILLIAM SYDNEY PORTER (O. HENRY) (1862-1910)

1357 Clarkson, Paul S., ed. A BIBLIOGRAPHY OF WILLIAM SYDNEY PORTER (O. HENRY). Caldwell, Idaho: Caxton Printers, 1938. 161 p.

Contains a chronological list of works, contributions to books and periodicals, collective editions, dramatizations, periodical appearances, and biographical and critical sources.

1358 Current-Garcia, Eugene. O. HENRY (WILLIAM SYDNEY PORTER). TUSAS, no. 77. New York: Twayne, 1965. 192 p. Bibliog.

A scholarly and balanced treatment of the man and his work. The types, themes, and features of his stories which are related to the three major phases of his experience and to those experiences associated with his years in prison are analyzed, as are the structural and technical characteristics of his stories as a whole.

1359 Davis, Robert H., and Maurice, Arthur B. THE CALIPH OF BAGDAD: BEING ARABIAN NIGHTS FLASHES OF THE LIFE, LETTERS, AND WORK OF O. HENRY--WILLIAM SYDNEY PORTER. New York and London: Appleton, 1931. xi, 411 p. Illus.

An interesting memoir based on recollections of O. Henry by those who knew him, on letters, and on the Smith biography. Not a scholarly work.

1360 Ejxenbaum, B.M. O. HENRY AND THE THEORY OF THE SHORT STORY. Translated with notes and postscript by I.R. Titunik. Ann Arbor: University of Michigan Press, 1968. 41 p. Bibliog. note.

A Russian scholar's careful analysis of O. Henry's approach to short fiction. Written in 1925, the high-water mark of his popularity with Russian readers.

1361 Gallegly, Joseph. FROM ALAMO PLAZA TO JACK HARRIS'S SALOON: O. HENRY AND THE SOUTHWEST HE KNEW. The Hague and Paris: Mouton, 1970. 213 p. Illus., bibliog.

Valuable study of O. Henry's use in some of his stories of his experience of the Southwest.

1362 Langford, Gerald. ALIAS O. HENRY: A BIOGRAPHY OF WILLIAM SYDNEY PORTER. New York: Macmillan, 1957. xix, 294 p. Illus.

The fullest and most reliable biography yet to appear, it is the first to deal realistically with O. Henry's two marriages and the first to analyze adequately the evidence in the embezzlement trial.

1363 Long, E. Hudson. O. HENRY, AMERICAN REGIONALIST. Southern Writers Series, no. 3. Austin, Tex.: Steck-Vaughn, 1969. 43 p. Bibliog.

Deals with the writer's early life in Greensboro, North Carolina, and later in Texas, and with the time in prison and the life in New York.

1364 ______. O. HENRY: THE MAN AND HIS WORK. Philadelphia: University of Pennsylvania Press, 1949. xi, 158 p. Bibliog.

The best biography up to the time of its publication, but since superseded.

1365 O'Connor, Richard. O. HENRY: THE LEGENDARY LIFE OF WILLIAM S. PORTER. Garden City, N.Y.: Doubleday, 1970. x, 252 p. Illus. Bibliog.

A well-written and sympathetic biography which, however, adds nothing to Langford's (see no. 1362) earlier and more scholarly work.

1366 Smith, C. Alphonso. O. HENRY BIOGRAPHY. Garden City, N.Y.: Doubleday, Page, 1916. ix, 258 p. Illus.

The first full-length biography, it is still authoritative although authorized, but outdated in some respects.

EZRA POUND (1885-1972)

1367 Ackroyd, Peter. EZRA POUND AND HIS WORLD. New York: Scribner's, 1981. 127 p. Illus.

One of the best brief biographies, this also abounds in excellent photographs.

1368 Alexander, Michael. THE POETIC ACHIEVEMENT OF EZRA POUND. London and Boston: Faber and Faber, 1979. 247 p. Bibliog.

An introductory critical survey of Pound's verse as a whole, including the translations. This new reading of the poetry should be very useful to students.

1369 Amdur, Alice Steiner. THE POETRY OF EZRA POUND. Cambridge, Mass.: Harvard University Press, 1936. Reprint. New York: Russell and Russell, 1966. 106 p. Bibliog.

An early and sympathetic assessment of Pound's verses, although his thought is viewed as being quite limited.

1370 Baumann, Walter. THE ROSE IN THE STEEL DUST: AN EXAMINATION OF THE CANTOS OF EZRA POUND. Bern: Francke Verlag, 1967. 211 p. Bibliog.

The principal contribution here is the line for line interpretation of two of the key cantos, IV and LXXXII.

1371 Bornstein, George. THE POSTROMANTIC CONSCIOUSNESS OF EZRA POUND. Victoria, B.C.: University of Victoria, 1977. 84 p.

Argues that the achievement of Pound can be most profitably understood as a postromantic phenomenon, particularly in terms of the mental action of his poetry.

1372 Brooke-Rose, Christine. A ZBC OF EZRA POUND. London: Faber and Faber, 1971. x, 297 p. Bibliog.

Interesting insights to the poetry presented in the style of a classroom lecturer.

1373 Chace, William M. THE POLITICAL IDENTITIES OF EZRA POUND AND T.S. ELIOT. Stanford, Calif.: Stanford University Press, 1973. xviii, 238 p.

Both poets are seen as reactionaries, but also as radicals. Attempts to examine their politics, and concludes that they were "separated from society."

1374 Cornell, Julien. THE TRIAL OF EZRA POUND: A DOCUMENTED ACCOUNT OF THE TREASON CASE BY THE DEFENDANT'S LAWYER. New York: John Day, 1966. ix, 215 p.

The story of the trial, of Pound's confinement to St. Elizabeth's Hospital and his eventual release is told here, including the relevant documentary material from Cornell's files and public records, and the complete transcript of the trial.

1375 Davie, Donald. EZRA POUND: POET AS SCULPTOR. New York: Oxford University Press, 1964. viii, 261 p.

The emphasis in this valuable study is on Pound as translator.

1376 Davis, Earle. VISION FUGITIVE: EZRA POUND AND ECONOMICS. Lawrence and London: University Press of Kansas, 1968. xiv, 213 p.

Sees the economic theme as central to THE CANTOS and contends that they cannot be absorbed or judged without an attempt to understand the economic theories behind them. These theories are examined in some detail.

1377 DeNagy, N. Christoph. EZRA POUND'S POETICS AND LITERARY TRADITION. Bern, Switz.: Francke Verlag, 1966. 128 p. Bibliog.

The monograph is concerned primarily with the Conceptualized Poetics, and the method used is to elucidate them by means of comparisons with individual predecessors.

1378 _____. THE POETRY OF EZRA POUND: THE PRE-IMAGIST STAGE. Bern: Francke Verlag, 1960. 183 p. Bibliog.

Centers on Pound's relationship to the literary traditions with which he affiliated himself.

1379 Edwards, John Hamilton, and Vasse, William W., eds, with assistance from John J. Espey and Frederic Peachy. ANNOTATED INDEX TO THE CANTOS OF EZRA POUND, CANTOS I-LXXXIV. Berkeley and Los Angeles: University of California Press, 1957. xiv, 325 p.

Indispensable.

1380 Emery, Clark. IDEAS INTO ACTION: A STUDY OF POUND'S CANTOS. University of Miami Publications in English and American Literature, no. 111. Coral Gables, Fla.: University of Miami Press, 1958. xi, 196 p.

Approaches the poem indirectly, through Pound's prose that indicates the consistency of his ideas over the forty-year period that saw the growth of his major work. Then Emery shows the means employed to incorporate the ideas in the poem, and the means used to form the ninety-seven cantos written by the time of publication of this book into a unified whole.

1381 Espey, John. EZRA POUND'S MAUBERLY: A STUDY IN COMPOSITION. Berkeley, Los Angeles, and London: University of California Press, 1955. Paperback ed., 1974. 139 p.

Attempts to trace in detail the materials Pound reshaped, and to base a reading on the implications of his sources.

1382 Fraser, G.S. EZRA POUND. Edinburgh: Oliver and Boyd, 1960. Reprint. New York: Grove Press, 1961. 118 p. Bibliog.

A British introduction to the poet and his work, intended for students.

1383 Giovannini, G. EZRA POUND AND DANTE. Utrecht, Holland: Dekker and Van de Vegt, n.d. 18 p.

A lecture by a Fulbright scholar in American literature given at the University of Nijmegen in 1961. Pound's association with Dante is found to be more constant than that of any other poet writing in English.

1384 Goodwin, K.L. THE INFLUENCE OF EZRA POUND. London: Oxford University Press, 1966. xvi, 230 p.

Yeats and T.S. Eliot are seen as the major poets on whom Pound had considerable influence. Hart Crane, E.E. Cummings, William Carlos Williams, Marianne Moore, and Archibald MacLeish are others influenced in some measure. Part 1 studies Pound's interests and friends; part 2 applies a combined chronological and textual method to the influence on Yeats and Eliot; part 3 is a textual study of other poets influenced.

1385 Harmon, William. TIME IN EZRA POUND'S WORK. Chapel Hill: University of North Carolina Press, 1977. xiii, 165 p. Bibliog.

Argues that, "from his earliest criticism to his last peoms," an "emphatic insistence on the importance of time animates all of his work."

1386 Hesse, Eva, ed. NEW APPROACHES TO EZRA POUND: A CO-ORDINATED INVESTIGATION OF POUND'S POETRY AND IDEAS. Berkeley and Los Angeles: University of California Press, 1969. 406 p.

An excellent collection of interrelated essays by eminent scholars, with a helpful introduction by the editor.

1387 Homberger, Eric, ed. EZRA POUND: THE CRITICAL HERITAGE. Critical Heritage Series. London and Boston: Routledge and Kegan Paul, 1972. xix, 500 p. Bibliog.

Excellent collection of reviews and essays on Pound and his work, dating from 1904 through 1970.

1388 Hutchins, Patricia. EZRA POUND'S KENSINGTON: AN EXPLORATION 1885-1913. Chicago: Henry Regnery, 1965. 180 p. Illus.

A study of Pound's early life and of his period in London's Kensington section. Much of the material was gathered from interviews with Pound and those who knew him in the Kensington years.

1389 Kenner, Hugh. THE POETRY OF EZRA POUND. Norfolk, Conn.: New Directions, 1951. Reprint. Millwood, N.Y.: Kraus, 1974. 342 p.

A work of exposition intended to help the intelligent reader to understand Pound's poetry, the book performs well a valuable function. Divided into three parts: (1) "Ching Ming," (2) "Personae," and (3) "The Cantos."

1390 Knapp, James F. EZRA POUND. TUSAS, no. 348. Boston: Twayne, 1979. 177 p. Bibliog.

For the undergraduate student confronted with the complexities of Pound, this new book may well be the best general introduction available. Knapp believes that, when the poetry is seen whole, "it reveals a coherent intellectual quest, of central importance to our time."

1391 Makin, Peter. PROVENCE AND POUND. Berkeley, Los Angeles, and London: University of California Press, 1978. xiv, 428 p. Bibliog.

A very good presentation of Provencal culture and of Pound's interest in, and use of, it.

1392 Norman, Charles. THE CASE OF EZRA POUND. New York: Funk and Wagnalls, 1968. 209 p. Illus.

The treason trial and the events leading up to it.

1393 O'Connor, William Van. EZRA POUND. UMPAW, no. 26. Minneapolis: University of Minnesota Press, 1963. 48 p. Bibliog.

A generally unsympathetic view of Pound the man and of Pound the poet. O'Connor goes so far as to term him "mad."

1394 O'Connor, William Van, and Stone, Edward, eds. A CASEBOOK ON EZRA POUND. New York: Crowell, 1959. xi, 179 p. Bibliog.

A series of articles by various hands discussing aspects of Pound's career, the implications of his Bollinger Award, and the U.S. government's treatment of him. This is a text designed to suggest term papers for the college undergraduate.

1395 Olson, Charles. CHARLES OLSON & EZRA POUND: AN ENCOUNTER AT ST. ELIZABETHS. Edited by Catherine Seelye. New York: Grossman Publishers, 1975. xxvi, 147 p.

Olson's notes, published posthumously, on his visits to Pound while the latter was incarcerated in a Washington, D.C., hospital after having been declared insane by government alienists.

1396 Quinn, Sister Bernetta, O.S.F. EZRA POUND: AN INTRODUCTION TO THE POETRY. New York and London: Columbia University Press, 1972. xv, 191 p. Bibliog.

A sensitive and balanced judgment of the poetry from the early lyrics through the CANTOS, preceded by a compassionate analysis of Ezra Pound the man.

1397 Rosenthal, M.L. A PRIMER OF EZRA POUND. New York: Macmillan, 1960. 56 p. Bibliog.

Discusses the early poetry, Pound's basic thought frames, the Mauberley sequence, and the CANTOS. A good introduction to Pound, but all too short.

1398 Russell, Peter, ed. AN EXAMINATION OF EZRA POUND: A COLLECTION OF ESSAYS. London: Peter Nevill, 1950. Rev. ed. New York: Gordian Press, 1973. 307 p. Bibliog.

This revision contains nineteen essays, including ones by Eliot, Edith Sitwell, Allen Tate, Hemingway, Marshall McLuhan, and Wyndham Lewis.

1399 Sanders, Frederick K. JOHN ADAMS SPEAKING: POUND'S SOURCES FOR THE ADAMS CANTOS. Orono: University of Maine Press, 1975. iv, 530 p.

A persistent tracking down of the sources reveals Pound's astonishing scholarship and shows that the poetry is not difficult to understand if the reader is familiar with them. Sanders comments that these cantos "constitute the most elaborate tribute . . . that has ever been accorded John Adams by a major artist."

1400 Schneidau, Herbert N. EZRA POUND: THE IMAGE AND THE REAL. Baton Rouge: Louisiana State University Press, 1969. viii, 210 p.

A discussion of Pound's poetics treated in the context of two of the major efforts of his life: the imagist movement and his continual striving to reach "the poetry of reality." Within both efforts is seen "a reverence for the precisely presented particular."

1401 Sieburth, Richard. INSTIGATIONS: EZRA POUND AND REMY DE GOURMONT. Cambridge, Mass., and London: Harvard University Press, 1978. viii, 197 p.

Asserts that Gourmont provided for Pound, both by personal

example and by his works, "a range of instigations, a series of incitements to experiment and discovery."

1402 Stock, Noel. POET IN EXILE: EZRA POUND. New York: Barnes and Noble, 1964. xi, 273 p. Bibliog.

A British scholar aims to "cut through the tangle of opinions, favourable or unfavourable prejudices and the various irrelevancies stemming from Pound and others, which prevent many a reader of goodwill from getting at the best of his work." This aim is largely carried out.

1403 _____, ed. EZRA POUND: PERSPECTIVES. Chicago: Henry Regnery, 1965. xiii, 219 p. Illus.

A book of essays written in honor of Pound's eightieth birthday by a large group of distinguished poets and scholars, and introduced by the editor.

1404 Surette, Leon. A LIGHT FROM ELEUSIS: A STUDY OF EZRA POUND'S CANTOS. Oxford, Engl.: Clarendon Press, 1979. xiv, 306 p.

A "biography" of the poem, this study is a chronological examination of its development from 1915 to the 1960s, when the last fragments were composed. A most valuable work for the reader who is trying to understand a mind whose "restless galvanic energy . . . both fascinates and irritates."

1405 Watts, Harold H. EZRA POUND AND THE CANTOS. London: Routledge and Kegan Paul, 1952. 132 p.

Feels that the effect of reading THE CANTOS is that of freezing inertia. But it is a poem for which we should be grateful, for it is the record of a negative criticism of our society that we should not ignore, and of a real struggle with the interrelated artistic and political problems which our period presents.

1406 Woodward, Anthony. EZRA POUND AND THE PISAN CANTOS. London, Boston, and Henley, Engl.: Routledge and Kegan Paul, 1980. xi, 128 p. Bibliog.

An erudite and intelligent reading of what the author holds to be Pound's greatest achievement.

JOHN CROWE RANSOM (1888-1974)

1407 Buffington, Robert. THE EQUILIBRIST: A STUDY OF JOHN CROWE RANSOM'S POEMS, 1916-1963. Nashville: Vanderbilt University Press, 1967. ix, 160 p. Bibliog.

Offers close readings of a number of what Buffington considers to be the best poems. The first chapter is introductory, and the remaining three are titled "Poems About God," "The Accomplished Poet: CHILLS AND FEVER and TWO GENTLEMEN IN BONDS," and "The Later Poems."

1408 Magner, James E., Jr. JOHN CROWE RANSOM: CRITICAL PRINCIPLES AND PREOCCUPATIONS. The Hague and Paris: Mouton, 1971. 134 p. Bibliog.

Attempts to show "the philosophical roots of Ransom's critical principles, to show these principles as they come to grips with the poem itself and to show Ransom's critical estimate of some poets and critics of his own time." Magner exhibits a nicely balanced judgment and does well in pointing out where Ransom's critical strength and weakness lie.

1409 Parsons, Thornton H. JOHN CROWE RANSOM. TUSAS, no. 150. New York: Twayne, 1969. 170 p. Bibliog.

Claims to be the first book-length study of Ransom's poetry, but it is not. Buffington's book preceded it by two years and is not listed in the bibliography. No attention is paid to the prose, which Parsons feels has been adequately assessed elsewhere. He concludes that Ransom is "the most distinguished poet of his kind (the academic) that America has produced."

1410 Williams, Miller. THE POETRY OF JOHN CROWE RANSOM. New Brunswick, N.J.: Rutgers University Press, 1972. 125 p.

An enthusiastic essay in which Ransom is seen as "opposed to the science-oriented mentality of this century and an enemy of rational positivism." One must read his poems, Williams says, with the whole man in mind, "Southerner, Calvinist, scholar, poet and man, as the parts come together repeatedly in all of the poems."

1411 Young, Thomas Daniel. GENTLEMAN IN A DUSTCOAT: A BIOGRAPHY OF JOHN CROWE RANSOM. Baton Rouge: Louisiana State University Press, 1976. xx, 528 p. Illus.

The authorized biography, written with the assistance of Ransom, who met with the author daily for a month of four-hour sessions, and of his family and friends. Comparatively little space is devoted to discussion of the poems.

1412 _____. JOHN CROWE RANSOM. Southern Writers Series, no. 12. Austin, Tex.: Steck-Vaughn, 1971. 44 p. Bibliog.

The pamphlet offers an able introduction to the life and work.

1413 _____, ed. JOHN CROWE RANSOM: CRITICAL ESSAYS AND A BIBLIOGRAPHY. Baton Rouge: Louisiana State University Press, 1968. 290 p. Bibliog.

Sixteen essays by such well-known critics as Warren, Burgum, Delmore Schwartz, Cleanth Brooks, Jarrell, Matthiessen, Stauffer, Vivienne Koch, Louis Rubin, Jr., Graham Hough, and F.P. Jarvis. The bibliography of primary and secondary sources, by Mildred Brooks Peters, is excellent and exhaustive.

JAMES WHITCOMB RILEY (1849-1916)

1414 Carman, Bliss. JAMES WHITCOMB RILEY: AN ESSAY. Metuchen, N.J.: Charles F. Heartman, 1926. 86 p.

Written a year after Riley's death, the essay by his friend Carman says that Riley's "chief glory as a poet is that he, and he alone, enshrined in his work the very life of a large class, indeed of the most typical class, of Americans of that day." He was, says Carman, "a happy sentimentalist." Some letters from Riley are included.

1415 Crowder, Richard. THOSE INNOCENT YEARS: THE LEGACY AND INHERITANCE OF A HERO OF THE VICTORIAN ERA, JAMES WHITCOMB RILEY. Indianapolis and New York: Bobbs-Merrill, 1957. 288 p.

A straightforward and uncritical biography.

1416 Dickey, Marcus. THE YOUTH OF JAMES WHITCOMB RILEY: FORTUNE'S WAY WITH THE POET FROM INFANCY TO MANHOOD. Indianapolis: Bobbs-Merrill, 1919. vii, 425 p. Illus.

1417 _____. THE MATURITY OF JAMES WHITCOMB RILEY; FORTUNE'S WAY WITH THE POET IN THE PRIME OF LIFE AND AFTER. Indianapolis: Bobbs-Merrill, 1922. vii, 427 p. Illus.

These volumes, taken together, are the fullest biography of Riley. They are, however, uncritical and replete with sentimental adulation. The official biography.

1418 Mitchell, Minnie Belle. JAMES WHITCOMB RILEY AS I KNEW HIM: REAL INCIDENTS IN THE EARLY LIFE OF AMERICA'S BELOVED POET. Greenfield, Ind.: Old Swimmin' Hole Press, 1949. 224 p.

Reminiscences of a woman who knew Riley and his family in Greenfield.

1419 Nolan, Jeanette Covert; Gregory, Horace; and Farrell, James T. POET OF THE PEOPLE: AN EVALUATION OF JAMES WHITCOMB RILEY. Bloomington: Indiana University Press, 1951. 106 p.

Three essays originally presented as a symposium at Indiana University in connection with the 1949 centennial of Riley's birth: "Riley as a Children's Poet," "James Whitcomb Riley--A Victorian American," and "The Frontier and James Whitcomb Riley."

1420 Revell, Peter. JAMES WHITCOMB RILEY. TUSAS, no. 159. New York: Twayne, 1970. 174 p. Bibliog.

The aim in this pioneer critical examination of Riley's verse and prose is to discover "the sources from which Riley created his money-making poetic styles, and to analyze the ways in which the poet adapted his sources in order to achieve popular acceptance."

1421 Russo, Anthony J., and Russo, Dorothy R., comps. A BIBLIOGRAPHY OF JAMES WHITCOMB RILEY. Indianapolis: Indiana Historical Society, 1944. xxi, 351 p. Illus.

The fullest and most descriptive bibliography extant.

ANNA CORA MOWATT RITCHIE (1819-1870)

1422 Barnes, Eric Wöllencott. THE LADY OF FASHION: THE LIFE AND THE THEATRE OF ANNA CORA MOWATT. New York: Scribner's, 1954. xiv, 402 p. Illus.

The only full-length biography of the author of the popular comedy, FASHION, of 1845. The book is largely based on Mrs. Mowatt Ritchie's lengthy autobiography.

1423 Blesi, Marius. THE LIFE AND LETTERS OF ANNA CORA MOWATT. Charlottesville: University of Virginia Press, 1938.

The most exhaustive treatment of the literary career.

EDWIN ARLINGTON ROBINSON (1869-1935)

1424 Anderson, Wallace L. EDWIN ARLINGTON ROBINSON: A CRITICAL INTRODUCTION. Cambridge, Mass.: Harvard University Press, 1968. xvi, 175 p. Bibliog.

A thorough examination of Robinson's work in which Anderson concludes that "Robinson's most notable achievement lies in his perception and depiction of character." He wrote "with penetrating psychological insight." Of his contemporaries only Frost and Eliot are seen as of comparable stature.

1425 Barnard, Ellsworth. EDWIN ARLINGTON ROBINSON: A CRITICAL STUDY. New York: Macmillan, 1952. xiii, 318 p.

The emphasis is on the earlier work. Robinson's diction, characterization, poetic forms, and philosophical stance are analyzed, with attention also to his frequent obscurities.

1426 _____, ed. EDWIN ARLINGTON ROBINSON: CENTENARY ESSAYS. Athens: University of Georgia Press, 1969. xvii, 192 p. Bibliog.

A dozen essays by Robinson scholars.

1427 Bates, Esther Willard. EDWIN ARLINGTON ROBINSON AND HIS MANUSCRIPTS. Waterville, Maine: Colby College Library, 1944. 32 p.

One of Robinson's fellow colonists at Peterborough's MacDowell Colony who served him as a typist writes about his work habits and about the meticulous condition in which she received his hand-written manuscripts. He did not revise much.

1428 Beebe, Lucius, and Bulkley, Robert J., Jr., eds. A BIBLIOGRAPHY OF THE WRITINGS OF EDWIN ARLINGTON ROBINSON. Cambridge, Mass.: Dunster House Bookshop, 1931. 59 p.

Items through 1931 are described.

1429 Brown, Rollo Walter. NEXT DOOR TO A POET. New York and London: Appleton-Century, 1937. 98 p.

Interesting reminiscences of one who knew Robinson well at the MacDowell Colony.

1430 Cary, Richard, ed. APPRECIATION OF EDWIN ARLINGTON ROBINSON: 28 INTERPRETIVE ESSAYS. Waterville, Maine: Colby College Press, 1969. xiii, 356 p.

An excellent collection, by well-known scholars and critics.

1431 _____. EARLY RECEPTION OF EDWIN ARLINGTON ROBINSON: THE FIRST TWENTY YEARS. Waterville, Maine: Colby College Press, 1974. xi, 321 p.

Reprints reviews of THE TORRENT AND THE NIGHT BEFORE

(1896), THE CHILDREN OF THE NIGHT (1897), CAPTAIN CRAIG (1902), THE CHILDREN OF THE NIGHT (1905 edition), THE TOWN DOWN THE RIVER (1910), and CAPTAIN CRAIG (1915 edition).

1432 Coxe, Louis. EDWIN ARLINGTON ROBINSON. UMPAW, no. 17. Minneapolis: University of Minnesota Press, 1962. 48 p. Bibliog.

A general introduction in which the opinion is advanced that Robinson's reputation suffered because of the large number of mediocre poems he published in the second half of his career. Nevertheless Coxe concludes that "he is in the very front rank of American writers."

1433 ______. EDWIN ARLINGTON ROBINSON: THE LIFE OF POETRY. New York: Pegasus, 1969. 188 p. Bibliog.

Far superior to Coxe's UMPAW pamphlet (see no. 1432), this is a discerning study of Robinson's life and of his poetic achievement. He is seen as "an old-line Yankee" who would not play the game of materialism but insisted on being only what he was--a poet in a society that did not value poetry.

1434 Franchere, Hoyt C. EDWIN ARLINGTON ROBINSON. TUSAS, no. 137. New York: Twayne, 1968. 161 p. Bibliog.

An interesting and valuable study of the life and work.

1435 Fussell, Edwin S. EDWIN ARLINGTON ROBINSON: THE LITERARY BACKGROUND OF A TRADITIONAL POET. Berkeley and Los Angeles: University of California Press, 1954. Reprint. New York: Russell and Russell, 1970. x, 211 p.

A study of literary influences on Robinson. Two principal chapters treat American and British influences. European naturalism, classical literature, and the English Bible are considered more briefly. The final chapter deals with his use of tradition compared with Eliot's.

1436 Hagedorn, Hermann. EDWIN ARLINGTON ROBINSON: A BIOGRAPHY. New York: Macmillan, 1938. xii, 402 p.

The authorized biography, written by a friend of twenty-five years, it is based on Robinson's letters, the recollections of friends, and Hagedorn's own memories. Three fourths of the book treats the years before 1916.

1437 Hogan, Charles Beecher, ed. A BIBLIOGRAPHY OF EDWIN ARLINGTON ROBINSON. New Haven, Conn.: Yale University Press, 1936. 221 p.

The standard bibliography. Also includes biographical and critical material. Updated through 1970 by William White's EDWIN ARLINGTON ROBINSON: A SUPPLEMENTARY BIBLIOGRAPHY, (Serif Series of Bibliographies and Checklists, no. 17. Kent, Ohio: Kent State University Press, 1971. 168 p.).

1438 Joyner, Nancy Carol, ed. EDWIN ARLINGTON ROBINSON: A REFERENCE GUIDE. Boston: G.K. Hall, 1978. xv, 223 p.

Indispensable. This well-annotated guide includes a list of books by Robinson, a list of articles about him 1894-1915, selected from Cary's book, and writings about Robinson, 1916-76, the major part of the bibliography.

1439 Kaplan, Estelle. PHILOSOPHY IN THE POETRY OF EDWIN ARLINGTON ROBINSON. New York: Columbia University Press, 1940. Reprint. New York: AMS Press, 1966. 162 p. Bibliog.

The work is divided in two parts: (1) the sources of Robinson's idealism, discerned as Emersonian idealism as modified by Royce's interpretation of Schopenhauer; and (2) philosophical analysis of many of the longer poems.

1440 Lippincott, Lillian, comp. A BIBLIOGRAPHY OF THE WRITINGS AND CRITICISM OF EDWIN ARLINGTON ROBINSON. Boston: F.W. Faxon, 1937. 86 p.

In seven parts: (1) significant dates in Robinson's life; (2) the books of poetry, the individual poems, and the prose; (3) criticisms of Robinson, including books on him, parts of books about him, and theses on him; (4) periodical articles on him; (5) biographical articles; (6) photographs of him; and (7) sources of the bibliography.

1441 Murphy, Francis, ed. EDWIN ARLINGTON ROBINSON: A COLLECTION OF CRITICAL ESSAYS. Englewood Cliffs, N.J.: Prentice-Hall, 1970. 186 p. Bibliog.

An excellent collection of thirteen essays with a good introduction by the editor.

1442 Neff, Emery. EDWIN ARLINGTON ROBINSON. American Men of Letters. New York: Sloane Associates, 1948. xviii, 286 p.

A critical biography that contributes nothing new to the life story, but which does bring occasional fresh insights to the reading of the poems.

1443 Robinson, W.R. EDWIN ARLINGTON ROBINSON: A POETRY OF THE ACT. Cleveland, Ohio: Press of Western Reserve University, 1967. 183 p.

A close examination of Robinson's aesthetic, early, middle, and late, with emphasis on the later poetry. Robinson is viewed as an existentialist; "with the only certainty his immediate concrete experience, his life's value is his own doing." For Robinson this doing was, early and late, the creation of poetry.

1444 Smith, Chard Powers. WHERE THE LIGHT FALLS: A PORTRAIT OF EDWIN ARLINGTON ROBINSON. New York: Macmillan, 1965. xx, 420 p. Illus.

Partly memoir and partly literary criticism, the book is by a friend who first met Robinson in 1924 at the MacDowell Colony. The majority of the poems are seen as autobiographical. The impetus for most of them is said to be the loss of Emma, the only woman he ever loved, to his brother Herman.

1445 Van Doren, Mark. EDWIN ARLINGTON ROBINSON. New York: Literary Guild of America, n.d. Reprint. New York: Haskell House, 1975. 93 p. Bibliog.

A critical study in four chapters: (1) "The Man and His Career," (2) "The Shorter Poems," (3) "The Longer Poems," (4) "TRISTRAM." Written to coincide with the publication of TRISTRAM by the Literary guild.

1446 Winters, Yvor. EDWIN ARLINGTON ROBINSON. 1947. Rev. ed. New York: New Directions, 1971. 180 p. Bibliog.

A brilliant analysis of the poetry in which the virtues and vices are amply exhibited. Robinson is seen as the "last great American writer" of the tradition of Henry James, Edith Wharton, Motley and Parkman. He is marked as a poet with a deficiency--a lack of richness in language--but with an impersonal greatness of style seldom achieved in the twentieth century.

THEODORE ROETHKE (1908-1963)

1447 Blessing, Richard Allen. THEODORE ROETHKE'S DYNAMIC VISION. Bloomington and London: Indiana University Press, 1974. x, 240 p. Bibliog.

Attempts to discover by what techniques Roethke was able to present dynamism successfully in a work of art. Thus the book is a study of Roethke's style: of his use of rhythm, rhyme, diction, imagery, verb forms, pun, paradox, compression, repetition. Also it is a study of his treatment of time and space, and of his search for appropriately energetic subject matter.

1448 Lane, Gary, ed., and Dedekind, Roland, programmer. CONCORDANCE TO THE POEMS OF THEODORE ROETHKE. Metuchen, N.J.: Scarecrow Press, 1972. v, 484 p.

A computerized concordance correlated to THE COLLECTED POEMS OF THEODORE ROETHKE.

1449 Malkoff, Karl. THEODORE ROETHKE: AN INTRODUCTION TO THE POETRY. New York and London: Columbia University Press, 1966. viii, 245 p. Bibliog.

Attempts a comprehensive survey to place "each poem in the context of the poet's total development." Both form and content are considered, and there is denial of the contention of some critics, "especially British," that Roethke wrote low-grade nonsense verse that meant nothing.

1450 Mills, Ralph J., Jr. THEODORE ROETHKE. UMPAW, no. 30. Minneapolis: University of Minnesota Press, 1963. 47 p. Bibliog.

Uses poems from each of Roethke's books, as well as his biography, to show that Roethke's work cannot very well be classified. Argues that it focuses on the Self and its relation to the Creative Act.

1451 Moul, Keith R., ed. THEODORE ROETHKE'S CAREER: AN ANNOTATED BIBLIOGRAPHY. Boston: G.K. Hall, 1977. xxi, 254 p.

In two parts: (1) writings by Roethke, including books, essays and nonfiction, poetry, and poems and prose fragments from the notebooks; and (2) writings about Roethke, 1922-73, organized by year and annotated. Indispensable.

1452 Parini, Jay. THEODORE ROETHKE: AN AMERICAN ROMANTIC. Amherst: University of Massachusetts Press, 1979. xi, 203 p.

Tries to isolate major patterns in Roethke's work, to discover his mythos, and to relate his writing to the Romantic tradition. The central image in his work, and its subject from beginning to end, is perceived to be the autobiographical myth of the greenhouse Eden. Emerson and Whitman are seen as his "primary ancestors" and Stevens as a strong contemporary influence.

1453 Seager, Allan. THE GLASS HOUSE: THE LIFE OF THEODORE ROETHKE. New York: McGraw-Hill, 1968. 301 p.

Written after access to the Roethke manuscripts in the University of Washington collection, this is a full and well-written biography which provides a vivid picture of the poet. Unfortunately, there is no documentation nor are there any notes.

1454 Stein, Arnold, ed. THEODORE ROETHKE: ESSAYS ON THE POETRY. Seattle and London: University of Washington Press, 1965. xx, 199 p.

Excellent collection with a good introduction by Stein. Those included are Stephen Spender, Louis L. Martz, William Meredith, John Wain, W.D. Snodgrass, Frederick J. Hoffman, Ralph J. Mills, Jr., Denis Donoghue, and Roy Harvey Pearce.

1455 Sullivan, Rosemary. THEODORE ROETHKE: THE GARDEN MASTER. Seattle and London: University of Washington Press, 1975. xv, 220 p. Bibliog.

An extensive review of the work, bringing together the insights provided by Seager's biography (see no. 1453) and Roethke's own letters and notebooks. Among themes treated are Roethke's sensitivity to nature; his relationship to his dead father; his attempts to explore modes of consciousness that carried him to the edge of psychic disaster; his interest in mysticism; his debts to earlier poets; and the calm joyousness at the core of his work.

1456 Williams, Harry. "THE EDGE IS WHAT I HAVE": THEODORE ROETHKE AND AFTER. Lewisburg, Pa.: Bucknell University Press, 1977. 219 p. Bibliog.

Provides a critical assessment of the long poems and proceeds to a comparison of Roethke with five poets seen to be strongly influenced by him: James Wright, Robert Bly, James Dickey, Sylvia Plath, and Ted Hughes.

CARL SANDBURG (1878-1967)

1457 Allen, Gay Wilson. CARL SANDBURG. UMPAW, no. 101. Minneapolis: University of Minnesota Press, 1972. 48 p. Bibliog.

A good brief introduction to Sandburg's life and work. Allen, Whitman's best biographer, sees Sandburg as different from Whitman in their attitude toward death.

1458 Callahan, North. CARL SANDBURG: LINCOLN OF OUR TIME. New York: New York University Press, 1970. xv, 253 p.

A sound scholarly biography of the poet, with valuable critical appraisal of his work.

1459 Crowder, Richard. CARL SANDBURG. TUSAS, no. 47. New York: Twayne, 1964. 176 p. Bibliog.

The best introduction to Sandburg's life and work yet available. Includes a long chapter on his life of Lincoln.

1460 Golden, Harry. CARL SANDBURG. Cleveland, Ohio, and New York: World, 1961. 287 p. Illus.

An affectionate portrait by the author of ONLY IN AMERICA, who considered Sandburg his best friend.

1461 Hoffman, Daniel. "MOONLIGHT DRIES NO MITTENS": CARL SANDBURG RECONSIDERED. Washington, D.C.: Library of Congress, 1979. Unpaged.

A lecture delivered at the Library of Congress in 1978. Sandburg is seen as "a writer who prized direct experience over literary tradition, raw power over finesse." Hoffman contends that, at his best, Sandburg contrived his own form without being aware that it was form at all.

1462 Sandburg, Helga. A GREAT AND GLORIOUS ROMANCE: THE STORY OF CARL SANDBURG AND LILIAN STEICHEN. New York and London: Harcourt Brace Jovanovich, 1978. 319 p. Illus.

Not a formal biography, but the loving filial recollections of the almost sixty years together of the author's father and mother. Sandburg's brother-in-law was the famous photographer, Edward Steichen.

1463 Sutton, William A. CARL SANDBURG REMEMBERED. Metuchen, N.J., and London: Scarecrow Press, 1979. vii, 304 p.

In two parts. Part 1, entitled "The Perry Friendship," prints sections of a hitherto unpublished manuscript of Mrs. Lilla Perry, who had known Sandburg for years; part 2 contains seventy-six reminiscences of persons who had had personal experience of the poet.

1464 Van Doren, Mark. CARL SANDBURG. Washington, D.C.: Library of Congress, 1969. Unpaged. Bibliog.

A good critical estimate with the most extensive bibliography of Sandburg to date.

See also no. 1003.

WILLIAM SAROYAN (1908-1981)

1465 Floan, Howard R. WILLIAM SAROYAN. TUSAS, no. 100. New York: Twayne, 1966. 176 p. Bibliog.

The first book-length study of Saroyan and his work, the early writing is treated in most detail. Saroyan is seen as a writer whose "inherited attitudes and tastes have placed him outside the mainstream of American culture," which has Anglo-Saxon origins. Instead of being a literature of denial or of anger, his is one of affirmation.

WILLIAM GILMORE SIMMS (1806-1870)

1466 Kibler, James E., Jr. PSEUDONYMOUS PUBLICATIONS OF WILLIAM GILMORE SIMMS. Athens: University of Georgia Press, 1976. ix, 102 p.

Lists an amazing number of items published under pseudonyms, particularly poetry. In his introduction, Kibler states his belief that the chief reason for Simms's practice is that the bulk of this work appeared in his own magazines and newspapers.

1467 _____, comp. THE POETRY OF WILLIAM GILMORE SIMMS: AN INTRODUCTION AND BIBLIOGRAPHY. Spartanburg, S.C.: Reprint Co., 1979. xiv, 478 p. Illus.

A lengthy introduction to Simms the poet is followed by a descriptive bibliography divided into three parts: "Proved Poems," "Questionable Attributions," and "Sources Checked."

1468 Parks, Edd Winfield. WILLIAM GILMORE SIMMS AS LITERARY CRITIC. University of Georgia Monographs, no. 7. Athens: University of Georgia Press, 1961. viii, 152 p.

Chapters on Simms's criticism of novels and novelists, of

poetry and poets, of dramas and dramatists, of nationalism and sectionalism. In sum, Simms is seen as a good but not great critic, who "tried always to be genial but just."

1469 Salley, A.S., ed. CATALOGUE OF THE SALLEY COLLECTION OF THE WORKS OF WILLIAM GILMORE SIMMS. Columbia, S.C.: Privately printed, 1943. 121 p.

Although incomplete, this catalog is the fullest bibliography of Simms's work in print.

UPTON SINCLAIR (1878-1968)

1470 Bloodworth, William A., Jr. UPTON SINCLAIR. TUSAS, no. 294. Boston: Twayne, 1977. 178 p. Bibliog.

An excellent introduction to the life and times, with considerable attention to Sinclair's best works of fiction: THE JUNGLE, KING COAL, OIL! and BOSTON. He is seen as "an energetic, persistent, and generally articulate voice of pre-World War I reform," a life-long propagandist for social justice.

1471 Dell, Floyd. UPTON SINCLAIR: A STUDY IN SOCIAL PROTEST. New York: Doran, 1927. Reprint. New York: AMS Press, 1970. 194 p. Bibliog.

A balanced and generally sympathetic view of Sinclair and his work. He is seen in the mid-twenties as "the fearless and robust transcriber of the tragi-comic welter which is contemporary America."

1472 Gottesman, Ronald, and Silet, Charles L.P., eds. THE LITERARY MANUSCRIPTS OF UPTON SINCLAIR. Columbus: Ohio State University Press, 1972. xxiii, 470 p.

Detailed description of the extant manuscripts.

1473 Gottesman, Ronald, ed. UPTON SINCLAIR: AN ANNOTATED CHECKLIST. Serif Series of Bibliographies and Checklists, no. 24. Kent, Ohio: Kent State University Press, 1973. xx, 544 p.

Indispensable for Sinclair scholarship. In four parts: (1) "Sinclair in English," (2) "Sinclair in Translation and Foreign Editions," (3) "Selected Publications about Sinclair," and (4) "Supplementary Material."

1474 Harris, Leon. UPTON SINCLAIR: AMERICAN REBEL. New York: Crowell, 1975. x, 435 p. Illus., bibliog. notes.

The only full-scale biography, it is an enthusiastic rendition of a life devoted to social justice and reform. Holds that, from 1905 to 1945, Sinclair was America's most important writer, but by the time of his death in 1968, he was again virtually unknown.

1475 Yoder, Jon A. UPTON SINCLAIR. Modern Literature Monographs. New York: Frederick Ungar, 1975. ix, 134 p. Bibliog.

Sees two reasons for the meagre reputation of Sinclair, whom Yoder regards as "one of America's most significant writers": his socialism and the fact that his writing does not meet current academic literary standards. Unfortunately, because of the series' format, the book is much briefer than it deserves to be.

GERTRUDE STEIN (1874-1946)

1476 Bridgman, Richard. GERTRUDE STEIN IN PIECES. New York: Oxford University Press, 1970. xvi, 411 p. Bibliog.

An impressive descriptive reading of Stein's work, this is perhaps the most important and indispensable volume of criticism on Stein to be published to date.

1477 Brinnin, John Malcolm. THE THIRD ROSE: GERTRUDE STEIN AND HER WORLD. Boston: Little, Brown, 1959. xviii, 427 p. Reprint. Gloucester, Mass.: P. Smith, 1968. Illus., bibliog.

The fullest and most readable of the early biographies. Some errors in fact exist, but the life story is well told.

1478 Burnett, Avis. GERTRUDE STEIN. New York: Atheneum, 1972. viii, 187 p. Illus., bibliog.

The biographical facts are enhanced by a series of dialogues written with "poetic license."

1479 Copeland, Carolyn Faunce. LANGUAGE & TIME & GERTRUDE STEIN. Iowa City: University of Iowa Press, 1975. 182 p. Bibliog.

In three parts: "The Early Years (1903-1912)," "The Middle Years (1913-1932)," and "The Later Years (1932-1944)." The aim is to reveal Stein as an important experimental writer "who deserves better than she has received from critical analysis."

1480 Hobhouse, Janet. EVERYBODY WHO WAS ANYBODY: A BIOGRAPHY OF GERTRUDE STEIN. New York: Putnam, 1975. xii, 244 p. Illus., bibliog.

Adds nothing important, but does treat Stein's lesbianism more explicitly than does any other biography.

1481 Hoffman, Frederick J. GERTRUDE STEIN. UMPAW, no. 10. Minneapolis: University of Minnesota Press, 1961. 48 p. Bibliog.

Holds that Stein's major contribution to twentieth-century literature was methodological. She "was engaged in an analysis of the mind in its precise function of apprehending and experiencing objects." The strict limitations of space in this series hamper Hoffman in dealing with the vast quantity of Stein's work.

1482 _____. THE DEVELOPMENT OF ABSTRACTIONISM IN THE WRITINGS OF GERTRUDE STEIN. Philadelphia: University of Pennsylvania Press, 1965. 229 p.

A detailed account of the progressive development of Stein's style.

1483 Hoffman, Michael J. GERTRUDE STEIN. TUSAS, no. 268. Boston: Twayne, and London: George Prior, 1976. 159 p. Bibliog.

Examines a considerable part of the huge corpus of Stein's work and concludes that she "is a major writer historically and intrinsically and that she has written some of the finest and most complex books of our time."

1484 Liston, Maureen R., ed. GERTRUDE STEIN: AN ANNOTATED CRITICAL BIBLIOGRAPHY. Serif Series of Bibliographies and Checklists, no. 35. Kent, Ohio: Kent State University Press, 1979. xiii, 230 p.

Indispensable. In two main parts: (1) bibliographical and biographical material and (2) analytical and critical material, including critical books and typescripts, dissertations, critical articles, chapters of books, introductions to Stein's works, and reviews.

1485 Mellow, James R. CHARMED CIRCLE: GERTRUDE STEIN AND COMPANY. New York: Praeger, 1974. 528 p. Bibliog.

Without doubt the definitive biography. The most complete, accurate, and scholarly of all the accounts of Stein's life, it is also an extremely readable book.

1486 Miller, Rosalind S. GERTRUDE STEIN: FORM AND INTELLIGIBILITY. New York: Exposition Press, 1949. 162 p. Bibliog.

An early attempt to assist the "average reader" to understand Stein's work. Although helpful, it is quite limited. In a second section the Radcliffe Manuscripts, Stein's student themes, are printed for the first time.

1487 Neuman, S.C. GERTRUDE STEIN: AUTOBIOGRAPHY AND THE PROBLEM OF NARRATION. English Literary Studies. Victoria, B.C.: University of Victoria, 1979. 88 p.

Detailed examination of THE AUTOBIOGRAPHY OF ALICE B. TOKLAS, EVERYBODY'S AUTOBIOGRAPHY, PARIS, FRANCE, and WARS I HAVE SEEN demonstrates that Stein "uses autobiography to provide a particular construct of the self that is certainly not 'true' in an absolute sense" but which is impersonal and which arises from a theory of literature which she had advanced in early works.

1488 Reid, Benjamin L. ART BY SUBTRACTION; A DISSENTING OPINION OF GERTRUDE STEIN. Norman: University of Oklahoma Press, 1958. xiii, 224 p. Bibliog.

The first full-scale attempt to present an adverse judgment on Stein's work. Unfortunately, Reid indulges at times in the tactics of a prosecuting attorney.

1489 Steiner, Wendy. EXACT RESEMBLANCE TO EXACT RESEMBLANCE: THE LITERARY PORTRAITURE OF GERTRUDE STEIN. Yale Studies in English, no. 189. New Haven, Conn.: Yale University Press, 1978. x, 225 p. Bibliog.

1490 Steward, Samuel M., ed. DEAR SAMMY: LETTERS FROM GERTRUDE STEIN AND ALICE B. TOKLAS, EDITED WITH A MEMOIR. Boston: Houghton Mifflin, 1977. x, 260 p. Illus.

The memoir, based on the author's meetings with Stein and Toklas, occupies about half the space of the book and presents a vivid picture of both women.

1491 Stewart, Allegra. GERTRUDE STEIN AND THE PRESENT. Cambridge, Mass.: Harvard University Press, 1967. ix, 223 p.

Focuses on the experience of contemplation and creative dissociation that determined, the author believes, not only Stein's metaphysical outlook but also her poetic practices and purposes. There is extended Jungian analysis of Stein's opera libretto, DOCTOR FAUSTUS LIGHTS THE LIGHTS.

1492 Sutherland, Donald. GERTRUDE STEIN: A BIOGRAPHY OF HER WORK. New Haven, Conn.: Yale University Press, 1951. 218 p.

The first book-length study of Stein's work, this is a point of departure for later studies. Sutherland is, however, far from objective in his evaluations, being almost rabidly an advocate of Stein.

1493 Toklas, Alice B. WHAT IS REMEMBERED. New York, Chicago, and San Francisco: Holt, Rinehart and Winston, 1963. 186 p.

Stein, as her long-time companion remembers her.

1494 Wilson, Robert A.J., comp. GERTRUDE STEIN: A BIBLIOGRAPHY. Phoenix Bibliographies, no. 7. New York: Phoenix Bookshop, 1974. xii, 227 p.

The most complete bibliography.

JOHN STEINBECK (1902-1968)

1495 Astro, Richard. JOHN STEINBECK AND EDWARD F. RICKETTS: THE SHAPING OF A NOVELIST. Minneapolis: University of Minnesota Press, 1973. xii, 259 p.

Study of the life, work, and ideas of Steinbeck's closest personal and intellectual companion for almost two decades. Their relationship is discussed in detail, and Ricketts is seen as the source of Steinbeck's personae in six novels: IN DUBIOUS BATTLE, THE GRAPES OF WRATH, THE MOON IS DOWN, CANNERY ROW, BURNING BRIGHT, and SWEET THURSDAY.

1496 Astro, Richard, and Hayashi, Tetsumaro, eds. STEINBECK: THE MAN AND HIS WORK. Corvallis: Oregon State University Press, 1971. ix, 183 p.

Proceedings of the 1970 Steinbeck Conference. Ten papers on various themes.

1497 Davis, Robert Murray, ed. STEINBECK: A COLLECTION OF CRITICAL ESSAYS. Twentieth Century Views. Englewood Cliffs, N.J.: Prentice-Hall, 1972. 183 p. Bibliog.

Excellent collection of twelve essays with a good introduction by Davis.

1498 Fensch, Thomas. STEINBECK AND COVICI: THE STORY OF A FRIENDSHIP. Middlebury, Vt.: Paul S. Eriksson, 1979. 248 p. Bibliog.

Traces the long friendship between Steinbeck and his editor largely through their correspondence. Unfortunately Fensch commits blunders that shake the reader's confidence, as in his repeated references to the poet Edward [sic] Arlington Robinson.

1499 Fontenrose, Joseph. JOHN STEINBECK: AN INTRODUCTION AND

INTERPRETATION. New York: Barnes and Noble, 1964. ix, 150 p. Illus., bibliog.

Useful for undergraduates.

1500 French, Warren. JOHN STEINBECK. TUSAS, no. 2. 2d ed. Rev. Boston: Twayne, 1975. 189 p. Bibliog.

A complete revision of the 1961 edition, done from a new point of view. Steinbeck's writing is now seen as illustrating "the drama of consciousness." The dividing line between the concepts of human destiny displayed in the earlier work and those observed in the later is viewed as 1945.

1501 ______, ed. A COMPANION TO THE GRAPES OF WRATH. New York: Viking, 1963. xi, 243 p. Bibliog.

Reprints essays on the background, the reception, and the reputation of Steinbeck's best-known novel. Useful for undergraduate papers.

1502 Goldstone, Adrian H., and Payne, John R., eds. JOHN STEINBECK: A BIBLIOGRAPHICAL CATALOGUE OF THE ADRIAN H. GOLDSTONE COLLECTION. Austin: University of Texas Humanities Research Center, 1974. 240 p.

Bibliography based on one of the world's most complete collections of Steinbeck materials. Sections on books, contributions to books, contributions to periodicals, translations, stage, screen, television and radio, and books about Steinbeck.

1503 Gray, James. JOHN STEINBECK. UMPAW, no. 94. Minneapolis: University of Minnesota Press, 1971. 48 p. Bibliog.

A very good brief introduction to Steinbeck's work.

1504 Hayashi, Tetsumaro, ed. JOHN STEINBECK: A DICTIONARY OF HIS FICTIONAL CHARACTERS. Metuchen, N.J.: Scarecrow Press, 1976. ix, 222 p.

All of Steinbeck's characters are listed alphabetically and are identified in some detail. Prefaced by a biographical portrait written by Richard Astro.

1505 ______. A NEW STEINBECK BIBLIOGRAPHY, 1929-1971. Metuchen, N.J.: Scarecrow Press, 1973. 225 p.

Supersedes Hayashi's earlier JOHN STEINBECK: A CONCISE BIBLIOGRAPHY (1930-1965) (Metuchen, N.J.: Scarecrow Press, 1967). Quite complete, it is in two parts:

(1) primary material, with 379 items; and (2) secondary material, with 1,805 items. Unannotated.

1506 _____. STEINBECK'S LITERARY DIMENSION: A GUIDE TO COMPARATIVE STUDIES. Metuchen, N.J.: Scarecrow Press, 1973. viii, 191 p. Bibliog.

In two parts: (1) comparative essays by Steinbeck scholars comparing him with the following: Dickens, Faulkner, Hemingway, Kazantzakis, D.H. Lawrence, Daniel Mainwaring, Milton, Salinger, Adlai Stevenson, Robert Penn Warren, and Zola; and (2) criticism and bibliography.

1507 _____. A STUDY GUIDE TO STEINBECK: A HANDBOOK TO HIS MAJOR WORKS. Metuchen, N.J.: Scarecrow Press, 1974. xvi, 316 p.

For each work a Steinbeck scholar provides (1) background of the work, (2) plot synopsis, (3) critical explication, and (4) apparatus for research papers. Designed for undergraduates.

1508 Jain, Sunita. JOHN STEINBECK'S CONCEPT OF MAN: A CRITICAL STUDY OF HIS NOVELS. New Delhi: New Statesman Publishing Co., 1979. viii, 102 p. Bibliog.

The concept that man is at the same time an individual and a group animal informs the meaning and controls the artistic material of his novels throughout his career. All of the sixteen novels are analyzed according to this thesis.

1509 Kallapur, S.T. JOHN STEINBECK. Dharwad, India: Karnatak University, 1978. 182 p.

Attempts to make the case for considerable influence of Hindu thought in Steinbeck's work. Contends that a study of his novels provides substantial internal evidence of his knowledge of Indian books.

1510 Kiernan, Thomas. THE INTRICATE MUSIC: A BIOGRAPHY OF JOHN STEINBECK. Boston and Toronto: Little, Brown, 1979. xvii, 331 p.

The first full-scale biography to be published. It is clearly written and easy to read, and graphically demonstrates the vital importance of Steinbeck's friendship with Ed Ricketts. Kiernan is enthusiastic about Steinbeck as a writer but has reservations about him as a man.

1511 Lisca, Peter. THE WIDE WORLD OF JOHN STEINBECK. New Brunswick, N.J.: Rutgers University Press, 1958. 326 p. Bibliog.

Carefully analyzes the fiction through PIPPIN. Perceives a decline in Steinbeck's artistry after World War II, partly attributable to the death of his close friend, Ed Ricketts.

1512 McCarthy, Paul. JOHN STEINBECK. Modern Literature Monographs. New York: Frederick Ungar, 1980. xi, 163 p. Bibliog.

A very good review of Steinbeck's life and work, which concludes that his "strongest convictions and passions appear in his fundamental belief in humanity, in his expectation that man will endure, and that the creative forces of the human spirit will prevail."

1513 Marks, Lester Jay. THEMATIC DESIGN IN THE NOVELS OF JOHN STEINBECK. The Hague and Paris: Mouton, 1969. 144 p. Bibliog.

Contends that Steinbeck's ideas may be seen in three thematic patterns which recur throughout his novels: that man is a religious creature; that man is a "group animal" having an individual will and intelligence; and that man lives without knowledge of the cause of his existence, but is spurred on by the mystery of life to search for human values.

1514 Moore, Harry Thornton. THE NOVELS OF JOHN STEINBECK: A FIRST CRITICAL STUDY. Chicago: Normandie House, 1939. 102 p. 2d ed. with a Contemporary Epilogue. Port Washington, N.Y.: Kennikat Press, 1968. 106 p.

Treats the novels through THE GRAPES OF WRATH. Prefers the lyrical tone of the earlier work to the more sociological tone that Steinbeck seemed to be adopting.

1515 O'Connor, Richard. JOHN STEINBECK. American Writers Series. New York: McGraw-Hill, 1970. 128 p. Bibliog.

A relatively juvenile biography that adds nothing new.

1516 Prabhakar, S.S. JOHN STEINBECK: A STUDY (MOTIFS OF DREAM AND DISILLUSIONMENT). Hyderabad, India: Academic Publishers, 1976. vi, 216 p. Bibliog.

The thesis of this clumsily written book is that Steinbeck was a dreamer, but of an authentic American variety--"a dreamer of practical idealism."

1517 Pratt, John Clark. JOHN STEINBECK: A CRITICAL ESSAY. Contemporary Writers in Christian Perspective Series. Grand Rapids, Mich.: William B. Eerdmans, 1970. 48 p. Bibliog.

Attempts to synthesize Steinbeck's view of Christianity.

1518 Satyanarayana, M.R. JOHN STEINBECK: A STUDY IN THE THEME OF COMPASSION. Hyderabad, India: Osmania University, 1977. ii, 152 p., v. Bibliog.

An Indian scholar's view of Steinbeck as believing in compassion and love in spite of a lack of faith in God.

1519 Steinbeck, Elaine, and Wallsten, Robert, eds. STEINBECK, A LIFE IN LETTERS. New York: Viking, 1975. xv, 906 p.

Edited by Steinbeck's widow and a friend, this is a carefully selected and edited collection of Steinbeck's letters, intended to present the more favorable side of the writer. The letters chosen are accompanied by minimal commentary.

1520 Watt, F.W. STEINBECK. Edinburgh: Oliver and Boyd, 1962. New York: Grove Press, 1962. 117 p. Bibliog.

A British introduction to the writer and his work which adopts a balanced and sophisticated stance.

WALLACE STEVENS (1879-1955)

1521 Baird, James. THE DOME AND THE ROCK: STRUCTURE IN THE POETRY OF WALLACE STEVENS. Baltimore: Johns Hopkins University Press, 1968. xxxi, 334 p.

An erudite study of the entire range of Stevens's poetry which, Baird contends, adds up to the Grand Poem. "The separate poems of Stevens are all parts of the total poem, 'proofs' of one another and of the whole."

1522 Beckett, Lucy. WALLACE STEVENS. London: Cambridge University Press, 1974. 222 p. Bibliog.

A competent review of the full range of the poetry.

1523 Benamou, Michel. WALLACE STEVENS AND THE SYMBOLIST IMAGINATION. Princeton, N.J.: Princeton University Press, 1972. xxvii, 154 p.

Suggests affinities between Stevens and Jules Laforgue, Baudelaire, and Mallarmé as well as the influence of painting on his poetry.

1524 Blessing, Richard Allen. WALLACE STEVENS' "'WHOLE HARMONIUM.'" Syracuse, N.Y.: Syracuse University Press, 1970. xi, 185 p. Bibliog.

Attempts to illustrate the unity of THE COLLECTED POEMS, which is seen as "a single, unified, grand poem."

1525 Bloom, Harold. WALLACE STEVENS: THE POEMS OF OUR CLIMATE. Ithaca, N.Y., and London: Cornell University Press, 1977. viii, 413 p.

A full commentary on nearly all of Stevens's poetic canon. Emphasis is on the long poems and sequences and their complex relations to one another and to the work of Wordsworth, Shelley, Keats, Emerson, and "most crucially," Whitman. One of the most ambitious attempts to explicate Stevens.

1526 Borroff, Marie, ed. WALLACE STEVENS: A COLLECTION OF CRITICAL ESSAYS. Twentieth Century Views. Englewood Cliffs, N.J.: Prentice-Hall, 1963. 181 p. Bibliog.

A useful collection of essays by Stevens scholars.

1527 Brown, Ashley, and Haller, Robert S., eds. THE ACHIEVEMENT OF WALLACE STEVENS. Philadelphia and New York: Lippincott, 1962. 287 p. Bibliog.

Rewarding collection of essays by well-known writers and scholars.

1528 Brown, Merle E. WALLACE STEVENS: THE POEM AS ACT. Detroit: Wayne State University Press, 1970. 219 p.

Expressing dissatisfaction with the New Criticism, Brown contends that all of Stevens's genuine poems may be called poems--in Stevens's own words--"of the mind in the act of finding what will suffice." Many of Brown's favorite poems are explicated.

1529 Burney, William. WALLACE STEVENS. TUSAS, no. 127. Boston: Twayne, 1968. 190 p. Bibliog.

Written for undergraduates, this is, as Burney admits, largely an exercise in paraphrase. Chapter 1 treats the plays and HARMONIUM, (2) the middle period, (3) TRANSPORT TO SUMMER, (4) THE AURORAS OF AUTUMN and THE ROCK, and (5) prose and uncollected poems.

1530 Buttel, Robert. WALLACE STEVENS, THE MAKING OF "HARMONIUM." Princeton, N.J.: Princeton University Press, 1967. xv, 269 p.

A study of Stevens's undergraduate pieces and the manuscripts leading to and making up the poems of HARMONIUM reveals the development of a major poet.

1531 Doggett, Frank. STEVENS' POETRY OF THOUGHT. Baltimore: Johns Hopkins University Press, 1966. xiii, 223 p.

Major emphasis is on the nature and function of idea in Stevens's poetry. The purpose is illumination of the poems. Many helpful readings are provided.

1532 ______. WALLACE STEVENS: THE MAKING OF THE POEM. Baltimore and London: Johns Hopkins University Press, 1980. 160 p.

Through a study of Stevens's theories and memories, and through analysis of elements of his artistry and his disclosures of his creative intuitions, this recent book attempts a fresh view of the poetry. Stevens's explanations of them are used here in connection with the explication of many of the poems.

1533 Doggett, Frank, and Buttel, Robert, eds. WALLACE STEVENS: A CELEBRATION. Princeton, N.J.: Princeton University Press, 1980. xx, 361 p.

Published to commemorate the centennial of Stevens's birth, this is a collection of nineteen pieces, three by the poet himself, others by leading Stevens scholars.

1534 Enck, John J. WALLACE STEVENS: IMAGES AND JUDGMENTS. Carbondale: Southern Illinois University Press, 1964. xii, 258 p.

A study of the Stevens canon that concludes that his special vocabulary and structure comprise his basic traits and that indifference to academic references removes him from the more celebrated imagists. His knowledge, however, is seen as wide, if eclectic.

1535 Fuchs, Daniel. THE COMIC SPIRIT OF WALLACE STEVENS. Durham, N.C.: Duke University Press, 1963. vii, 201 p. Bibliog.

Contends that the comic spirit is central and, without a sense of it, there can be no true understanding of Stevens. The study is interpretive and proceeds thematically.

1536 Hines, Thomas J. THE LATER POETRY OF WALLACE STEVENS: PHENOMENOLOGICAL PARALLELS WITH HUSSERL AND HEIDEGGER. Lewisburg, Pa.: Bucknell University Press, 1976. 298 p. Bibliog.

An interesting attempt to make Stevens's later work more accessible to the reader by showing, through the concepts of the two German philosophers, "some of the meditational processes . . . and some of the visionary forms that Stevens incorporates in his poems."

1537 Kermode, Frank. WALLACE STEVENS. Edinburgh and London: Oliver and Boyd, 1960. 134 p. Bibliog.

The best short introduction to Stevens's work.

1538 Kessler, Edward. IMAGES OF WALLACE STEVENS. New Brunswick, N.J.: Rutgers University Press, 1972. 267 p.

Argues that "Stevens' poetry reveals no linear development of the sort that characterizes the works of Yeats or Eliot or more recently Robert Lowell; rather, the poems eddy around certain fixed ideas revealed in a recurring pattern of imagery." The study proceeds to a discussion of Stevens's major or controlling images.

1539 Litz, A. Walton. INTROSPECTIVE VOYAGER: THE POETIC DEVELOPMENT OF WALLACE STEVENS. New York: Oxford University Press, 1972. xiii, 326 p.

The aim is to evaluate and place in perspective the poems of 1914-37, which are, Litz feels, in danger of being swallowed up by the concentration of recent critical attention on the later poetry. He suggests that the best reader of the last volumes is the reader instructed in the earlier poems.

1540 Morris, Adalaide Kirby. WALLACE STEVENS: IMAGINATION AND FAITH. Princeton, N.J.: Princeton University Press, 1974. xi, 204 p. Bibliog.

An important study of Stevens and religion. Considers the forces of Stevens's background that "made him turn instinctively to religion for sanction and solace"; his critique of the old faith and his efforts to build a new, personal, and more expansive one; and the core of this new faith, in which God becomes one with the imagination.

1541 Morse, Samuel French. WALLACE STEVENS: POETRY AS LIFE. Pegasus American Authors Series. New York: Pegasus, 1970. xv, 232 p. Bibliog.

Stevens's official biographer presents here a biocritique that tries "to bring into focus some of the apparent contradictions and inconsistencies, as well as the steadfast convictions he expressed in both his life and his work."

1542 Morse, Samuel French, et al., eds. WALLACE STEVENS CHECKLIST AND BIBLIOGRAPHY OF STEVENS CRITICISM. Denver: Alan Swallow, 1963. 98 p.

A preface contains lists of books and pamphlets by Stevens, his contribution to books and to periodicals. An index contains titles by Stevens, and other titles. Stevens criticism is listed by type. Coedited by Jackson R. Bryer and Joseph N. Riddel.

1543 Nassar, Eugene Paul. WALLACE STEVENS: AN ANATOMY OF FIGURATION. Philadelphia: University of Pennsylvania Press, 1965. 229 p. Bibliog.

A close study of Stevens's figures. He is shown as often exploiting "the possibilities of mixed metaphor, the very real power of imaginative, illogical, irrational linkages."

1544 O'Connor, William Van. THE SHAPING SPIRIT: A STUDY OF WALLACE STEVENS. Chicago: Henry Regnery, 1950. ix, 146 p. Bibliog.

One of the earliest book-length studies, it remains a valuable work, with many intuitive insights that have worn well under the scrutiny of later critical works.

1545 Pack, Robert. WALLACE STEVENS: AN APPROACH TO HIS POETRY AND THOUGHT. New Brunswick, N.J.: Rutgers University Press, 1958. xvi, 203 p.

Stevens is seen as "the perfect example of the contemporary Western sophisticate." Not obsessed with any social or political ideology, he defends what is and finds "the point of life in the satisfactions of life. He is more interested in continuity than in progress, for the life of the imagination does not improve."

1546 Pearce, Roy Harvey, and Miller, J. Hillis, eds. THE ACT OF THE MIND: ESSAYS ON THE POETRY OF WALLACE STEVENS. Baltimore: Johns Hopkins Press, 1965. xi, 287 p.

Four of the twelve essays are published herein for the first time. The collection is generally excellent.

1547 Perlis, Alan. WALLACE STEVENS: A WORLD OF TRANSFORMING SHAPES. Lewisburg, Pa.: Bucknell University Press, 1976. 160 p. Bibliog.

Argues that the poet "transforms the external world that he perceives to the shape of imaginary constructs." Provides a series of close readings to demonstrate the thesis.

1548 Riddel, Joseph N. THE CLAIRVOYANT EYE: THE POETRY AND POETICS OF WALLACE STEVENS. Baton Rouge: Louisiana State University Press, 1965. ix, 308 p.

Interesting readings of the poems, individually and chronologically. Also presents an account of the poet's theory of imagination and how it relates to the development of his style. An important book.

1549 Stern, Herbert J. WALLACE STEVENS: ART OF UNCERTAINTY. Ann Arbor: University of Michigan Press, 1966. x, 206 p.

The premise is that "the excellence of Stevens's art issued from his ability to cast opposing aspects of his mind against one another, and to distil from these internal struggles a poetry whose vitality is in its own self-questioning." Stevens's passion for philosophical and aesthetic speculation is seen as inherent in his poetry from the beginning. Stevens as hedonist, as humanist, as skeptic, and as romantic meliorist was one and the same.

1550 Stevens, Holly. SOUVENIRS AND PROPHECIES: THE YOUNG WALLACE STEVENS. New York: Knopf, 1977. vii, 288 p.

Close study of the journals Stevens kept beginning in 1898 enable his daughter to present an excellent picture of him in his earlier years. The journals are printed in full, along with her enlightening commentary.

1551 Tindall, William York. WALLACE STEVENS. UMPAW, no. 11. Minneapolis: University of Minnesota Press, 1961. 47 p. Bibliog.

A provocative and witty essay in which Tindall contends that Stevens's poems are of two kinds: one, "strange and imagistic"; the other, "lean and discursive." Analogy and interaction are seen as his principles throughout his career, and Tindall observes "little real development in theme or method."

1552 Vendler, Helen Hennessy. ON EXTENDED WINGS: WALLACE STEVENS' LONGER POEMS. Cambridge, Mass.: Harvard University Press, 1969. x, 334 p.

One of the more important books on Stevens, it follows, through study of many of the long poems, some of the experiments in style Stevens undertook--experiments in diction, rhetoric, syntax, genre, imagery, voice, and meter.

1553 Walsh, Thomas F., ed. CONCORDANCE TO THE POETRY OF WALLACE STEVENS. University Park: Pennsylvania State University Press, 1963. xx, 341 p.

Essential. Based on THE COLLECTED POEMS, THE NECESSARY ANGEL, and OPUS POSTHUMOUS.

1554 Wells, Henry W. INTRODUCTION TO WALLACE STEVENS. Bloomington: Indiana University Press, 1964. 218 p.

The poems studied are Wells's selection of "the best and most typical of Stevens' poetic accomplishment." Although the interpretations are often quite opinionated, they display frequent rewarding insights.

1555 Willard, Abbie F. WALLACE STEVENS: THE POET AND HIS CRITICS. Chicago: American Library Association, 1978. xiii, 270 p.

Selects, arranges, and assesses criticism that continues to proliferate as Stevens's reputation grows. Chapter 1 discusses Stevens's chronological development from the three perspectives most frequently found in critical studies; (2) examines the influences on his development with emphasis on literary movements; (3) tries to define the aesthetic forms he chose to employ; (4) discusses his world view as interpreted by the critics; and (5) reviews his own comments on himself and his world.

See also no. 1730.

HARRIET BEECHER STOWE (1811-1896)

1556 Adams, John R. HARRIET BEECHER STOWE. TUSAS, no. 42. New York: Twayne, 1963. 172 p. Bibliog.

A critical biography that includes readings of all Stowe's more important literary work. Believes OLDTOWN FOLKS to be her best and most realistic book, and UNCLE TOM'S CABIN to be an hysterical vision done with emotional power.

1557 Ammons, Elizabeth, ed. CRITICAL ESSAYS ON HARRIET BEECHER STOWE. Boston: Twayne, 1980. 307 p. Bibliog.

A far-ranging collection that includes pieces by such contemporaries as George Sand, George Eliot, Bret Harte, Howells, and James; such black writers as Paul Laurence Dunbar, Langston Hughes, and James Baldwin; and such modern scholars as Constance Rourke, Leslie Fiedler, Edmund Wilson, and Anthony Burgess.

1558 Ashton, Jean W., ed. HARRIET BEECHER STOWE: A REFERENCE GUIDE. Boston: G.K. Hall, 1977. xxii, 168 p.

Contains a list of Stowe's writings, followed by the main text, an annotated listing of writings about Stowe from 1843 through 1974. Three appendixes are concerned with (1) fictional responses to UNCLE TOM'S CABIN, (2) plays based on the life of Stowe, and (3) UNCLE TOM'S CABIN on the stage.

1559 Birdoff, Harry. THE WORLD'S GREATEST HIT--UNCLE TOM'S CABIN. New York: S.F. Vanni, 1947. xiv, 440 p. Illus.

The history of Stowe's famous story on the stage and in the movies. Illustrated with old-time playbills, daguerrotypes, vignettes, music sheets, poems, and cartoons.

1560 Crozier, Alice C. THE NOVELS OF HARRIET BEECHER STOWE. New York: Oxford University Press, 1969. x, 235 p.

One of the best books on Stowe. Individual chapters deal with UNCLE TOM'S CABIN and DRED, and a third with the artistic point of view in both novels. Two other chapters treat the New England novels and the novels concerned with the social status of woman, and a final chapter analyzes Stowe's article "The True Story of Lady Byron's Life" and the storm it aroused.

1561 Fields, Annie, ed. LIFE AND LETTERS OF HARRIET BEECHER STOWE. Boston: Houghton, Mifflin, 1897. Reprint. Detroit: Gale Research Co., 1970. 406 p.

Based on the biography of Mrs. Stowe's son, Rev. C.E. Stowe, but filled out with many letters and other material that had since come to light.

1562 Foster, Charles H. THE RUNGLESS LADDER: HARRIET BEECHER STOWE AND NEW ENGLAND PURITANISM. Durham, N.C.: Duke University Press, 1954. xviii, 278 p. Bibliog.

A critical study of Stowe's novels and their relationship to her religious heritage. She is seen as more within the New England tradition than is Hawthorne. Foster believes that her permanently significant contribution to American culture lay in her ability "to give us a balanced and immediate sense of the vital and complex Puritan past."

1563 Gerson, Noel B. HARRIET BEECHER STOWE: A BIOGRAPHY. New York: Praeger, 1976. 218 p. Bibliog.

A somewhat pedestrian biography that offers nothing new, but does tell the story of Mrs. Stowe with objectivity.

1564 Gilbertson, Catherine. HARRIET BEECHER STOWE. New York and London: Appleton-Century, 1937. Reprint. Port Washington, N.Y.: Kennikat Press, 1968. xii, 330 p. Illus.

A biography written with the aim of steering a middle course between adulation and condemnation. Places Stowe within the genteel tradition and sees her writing, especially UNCLE TOM'S CABIN, as a projection of her domestic and emotional suffering. Praises the New England novels.

1565 Hildreth, Margaret Holbrook, ed. HARRIET BEECHER STOWE: A BIBLIOGRAPHY. Hamden, Conn.: Archon, 1976. xiv, 257 p.

Indispensable. Part 1 contains a listing of writings by Stowe, including translations of her work. Part 2 contains a listing of writings about Stowe in both English and foreign languages. Unannotated.

1566 Johnston, Johanna. RUNAWAY TO HEAVEN: THE STORY OF HARRIET BEECHER STOWE. Garden City, N.Y.: Doubleday, 1963. viii, 490 p. Illus. Bibliog.

A popular biography that adds little that is new. Tries to present Stowe against the background of her time.

1567 Kirkham, E. Bruce. THE BUILDING OF UNCLE TOM'S CABIN. Knoxville: University of Tennessee Press, 1977. x, 264 p. Illus., bibliog.

Although Kirkham presents a biography of Mrs. Stowe, the emphasis is on the making of her famous book. The manuscripts of the novel and her revisions are closely studied, to reveal that she was neither a careless nor a hasty writer.

1568 Stowe, Charles Edward, and Stowe, Lyman Beecher. HARRIET BEECHER STOWE: THE STORY OF HER LIFE. Boston and New York: Houghton Mifflin, 1911. vi, 313 p. Illus.

A memorial biography by Stowe's son and grandson that concentrates on her character rather than on her work. Adds nothing to earlier biographies.

1569 Wagenknecht, Edward. HARRIET BEECHER STOWE: THE KNOWN AND THE UNKNOWN. New York: Oxford University Press, 1965. 267 p. Bibliog.

Another of Wagenknecht's "psychographs" or character studies, this is based partly on unpublished letters. Mrs. Stowe is seen as first and foremost daughter, sister, wife, and mother. Her art was the next most important thing to her. Her literary affinities are viewed as being with Twain and Cable. The lengthy notes are very helpful.

1570 Wilson, Forrest. CRUSADER IN CRINOLINE: THE LIFE OF HARRIET BEECHER STOWE. Philadelphia, London, and New York: Lippincott, 1941. 706 p. Illus.

The fullest biography yet published, it is a scholarly and very readable account based on earlier biographies, unpublished letters, newspaper files, and reminiscences of literary persons. Despite the length of the work, relatively little space is devoted to Stowe's literary achievement.

WILLIAM STYRON (1925--)

1571 Bryer, Jackson, ed., assisted by Mary Beth Hatem. WILLIAM STYRON: A REFERENCE GUIDE. Boston: G.K. Hall, 1978. xiv, 155 p.

An indispensable reference work containing a well-annotated list of writings about Styron organized by year from 1946 through 1978.

1572 Clarke, John Henrik, ed. WILLIAM STYRON'S NAT TURNER: TEN BLACK WRITERS RESPOND. Boston: Beacon Press, 1968. x, 120 p.

Essays by Lerone Bennett, Jr., Alvin F. Poussaint, M.D., Vincent Harding, John Oliver Killens, John A. Williams, Ernest Kaiser, Loyle Hairston, Charles V. Hamilton, Mike Thelwell, and an introduction by the editor.

1573 Fossum, Robert H. WILLIAM STYRON: A CRITICAL ESSAY. Contemporary Writers in Christian Perspective. Grand Rapids, Mich.: William B. Eerdmans, 1968. 48 p. Bibliog.

Readings of the novels LIE DOWN IN DARKNESS, THE LONG MARCH, SET THIS HOUSE ON FIRE, and THE CONFESSIONS OF NAT TURNER that focus on Styron's responses to the "absence of God." He is seen as suggesting that "God is not absent after all."

1574 Friedman, Melvin J. WILLIAM STYRON. Bowling Green, Ohio: Bowling Green University Popular Press, 1974. viii, 72 p. Bibliog.

Discusses the reception of Styron's novels and examines the influence of Faulkner, Hemingway, Proust, Camus, and Fitzgerald on his work. He is also seen as having both a thematic and technical kinship with contemporary French writers such as Robbé-Grillet, Butor, and Simon.

1575 Mackin, Cooper R. WILLIAM STYRON. Southern Writers Series, no. 7. Austin, Tex.: Steck-Vaughn, 1969. 43 p. Bibliog.

Provides a brief biographical sketch and readings of the four novels through NAT TURNER as distinctly southern. Styron's protagonists are all seen as southern rebels.

1576 Morris, Robert K., and Malin, Irving, eds. THE ACHIEVEMENT OF WILLIAM STYRON. Athens: University of Georgia Press, 1975. 280 p. Bibliog.

Eleven essays by Styron scholars on various aspects of his work, with a fine bibliography by Jackson R. Bryer on Styron's works and on works about him.

1577 Ratner, Marc L. WILLIAM STYRON. TUSAS, no. 196. New York: Twayne, 1972. 170 p. Bibliog.

Traces the development of Styron's fiction chronologically, and shows the struggle toward self-realization to be his main theme. Styron's views on sex and violence are studied for their use in connection with the death of love. His use of satire and his sense of the spiritual malaise afflicting American life are also remarked, as is the critical mistake of viewing him as a regional writer limited to a southern tradition and past.

1578 West, James L.W., III, ed. WILLIAM STYRON: A DESCRIPTIVE BIBLIOGRAPHY. Boston: G.K. Hall, 1977. xxxvii, 252 p.

A remarkably complete and thoroughly described bibliography with a charming preface by Styron and a good introduction by West. The contents are organized thus: (1) "Editions in English," (2) "Editions in French," (3) "Previously Unpublished Contributions to Books and Other Publications," (4) "Republished Contributions to Books," (5) "Appearances in Periodicals and Newspapers," (6) "Published Letters," (7) "Blurbs," (8) "Non-French Translations."

ALLEN TATE (1899-1979)

1579 Bishop, Ferman. ALLEN TATE. TUSAS, no. 124. New York: Twayne, 1967. 172 p. Bibliog.

In a balanced study of the man and his work, Tate is viewed as "one of a very small number of American writers who have had the ability to present the intellectual as well as the emotional side of the American experience." His poetry, fiction, and criticism are all examined, as are his Civil War biographies.

1580 Hemphill, George. ALLEN TATE. UMPAW, no. 39. Minneapolis: University of Minnesota Press, 1964. 48 p. Bibliog.

A good brief introduction that challenges the view of Tate as a professional southerner.

1581 Squires, Radcliffe. ALLEN TATE: A LITERARY BIOGRAPHY. Pegasus American Authors Series. New York: Pegasus, 1971. ix, 231 p. Bibliog.

Although the main events of Tate's life are amply covered, the emphasis is on discussion of his writing, particularly the poetry. The book provides the best introduction to Tate and his work published to date.

1582 ______, ed. ALLEN TATE AND HIS WORK: CRITICAL EVALUATIONS. Minneapolis: University of Minnesota Press, 1972. 355 p. Bibliog.

Following a knowledgeable introduction by Squires, the book falls into four sections: (1) "The Man," (2) "The Essayist," (3) "The Novelist," and (4) "The Poet." The critical essays, thirty-five in number, are by well-known critics and scholars, and there are excellent bibliographies of Tate's works and of writing about him.

BAYARD TAYLOR (1825-1878)

1583 Beatty, Richmond Croom. BAYARD TAYLOR: LAUREATE OF THE GILDED AGE. Norman: University of Oklahoma Press, 1936. xv, 379 p. Bibliog. note.

"His is the story of a man who lived from his youth to his premature death within a maelstrom," a "martyr to the American way of life." He is seen as almost the proto-typical modern American, "rootless, in practice godless, eternally restless, harassed by debt and the sense of a fading, outraged purpose," rushing through life and never finding the peace he sought.

1584 Cary, Richard. THE GENTEEL CIRCLE: BAYARD TAYLOR AND HIS NEW YORK FRIENDS. Ithaca, N.Y.: Cornell University Press, 1952. 44 p.

Examines Taylor's relationship with Richard Henry Stoddard, Edmund Clarence Stedman, and Thomas Bailey Aldrich, the other members of the New York group of romantic senti-mentalist poets who worshipped at the shrine of Emerson, Longfellow, and Holmes, and who looked to Taylor as their leader. His flaws are seen as his essential mediocrity, his hunger for fame, and his subservience to the cult of the genteel.

1585 Krumpelmann, John T. BAYARD TAYLOR AND GERMAN LETTERS. Hamburg: Cram, de Gruyter and Co., 1959. 235 p. Bibliog.

The purpose of the study is to show that, after 1844, Taylor occupied himself with German literature throughout his career and became the foremost literary intermediary between America and Germany. The book is in three parts: (1) the origin and development of Taylor's interest in German letters, with its manifestation in his works; (2) Taylor as a disseminator of the knowledge of German literature; and (3) Taylor as a writer in German and as a representative of American letters in Germany.

1586 Smyth, Albert H. BAYARD TAYLOR. American Men of Letters. Boston and New York: Houghton Mifflin, 1896. 320 p. Bibliog.

A generally accurate assessment despite the author's own total acceptance of genteel values.

1587 Wermuth, Paul C. BAYARD TAYLOR. TUSAS, no. 228. New York: Twayne, 1973. 199 p. Bibliog.

Primarily a study of Taylor's published works, it does include a good biographical sketch. There are chapters on Taylor and the genteel tradition, travel writings, fiction, poetry, and criticism. He is considered important because he was so typical of his age, both in his work and in his person.

EDWARD TAYLOR (1642?-1729)

1588 Gefvert, Constance J., ed. EDWARD TAYLOR: AN ANNOTATED BIBLIOGRAPHY, 1668-1970. Serif Series of Bibliographies and Checklists, no. 19. Kent, Ohio: Kent State University Press, 1971. xxxiii, 83 p.

Indispensable. An introductory essay evaluates Taylor scholarship between 1937 and 1970. The main text is divided into two parts: (1) primary sources, including editions of Taylor's works, letters, and manuscripts; and (2) secondary sources: bibliographies, biography and genealogy, critical books and articles, and dissertations and theses.

1589 Grabo, Norman S. EDWARD TAYLOR. TUSAS, no. 8. New Haven, Conn.: College and University Press, 1961. 192 p. Bibliog.

The first book-length treatment of Taylor, it attempts to define the character of his poetry analytically, and to place it in the context of the life that produced it. The quality of Taylor's unifying mysticism, the structure of his thought, and the poetic and critical theory he evolved are all explored. Taylor stands revealed as a gifted and complex poet.

1590 Stanford, Donald E. EDWARD TAYLOR. UMPAW, no. 52. Minneapolis: University of Minnesota Press, 1965. 46 p. Bibliog.

A general introduction to Taylor and his poetry, it emphasizes his orthodoxy and concludes that, although his work is not up to the standards of the English metaphysical poets, it nonetheless is an "impressive body of poetry."

SARA TEASDALE (1884-1933)

1591 Carpenter, Margaret Haley. SARA TEASDALE: A BIOGRAPHY. New York: Schulte Publishing Co., 1960. xix, 377 p. Illus. Bibliog.

The first full-scale biography, this is well-researched and competently presented. Vachel Lindsay's letters to Sara are here published for the first time and reveal the importance of Teasdale to him. Carpenter's judgment of her poetry is that it is pure music, pure emotion, and pure beauty.

1592 Drake, William D. SARA TEASDALE, WOMAN AND POET. New York: Harper and Row, 1979. xiv, 304 p. Illus., bibliog.

The most recent biographical study, this is nicely balanced between discussion of the life and of the poetry.

HENRY DAVID THOREAU (1817-1862)

1593 Anderson, Charles R. THE MAGIC CIRCLE OF WALDEN. New York, Chicago, and San Francisco: Holt, Rinehart and Winston, 1968. x, 306 p.

A detailed and imaginative reading of WALDEN in which the work is presented as an extended poem.

1594 Bazalgette, Leon. HENRY THOREAU, BACHELOR OF NATURE. Translated by Van Wyck Brooks. New York: Harcourt, Brace, 1924. iii, 357 p.

Thoreau's French biographer shows his subject as a man spiritually attuned to nature. The approach is distinctly romantic.

1595 Cameron, Kenneth Walter, ed. THOREAU'S HARVARD YEARS: MATERIALS INTRODUCTORY TO NEW EXPLORATIONS. Hartford, Conn.: Transcendental Books, 1966. 130 p.

Reproduces numerous documents such as the calendars for the Harvard years, Thoreau in the college records, and a list of his textbooks.

1596 _____. YOUNG THOREAU AND THE CLASSICS: A REVIEW--THE CURRICULUM OF THE CONCORD ACADEMY, PROBABILITIES AND EVIDENCE. Hartford, Conn.: Transcendental Books, 1975. 129 p.

Reprints some of the materials used in training pupils in the classics at the school young Thoreau attended.

1597 Canby, Henry Seidel. THOREAU. Boston: Houghton Mifflin, 1939. xx, 508 p. Illus., bibliog.

Prior to Harding's (see no. 1605), the fullest and most scholarly biography. Canby tries to show the sides of Thoreau not revealed by his earlier biographers, such as Channing (see no. 1598) and Sanborn (see no. 1623), who viewed him as poet-naturalist. Thus he attempts to present him as would-be lover, home-bred philosopher, and dynamic individualist.

1598 Channing, William Ellery. THOREAU, THE POET-NATURALIST. 1873. New ed. Enl. Edited by F.B. Sanborn. Boston: Charles E. Goodspeed, 1902. xx, 397 p.

Thoreau is here portrayed by a friend who observed him closely. He was not, Channing says, in the usual sense a scientific man, his talent being literary, but "in no narrow view, a naturalist."

1599 Christie, John Aldrich. THOREAU AS WORLD TRAVELER. New York and London: Columbia University Press, 1965. xiii, 358 p. Illus., bibliog.

A fascinating study of Thoreau's reading of travel literature, with a lengthy bibliography of travel works read by him.

1600 Cook, Reginald L. PASSAGE TO WALDEN. Boston: Houghton Mifflin, 1949. xvi, 238 p. 2d ed. New York: Russell and Russell, 1966. xvi, 253 p.

A thorough study of Thoreau's relation to nature. The second edition contains a key to references and citations.

1601 Edel, Leon. HENRY D. THOREAU. UMPAW, no. 90. Minneapolis: University of Minnesota Press, 1970. 47 p. Bibliog.

The biographer of Henry James shares the Master's opinion of Thoreau: "He was worse than provincial, he was parochial." Consequently, this introduction to Thoreau is marked by antagonism and denigration.

1602 Emerson, Edward Waldo. HENRY THOREAU AS REMEMBERED BY A YOUNG FRIEND. Boston and New York: Houghton Mifflin, 1917. viii, 152 p. Illus.

Reminiscences of Emerson's son, who knew Thoreau intimately and admired him greatly. Dr. Emerson also sought out residents of Concord who had known Thoreau and repeated their stories. His reason for writing this memoir was to defend Thoreau's name against critics, such as Lowell, who had defamed it.

1603 Garber, Frederick. THOREAU'S REDEMPTIVE IMAGINATION. New York: New York University Press, 1977. x, 229 p.

A study of those Thoreau texts "that most clearly illuminate the successes and frustrations of Thoreau's redemptive imagination as it seeks to make a place for the self in American nature." THE MAINE WOODS and "Walking" are seen as crucial texts in this connection.

1604 Glick, Wendell, ed. THE RECOGNITION OF HENRY DAVID THOREAU: SELECTED CRITICISM SINCE 1848. Ann Arbor: University of Michigan Press, 1969. xxi, 381 p.

A reprinting of Thoreau criticism beginning with James Russell Lowell in A FABLE FOR CRITICS of 1848 and ending with Joseph Moldenhauer's "Paradox in WALDEN" of 1964. Forty-six pieces in all are reprinted.

1605 Harding, Walter. THE DAYS OF HENRY THOREAU. New York: Knopf, 1965. xvi, 472 p., xvi. Illus. Bibliog. note.

As close to a definitive biography as we are likely to get. Harding has unearthed almost every fact about Thoreau that will probably come to light. The result is an indispensable book for Thoreau scholars.

1606 _____. A THOREAU HANDBOOK. New York: New York University Press, 1959. xviii, 229 p.

A useful guide to scholarship on Thoreau.

1607 _____, ed. THOREAU: A CENTURY OF CRITICISM. Dallas: Southern Methodist University Press, 1954. x, 205 p.

An interesting collection of essays beginning with George Ripley's review of A WEEK and ending with Philip and Kathryn Whitford's "Thoreau: Pioneer Ecologist and Conservationist." The essays on Thoreau of Emerson, Lowell, Alcott, and Stevenson are included, as are the views of more modern writers like Sinclair Lewis and Henry Miller.

1608 _____. THOREAU'S LIBRARY. Charlottesville: University of Virginia Press, 1957. 102 p.

A helpful descriptive catalog of Thoreau's personal library.

1609 _____. THE THOREAU CENTENNIAL: PAPERS MARKING THE OBSERVANCE IN NEW YORK CITY OF THE ONE HUNDREDTH ANNIVERSARY OF THE DEATH OF HENRY DAVID THOREAU. N.p.: State University of New York Press, 1964. Unpaged.

Carl F. Hovde, Joseph J. Moldenhauer, Walter Harding, Raymond Adams, J. Lyndon Shanley, Reginald L. Cook, Howard Mumford Jones, Donald S. Harrington, and Braj Kumar Nehru are those represented.

1610 Harding, Walter, ed., and Advena, Jean Cameron, comp. A BIBLIOGRAPHY OF THE THOREAU SOCIETY BULLETIN BIBLIOGRAPHIES 1941-1969. Troy, N.Y.: Whitston Publishing Co., 1971. viii, 323 p.

A most useful annotated bibliography that provides a cumulation and index of the items printed in the quarterly bulletins of the society from its beginning through 1969.

1611 Hicks, John H., ed. THOREAU IN OUR SEASON. Amherst: University of Massachusetts Press, 1966. 176 p.

Most of the essays here reprinted appeared initially in THE MASSACHUSETTS REVIEW for autumn 1962 under the title "A Centenary Gathering for Henry David Thoreau." Various facets of Thoreau are examined, and there is a clash of views about the man and his work.

1612 Hough, Henry Beetle. THOREAU OF WALDEN: THE MAN AND HIS EVENTFUL LIFE. New York: Simon and Schuster, 1956. viii, 275 p.

Written by a country editor with a vast enthusiasm for Thoreau, the biography adds nothing to our knowledge of his life, but can be useful as an introduction to the man and his work.

1613 Howarth, William L. THE LITERARY MANUSCRIPTS OF HENRY DAVID THOREAU. Calendars of American Literary Manuscripts Series, no. 3. Columbus: Ohio State University Press, 1974. xxxvii, 408 p. Illus.

The known Thoreau manuscripts are located as to repository, and each manuscript entry contains the following information: citation, title, first line, collation, date, and contents.

1614 Krutch, Joseph Wood. HENRY DAVID THOREAU. American Men of Letters. New York: William Sloane Associates, 1948. Reprint. Westport, Conn.: Greenwood Press, 1973. xiii, 298 p.

A biocritical study that is enthusiastic about its subject. Krutch recognizes the conflicts within Thoreau between his pantheistic tendencies and his moral ideas, for example; however, he contends that they lend a richness to his writing, the hallmark of which is a unity of sensibility.

1615 Lebeaux, Richard. YOUNG MAN THOREAU. Amherst: University of Massachusetts Press, 1977. 262 p. Bibliog.

An interesting and valuable new study of Thoreau's formative years that takes an Eriksonian approach to understanding the "identity crisis" of the complex person Henry Thoreau was. Studies his progress from birth up to the beginning of the Walden experiment in 1845.

1616 McIntosh, James. THOREAU AS ROMANTIC NATURALIST: HIS SHIFTING STANCE TOWARD NATURE. Ithaca, N.Y., and London: Cornell University Press, 1974. 310 p. Illus.

Thoreau is seen as a romantic naturalist in that "he regards man's communication with nature as spiritual, not as destructive of the human spirit." Examination of the WEEK, THE MAINE WOODS, and WALDEN reveals that he shifts his attitudes within each work, showing a kind of ambivalence resulting from his wish for involvement with nature and his sense of separation from it.

1617 Marble, Annie Russell. THOREAU: HIS HOME, FRIENDS AND BOOKS. New York: Crowell, 1902. Reprint. New York: AMS Press, 1969. viii, 343 p. Illus.

This book goes a bit beyond the title's announced range to include chapters on Thoreau as naturalist and on Thoreau's service and rank in literature.

1618 Metzger, Charles R. THOREAU AND WHITMAN: A STUDY OF THEIR ESTHETICS. Seattle: University of Washington Press, 1961. v, 113 p. Bibliog.

The esthetics of the two are seen as having a great deal in common; both, for example, "were deeply concerned with salvation, and particularly with the role which art can play in contributing to it." Thoreau is believed to be more conventional than Whitman in his art forms.

1619 Miller, Perry. CONSCIOUSNESS IN CONCORD: THE TEXT OF THOREAU'S HITHERTO "LOST JOURNAL" (1840-1841) TOGETHER WITH NOTES AND A COMMENTARY. Boston: Houghton Mifflin, 1958. xi, 243 p.

Well over half the book is devoted to the commentary, which affords Miller ample opportunity to display his dislike, amounting to occasional hostility, of Thoreau as human being.

1620 Oehlschlaeger, Fritz, and Hendrick, George, eds. TOWARD THE MAKING OF THOREAU'S MODERN REPUTATION: SELECTED CORRESPONDENCE OF S.A. JONES, A.W. HOSMER, H.S. SALT, H.G.O. BLAKE, and D. RICKETSON. Urbana, Chicago, and London: University of Illinois Press, 1979. xix, 413 p.

A lengthy introduction to the letters identifies the correspondents and attempts to establish the case for them as laying the foundation for Thoreau's modern reputation.

1621 Paul, Sherman. THE SHORES OF AMERICA: THOREAU'S INWARD EXPLORATION. Urbana: University of Illinois Press, 1958. xi, 433 p.

A generally successful attempt at a "spiritual biography," a study of Thoreau's inner life based on close reading of what he wrote. For Paul, Thoreau is the most interesting of the Transcendentalists, for he tested their ideas by living them.

1622 _____, ed. THOREAU: A COLLECTION OF CRITICAL ESSAYS. Englewood Cliffs, N.J.: Prentice-Hall, 1962. 188 p. Bibliog.

Reprints fourteen well-chosen essays, with a sound introduction.

1623 Sanborn, F.B. THE LIFE OF HENRY DAVID THOREAU. American Men of Letters Series. Boston: Houghton Mifflin, 1882. 324 p.

Written by one of Thoreau's close friends, it provides an interesting portrait.

1624 Sayre, Robert F. THOREAU AND THE AMERICAN INDIANS. Princeton, N.J.: Princeton University Press, 1977. xix, 239 p.

A study of the similarity of the pronouncements of Thoreau and of the "great Indian chiefs" on the ecology. It traces Thoreau's fascination with Indian life, his attempts to learn about and to imitate it, and some of the differences between Indians as he read and wrote about them and as they were.

1625 Seybold, Ethel. THOREAU: THE QUEST AND THE CLASSICS. Yale Studies in English, vol. 116. New Haven, Conn.: Yale University Press, 1951. x, 148 p. Bibliographical footnotes.

A fine study of the relation of Thoreau's spiritual development to his reading in classical literature.

1626 Shanley, J. Lyndon. THE MAKING OF WALDEN, WITH THE TEXT OF THE FIRST VERSION. Chicago: University of Chicago Press, 1957. vii, 208 p.

The story of the successive versions of WALDEN, with the complete text of the first version and an appendix which compares it with the published text.

1627 Stoller, Leo. AFTER WALDEN: THOREAU'S CHANGING VIEWS ON ECONOMIC MAN. Stanford, Calif.: Stanford University Press, 1957. 163 p.

An important study that treats the development of Thoreau's thought, with emphasis on his economic theories.

1628 Taylor, J. Golden. NEIGHBOR THOREAU'S CRITICAL HUMOR. Monograph Series, vol. 6, no. 1. Logan: Utah State University, 1958. 91 p.

Contends that Thoreau was "neither hermit, anarchist, nor misanthrope: he lived and wrote with the solicitude and prerogative of a neighbor." The main purpose here is to identify Thoreau's serious humor and to show how it is the chief vehicle of his social criticism.

1629 Timpe, Eugene F., ed. THOREAU ABROAD: TWELVE BIBLIOGRAPHICAL ESSAYS. Hamden, Conn.: Archon Books, 1971. 203 p.

Essays on the publication and reception of Thoreau in France, the Netherlands, Germany, Switzerland, Italy, Bohemia, Russia, Israel, India, Japan, and Australia.

1630 Van Doren, Mark. HENRY DAVID THOREAU, A CRITICAL STUDY. Boston and New York: Houghton Mifflin, 1916. Reprint. New York: Russell and Russell, 1961. viii, 138 p. Bibliog. note.

Based on examination of Thoreau's journal. Thoreau, Van Doren holds, should not be taken literally. "By creating a classic image of the cynic hermit in ideal solitude" he "demonstrated some of the meannesses of Time and Matter, and furnished the spirit and will for social criticism."

1631 Whicher, George F. WALDEN REVISITED: A CENTENNIAL TRIBUTE TO HENRY DAVID THOREAU. Chicago: Packard, 1945. 93 p.

This heartfelt tribute may well serve as one of the best brief introductions to Thoreau.

MARK TWAIN. See SAMUEL LANGHORNE CLEMENS.

ROYALL TYLER (1757-1826)

1632 Tanselle, G. Thomas. ROYALL TYLER. Cambridge, Mass.: Harvard University Press, 1967. xvi, 281 p. Illus., bibliog.

The first book on Tyler, author of THE CONTRAST, the first native comedy professionally produced (1787), and a dauntless encourager of a truly American literature, this study begins with a fifty-page biographical sketch, and then takes up in successive chapters THE CONTRAST, later plays, Tyler as poet, as novelist, and as essayist.

JOHN UPDIKE (1932--)

1633 Burchard, Rachael C. JOHN UPDIKE: YEA SAYINGS. Crosscurrents/ Modern Critiques. Carbondale and Edwardsville: Southern Illinois University Press, 1971. xii, 172 p. Bibliog.

> Reviews the poetry, the five novels through COUPLES, and the short stories. Finds Updike important "because of his superb literary artistry and because he has something to say." His yea sayings are: there is some virtue in man; goodness lives; the individual is at least minutely significant; and life in all its complexity can be good. Above all, Updike asserts that God exists.

1634 Detweiler, Robert. JOHN UPDIKE. TUSAS, no. 214. New York: Twayne, 1972. 183 p. Bibliog.

> A study devoted exclusively to Updike's fiction in which the author tries to demonstrate the qualities of irony and self-consciousness inherent in what he terms Updike's art of "secular baroque." The six novels published through RABBIT REDUX are explicated in depth.

1635 Hamilton, Alice, and Hamilton, Kenneth. THE ELEMENTS OF JOHN UPDIKE. Grand Rapids, Mich.: William B. Eerdmans, 1970. 267 p. Bibliog.

> The first book-length study of Updike, this attempts to outline his thought as it emerges from his poems, articles, short stories, and novels. Updike is viewed as an essentially religious writer who "directs us to those aspects of earth which can speak to us of heaven and show us how to relate ourselves qualitatively to it."

1636 Markle, Joyce B. FIGHTERS AND LOVERS: THEME IN THE NOVELS OF JOHN UPDIKE. New York: New York University Press, 1973. 205 p. Bibliog.

> The thesis is that Updike deals with the same problems in each of the novels through RABBIT REDUX except for BECH (which is seen as a comic, not a serious, novel); namely, the flight from death; the need for "lovers" (characters who make others feel "special"); evidence of man's impact on his world; the sources of man's sense of importance; and man's abilities and responsibilities in relating to the members of his society.

1637 Olivas, Michael A., ed. AN ANNOTATED BIBLIOGRAPHY OF JOHN UPDIKE CRITICISM, 1967-1973, AND A CHECKLIST OF HIS WORKS. New York and London: Garland, 1975. x, 91 p.

Supplements the Taylor bibliography of 1968 (see no. 1639), using the same style and critical approach.

1638 Samuels, Charles Thomas. JOHN UPDIKE. UMPAW, no. 79. Minneapolis: University of Minnesota Press, 1969. 46 p. Bibliog.

A brief introduction to Updike's works. Each novel, through COUPLES, is discussed.

1639 Taylor, C. Clarke, ed. JOHN UPDIKE: A BIBLIOGRAPHY. Serif Series of Bibliographies and Checklists. Kent, Ohio: Kent State University Press, 1968. vii, 82 p.

Thirty pages are devoted to listing primary sources; the remainder to an annotated list of secondary sources through 1966.

1640 Thorburn, David, and Eiland, Howard, eds. JOHN UPDIKE: A COLLECTION OF CRITICAL ESSAYS. Englewood Cliffs, N.J.: Prentice-Hall, 1979. ix, 222 p. Bibliog.

Twenty-three essays grouped in five sections: (1) "The Rabbit Novels," (2) "Marriage Novels," (3) "Olinger Novels," (4) "THE COUP," and (5) "The Short Stories." An excellent collection, well introduced by Thorburn.

1641 Uphaus, Suzanne Henning. JOHN UPDIKE. Modern Literature Monographs. New York: Frederick Ungar, 1980. x, 149 p. Bibliog.

This latest study of Updike's work covers its full range and finds him a writer of great variety with a remarkable mastery of language. The best of his novels are perceived to be RABBIT, RUN, THE CENTAUR, RABBIT REDUX, A MONTH OF SUNDAYS, and THE COUP.

1642 Vargo, Edward P. RAINSTORMS AND FIRE: RITUAL IN THE NOVELS OF JOHN UPDIKE. National Universities Publications Series in Literary Criticism. Port Washington, N.Y., and London: Kennikat Press, 1973. 229 p. Bibliog.

Carefully analyzes, in a chapter devoted to each, THE POORHOUSE FAIR, RABBIT, RUN, THE CENTAUR, OF THE FARM, COUPLES, and RABBIT REDUX. Also reviews many critical estimates of Updike's work. Concludes that, in all his novels, Updike reveals "that even in twentieth century America man instinctively returns to rituals to answer his fear of death and his need for ecstasy and wholeness."

JONES VERY (1813-1880)

1643 Bartlett, William Irving. JONES VERY, EMERSON'S "BRAVE SAINT." Durham, N.C.: Duke University Press, 1942. xiii, 237 p. Illus., bibliog.

The only book-length complete life of Very, although not able to take advantage of some materials used by Gittleman twenty-five years later. Emphasis is on the relationship with Emerson and Elizabeth Peabody.

1644 Gittleman, Edwin. JONES VERY: THE EFFECTIVE YEARS, 1833-1840. New York and London: Columbia University Press, 1967. xx, 436 p. Bibliog.

This full-scale, excellent biography ceases with the year 1840 although Very lived until 1880. Gittleman's reason is that Very's "effective" life was over when he was only twenty-seven years old. After that he was "cut off by choice and circumstance from the ideas, people, and activities which gave special meaning to his earlier life." Traces his growth as poet and essayist.

ROBERT PENN WARREN (1905--)

1645 Bohner, Charles H. ROBERT PENN WARREN. TUSAS, no. 69. New York: Twayne, 1964. 175 p. Bibliog.

Provides "an overview of Warren's literary career, an analysis of the themes which have preoccupied him, and an account of the development of his art as it has deepened and matured."

1646 Casper, Leonard. ROBERT PENN WARREN: THE DARK AND BLOODY GROUND. Seattle: University of Washington Press, 1960. xix, 212 p. Bibliog.

The first book-length study, it offers a critical evaluation of Warren's works, which are treated chronologically within genres. The bibliography is excellent, being in two parts: primary and secondary sources.

1647 Clark, William Bedford, ed. CRITICAL ESSAYS ON ROBERT PENN WARREN. Boston: Twayne, 1981. 280 p. Bibliog.

The most comprehensive collection on Warren to appear. He is treated as novelist, poet, critic, and social commentator. Malcolm Cowley, John Crowe Ransom, Henry Nash Smith, and Carlos Baker are among the essayists.

1648 Gray, Richard, ed. ROBERT PENN WARREN: A COLLECTION OF CRITICAL ESSAYS. Englewood Cliffs, N.J.: Prentice-Hall, 1980. viii, 206 p. Bibliog.

An excellent new collection of sixteen essays, ably introduced by the editor. Among those represented are Cleanth Brooks, Arthur Mizener, James H. Justus, Barnett Guttenberg, Frederick P.W. McDowell, and John Hicks.

1649 Guttenberg, Barnett. WEB OF BEING: THE NOVELS OF ROBERT PENN WARREN. Nashville: Vanderbilt University Press, 1975. xiii, 173 p. Bibliog.

Devotes a chapter each to probing readings of NIGHT RIDER, AT HEAVEN'S GATE, ALL THE KING'S MEN, WORLD ENOUGH AND TIME, BAND OF ANGELS, THE CAVE, WILDERNESS, FLOOD, and MEET ME IN THE GREEN GLEN. Concludes that "the story at the heart of Warren's fiction traces the search for selfhood." It is a fiction that will endure, Guttenberg believes, because "it deals incisively with the dissociation of being which has become a central issue of the twentieth century."

1650 Huff, Mary Nance. ROBERT PENN WARREN: A BIBLIOGRAPHY. New York: David Lewis, 1968. xi, 171 p.

The volume is divided into eight sections: (1) books by Warren, (2) translations of his books, (3) short stories, (4) poems, (5) essays and articles, (6) book reviews by Warren, (7) miscellanea, (8) biographical and critical material on Warren, with brief descriptive annotation.

1651 Longley, John Lewis, Jr. ROBERT PENN WARREN. Southern Writers Series, no. 2. Austin, Tex.: Steck-Vaughn, 1969. 43 p. Bibliog.

Stresses the "southernness" of Warren and his work.

1652 Newton, Thomas A., ed. A CHARACTER INDEX OF ROBERT PENN WARREN'S LONG WORKS OF FICTION. Emporia State Research Studies, vol. 26, no. 3. Emporia, Kans.: Emporia State University, 1978. 104 p.

Identifies the characters in all the novels.

1653 Strandberg, Victor H. A COLDER FIRE: THE POETRY OF ROBERT PENN WARREN. Lexington: University of Kentucky Press, 1965. xii, 292 p.

Following an introduction on the themes of Warren's poetry, the book proceeds to a chronological discussion of the poetry through YOU, EMPERORS, AND OTHERS. BROTHER TO DRAGONS is seen as Warren's best book of poems.

1654 Walker, Marshall. ROBERT PENN WARREN: A VISION EARNED. New York: Barnes and Noble, 1979. 279 p. Bibliog.

An enthusiastic and scholarly British study of the full range of Warren's writing: poetry, short stories, novels, and literary criticism. Up to date and indispensable.

EUDORA WELTY (1909--)

1655 Appel, Alfred, Jr. A SEASON OF DREAMS: THE FICTION OF EUDORA WELTY. Baton Rouge: Louisiana State University Press, 1965. xvi, 274 p. Bibliog.

A thorough study of the fiction through THE BRIDE OF INNISFALLEN (1955), although DELTA WEDDING is given incomprehensibly short shrift. Among topics discussed are the theme of human isolation, Welty's comic modes, her use of the grotesque and the Gothic, her literary techniques, her characterization of the Negro, and the elusive nature of some of the later stories. The importance of sense of place in her fiction is stressed.

1656 Bryant, J.A., Jr. EUDORA WELTY. UMPAW, no. 66. Minneapolis: University of Minnesota Press, 1968. 48 p. Bibliog.

Briefly reviews the short stories and novels and comments on Welty's keen visual imagination and penchant for "seeing things in their connectedness." Being southern is at once the most important and least important thing about her. She is "not without the Southern writer's sense of the past or feeling for the metaphysical," but she is never partisan in either of these areas, Bryant believes.

1657 Desmond, John F., ed. A STILL MOMENT: ESSAYS ON THE ART OF EUDORA WELTY. Metuchen, N.J., and London: Scarecrow Press, 1978. viii, 142 p.

A series of essays by various hands intended to assist the reader to understand Welty's metaphysical vision.

1658 Dollarhide, Louis, and Abadie, Ann J., eds. EUDORA WELTY: A FORM OF THANKS. Jackson: University Press of Mississippi, 1979. xiii, 138 p.

Essays by Cleanth Brooks and others on various aspects of Welty's work, read at a symposium held to honor her and to inaugurate the Center for the Study of Southern Culture at the University of Mississippi in 1977.

1659 Howard, Zelma Turner. THE RHETORIC OF EUDORA WELTY'S SHORT STORIES. Jackson: University and College Press of Mississippi, 1973. 128 p. Bibliog.

Analyzes representative stories from the collections A CURTAIN OF GREEN (1941), THE WIDE NET (1943), and THE GOLDEN APPLES (1949), using the methods and terminology of Wayne C. Booth's THE RHETORIC OF FICTION (1961). A chapter is devoted to each of the following: the narrative voice, the archetype and semantics as rhetorical devices, use of rhetoric to individualize experience, and time as a rhetorical device.

1660 Isaacs, Neil. EUDORA WELTY. Southern Writers Series, no. 8. Austin, Tex.: Steck-Vaughn, 1969. 43 p. Bibliog.

Emphasizes the sense of place in Welty's stories. Plot summaries are provided for several of the stories and novels, but critical commentary is limited by the space demands of this series.

1661 Kreyling, Michael. EUDORA WELTY'S ACHIEVEMENT OF ORDER. Baton Rouge and London: Louisiana State University Press, 1980. xxii, 188 p. Bibliog.

The latest full-scale study of the fiction, this is the first to include analysis of the novels LOSING BATTLES (1970) and THE OPTIMIST'S DAUGHTER (1972). In the latter Kreyling finds a strong affinity with Virginia Woolf's TO THE LIGHTHOUSE and believes that Welty learned much of her own art of fiction by reading Woolf. A prime objective of this sensitive study is to remove the label "regional writer" from Welty and have her considered "with her peers--Woolf, Bowen, and Forster, among others."

1662 Manz-Kunz, Marie-Antoinette. EUDORA WELTY: ASPECTS OF REALITY IN HER SHORT FICTION. Bern, Switz.: Francke Verlag, 1971. 124 p. Bibliog.

Analyzes a number of the short stories in an attempt to characterize some of the attitudes toward reality entertained by Welty's protagonists in their pursuit of experience. Chapter headings are (1) "The Writer and Her Work," (2) "Reality as an Experience of Rhythm," (3) "The Secrets in the World," (4) "Lone Wanderers of Experience," (5) "Hegira into Fantasy," and (6) "The Aspects of Reality."

1663 Prenshaw, Peggy Whitman, ed. EUDORA WELTY: CRITICAL ESSAYS. Jackson: University Press of Mississippi, 1979. xviii, 446 p.

A valuable collection on a range of topics pertaining to

Welty, the book is divided under four main headings: (1) general studies, such as, Chester Eisinger's "Traditionalism and Modernism in Eudora Welty"; (2) early fiction, e.g., Brenda Cornell's "Ambiguous Necessity: A Study of THE PONDER HEART; (3) later fiction, e.g., Robert Heilman's "LOSING BATTLES and Winning the War"; (4) photography and criticism, e.g., Barbara McKenzie's "The Eye of Time: The Photographs of Eudora Welty."

1664 Thompson, Victor H., ed. EUDORA WELTY: A REFERENCE GUIDE. Boston: G.K. Hall, 1976. xviii, 175 p.

A well-annotated list of writings about Welty organized chronologically from 1936 through 1975. Indispensable.

1665 Vande Kieft, Ruth M. EUDORA WELTY. TUSAS, no. 15. New York: Twayne, 1962. 203 p. Bibliog.

The first extended critical study of Welty's fiction, this remains the best introduction to her work through THE BRIDE OF INNISFALLEN. Discusses in detail her central themes; her emphasis on the mysteries of the universe, of personal identity and of human relationships; her methods of conveying these mysteries; her use of comedy; her projection of the world of dream and fantasy; and the development of her technique and artistic vision. A final chapter relates Welty to southern and other contemporary fiction writers and provides a general appraisal of her achievement. Feeling that her stories "require the kind of patient and loving scrutiny we apply to poems," Vande Kieft explicates them in detail.

NATHANAEL WEST (1903-1940)

1666 Comerchero, Victor. NATHANAEL WEST: THE IRONIC PROPHET. Syracuse, N.Y.: Syracuse University Press, 1964. xii, 189 p.

Emphasizes the influence of Freud, the French surrealists and symbolists, and the concepts of the quest and the wasteland. Sees T.S. Eliot as the most important influence of all.

1667 Hyman, Stanley Edgar. NATHANAEL WEST. UMPAW, no. 21. Minneapolis: University of Minnesota Press, 1962. 48 p. Bibliog.

Sees MISS LONELYHEARTS as not only West's best book, but one of the three greatest books of the twentieth century, along with THE GREAT GATSBY and THE SUN ALSO RISES. Discovers "latent homosexuality" in the character of Miss Lonelyhearts, along with an Oedipal complex.

1668 Jackson, Thomas H., ed. TWENTIETH CENTURY INTERPRETATIONS OF MISS LONELYHEARTS: A COLLECTION OF CRITICAL ESSAYS. Englewood Cliffs, N.J.: Prentice-Hall, 1971. viii, 112 p. Bibliog.

The essays are divided into two groups: "Interpretations" and "View Points." Eleven in all, introduced by the editor.

1669 Light, James F. NATHANAEL WEST: AN INTERPRETATIVE STUDY. 2d ed., rev. and enl. Evanston, Ill.: Northwestern University Press, 1971. xxv, 236 p.

An updating and enlargement of the first edition of 1961 that takes advantage of the more recent West scholarship. A thorough biocritical study that includes discussion of not only the novels and short stories but also of West's movie scripts and his play.

1670 Malin, Irving. NATHANAEL WEST'S NOVELS. Crosscurrents/Modern Critiques. Carbondale and Edwardsville: Southern Illinois University Press, 1972. ix, 141 p.

Devotes a chapter to each of the four novels, and an opening chapter suggests approaches to them. Concentrates on explication of texts. Concludes that, although the novels vary in quality, with MISS LONELYHEARTS and THE DAY OF THE LOCUST being the most powerful, they are remarkably alike in theme, character, and symbol, all of them resembling lyrics.

1671 Martin, Jay. NATHANAEL WEST: THE ART OF HIS LIFE. New York: Farrar, Straus & Giroux, 1970. 435 p. Illus.

The official biography, and the best. Martin took full advantage of the materials provided him by West's sister and brother-in-law, S.J. Perelman. Has an appendix on West's screen writing.

1672 ______, ed. NATHANAEL WEST: A COLLECTION OF CRITICAL ESSAYS. Twentieth Century Views. Englewood Cliffs, N.J.: Prentice-Hall, 1971. viii, 176 p. Bibliog.

The best collection available, it includes twenty-one items and a good introduction by Martin.

1673 Reid, Randall. THE FICTION OF NATHANAEL WEST: NO REDEEMER, NO PROMISED LAND. Chicago and London: University of Chicago Press, 1967. viii, 174 p. Bibliog.

Sees the power of art to shape reality as a persistent theme in West's novels. Dreams were his special subject, "but absolute clarity was his special tool, and clarity is not kind to dreams." Contends that parody was, for West, a diagnostic instrument that he used to identify the familiar themes of our culture, to expose their weaknesses and to express their decadence.

1674 Scott, Nathan A., Jr. NATHANAEL WEST, A CRITICAL ESSAY. Contemporary Writers in Christian Perspective. Grand Rapids, Mich.: William B. Eerdmans, 1971. 47 p. Bibliog.

Sketches West's life and works and views him as an "extraordinarily competent analyst of our modern penchant for fighting misery with dreams and of 'the breakdown of the American dream.'"

1675 Vannatta, Dennis P. NATHANAEL WEST: AN ANNOTATED BIBLIOGRAPHY OF THE SCHOLARSHIP AND WORKS. New York and London: Garland Publishing, 1976. xv, 165 p.

In twelve parts: "Master Checklist of Scholarship," "Bibliographical Studies," "The State of West Scholarship," "Biographical Studies," "Biographical Criticism," "Source Studies," "Influence Studies," "Genre Studies," "Studies in the History of Ideas," "Historical-Sociological Criticism," "Comparative Studies," and "General Criticism." An appendix lists West's works. Indispensable.

1676 White, William, ed. NATHANAEL WEST: A COMPREHENSIVE BIBLIOGRAPHY. Serif Series of Bibliographies and Checklists, no. 32. Kent, Ohio: Kent State University Press, 1975. xi, 209 p. Illus.

Includes books by West, works by him published in books containing works by others, plays (unpublished), movies, work published in periodicals, unpublished stories and other writings, selections in anthologies, and a final section of biographical and critical material about West, including theses and dissertations. Unannotated.

EDITH WHARTON (1862-1937)

1677 Auchincloss, Louis. EDITH WHARTON. UMPAW, no. 12. Minneapolis: University of Minnesota Press, 1961. 46 p. Bibliog.

A brief review of Wharton's fiction, which concludes that "she will be remembered primarily for her two great novels of manners: THE HOUSE OF MIRTH, and THE AGE OF INNOCENCE."

1678 ______. EDITH WHARTON: A WOMAN IN HER TIME. New York: Viking, 1971. 191 p. Illus.

A biography that is valuable primarily for the photographs which illustrate it.

1679 Bell, Millicent. EDITH WHARTON & HENRY JAMES: THE STORY OF THEIR FRIENDSHIP. New York: George Braziller, 1965. 384 p.

Based largely on the correspondence of the two writers, this is a detailed and often fascinating account of their personal relationship and of their literary relationship.

1680 Brenni, Vito J., ed. EDITH WHARTON: A BIBLIOGRAPHY. Morgantown: West Virginia University Library, 1966. xvi, 99 p.

Includes novels, short stories, poems, nonfiction, and translations of Wharton's writing. Other sections are about drama based on her writings, reviews of her books, biographical and critical writing about her, theses and dissertations, and bibliographies, obituaries and portraits. Largely unannotated.

1681 Howe, Irving, ed. EDITH WHARTON: A COLLECTION OF CRITICAL ESSAYS. Englewood Cliffs, N.J.: Prentice-Hall, 1962. vi, 181 p. Bibliog.

An introductory essay by Howe on "The Achievement of Edith Wharton" is followed by sixteen essays by eminent critics and scholars such as Edmund Wilson, Louis Auchincloss, Percy Lubbock, Q.D. Leavis, Alfred Kazin, E.K. Brown, Blake Nevius, Lionel and Diana Trilling, Henry James, V.L. Parrington, and Louis Coxe. An excellent collection.

1682 Kellogg, Grace. THE TWO LIVES OF EDITH WHARTON: THE WOMAN AND HER WORK. New York: Appleton-Century, 1965. xiv, 332 p. Bibliog.

The interrelationship of Wharton's writing and her social life is the theme of this biography. "In its warping of her life and its containment of her work, for the author no less than for Lily Bart [heroine of THE HOUSE OF MIRTH], the Cage was a determining limitation." The letters to Louis Bromfield are the main contribution of this study.

1683 Lawson, Richard H. EDITH WHARTON AND GERMAN LITERATURE. Bonn: Bouvier Verlag Herbert Grundmann, 1974. 146 p. Bibliog.

Studies Wharton's reading of German literature and its influence on her work. Sudermann and Nietzsche are seen as exerting strong influence, Goethe less substantially. A case is made for her assimilation of Gottfried Keller's ROMEO UND JULIA AUF DEM DORFE in her own book, SUMMER.

1684 Lewis, R.W.B. EDITH WHARTON: A BIOGRAPHY. New York: Evanston, Ill., San Francisco, and London: Harper and Row, 1975. xiv, 592 p. Illus.

The definitive life, it is based on much information previously unknown or unavailable, including the tempestuous love affair with Morton Fullerton. The study of Mrs. Wharton is detailed, scholarly, and generally objective. Basic to all future work on her.

1685 Lovett, Robert Morss. EDITH WHARTON. New York: Robert M. McBride, 1925. Reprint. Folcroft, Pa.: Folcroft Press, 1969. 91 p. Bibliog.

An early critical study that compares Wharton with Jane Austen as social critic to Wharton's disadvantage. The difference is seen to lie in their respective societies: Austen's "stable, self-perpetuating, permanent," Wharton's "transitory, imitative, sterile."

1686 Lubbock, Percy. PORTRAIT OF EDITH WHARTON. New York: Appleton-Century, 1947. vii, 249 p.

An informal portrait by a close friend that is impressionistic rather than realistic in its approach.

1687 Lyde, Marilyn. EDITH WHARTON: CONVENTION AND MORALITY IN THE WORK OF A NOVELIST. Norman: University of Oklahoma Press, 1959. xix, 194 p. Bibliog.

Provides a full account of Wharton's views on changing social conventions in the light of her moral philosophy.

1688 McDowell, Margaret B. EDITH WHARTON. TUSAS, no. 265. Boston: Twayne, 1976. 158 p. Bibliog.

A very good introduction that includes an adequate biographical sketch and a reasonably inclusive review of Wharton's work.

1689 Nevius, Blake. EDITH WHARTON: A STUDY OF HER FICTION. Berkeley and Los Angeles: University of California Press, 1953. xi, 271 p. Bibliog.

Despite its years, this remains one of the best critiques of Wharton's work. Two themes are stressed: the sensitive person is destroyed by less refined people, and the sensitive person falls victim to a conflict between his craving for individual freedom and his obligation to assume social responsibility.

1690 Walton, Geoffrey. EDITH WHARTON: A CRITICAL INTERPRETATION. Rutherford, N.J.: Fairleigh Dickinson University Press, 1971. 216 p. Bibliog.

A detailed and indispensable criticism of the full range of Wharton's work. The evaluations are done from a fresh perspective.

1691 Wolff, Cynthia Griffin. A FEAST OF WORDS: THE TRIUMPH OF EDITH WHARTON. New York: Oxford University Press, 1977. viii, 453 p. Illus., bibliog.

An interesting psychological study of Wharton, who is seen as a sexually repressed woman finally liberated at the age of forty-five through her affair with Morton Fullerton. Her fiction is closely analyzed, and the theme runs through the analysis that Wharton uses language as an outlet for the repressed self beginning with her childhood, continuing through her marriage, until her eventual release in the Fullerton affair. "The adult author unleashes the voice of rebellion that the little girl had so fearfully stilled." Greatly indebted to Lewis's (see no. 1684) biography.

See also no. 307.

WALT WHITMAN (1819-1892)

1692 Allen, Gay Wilson. THE NEW WALT WHITMAN HANDBOOK. Chicago: Packard and Co., 1946. Reprint. New York: New York University Press, 1975. xxi, 423 p. Illus. Bibliog.

A completely revised, rewritten, and updated version of the original handbook. Five chapters follow a chronological table: (1) "The Growth of Whitman Biography," (2) "The Growth of LEAVES OF GRASS," (3) "The Realm of Whitman's Ideas," (4) "Literary Techniques in LEAVES OF GRASS," and (5) "Whitman and World Literature." The bibliography is extensive.

1693 _____. A READER'S GUIDE TO WALT WHITMAN. New York: Farrar, Straus and Giroux, 1970. xiii, 234 p. Bibliog.

Intended as an introduction to intelligent reading and study, the book is neither an exhaustive analysis nor a definitive critical evaluation. Attention is paid to changing critical views about Whitman.

1694 _____. THE SOLITARY SINGER: A CRITICAL BIOGRAPHY OF WALT WHITMAN. New York: Macmillan, 1955. Rev. ed. New York: New York University Press, 1967. xii, 616 p. Illus.

Allen's biography comes as close as we have to being "definitive." There are more facts here about Whitman's life than are to be found in any other book. The criticism of the poetry, however, is somewhat pedestrian.

1695 _____. WALT WHITMAN. New York: Grove Press, 1961. Rev. ed. Detroit: Wayne State University Press, 1969. 251 p. Illus., bibliog.

A profile written originally for the Evergreen Profile Series and here revised and updated. A profusely illustrated book for the nonspecialist, it includes, besides a biographical essay, excerpts from Whitman's work, and selected criticism.

1696 _____. WALT WHITMAN AS MAN, POET, AND LEGEND WITH A CHECKLIST OF WHITMAN PUBLICATIONS 1945-1960 BY EVIE ALLISON ALLEN. Carbondale: Southern Illinois University Press, 1961. xii, 260 p.

Something of a reprise on earlier Allen. In three parts: (1) "The Man," (2) "The Poet," and (3) "The Legend," which concerns Whitman's image in the twentieth century. The checklist is quite valuable.

1697 _____, ed. WALT WHITMAN ABROAD: CRITICAL ESSAYS FROM GERMANY, FRANCE, SCANDINAVIA, RUSSIA, ITALY, SPAIN AND LATIN AMERICA, ISRAEL, JAPAN, AND INDIA. Syracuse: Syracuse University Press, 1955. xii, 290 p. Bibliog.

An impressive collection, translated into English by various hands.

1698 Arvin, Newton. WHITMAN. New York: Macmillan, 1938. viii, 320 p. Bibliog.

A portrait rather more than a biography, it emphasizes Whitman's political and economic views.

1699 Asselineau, Roger. THE EVOLUTION OF WALT WHITMAN: THE CREATION OF A BOOK. Cambridge, Mass.: Belknap Press of Harvard University Press, 1962. viii, 392 p.

This book, by a French scholar, traces in part 1 the main themes of LEAVES OF GRASS, and in part 2 the progress of Whitman's art.

1700 Bailey, John. WALT WHITMAN. English Men of Letters. London: Macmillan, 1926. v, 220 p.

A British introduction to the life and work, it is somewhat patronizing in tone, particularly in the comments on the vulgarities of Whitman's language and his disregard of the rules of grammar, arising from ignorance or carelessness. Whitman is also taken to task for his use of foreign words.

1701 Barrus, Clara. WHITMAN AND BURROUGHS, COMRADES. Boston and New York: Houghton Mifflin, 1931. xxx, 392 p. Illus.

Reveals how Whitman's concept of comradeship worked in his personal life, with special emphasis on John Burroughs as "the most complete embodiment of the Whitman ideal of comradeship." Valuable as a source for documents.

1702 Beaver, Joseph. WALT WHITMAN--POET OF SCIENCE. New York: King's Crown Press, 1951. xv, 178 p. Bibliog.

An examination of Whitman's work leads Beaver to conclude that he was the first American poet to embody modern scientific concepts in a poetic manner. Shows how Whitman went about reconciling science with poetry, and evaluates the degree of success achieved.

1703 Binns, Henry Bryan. WALT WHITMAN AND HIS POETRY. London: George G. Harrap, 1920. Reprint. Folcroft, Pa.: Folcroft Press, 1969. 167 p.

A British evaluation of the man and his poems which includes a printing of many of them in whole or in part.

1704 Black, Stephen A. WHITMAN'S JOURNEYS INTO CHAOS: A PSYCHOANALYTIC STUDY OF THE POETIC PROCESS. Princeton, N.J.: Princeton University Press, 1975. xv, 255 p. Bibliog.

Neither a biography nor an interpretation of LEAVES OF GRASS, this is a psychoanalytic investigation of Whitman's poetic processes between 1855 and 1865. The chaos referred to in the title supposedly existed in Whitman's unconscious, "where his fantasies and poetic impulses originated; the journeys into this chaos are the poems." Interesting, if inconclusive.

1705 Blodgett, Harold. WALT WHITMAN IN ENGLAND. Ithaca, N.Y.: Cornell University Press, 1934. ix, 244 p. Bibliog.

Reviews the attitudes toward Whitman of William M. Rossetti, Dowden, Symonds, Buchanan, Anne Gilchrist, Swinburne, Tennyson, and several more minor poets, as well as Edward Carpenter, Havelock Ellis, and "professors and journalists."

1706 Brasher, Thomas L. WHITMAN AS EDITOR OF THE BROOKLYN DAILY EAGLE. Detroit: Wayne State University Press, 1970. 264 p.

An interesting study that presents a comprehensive picture

of Whitman during his two years as editor of the EAGLE. He is vindicated as a highly professional journalist, and some of the ideas expressed in his editorials are seen as foreshadowing ideas expressed in LEAVES OF GRASS.

1707 Burroughs, John. WHITMAN, A STUDY. Boston: Houghton Mifflin, 1896. Reprint. New York: AMS Press, 1969. 268 p.

Written by Whitman's naturalist friend, this examines Walt's relation to art and literature, to life and morals, to culture, to his country and his times, to science and religion, with chapters on his life, his ruling ideas and aims, and on his self-reliance.

1708 Canby, Henry Seidel. WALT WHITMAN, AN AMERICAN: A STUDY IN BIOGRAPHY. Boston: Houghton Mifflin, 1943. viii, 381 p. Illus., bibliog.

Whitman is here stressed as the great poet of democracy, seen as "self-revealing beyond all of his contemporaries in his poetry."

1709 Chari, V.K. WHITMAN IN THE LIGHT OF VEDANTIC MYSTICISM. Lincoln: University of Nebraska Press, 1964. xiii, 176 p.

An Indian scholar's attempt to present a consistent account of Whitman's poetic thought and belief, proceeding from the central standpoint of the self. The unity of thought and experience in Whitman is explained in terms of Vedantic philosophy.

1710 Chase, Richard. WALT WHITMAN. UMPAW, no. 9. Minneapolis: University of Minnesota Press, 1961. 48 p. Bibliog.

A good synthesis of Chase's earlier writing on Whitman.

1711 ______. WALT WHITMAN RECONSIDERED. New York: William Sloane Associates, 1955. 191 p.

A highly imaginative interpretation of Whitman and his poetry. "Song of Myself," for example, is analyzed primarily as a comic poem. Chase, like most others who have written about him, concludes that Whitman is impossible to pin down, to define absolutely.

1712 Clark, Leadie M. WALT WHITMAN'S CONCEPT OF THE AMERICAN COMMON MAN. New York: Philosophical Library, 1955. xiv, 178 p. Bibliog.

It implied, Clark holds, "a theory of racial superiority";

indeed, Whitman's common man appears to be a WASP. Whitman is also taken to task for not teaching an intellectual philosophy "whereby the reader can become great." He is seen as espousing the larger view of liberty, fraternity, and spiritual equality but as providing no social or political philosophy to "help the reader adjust to his present environment."

1713 Coyle, William. THE POET AND THE PRESIDENT: WHITMAN'S LINCOLN POEMS. New York: Odyssey Press, 1962. xiii, 334 p.

The aim here is to afford composition and literature classes a wide range of materials for research and for critical analysis. The four poems in "Memories of President Lincoln" are reprinted together with a selection of criticism, explication, and biographical data bearing on the poems.

1714 Crawley, Thomas Edward. THE STRUCTURE OF LEAVES OF GRASS. Austin and London: University of Texas Press, 1970. xii, 256 p. Bibliog.

Sees an effective unifying principle at work in LEAVES OF GRASS. There are chapters on Whitman's organic principle and poet-prophet, on the Christ symbol in LEAVES OF GRASS, on a structural analysis of the book, and on its evolution.

1715 DeSelincourt, Basil. WALT WHITMAN: A CRITICAL STUDY. New York: Mitchell Kennerley, 1914. Reprint. New York: Russell and Russell, 1965. 251 p.

Although a pioneer study, it has retained much of its value. Whitman is seen as carrying with him to the last "a faculty of trance-like perception which enabled him to throw a gleam of poetry over any and every detail of his experience."

1716 Dutton, Geoffrey. WHITMAN. Writers and Critics Series. Edinburgh and London: Oliver and Boyd, 1961. 120 p. Bibliog.

A sensible British introduction divided into three parts: (1) "The Man and the Prose," (2) "The Poetry," and (3) "The Critics."

1717 Faner, Robert D. WALT WHITMAN AND OPERA. Philadelphia: University of Pennsylvania Press, 1951. xi, 249 p. Bibliog.

An excellent study which shows that grand opera was a major influence on the development of Whitman's poetry. Part 1 is devoted to background material such as the music Whitman heard or knew and the extent of his technical knowledge of music, as well as his understanding of, and response to, the art of opera. Part 2 examines representative poems to show how opera influenced their form and content.

1718 Golden, Arthur, ed. WALT WHITMAN: A COLLECTION OF CRITICISM. New York: McGraw-Hill Paperbacks, 1974. viii, 152 p. Bibliog.

In four parts: (1) "The Long Foreground," (2) "The Creative Process: Literary Techniques and Achievement," (3) "The Revisory Process," and (4) "Democratic Vistas." Gay Wilson Allen, Roger Asselineau, Stanley K. Coffman, Jr., Edwin Haviland Miller, Stephen E. Whicher, James E. Miller, Jr., Richard Chase, and the editor are the critics represented.

1719 Hindus, Milton, ed. LEAVES OF GRASS ONE HUNDRED YEARS AFTER: NEW ESSAYS BY WILLIAM CARLOS WILLIAMS, RICHARD CHASE, LESLIE A. FIEDLER, KENNETH BURKE, DAVID DAICHES, AND J. MIDDLETON MURRY. Stanford, Calif.: Stanford University Press, 1955. 149 p.

An important collection.

1720 ______. WALT WHITMAN, THE CRITICAL HERITAGE. Critical Heritage Series. London: Routledge and Kegan Paul, 1971. xi, 292 p. Bibliog.

Divided into three sections 1855-60, 1865-92, and 1893-1914, this reprints essays and reviews, British and American, appearing during those time spans.

1721 Holloway, Emory. FREE AND LONESOME HEART: THE SECRET OF WALT WHITMAN. New York: Vantage Press, 1960. 232 p.

A fascinating, if controversial, study of "Whitman's nature, his knowledge and poetic treatment of sex and friendship, and the influence such treatment had in turn on his own life." Whitman's various affairs of the heart, alternating between the male and the female, are explored, and Holloway presents evidence that Whitman had at least one child, a son named John Whitman Wilder.

1722 ______. WHITMAN; AN INTERPRETATION IN NARRATIVE. New York and London: Knopf, 1926. xv, 330 p. Illus.

The first of the modern biographies, this is written primarily for the general reader who knows little or nothing about Whitman; therefore, the scholarly apparatus of footnotes and documentation is dispensed with. It is, however, based on solid scholarship.

1723 Kaplan, Justin. WALT WHITMAN: A LIFE. New York: Simon and Schuster, 1981. 429 p. Illus.

Engagingly written, this latest biography of Whitman departs from the biographical norm as did Kaplan's biography of Mark Twain. It begins with the poet's final years in Camden and provides a meticulously documented account of this period; then it flashes back to Whitman's beginnings and continues from there. Although dramatic in effect, the work offers little that is not to be found in Allen's THE SOLITARY SINGER, and omits much that is to be found there.

1724 Kennedy, William Sloane. THE FIGHT OF A BOOK FOR THE WORLD: A COMPANION VOLUME TO LEAVES OF GRASS. West Yarmouth, Mass.: Stonecroft Press, 1926. xvi, 304 p.

One of Whitman's friends created this book as "an armory of weapons against his enemies and a box of tools for the service of his friends." It is, in essence, an early handbook of more than historical interest.

1725 Lewis, R.W.B., ed. THE PRESENCE OF WALT WHITMAN: SELECTED PAPERS FROM THE ENGLISH INSTITUTE. New York and London: Columbia University Press, 1962. xvi, 215 p.

Seven essays by Stephen E. Whicher, Paul Fussell, Jr., Richard Chase, Roy Harvey Pearce, Samuel Hynes, James E. Miller, Jr., and James A. Wright, dominated by the elements of Whitman as poet and as self.

1726 McLeod, A.L., ed. WALT WHITMAN IN AUSTRALIA AND NEW ZEALAND: A RECORD OF HIS RECEPTION. Sydney: Wentworth Press, 1964. 161 p.

A reprint of public lectures and essays and notices published in Australian and New Zealand newspapers and periodicals from 1891 through 1907.

1727 Marinacci, Barbara. O WONDROUS SINGER! AN INTRODUCTION TO WALT WHITMAN. New York: Dodd, Mead, 1970. 371 p. Illus. Bibliog.

A rather simplified introduction to a very complicated poet. Adds nothing to our knowledge of Whitman.

1728 Masters, Edgar Lee. WHITMAN. New York: Scribner's, 1937. 342 p.

An adequate but rather plodding biography that adds nothing new to the life story and pays surprisingly little attention to the poetry.

1729 Mendelson, Maurice. LIFE AND WORK OF WALT WHITMAN: A SOVIET VIEW. Translated from Russian by Andrew Bromfield. Moscow: Progress Publishers, 1976. 347 p.

Instructive for American readers in that they may have at

first-hand a Marxist view of Whitman and his poetry. Whitman is seen as a champion of collectivism. For example, we are told that Whitman, aware of Thoreau's individualism, "took him sharply to task for his insufficient democratic commitment."

1730 Middlebrook, Diane Wood. WALT WHITMAN AND WALLACE STEVENS. Ithaca, N.Y., and London: Cornell University Press, 1974. 238 p.

The two poets are seen as having made analagous contributions to American literature and to modern poetry. Stevens admired and sought to achieve in his own writing two characteristics of Whitman: concreteness and elan. His resemblance to Whitman lies "in the area of a shared theory of poetry which derives ultimately from Coleridge's concept of the imagination, and was translated into American idioms in the writing of Ralph Waldo Emerson."

1731 Miller, Edwin Haviland, ed. A CENTURY OF WHITMAN CRITICISM. Bloomington and London: Indiana University Press, 1969. xliii, 368 p.

An excellent collection, beginning with Emerson's 1855 letter to Whitman extolling LEAVES OF GRASS, and ending with the editor's own 1968 explication of "The Sleepers."

1732 Miller, Edwin H., and Miller, Rosalind S., eds. WALT WHITMAN'S CORRESPONDENCE: A CHECKLIST. New York: New York Public Library, 1957. x, 161 p.

A chronological list beginning with 1842 and ending with 1890.

1733 Miller, James E., Jr. A CRITICAL GUIDE TO LEAVES OF GRASS. Chicago: University of Chicago Press, 1957. xi, 268 p.

This helpful guide is divided into two parts: (1) "Close-ups: The Dramatic Structure" examines individual sections; and (2) "Panorama: The Structure of LEAVES OF GRASS examines the basic unity of the entire work and the relationship of its parts.

1734 ______. WALT WHITMAN. TUSAS, no. 20. New York: Twayne, 1962. 188 p. Bibliog.

An interesting introduction to Whitman and his poetry. In seven chapters: (1) sets forth the various roles he assumed, (2) deals with the growth of LEAVES OF GRASS through nine editions, (3) with the prose works that were concerned with a "poetics for Democracy," (4) with the epic structure of LEAVES OF GRASS, (5) with its greatest individual poems, (6) with its recurring images, (7) with its language and its wit, and (8) with its bardic voice.

1735 Miller, James E., Jr., with Karl Shapiro and Bernice Slote. START WITH THE SUN. Lincoln: University of Nebraska Press, 1960. viii, 260 p. Bibliog.

Essays by the three authors on the Whitman tradition in poetry. Important essays deal with Whitman's influence on the poetry of D.H. Lawrence, Hart Crane, and Dylan Thomas.

1736 Nambiar, O.K. WALT WHITMAN AND YOGA. Bangalore, India: Jeevan Publications, 1966. xii, 183 p.

A Hindu scholar contends that section 5 of "Song of Myself" describes the whole Yogic movement, and that the incidents and symbols he refers to are similar to those mentioned in Yogic works on Kundalini (a psychophysical energy present in each individual).

1737 Pearce, Roy Harvey, ed. WHITMAN: A COLLECTION OF CRITICAL ESSAYS. Englewood Cliffs, N.J.: Prentice-Hall, 1962. viii, 183 p. Bibliog.

Fourteen essays that discuss various aspects of the man and his work. Except for Ezra Pound and D.H. Lawrence, the critics are all fairly well-known Whitman scholars.

1738 Perry, Bliss. WALT WHITMAN. American Men of Letters. Boston and New York: Houghton Mifflin, 1906. viii, 334 p.

An ably written biocritical study that may still serve as an adequate introduction to Whitman.

1739 Rajasekharaiah, T.R. THE ROOTS OF WHITMAN'S GRASS. Rutherford, Madison, and Teaneck, N.J.: Fairleigh Dickinson University Press, 1970. 522 p. Bibliog.

An Indian scholar attempts to demonstrate the influence of Indian thought as paramount in the making of LEAVES OF GRASS. He contends that internal evidence proves that Whitman made use of Indian scripture in writing his book.

1740 Rubin, Joseph Jay. THE HISTORIC WHITMAN. University Park and London: Pennsylvania State University Press, 1973. 406 p.

An excellent recreation of Whitman's life up to the publication in 1855 of the first edition of LEAVES OF GRASS. The emphasis is on the richness and variety of life Whitman encountered during these early years. Also collects and reprints for the first time "Letters from a Travelling Bachelor," appearing in the New York Sunday DISPATCH from 14 October 1849 through 6 January 1850.

1741 Schyberg, Frederik. WALT WHITMAN. Copenhagen: Gyldendal, 1933. Translated from Danish by Evie Allison Allen. New York: Columbia University Press, 1951. xv, 387 p. Bibliog.

Initially published in Danish in 1933, it is valuable in its tracing of the development of LEAVES OF GRASS through its nine editions and in its attempt to reconstruct Whitman's life as it is revealed in his book. His place in world literature is discussed in a final chapter. He is seen as having broken quite intentionally with European academic tradition in both style and content. He celebrated modern reality as well as modern America and its democracy.

1742 Shephard, Esther. WALT WHITMAN'S POSE. New York: Harcourt, Brace, 1938. xii, 453 p. Illus.

An attempt to debunk Whitman by portraying him as a poseur, "charlatan and arch-egotist or victim of an extreme case of schizophrenia." Shephard, among other idiocies, protests to have discovered the source of LEAVES OF GRASS in the epilogue to George Sand's THE COUNTESS OF RUDOLSTADT.

1743 Smuts, Jan Christian. WALT WHITMAN: A STUDY IN THE EVOLUTION OF PERSONALITY. Detroit: Wayne State University, 1973. 205 p.

A pioneer study, written in 1895, when the future prime minister of the Union of South Africa was only twenty-four, and unpublished until almost a quarter century after his death.

1744 Stavrou, C.N. WHITMAN AND NIETZSCHE: A COMPARATIVE STUDY OF THEIR THOUGHT. Chapel Hill: University of North Carolina Press, 1964. xi, 231 p. Bibliog.

A rewarding study in which many parallelisms are found between the expressed thought of Whitman and that of the German philosopher. Differences between them are also pointed out, as, for example, Whitman's seeing as he grew older both the limitations of absolute individualism and the pitfalls of democracy, whereas Nietzsche never wavered in his belief that the state, any state, blocks man's path to self-fulfillment.

1745 Stovall, Floyd. THE FOREGROUND OF LEAVES OF GRASS. Charlottesville: University Press of Virginia, 1974. x, 320 p.

This is the fascinating story of Whitman's intellectual and cultural development, especially during the years preceding the first two or three editions of LEAVES OF GRASS. It deals, among other things, with his reading, with the influence of the New York stage and the New York opera, with science, phrenology, geography, ancient and medieval history and literature, German romantic philosophy, French and British literary influences, and Emerson.

1746 Symonds, John Addington. WALT WHITMAN: A STUDY. London: John C. Nimmo, 1893. Reprint. New York: AMS Press, 1968. xxxv, 160 p.

An enthusiastic interpretation of Whitman and his poetry by a British critic.

1747 Tanner, James T.F., ed. WALT WHITMAN: A SUPPLEMENTARY BIBLIOGRAPHY: 1961-1967. Serif Series of Bibliographies and Checklists. Kent, Ohio: Kent State University Press, 1968. vi, 59 p.

An unannotated bibliography of works about Whitman that is intended to update the Evie Allison Allen bibliography (see no. 1696) included in Gay Wilson Allen's WALT WHITMAN AS MAN, POET, AND LEGEND (1961), covering the years 1945-60.

1748 Thomson, James. WALT WHITMAN, THE MAN AND THE POET. London: Bertram Dobell, 1910. xxxv, 106 p.

A spirited defense of Whitman by the author of "The City of Dreadful Night."

1749 Traubel, Horace. WITH WALT WHITMAN IN CAMDEN. 5 vols. Vol. 1, 28 March-14 July 1888. Boston: Small, Maynard, 1906. xiv, 473 p. Illus. Vol. 2, 15 July-31 October 1888. New York: Appleton, 1908. xi, 570 p. Illus. Vol. 3, 1 November 1888-20 January 1889. New York: Mitchell Kennerley, 1914. viii, 590 p. Illus. Vol. 4, 21 January-7 April 1889. Edited by Sculley Bradley. Carbondale: Southern Illinois University Press, 1959. xviii, 528 p. Illus. Vol. 5, 8 April-14 September 1889. Edited by Gertrude Traubel. Carbondale: Southern Illinois University Press, 1964. xii, 524 p. Illus.

Indispensable for students of Whitman. Whitman's young Camden neighbor, Horace Traubel, began taking notes of his almost daily visits to and conversations with Whitman through most of 1888 and 1889. These volumes are the virtually unedited version of those hundreds of scribbled notes, constituting a unique and unvarnished portrait of the great poet in his old age.

1750 Waskow, Howard J. WHITMAN: EXPLORATIONS IN FORM. Chicago and London: University of Chicago Press, 1966. ix, 279 p. Bibliog.

In two parts: (1) "Whitman's Habit of Mind," and (2)

"Whitman at Work." Tries to define individual poems by showing how they work, and to define Whitman's poetry by demonstrating the relationship among the various ways of working.

1751 Willard, Charles B. WHITMAN'S AMERICAN FAME: THE GROWTH OF HIS REPUTATION IN AMERICA AFTER 1892. Providence: Brown University, 1950. 269 p. Bibliog.

Whitman is seen as emerging, in the years since his death, "slowly and doubtfully at first, then with rapid and complete recognition, as our greatest poet, the true American Giant." The book summarizes and discusses the major aspects of this solidification of reputation.

1752 Winwar, Frances. AMERICAN GIANT: WALT WHITMAN AND HIS TIMES. New York and London: Harper, 1941. xiv, 341 p. Illus. Bibliog.

A somewhat popularized biography that attempts to make Whitman's life more sensational than it apparently was.

See also no. 1618.

JOHN GREENLEAF WHITTIER (1807-1892)

1753 Bennett, Whitman. WHITTIER, BARD OF FREEDOM. Chapel Hill: University of North Carolina Press, 1941. xv, 359 p. Illus.

An interpretative biography that is over-laudatory. Whittier is called "an astute editor, a graceful essayist, a thundering prose controversialist, and . . . a truly masterful indigenous poet." He is seen also as a progressive and a liberal of his times, and the greatest teacher of "the American Way" who ever lived. This sympathetic study, which has enthusiasm for its subject to recommend it, is marred by Bennett's blunderbuss attack on Mordell's biography.

1754 Carpenter, George Rice. JOHN GREENLEAF WHITTIER. American Men of Letters. Boston and New York: Houghton, Mifflin, 1903. viii, 311 p.

Despite its age, this remains quite possibly the best short biography. It is the first study of Whittier to observe that his poetic career was determined by the rising tide of romanticism. The emphasis is on the poet rather than on Whittier the abolitionist.

1755 Claflin, Mary B. PERSONAL RECOLLECTIONS OF JOHN G. WHITTIER. New York: Crowell, 1893. 95 p.

A chatty string of reminiscences by the wife of the governor of Massachusetts, in whose home Whittier was frequently entertained.

1756 Currier, Thomas Franklin, ed. A BIBLIOGRAPHY OF JOHN GREENLEAF WHITTIER. Cambridge, Mass.: Harvard University Press, 1937. xvi, 692 p.

The fullest and best bibliography of Whittier's works, it is a model for this kind of book. Also includes secondary sources up to 1937, but they are not annotated.

1757 Hawkins, Chauncey J. THE MIND OF WHITTIER: A STUDY OF WHITTIER'S FUNDAMENTAL RELIGIOUS IDEAS. New York: Thomas Whittaker, 1904. Reprint. New York: Haskell House, 1973. 114 p.

The fullest and best consideration of Whittier as religious poet, the book contains chapters on "The Inner Light" and on its nature, on "Jesus Christ," on "Optimism," on "Religion and Humanity," on "Nature," and on "Future Life." Hawkins was minister of the First Congregational Church of Spencer, Massachusetts.

1758 Higginson, Thomas Wentworth. JOHN GREENLEAF WHITTIER. English Men of Letters. New York: Macmillan, 1902. viii, 196 p.

The best part of this brief biography by a close friend of the poet is that which deals with Whittier's political and abolitionist activities. It is also good in discussing his religious beliefs. Evaluation of the poetry is disappointing.

1759 Kennedy, W. Sloane. JOHN GREENLEAF WHITTIER: HIS LIFE, GENIUS, AND WRITINGS. Rev. and enl. Boston: D. Lothrop, 1892. Reprint. New York: Haskell House, 1973. 373 p. Bibliog.

Originally published in 1882, it was hurriedly republished shortly after Whittier's death with the addition of a final chapter treating the death, funeral, and some personal reminiscences. The main portion of this first biography of Whittier is divided into two equal parts: the life and the writings (prose and poetry). The biographical portion is sketchy and inaccurate, and the criticism of the poetry is colored by Kennedy's dislike of Whittier's religious beliefs. He saw "the reform craze, the religious craze, and the rhyme craze" as nearly destroying the major part of his poetry.

1760 Kribbs, Jayne K., ed. CRITICAL ESSAYS ON JOHN GREENLEAF WHITTIER. Boston: Twayne, 1980. 272 p. Bibliog.

The first collection to bring together 150 years of reviews, articles, and essays on Whittier's life and work.

1761 Leary, Lewis. JOHN GREENLEAF WHITTIER. TUSAS, no. 6. New York: Twayne, 1961. 189 p. Bibliog.

A not altogether reliable introduction to the man and his works, the book is divided into almost equal segments, the first being biographical, the second reviewing and discussing the poetry. The biographical section contains some errors of fact and the critical section takes a somewhat patronizing view of the poetry.

1762 Mordell, Albert. QUAKER MILITANT: JOHN GREENLEAF WHITTIER. Boston and New York: Houghton Mifflin, 1933. xxi, 354 p. Illus., bibliog.

The first of the "modern" biographies of Whittier, it is a product of extensive scholarship, resulting in a new view of the poet. Infatuated with Freudian analysis, Mordell sees Whittier, following his youthful rejection by Mary Emerson Smith, as a life-long celibate whose sexual repression led him to neurosis and to philandering with a series of women writers whom he had no intention of marrying. Mordell has, however, great admiration for him as politician, reformer, and poet. The flaming poems for freedom he regards as the best and likens Whittier to Milton rather than to Burns, and finally places him with Whitman "among our great American poets."

1763 Pickard, John B. JOHN GREENLEAF WHITTIER: AN INTRODUCTION AND INTERPRETATION. New York: Barnes and Noble, 1961. xiii, 145 p. Illus., bibliog.

The best balanced short introduction. The biographical sketch is reliable, and the analysis of the poetry is useful. Whittier is viewed as a minor poet with a solid core of enduring poetry. John B. Pickard is the grandson of S.T. Pickard.

1764 ______, ed. MEMORABILIA OF JOHN GREENLEAF WHITTIER. Hartford: Emerson Society, 1968. 167 p. Illus.

Includes eighteen articles from a symposium on Whittier, along with a section of twenty photographs of him that form a pictorial biography from age twenty-one to age eighty-two.

1765 Pickard, Samuel T. LIFE AND LETTERS OF JOHN GREENLEAF WHITTIER. 2 vols. Boston and New York: Houghton, Mifflin, 1895. Reprint. New York: Haskell House, 1969. vi, 802 p. Illus.

The indispensable biography, basic to all later scholarship, this was authorized by Whittier and undertaken by the husband of his niece. A well-written and generally objective account, it contains the first full examination of the relation of Whittier's political life to his poetry.

1766 Pollard, John A. JOHN GREENLEAF WHITTIER, FRIEND OF MAN. Boston: Houghton Mifflin, 1949. xviii, 615 p. Bibliog.

The fullest modern biography, it is well documented and is a desirable supplement to S.T. Pickard's life (see no. 1765). Sees the central fact of Whittier's life as his strong faith in democracy.

1767 Pray, Frances Mary. A STUDY OF WHITTIER'S APPRENTICESHIP AS A POET. State College (now University Park): Pennsylvania State College, 1930. 268 p.

Deals with poems written between 1825 and 1835 that were not included in Whittier's collected works.

1768 Sparhawk, Frances Campbell. WHITTIER AT CLOSE RANGE. Boston: Riverdale Press, 1925. 181 p.

The daughter of Whittier's physician and close friend provides intimate glimpses of the poet's life and character.

1769 Stevens, James Stacy, comp. WHITTIER'S USE OF THE BIBLE. University of Maine Studies, 2d Series, no. 16. Orono: University of Maine Press, 1930. 103 p.

A valuable although incomplete compendium of 816 passages from the poetry, arranged alphabetically by title of poem, that are associated with their Bible sources.

1770 Underwood, Francis H. JOHN GREENLEAF WHITTIER: A BIOGRAPHY. Boston: James R. Osgood, 1884. xvi, 413 p. Illus.

Written with the approval of the poet, this early biography was completed before its subject's death and is a portrait rather than a full life. Underwood, an abolitionist leader and later a U.S. consul in Scotland, knew Whittier well and undertook herein a critique of the poetry as well as of the man. Both receive high marks.

1771 von Frank, Albert J., ed. WHITTIER: A COMPREHENSIVE ANNOTATED BIBLIOGRAPHY. New York and London: Garland Publishing, 1976. 273 p.

An admirable and indispensable work, whose annotations reveal careful reading and analysis. There are ten chapters: "Biographies"; "Biographical Studies" (essays, etc.); "Standard Editions"; "Bibliographies and Guides to Manuscripts"; "Literary Influences and Associations"; "Politics, Journalism, and Anti-Slavery Crusade"; "Whittier's Religion"; "Reminiscences"; "Commentary on Individual Works"; "General Assessments and Reputation Studies."

1772 Wagenknecht, Edward. JOHN GREENLEAF WHITTIER: A PORTRAIT IN PARADOX. New York: Oxford University Press, 1967. viii, 262 p. Bibliog.

One of the best of Wagenknecht's "psychographs," its thesis is well stated in the title. The religious mysticism and the political realism; the love of power and the love of mankind; the saintly disposition and the passionate nature; the love of beauty and the fear of it--these and many other paradoxes are stated but never quite explained.

1773 Warren, Robert Penn. JOHN GREENLEAF WHITTIER'S POETRY: AN APPRAISAL AND A SELECTION. Minneapolis: University of Minnesota Press, 1971. xii, 208 p.

The first third of the book is an essay on Whittier's life and poetry, with the discussion of "Snow-Bound" the most rewarding portion. Warren makes several errors of fact concerning Whittier and seems to adopt and push the Mordell Freudian thesis a bit further.

THORNTON WILDER (1897-1975)

1774 Burbank, Rex. THORNTON WILDER. TUSAS, no. 5. Boston: Twayne, 1961. 156 p. Bibliog.

The best introduction to Wilder's life and work available. He is seen as within the humanist tradition, but as one who avoided making humanism a dogmatic, systematic philosophy. Full and balanced analyses of the novels and plays except for those written after 1960, such as THE EIGHTH DAY and THEOPHILUS NORTH.

1775 Goldstein, Malcolm. THE ART OF THORNTON WILDER. Lincoln: University of Nebraska Press, 1965. x, 179 p. Bibliog. note.

Provides biographical background to a study of Wilder's work. The primary aim is to create a useful guide to the plays and novels. Each is treated chronologically, the specific literary sources of each are traced, and the ideas underlying Wilder's writing as a whole are investigated. He is viewed as a major writer who has been neglected.

1776 Goldstone, Richard H. THORNTON WILDER: AN INTIMATE PORTRAIT. New York: Saturday Review Press and Dutton, 1975. xvii, 299 p. Illus., bibliog.

Published in the year of Wilder's death, and completed before that event, this is a full and excellent portrait of the writer based upon Goldstone's long friendship with him and on extensive research. Wilder emerges as a man "shaped and straitjacketed by the traditions that bred him," who fought loose from them to the extent possible for him.

1777 Grebanier, Bernard. THORNTON WILDER. UMPAW, no. 34. Minneapolis: University of Minnesota Press, 1964. 48 p. Bibliog.

Reviews the career briefly and provides cursory examination of the plays and novels. "No writer of his time has been more uniformly concerned with moral issues; none is less didactic."

TENNESSEE WILLIAMS (1914--)

1778 Donahue, Francis. THE DRAMATIC WORLD OF TENNESSEE WILLIAMS. New York: Frederick Ungar, 1964. viii, 243 p.

Interweaves Williams's life and works, giving a quite full account of the plays and the critical reaction to them, as well as an appraisal of the short stories and poetry. Contends that, behind Williams's "outer dramatic world of sex, violence, neuroticism, homosexuality and personal frustration, lie such basic themes as the conflict between reality and illusion, the destruction of the sensitive by the insensitive and the human corrosion wrought by time."

1779 Falk, Signi. TENNESSEE WILLIAMS. Rev. ed. TUSAS, no. 10. Boston: Twayne, 1978. 194 p. Bibliog.

An updating of the 1961 edition, this is an objective analysis of the plays and fiction. Also contains a wide sampling of critical comment, and provides play summaries. Very useful.

1780 Fedder, Norman J. THE INFLUENCE OF D.H. LAWRENCE ON TENNESSEE WILLIAMS. London, The Hague, and Paris: Mouton, 1966. 131 p. Bibliog.

Contends that Lawrence has been the most significant literary influence on Williams's work in poetry, fiction, and drama. The bulk of the study consists of a pointing out of textual parallels.

1781 Gunn, Drewey Wayne, ed. TENNESSEE WILLIAMS: A BIBLIOGRAPHY. Scarecrow Author Bibliographies, no. 48. Metuchen, N.J., and London: Scarecrow Press, 1980. xiii, 255 p.

In six parts: (1) Williams's publications of all kinds; (2)

his writings subdivided by genre, including unpublished items; (3) his manuscripts; (4) important productions; (5) biographical information; and (6) criticism, including bibliographies, critical articles and books, and dissertations. Indispensable although most items are not annotated.

1782 Hirsch, Foster. A PORTRAIT OF THE ARTIST: THE PLAYS OF TENNESSEE WILLIAMS. Port Washington, N.Y., and London: Kennikat Press, 1979. 121 p. Bibliog.

Discusses all the plays against a backdrop of the playwright's self-confessed homosexuality. Sees almost all of them as homosexual fantasies, and believes that between Williams and his ravenous female characters "there is a deep emotional connection." Hirsch's estimate of Williams as a writer is ambiguous. On the one hand, his writing is seen as "a blend of florid imagery, incantatory repetition, and labyrinthine syntax." On the other, he must be acknowledged as having "created more great parts for actors than any other modern playwright."

1783 Londre, Felicia Hardison. TENNESSEE WILLIAMS. World Dramatists Series. New York: Frederick Ungar, 1979. 213 p. Bibliog.

A valuable examination of all the plays. In five chapters: "Early One-Act Plays," "Full-Length Plays from BATTLE OF ANGELS through THE NIGHT OF THE IGUANA," "Later One-Act Plays," "Later Full-Length Plays," "Works in Progress." Londre feels that the most important influences on his work are his family, his southern background, and the presence of death in his life.

1784 Maxwell, Gilbert. TENNESSEE WILLIAMS AND FRIENDS. Cleveland, Ohio, and New York: World Publishing, 1965. xiii, 333 p. Illus.

A close friend portrays Williams as predominantly a good, generous, compassionate and kindly man, and as a playwright primarily concerned with showing people the horrors of the world they've made so that they can do something about them. Many interesting anecdotes.

1785 Stanton, Stephen S., ed. TENNESSEE WILLIAMS: A COLLECTION OF CRITICAL ESSAYS. Twentieth Century Views. Englewood Cliffs, N.J.: Prentice-Hall, 1977. x, 194 p. Bibliog.

Excellent collection, in three parts: (1) plays, (2) themes, and (3) work in progress. Good introduction by Stanton.

1786 Steen, Mike. A LOOK AT TENNESSEE WILLIAMS. New York: Hawthorn Books, 1969. xvi, 318 p. Illus.

An illuminating series of interviews between Steen and friends of Williams in the theater and film industry who have "happy memories" of him.

1787 Tharpe, Jac, ed. TENNESSEE WILLIAMS: A TRIBUTE. Jackson: University Press of Mississippi, 1977. xv, 896 p. Bibliog.

The authors of the more than fifty essays here collected are all academics, suggesting the broad interest in Williams's work that exists on the country's campuses. The sections of the book are (1) "Introductory," (2) "The Plays" [seven on STREETCAR], (3) "European Contexts," (4) "Themes," (5) "Prose and Poetry," (6) "Techniques," (7) "Assessment."

1788 Tischler, Nancy M. TENNESSEE WILLIAMS: REBELLIOUS PURITAN. New York: Citadel Press, 1961. 319 p. Bibliog.

A detailed biography that suffers only from an absence of documentation. There is, however, fine analysis and critical evaluation of plays from BATTLE OF ANGELS through SWEET BIRD OF YOUTH, with consideration of symbolic meanings. Williams is seen as much closer to Strindberg's love-hate than to D.H. Lawrence's cerebral sexuality.

1789 Weales, Gerald. TENNESSEE WILLIAMS. UMPAW, no. 53. Minneapolis: University of Minnesota Press, 1965. 46 p. Bibliog.

The thesis is that Williams, "a playwright who has a sharp eye for the nuances of speech and gesture which have always been of great importance to the realistic dramatist has consistently chosen to work in the nonrealistic tradition."

1790 Williams, Edwina Dakin, as told to Lucy Freeman. REMEMBER ME TO TOM. New York: Putnam, 1963. 255 p. Illus.

The story of her life and her relations with her famous son told by Williams's mother. Of particular interest is her version of her unhappy marriage and her husband's treatment of his family.

1791 Yacowar, Maurice. TENNESSEE WILLIAMS AND FILM. New York: Frederick Ungar, 1977. viii, 168 p. Bibliog.

An interesting study of the films made from Williams's plays, which concludes that his success in the theater eased his acceptance in film and that these films, bolstered by their theatrical prestige, enabled American filmmakers to treat other adult, even sensational, themes. In short, Williams was a liberalizing force in our cinema.

WILLIAM CARLOS WILLIAMS (1883-1963)

1792 Angoff, Charles, ed. WILLIAM CARLOS WILLIAMS. n.d. Unpaged.

Papers delivered at the Leverton Lecture Series at Fairleigh-Dickinson University: Kenneth Burke on "William Carlos Williams: A Critical Appreciation"; Emily Wallace on "The Forms of the Emotions . . . the Pointed Trees"; Norman Holmes Pearson on "The People Who Use the William Carlos Williams Collection at Yale"; and A.M. Sullivan on "Dr. William Carlos Williams, Poet and Humanist."

1793 Breslin, James E. WILLIAM CARLOS WILLIAMS: AN AMERICAN ARTIST. New York: Oxford University Press, 1970. 246 p.

Aims to provide a sense of the unity and range of Williams's writing. Studies his attempts to breathe new life into such standard forms as the lyric poem, historical essay, short story, novel, epic, and meditative poem. His reading of Whitman seen as helping him to discover and to affirm his creative powers. Examples of each type of Williams's writing are examined closely.

1794 Coles, Robert. WILLIAM CARLOS WILLIAMS: THE KNACK OF SURVIVAL IN AMERICA. New Brunswick, N.J.: Rutgers University Press, 1975. xv, 185 p.

A fellow physician and writer examines Williams's stories in LIFE ALONG THE PASSAIC and the Stecher trilogy. The latter is compared with Dos Passos's U.S.A. and found to be more effective and true to life because it is not polemical.

1795 Conarroe, Joel. WILLIAM CARLOS WILLIAMS' PATERSON: LANGUAGE AND LANDSCAPE. Philadelphia: University of Pennsylvania Press, 1970. 177 p. Bibliog.

The five books of the poem are read by locating the themes of man-city, river, mountains, economics, and the language and its search. The burden and the triumph of PATERSON are viewed as being the discovery, in the present, of a language commensurate with the present world.

1796 Dijkstra, Bram. THE HIEROGLYPHICS OF A NEW SPEECH: CUBISM, STIEGLITZ, AND THE EARLY POETRY OF WILLIAM CARLOS WILLIAMS. Princeton, N.J.: Princeton University Press, 1969. xviii, 218 p. Bibliog.

Contends that the immediate influence of certain developments in the visual arts on the poetry of Williams has been pervasive. Limits the evidence to the delineation of the two movements which, the author feels, had the earliest and most durable impact: Cubism and the work of Stieglitz and the painters and theorists who had grouped themselves around him. Limits discussion to the first twenty years of Williams's poetry.

1797 Guimond, James. THE ART OF WILLIAM CARLOS WILLIAMS: A DISCOVERY AND POSSESSION OF AMERICA. Urbana, Chicago, and London: University of Illinois Press, 1968. viii, 257 p. Bibliog.

A profound study that is based on Williams's attitudes toward America. Concludes that he believed the great tragedy of America "was that most men had responded to its newness with feelings of fear, greed, and disappointment rather than with awe and wonder." Williams is seen as a painstaking craftsman, determined to help make American poetry superior to that of any other nation.

1798 Koch, Vivienne. WILLIAM CARLOS WILLIAMS. Norfolk, Conn.: New Directions, 1950. Reprint. Millwood, N.Y.: Kraus Reprint Co., 1973. x, 278 p. Bibliog.

An early and careful study of the full range of Williams's writing, not only the poems but also the drama, fiction and nonfiction published through the late 1940s. His primary importance is seen to reside in his poetry.

1799 Mariani, Paul L. WILLIAM CARLOS WILLIAMS: THE POET AND HIS CRITICS. Chicago: American Library Association, 1975. xiii, 271 p.

An overview of the critical reception of Williams over the sixty years prior to the book's writing in the early 1970s. The focus is primarily on the American reception although a good look is also taken at the English reaction. Concludes that almost none of the published criticism is as perceptive as the kind of critical attention Williams himself paid to other poets.

1800 Mazzaro, Jerome. WILLIAM CARLOS WILLIAMS: THE LATER POEMS. Ithaca, N.Y., and London: Cornell University Press, 1973. xiv, 203 p. Bibliog.

A valuable study of the poetics, concentrating primarily on the late works: PATERSON, "Asphodel, That Greeny Flower," and "Pictures from Brueghel." These poems are seen as attempts to "link the phenomenal world of the older writer with the dreams he had in his youth."

1801 Paul, Sherman. THE MUSIC OF SURVIVAL: A BIOGRAPHY OF A POEM BY WILLIAM CARLOS WILLIAMS. Urbana, Chicago, and London: University of Illinois Press, 1968. xi, 141 p.

A close reading and examination of the making of "The Desert Music," a poem that Paul considers to be one of the finest and most complex Williams ever achieved. Williams's "autobiographical impulse" is also explored.

1802 Peterson, Walter Scott. AN APPROACH TO PATERSON. New Haven, Conn., and London: Yale University Press, 1967. xiii, 217 p.

Relates the body of the epic to the poet's earlier work, particularly IN THE AMERICAN GRAIN. Studies book 1 through 5. Book 5 is not included, for Peterson sees it as "at most a kind of coda to the poem."

1803 Riddel, Joseph N. THE INVERTED BELL: MODERNISM AND THE COUNTERPOETICS OF WILLIAM CARLOS WILLIAMS. Baton Rouge: Louisiana State University Press, 1974. xxv, 308 p.

Martin Heidigger, Jacques Derrida, and Claude Levi-Strauss are used to portray Riddel's sense of Williams's poetics. PATERSON is examined at length. It must, Riddel says, "turn the history of PATERSON inside out, and in doing so transgress the laws of teleological history in order to offer its own new fabric." Also the language of PATERSON, English is "turned inside out and thus disclosed to be not the fixed language of history but the elemental language of poetry." Unfortunately, this interesting, if unsympathetic, approach to the poetics refuses to let the poet speak for himself--as he did so fully in his essays on poetry.

1804 Sankey, Benjamin. A COMPANION TO WILLIAM CARLOS WILLIAMS' PATERSON. Berkeley, Los Angeles, and London: University of California Press, 1971. ix, 235 p. Bibliog.

An interpretation of the epic based on many readings and on a survey of what Williams had to say about it. The approach is a bit heavy.

1805 Tomlinson, Charles, ed. WILLIAM CARLOS WILLIAMS: A CRITICAL ANTHOLOGY. London: Penguin, 1972. 419 p. Bibliog.

Divided into the following sections: (1) "The Beginnings to the 1940's," (2) "The Debate on PATERSON," and (3) "The 1950's and 1960's." Contains a large number of valuable essays by eminent poets and critics.

1806 Townley, Rod. THE EARLY POETRY OF WILLIAM CARLOS WILLIAMS. Ithaca, N.Y., and London: Cornell University Press, 1975. 203 p.

Contends that Williams's work must be understood "somatically." The poems are seen as "finally inseparable, one from another, like the limbs of a man or of a tree." They are fragments "of the fluidic imaginative world in which we all live and dream" rather than unities within themselves. His best poems are rooted, Townley holds, in the true American frontier: "the exact place (on the page) where the mind and the continent meet, edge to edge."

1807 Wagner, Linda Welshimer. THE POEMS OF WILLIAM CARLOS WILLIAMS: A CRITICAL STUDY. Middletown, Conn.: Wesleyan University Press, 1964. 169 p. Bibliog.

The emphasis is on the poetic theory, with close reading of the poems. The technical aspects of the verse receive particular attention.

1808 ______. THE PROSE OF WILLIAM CARLOS WILLIAMS. Middletown, Conn.: Wesleyan University Press, 1970. xi, 234 p. Bibliog.

A companion volume to Wagner's study of the poems (see 1807), this is a comprehensive examination of the prose. Concluding chapters are on PATERSON and the late, triadic-line poems seen as the culmination of Williams's writing, both prose and poetry.

1809 ______, ed. WILLIAM CARLOS WILLIAMS: A REFERENCE GUIDE. Boston: G.K. Hall, 1978. xvii, 166 p.

Lists major works by Williams and provides the fullest annotated listing of works about him by year published, through 1976.

1810 Wallace, Emily Mitchell, ed. A BIBLIOGRAPHY OF WILLIAM CARLOS WILLIAMS. Middletown, Conn.: Wesleyan University Press, 1968. xxvii, 354 p.

The fullest bibliography of Williams's writings.

1811 Weaver, Mike. WILLIAM CARLOS WILLIAMS: THE AMERICAN BACKGROUND. Cambridge, Engl.: Cambridge University Press, 1971. xii, 228 p. Illus., bibliog.

Valuable as a contribution to literary biography, this adds much factual information about references throughout Williams's writing. The study of the Williams milieu is rich, but in presenting Williams's American viewpoint, Weaver abjures offering an evaluation of his work.

1812 Whitaker, Thomas R. WILLIAM CARLOS WILLIAMS. TUSAS, no. 143. New York: Twayne, 1968. 183 p. Bibliog.

Subordinates biography and literary history to discussion of Williams's works themselves. The poetry and prose are studied in roughly chronological order. A keen realization of Williams's concerns and of his artistic milieu is shown, and his growth as a poet is well established.

1813 Whittemore, Reed. WILLIAM CARLOS WILLIAMS, POET FROM JERSEY. Boston: Houghton Mifflin, 1975. xii, 404 p. Illus. Bibliog.

The first full-length biography, it owes a good deal to the Mike Weaver study (see no. 1811). Emphasis is placed on the poet's origins, his relationship to the New Jersey locale, and his importance to American poetry.

See also no. 1208.

EDMUND WILSON (1895-1972)

1814 Berthoff, Warner. EDMUND WILSON. UMPAW, no. 67. Minneapolis: University of Minnesota Press, 1968. 47 p. Bibliog.

An objective view of Wilson as critic and artist. Although Berthoff finds his service as a writer on literature and contemporary events to have been "singularly valuable," he finds him to be fundamentally a first-rate critical journalist--a handicap "in the serious prosecution of a sustained historical argument."

1815 Frank, Charles P. EDMUND WILSON. TUSAS, no. 152. New York: Twayne, 1970. 213 p. Bibliog.

A brief biographical sketch is followed by sound evaluation of much of Wilson's literary criticism, his poems and plays, and his fiction. Frank rates MEMOIRS OF HECATE COUNTY, PATRIOTIC GORE, THE AMERICAN EARTHQUAKE, and TO THE FINLAND STATION as his best books.

1816 Kriegel, Leonard. EDMUND WILSON. Carbondale and Edwardsville: Southern Illinois University Press, 1971. xi, 145 p. Bibliog.

Provides a balanced critical judgment of that part of Wilson's work treated: his criticism and reviewing; his political journalism and historical essays, his autobiographical writing, and those books containing records of his travels. I THOUGHT OF DAISY and MEMOIRS OF HECATE COUNTY are also assessed.

1817 Paul, Sherman. EDMUND WILSON: A STUDY OF LITERARY VOCATION IN OUR TIMES. Urbana: University of Illinois Press, 1965. 237 p. Bibliog. note.

The first book to be devoted entirely to Wilson, this is a useful biographical study.

1818 Ramsey, Richard David, comp. EDMUND WILSON: A BIBLIOGRAPHY. New York: David Lewis, 1971. ix, 345 p.

The most complete bibliography of work by and about Wilson. Includes books by him and edited by him, essays, book reviews, plays and dialogues, stories, poems, and translations by Wilson as well as of his works, miscellanea, manuscript locations, correspondence, items about Wilson, and theses and dissertations on him.

1819 Wain, John, ed. AN EDMUND WILSON CELEBRATION. Oxford, Engl.: Phaidon Press, 1978. x, 182 p. Checklist.

This group of lively essays in praise of Wilson is divided into three parts: "Edmund Wilson the Man," "The Artist as Critic," and "The Critic as Artist." Among those represented are Alfred Kazin, Angus Wilson, Larzer Ziff, John Updike, and Wain.

THOMAS WOLFE (1900-1938)

1820 Daniels, Jonathan. THOMAS WOLFE: OCTOBER RECOLLECTIONS. Columbia, S.C.: Bostick and Thornley, 1961. 26 p.

An address to the nineteenth Biennial Conference of the Southeastern Library Association held in Asheville, North Carolina. Wolfe and Daniels were at Chapel Hill together as students and remained friends until Wolfe's death. In this tribute, Daniels praises Wolfe primarily as a poet, and also tries to correct the legend that Max Perkins made him as a novelist.

1821 Field, Leslie A., ed. THOMAS WOLFE: THREE DECADES OF CRITICISM. New York: New York University Press, 1968. xxv, 304 p.

In four parts: (1) "His Major Themes," (2) "His Style," (3) "Specific Novels," and (4) "The Short Stories." With a selected checklist of criticism of Wolfe, by Maurice Beebe and Field. A very good collection.

1822 Holman, C. Hugh. THE LONELINESS AT THE CORE: STUDIES IN THOMAS WOLFE. Baton Rouge: Louisiana State University Press, 1975. xx, 184 p.

A collection of essays variously published before, but here revised and presented in a somewhat unified way.

1823 Johnson, Elmer D. THOMAS WOLFE: A CHECKLIST. Serif Series of Bibliographies and Checklists, no. 12. Kent, Ohio: Kent State University Press, 1970. xiii, 278 p.

Valuable, but unfortunately unannotated. Contains: books, articles, and parts of books by Wolfe; books and pamphlets, theses and dissertations, articles, and parts of books on Wolfe; poetry and fiction concerning Wolfe; and miscellaneous.

1824 Johnson, Pamela Hansford. HUNGRY GULLIVER: AN ENGLISH CRITICAL APPRAISAL OF THOMAS WOLFE. New York and London: Scribner's, 1948. 170 p.

Wolfe is seen as more American than Faulkner, Steinbeck or Hemingway, American in the sense that Whitman was. "Beside him Faulkner appears neurotic and obscure, Hemingway oversophisticated and Steinbeck . . . to have a certain recessive quality."

1825 Kennedy, Richard S. THE WINDOW OF MEMORY: THE LITERARY CAREER OF THOMAS WOLFE. Chapel Hill: University of North Carolina Press, 1962. xiv, 461 p.

The best biocritical study of Wolfe, this is an indispensable book for students of his work. Thoroughly documented, it presents his life and personality objectively, and analyzes his writing with sensitive perception. The creative editing of Edward Aswell on THE WEB AND THE ROCK and YOU CAN'T GO HOME AGAIN is demonstrated liberally.

1826 McElderry, Bruce R., Jr. THOMAS WOLFE. TUSAS, no. 50. New York: Twayne, 1964. 207 p. Bibliog.

A good introduction to the life and works. Examines Wolfe's use of autobiography and finds important differences between the actual experiences and Wolfe's fictional use of them.

1827 Muller, Herbert J. THOMAS WOLFE. Makers of Modern Literature. Norfolk, Conn.: New Directions, 1947. 196 p. Bibliog.

An early critical study that remains important for its insights. Wolfe is seen as America's closest approach to a Homer. His career is, Muller asserts, the myth of America. Even more than Whitman, Wolfe is said to be troubled by the disparity of the American dream and the ugly realities of life in America.

1828 Nowell, Elizabeth. THOMAS WOLFE: A BIOGRAPHY. Garden City, N.Y.: Doubleday, 1960. 456 p.

The first full-scale biography, it is of unusual interest because its author was Wolfe's literary agent and the recipient of his total confidence. Her portrait of him is fascinating and makes him come alive. In respect to his writing she says, "He was completely ignorant of how to shape a piece of writing and make it publishable, but he had a deep instinctive feeling for his work which rarely played him false."

1829 Payne, Ladell. THOMAS WOLFE. Southern Writers Series, no. 9. Austin, Tex.: Steck-Vaughn, 1969. 43 p. Bibliog.

Summarizes and comments briefly on Wolfe's life and four novels. Sees the novels as being like Dickens's in that they are parts of a continuum, and in their creating memorable characters and caricatures.

1830 Phillipson, John S., ed. THOMAS WOLFE: A REFERENCE GUIDE. Boston: G.K. Hall, 1977. xiii, 218 p.

Indispensable. Writings about Wolfe from 1929 through 1976 are listed and fully annotated. Lists of doctoral dissertations and works in foreign languages are provided.

1831 Raynolds, Robert. THOMAS WOLFE: MEMOIR OF A FRIENDSHIP. Austin and London: University of Texas Press, 1965. 154 p. Illus.

The record of a friendship that endured from 1932 until Wolfe's death in 1938. Wolfe is pictured as a good and gentle man and as "a religious poet."

1832 Reeves, Paschal. THOMAS WOLFE'S ALBATROSS: RACE & NATIONALITY IN AMERICA. Athens: University of Georgia Press, 1968. viii, 160 p. Bibliog.

Focuses on Wolfe's fiction, the ultimate goal of which was "an epic portrayal of his native land" to be achieved by projecting an "autobiographical self into a generic American." Wolfe is seen as failing in his aim, especially in the first two novels, because of his racial and nationalistic prejudices; only at the end does this albatross of prejudice fall away.

1833 _____, ed. THOMAS WOLFE: THE CRITICAL RECEPTION. New York: David Lewis, 1974. xxxiv, 256 p.

Reprints reviews and criticism of Wolfe's books, including the letters and notebooks, from 1929 through 1970.

1834 _____. THOMAS WOLFE AND THE GLASS OF TIME. Athens: University of Georgia Press, 1971. xiv, 166 p.

Proceedings of a symposium on the works of Wolfe. Papers by Richard S. Kennedy, Richard Walser, G. Hugh Holman, Fred W. Wolfe (the novelist's brother), Ladell Payne, and Paschal Reeves.

1835 Rubin, Louis D., Jr. THOMAS WOLFE: THE WEATHER OF HIS YOUTH. Baton Rouge: Louisiana State University Press, 1955. xiii, 183 p. Illus.

Rubin sees time as perhaps the major element in Wolfe's work, best exemplified in LOOK HOMEWARD, ANGEL, where it is "frozen" successfully. Wolfe is said to have shown in his four major novels how autobiography can be used effectively in fiction. He is seen as writing better about the town than the city, but having given perhaps the fullest characterization of the city in American fiction.

1836 ______, ed. THOMAS WOLFE: A COLLECTION OF CRITICAL ESSAYS. Englewood Cliffs, N.J.: Prentice-Hall, 1973. Bibliog. note.

Twelve essays by eminent scholars and critics with a good introduction by the editor. An excellent collection.

1837 Ryssel, Fritz Heinrich. THOMAS WOLFE. Translated by Helen Sebba. Modern Literature Monographs. New York: Frederick Ungar, 1972. ix, 117 p. Bibliog.

Published originally in Germany in 1963. Wolfe's greatness is seen to lie in "his humility and his courage, his awareness of the vanity of life, and his extraordinary fortitude." The novels are viewed as possessing an overarching unity.

1838 Snyder, William U. THOMAS WOLFE: ULYSSES AND NARCISSUS. Athens: Ohio University Press, 1971. xxiv, 234 p. Illus.

A psychobiography by a clinical psychologist who uses Freudian analysis. The three parts are significantly titled: (1) "Ulysses the Far-Wanderer--Wolfe's Relationships with Men," (2) "Narcissus and the Split Imago--Wolfe's Relationships with Women," and (3) "Diagnosis and Prognosis." Wolfe is seen as having great need for catharsis, as behaving compulsively and obsessively, as exhibiting manic-depressive behavior, and as having paranoidal tendencies.

1839 Turnbull, Andrew. THOMAS WOLFE. New York: Scribner's, 1967. x, 374 p. Illus.

The best biography, though not fully definitive. Extremely readable, and the portrayal of Wolfe is sensitive.

1840 Walser, Richard. THOMAS WOLFE UNDERGRADUATE. Durham, N.C.: Duke University Press, 1977. ix, 166 p. Illus.

Interesting account of Wolfe's days as an undergraduate at the University of North Carolina at Chapel Hill.

1841 Watkins, Floyd C. THOMAS WOLFE'S CHARACTERS: PORTRAITS FROM LIFE. Norman: University of Oklahoma Press, 1957. xiii, 194 p. Illus.

An interesting study of Wolfe's consistent use of persons and happenings from his own background for the creation of characters and events in his fiction. Watkins finds that Wolfe invented very little; his talent lay in reshaping what he had experienced or knew about.

1842 Wheaton, Mabel Wolfe, with LeGette Blythe. THOMAS WOLFE AND HIS FAMILY. Garden City, N.Y.: Doubleday, 1961. 336 p. Illus.

The rambling reminiscences of one of Wolfe's sisters as set down by Blythe from notes of conversations with her before her death in 1959, recordings by her, and correspondence and notes relating to the family.

RICHARD WRIGHT (1908-1960)

1843 Abcarian, Richard, ed. RICHARD WRIGHT'S NATIVE SON: A CRITICAL HANDBOOK. Belmont, Calif.: Wadsworth, 1970. x, 261 p. Bibliog.

In five parts: (1) "Essays by Wright," (2) "Reviews of NATIVE SON," (3) "Critical Essays," (4) "Related Essays," and (5) "Appendices (Chronology and Bibliography)."

1844 Baker, Houston A., Jr., ed. TWENTIETH CENTURY INTERPRETATIONS OF NATIVE SON. Englewood Cliffs, N.J.: Prentice-Hall, 1972. 124 p. Bibliog.

Helpful for student papers, this is a good collection of essays by generally well-known critics and writers.

1845 Bakish, David. RICHARD WRIGHT. Modern Literature Monographs. New York: Frederick Ungar, 1973. xiv, 114 p. Bibliog.

The best brief introduction to the life and work. The summaries of the fiction works are very ably done.

1846 Bone, Robert. RICHARD WRIGHT. UMPAW, no. 74. Minneapolis: University of Minnesota Press, 1969. 48 p. Bibliog.

A useful introduction to the life and work. NATIVE SON

is seen as a seriously flawed work of art, dissolving finally into Communist propaganda. Bone believes "The Man Who Lived Underground" to be Wright's most flawless work of fiction.

1847 Brignano, Russell Carl. RICHARD WRIGHT: AN INTRODUCTION TO THE MAN AND HIS WORKS. Pittsburgh: University of Pittsburgh Press, 1970. xiii, 201 p. Bibliog.

Wright is viewed as "neither a consistent, refined craftsman nor a stylistic innovator. His successes are colossal, his failures dreadful." Wright the artist is seen at his best from the standpoint of language, narration, and theme in the stories collected in UNCLE TOM'S CHILDREN (1938).

1848 Fabre, Michel. THE UNFINISHED QUEST OF RICHARD WRIGHT. Translated by Isabel Barzun. New York: William Morrow, 1973. xx, 652 p. Illus., bibliog.

In this remarkable French biography, admirably translated, the goal of the quest is seen as the awakening of the black man and the awakening of everyone to accepting the "black man" in himself so that all humanity will be brothers in a community of love.

1849 Fishburn, Katherine. RICHARD WRIGHT'S HERO: THE FACES OF A REBEL-VICTIM. Metuchen, N.J.: Scarecrow Press, 1977. viii, 225 p. Bibliog.

A thorough study of Wright's fiction hero, "a man beaten to the ground but determined to rise from his subjugation to join his fellow men in perhaps a godless world, but one where mutual respect gives life some dignity." Excellent primary and secondary source bibliography.

1850 Ray, David, and Farnsworth, Robert M., eds. RICHARD WRIGHT: IMPRESSIONS AND PERSPECTIVES. Ann Arbor: University of Michigan Press, 1973. xi, 207 p. Bibliog.

A reprinting in book form of the Richard Wright special issue of NEW LETTERS published by the University of Missouri in 1971.

1851 Rickels, Milton, and Rickels, Patricia. RICHARD WRIGHT. Southern Writers Series, no. 11. Austin, Tex.: Steck-Vaughn, 1970. ii, 44 p. Bibliog.

A very brief introduction to the life and works.

1852 Webb, Constance. RICHARD WRIGHT: A BIOGRAPHY. New York: Putnam, 1968. 443 p. Illus. Bibliog.

A generally competent biography, but not up to the level of Fabré's (see no. 1848).

ELINOR WYLIE (1885-1928)

1853 Gray, Thomas A. ELINOR WYLIE. TUSAS, no. 165. New York: Twayne, 1969. 171 p. Bibliog.

The first book-length study. Wylie is seen here as a poet who achieved early recognition more because of knowing the right people in the New York literary establishment than because of exceptional merit. In sum, she is pictured as a minor poet who was, at best, capable of affirming in her art the validity of the desire for quality in human life.

1854 Olson, Stanley. ELINOR WYLIE: A LIFE APART. New York: Dial Press and James Wade, 1979. vii, 376 p. Illus., bibliog.

The only full-scale scholarly biography, it presents a reliable picture of the poet and her life. There is, however, little critical analysis of the poetry.

Part 2

LANGUAGE

LANGUAGE

In comparison with the section of this guide devoted to books about American literature, the following section on books dealing with the American language is admittedly slender. It is so partly by design and partly because of the relative paucity of worthwhile books on the subject. Whereas there are quite literally thousands of scholarly works on American poets, dramatists, essayists, and fiction writers, there are only scores of such works on the American language or, as it is more frequently called, American English.

What I have attempted here is to present a representative group of volumes on various aspects of the language, with emphasis on the work of such leaders in the study of American English as Mencken, Craigie, Krapp, Mathews, and Marckwardt. What I have deliberately avoided is the inclusion of all of the many dictionaries that claim to be based on American usage, of all the grammars that make a similar claim, of all the guides to American usage or pronunciation, of all the works treating American dialects, or of all the attempts to render an account of the historical development of English in America. What I have included is, I believe, a reasonable selection of works that can lead the serious student of our language to a comprehensive and thorough knowledge of the subject. Highly popularized treatments or journalistic diatribes, which could have swollen considerably the number of volumes considered, have been generally excluded as of relatively small value and as frequently misleading. For such exclusion I offer no apology.

THE AMERICAN LANGUAGE

1855 Burkett, Eva M. AMERICAN ENGLISH DIALECTS IN LITERATURE. Metuchen, N.J., and London: Scarecrow Press, 1978. viii, 213 p.

> The purpose of this useful book is "to give students of American literature, language, sociology, and history the opportunity to understand and to realize the effectiveness of dialect as a literary language and to determine the relationship of the American-English language to American history and culture." Contains lists of writers and their works that provide examples of various forms of American-English dialects.

1856 Copperud, Roy H. AMERICAN USAGE: THE CONSENSUS. New York: Van Nostrand Reinhold, 1970. x, 292 p.

> Attempts to present the consensus of language authorities on disputed points. Seven current dictionaries of usage, as well as the leading conventional dictionaries, are compared.

1857 Craigie, William A. THE GROWTH OF AMERICAN ENGLISH I AND II. Westport, Conn.: Greenwood Press, 1971. 199-264 p. Originally published in 1940 as SOCIETY FOR PURE ENGLISH TRACTS LVI AND LVII by the Clarendon Press, Oxford, England.

> Observations by the editor of the DICTIONARY OF AMERICAN ENGLISH ON HISTORICAL PRINCIPLES, which was in the process of publication at the time.

1858 Craigie, William A., and Hulbert, James R., eds. A DICTIONARY OF AMERICAN ENGLISH ON HISTORICAL PRINCIPLES. Chicago: University of Chicago Press, 1938-44. 2,552 p. Bibliog.

> The most thorough and scientific work of its kind on the subject. The examples of historical usage often make for fascinating reading.

1859 Ehrlich, Eugene, with Stuart B. Flexner, Gorton Carruth, and Joyce M. Hawkins, eds. OXFORD AMERICAN DICTIONARY. New York and Oxford: Oxford University Press, 1980. 816 p.

A new dictionary that "has been prepared especially for those who need a compact, up-to-date guide to American English." Easy to use, but definitions are often excessively brief, and word derivations are not supplied.

1860 Evans, Bergen, and Evans, Cornelia, eds. A DICTIONARY OF CONTEMPORARY AMERICAN USAGE. New York: Random House, 1957. viii, 567 p.

Designed for people who speak a standard English but are uncertain about details. Definitions and discussions of words listed tend to be quite full and helpful. There is also a fairly detailed discussion of English grammar.

1861 Farmer, John S., comp. and ed. AMERICANISMS--OLD & NEW: A DICTIONARY OF WORDS, PHRASES AND COLLOQUIALISMS PECULIAR TO THE UNITED STATES, BRITISH AMERICA, THE WEST INDIES, ETC., THEIR DERIVATION, MEANING AND APPLICATION. London: Privately printed, 1889. Reprint. Detroit: Gale Research Co., 1976. xx, 564 p.

Although obviously dated, the book is most interesting in its list of words and phrases and in its definitions.

1862 Follett, Wilson. MODERN AMERICAN USAGE: A GUIDE. Edited and compiled by Jacques Barzun et al. New York: Hill and Wang, 1966. x, 436 p.

An excellent and sensible guide modeled on H.W. Fowler's A DICTIONARY OF MODERN ENGLISH USAGE, and written with at least a modicum of Fowler's wit.

1863 Francis, W. Nelson. THE STRUCTURE OF AMERICAN ENGLISH. New York: Ronald Press, 1958. vii, 614 p. Bibliog.

Attempts to bring together a synthesis of current linguistic knowledge, especially as applied to contemporary American English.

1864 Fries, Charles Carpenter. AMERICAN ENGLISH GRAMMAR; THE GRAMMATICAL STRUCTURE OF PRESENT-DAY AMERICAN ENGLISH WITH ESPECIAL REFERENCE TO SOCIAL DIFFERENCES OR CLASS DIALECTS. New York: Appleton-Century-Crofts, 1940. viii, 313 p.

Authorized by the National Council of Teachers of English. Although dated in many respects, it remains a very useful work.

1865 Horwill, H.W., ed. A DICTIONARY OF MODERN AMERICAN USAGE. 2d ed. Oxford: Clarendon Press, 1944. xxxi, 360 p.

A scholarly work by an English linguist who sees a "marked preference of American taste for the grandiloquent" in language.

1866 Krapp, George Philip. THE ENGLISH LANGUAGE IN AMERICA. 2 vols. New York: Modern Language Association, 1925. Reprint. New York: Frederick Ungar, 1960. Bibliog.

Volume 1 treats the history of the language with a discussion of Americanisms. Volume 2 deals with pronunciation and bibliography.

1867 _____. THE PRONUNCIATION OF STANDARD ENGLISH IN AMERICA. New York: Oxford University Press, 1919. Reprint. New York: AMS Press, 1969. xv, 235 p. Bibliog. note.

Although this book was first published in 1919, the chapters on the mechanism of speech, the description of sounds and sounds and their occurrence are still very useful.

1868 Laird, Charlton. LANGUAGE IN AMERICA. New York and Cleveland, Ohio: World, 1970. x, 543 p.

A largely undocumented but nevertheless scholarly and very readable account of the growth and development of language in the United States.

1869 Marckwardt, Albert H. AMERICAN ENGLISH. New York: Oxford University Press, 1958. xi, 194 p.

The principal aim of this excellent book is to present a synthesis of the growth and development of the English language in America.

1870 Mathews, Mitford M., ed. A DICTIONARY OF AMERICANISMS ON HISTORICAL PRINCIPLES. 2 vols. Chicago: University of Chicago Press, 1951. xvi, 1,946 p. Bibliog.

The purpose of this invaluable work is "to treat historically as many as possible of those words and meanings of words which have been added to the English language in the United States." The bibliography is extensive and most useful.

1871 Mencken, H.L. THE AMERICAN LANGUAGE: AN INQUIRY INTO THE DEVELOPMENT OF ENGLISH IN THE UNITED STATES. 4th ed., corr., enl. and rev. New York: Knopf, 1960. xi, 769 p., xxix.

The first edition was published in 1919. A work of enormous scholarship, the underlying thesis of which is that American English is decidedly the dominant force by now on the common language of the English-speaking world, and that it is vastly different from its British counterpart. The two streams of English are discussed, the beginnings of American, the period of growth, and the language today. There are chapters on American pronunciation, American spelling, American common speech, American slang, American proper names, and the future of the language.

1872 ______. THE AMERICAN LANGUAGE: SUPPLEMENT I. New York: Knopf, 1945. xvi, 739 p., xxxv.

Stresses the differences between American and English.

1873 ______. THE AMERICAN LANGUAGE: SUPPLEMENT II. New York: Knopf, 1948. xiii, 890 p., xliii.

Treats the pronunciation of American, American spelling, American common speech, proper names in America, and American slang.

1874 Moss, Norman, ed. WHAT'S THE DIFFERENCE? A BRITISH-AMERICAN DICTIONARY. New York: Harper and Row, 1973. 138 p.

A useful small book intended primarily to help Britons and Americans to communicate more effectively with each other. Presents lists of British words with their meanings in American, and lists of American words with their meanings in British English.

1875 Nicholson, Margaret, ed. A DICTIONARY OF AMERICAN-ENGLISH USAGE: BASED ON FOWLER'S MODERN ENGLISH USAGE. New York: Oxford University Press, 1957. xii, 671 p.

An adaptation of H.W. Fowler's book, a simplified version with American variations that retains as much of the original as space permits. Fowler's mannerisms and pedantries have been left untouched.

1876 Partridge, Eric, and Clark, John W. BRITISH AND AMERICAN ENGLISH SINCE 1900. London: Andrew Dakers, 1951. x, 341 p.

The section on American English is the work of Clark, who attempts to explain the characteristics of American English and their origin as well as to study its vocabulary, idiom and syntax, pronunciation, spelling, and dialects.

1877 Reed, Carroll E. DIALECTS OF AMERICAN ENGLISH. Cleveland, Ohio: World Pub. Co., 1967. Reprint. Amherst: University of Massachusetts Press, 1973. vii, 119 p.

A very good book for the student who has recently become aware of dialect variations.

1878 Taylor, Archer, and Whiting, Bartlett Jere, eds. A DICTIONARY OF AMERICAN PROVERBS AND PROVERBIAL PHRASES, 1820-1880. Cambridge, Mass.: Belknap Press of Harvard University Press, 1958. xxii, 418 p. Bibliog.

1879 Thomas, Charles Kenneth. AN INTRODUCTION TO THE PHONETICS OF AMERICAN ENGLISH. New York: Ronald Press, 1947. ix, 181 p.

A text for the study of pronunciation of English in the United States, designed for use in the elementary course in phonetics.

1880 Tibbetts, Arn, and Tibbetts, Charlene. WHAT'S HAPPENING TO AMERICAN ENGLISH? New York: Scribner's, 1978. xiii, 189 p.

A hard look at the plight of the language in present-day America. What the authors see as the decline of American English they also see as "the decline of the American as human being."

1881 Ward, Kendall K., and Kaltenborn, Arthur L., Jr. GUIDES FOR AMERICAN-ENGLISH PRONUNCIATION. Springfield, Ill.: Charles C Thomas, 1971. vii, 245 p.

A useful aid to the student in identifying the body of knowledge that exists regarding pronunciation of American English. The method used is to relate current pronunciation practices to the origin of a word and its component parts and to the function of the word in a sentence (noun, verb, adjective, etc.).

1882 Weingarten, Joseph A., comp. SUPPLEMENTARY NOTES TO THE DICTIONARY OF AMERICAN ENGLISH. New York: Privately printed, 1948. 95 p.

Provides further examples for a number of words in DICTIONARY OF AMERICAN ENGLISH (see no. 1858).

1883 Wentworth, Harold. AMERICAN DIALECT DICTIONARY. New York: Crowell, 1944. xv, 747 p.

Concerned primarily with variations--vocabular, phrasal, semantic, phonological, and morphological--in the English language as spoken and written by natives of North America, and especially with variations due to geography.

1884 Whiting, Bartlett Jere. EARLY AMERICAN PROBERBS AND PROVERBIAL PHRASES. Cambridge, Mass., and London: Belknap Press of Harvard University Press, 1977. lxiv, 555 p. Bibliog.

Covers the period from the colonial beginnings to 1820.

1885 Williamson, Juanita V., and Burke, Virginia M., eds. A VARIOUS LANGUAGE: PERSPECTIVES ON AMERICAN DIALECTS. New York: Holt, Rinehart and Winston, 1971. xix, 706 p. Bibliog.

An excellent collection of articles by language specialists arranged in six parts: (1) "A Various Language," (2) "Inherited Features," (3) "Literary Representations of American English Dialects," (4) "Aspects of Regional and Social Dialects," (5) "Selected Sounds and Forms," (6) "Studies of Urban Dialects."

INDEXES

AUTHOR INDEX

This index includes all authors, editors, compilers, translators, and other contributors to the books enumerated in the text. It is alphabetized letter by letter. References are to entry numbers.

A

B

D

E

F

G

H

L

M

Q

R

S

T

U

Y

Z

TITLE INDEX

This index includes all titles annotated in the text. In some instances, titles have been shortened as clarity permits. Where duplicate titles occur, the last names of authors have been parenthesized. The index is alphabetized letter by letter. References are to entry numbers.

A

B

C

D

E

G

H

I

J

K

L

M

N

O

P

Q

R

S

T

U

V

W

Y

Z

SUBJECT INDEX

This index includes subjects mentioned in the text. It also includes all titles mentioned in the text that are not listed in the Title Index of annotated works. Reference is to entry numbers. Alphabetizing is letter by letter.

A

B

G

H

K

L

Q

R

S

W

Y

Z